# Randy Newman's

# American Dreams

# Randy Newman's
# American Dreams

Kevin Courrier

ECW Press

Published by ECW PRESS
2120 Queen Street East, Suite 200, Toronto, Ontario, Canada M4E 1E2

LIBRARY AND ARCHIVES CANADA CATALOGUING IN PUBLICATION

Courrier, Kevin, 1954–
Randy Newman's American dreams / Kevin Courrier.

ISBN 1-55022-690-8

1. Composers — Biography.   2. Singers — Biography.   I. Title.

ML410.N554C86 2005    780'.92    C2004-907045-2

Editor: Kevin Connolly
Cover and Text Design: Tania Craan
Production and Typesetting: Mary Bowness
Printing: Printcrafters
Cover photo: © Jillian Edelstein/CORBIS SYGMA/MAGMA
Author photo: David Bidner

This book is set in Sabon and Oneloda.

The publication of *Randy Newman's American Dreams* has been generously supported
by the Ontario Arts Council, the Ontario Media Development Corporation, and the
Government of Canada through the Book Publishing Industry Development Program.
We acknowledge the support of the Canada Council for the Arts for our
publishing program. Canada

DISTRIBUTION
CANADA: Jaguar Book Group, 100 Armstrong Avenue, Georgetown, ON, L7G 5S4
UNITED STATES: Independent Publishers Group, 814 North Franklin Street,
Chicago, Illinois 60610

PRINTED AND BOUND IN CANADA

ECW PRESS
ecwpress.com

*For my mother and father who had the foresight to buy me a record player when I was eight.*

*In memory of Tom Fulton who taught me how to find my voice.*

# Table of Contents

# Acknowledgements

When I initially began this biography on Randy Newman, I assumed that I was simply writing about a cultural outsider who had cleverly carved a career for himself on the inside. It turned into something much more intricate than I first imagined. This river contained many tributaries. My research originally began with Greil Marcus's landmark essay on Newman, "Every Man Is Free," from his book, *Mystery Train*. But it was in his later *Invisible Republic: Bob Dylan's Basement Tapes*, about the subterranean cultural forces that shaped Dylan's 1967 recordings, that I encountered a reference he made to Constance Rourke's indispensable *American Humor: A Study of the National Character*. While subsequently examining that work, her apt metaphor of the mask and its singularly ambiguous role in American culture became an essential ingredient I needed in understanding Newman's own work. When he once described the character roles in his songs as those inhabited by an "untrustworthy narrator," I naturally turned next to Herman Melville's *The Confidence Man*, which, in part, became the skeleton key used to discover the inner voice of my own book.

It's often been conceded that writing a book is a lonely occupation. However, there were many people who actually helped with this project and made it less hermetic than it might have otherwise been. First of all, a deep gratitude to the folks at ECW Press for giving me the opportunity to pursue, with conviction, a project I passionately believed in. Thanks to Jack David for not only providing the green light, but also sharing my enthusiasm for a book about Randy Newman. My usual editor, Jen Hale, might have been busy becoming a parent, but she still found time to provide helpful feedback and located some rare songs I couldn't ferret out on my own. Tracey Millen, with her impeccable eye for detail, had an invaluable impact on the final copy-editing and indexing of this dense little tome. Special thanks to Kevin Connolly as the book's initial copy-editor. He not only encouraged my best instincts as a writer, but also caught some of my worst habits. My gratitude to Robyn Burnett, as well, for her dedicated effort to secure the best photos for this book.

There were a number of readers who kept me both honest and clear-headed. One of my most valued friends, Steve Vineberg, brought to this project an incisive, yet compassionate, professorial eye that helped me quickly cut to the core of the subject. In short, the book would be nowhere near as good without him. Brian Quinn asked all the right questions, as he had with *Dangerous Kitchen*, and contributed some compelling feedback, too — especially on the material set in the early sixties. Both *Dangerous Kitchen* and *Randy Newman's American Dreams* were, in part, borne out of ongoing discussions and debates over music, politics and art, with my good friend Donald Brackett. His insights and comments always pushed me deeper into these subjects than I sometimes thought I could go. My dear friend and colleague Shlomo Schwartzberg, who brings a principled professional dignity that is rare today in the business of film criticism, brought those same essential skills to the reading of this manuscript. David Churchill, who shares those same values, was equal to the task of helping me take this book further. His selfless involvement is a succinct illustration of the best of what true friendship can offer.

Many others showed their support in other incalculable ways. My brother Scott Courrier went beyond the call of duty to secure a rare copy of *Goldmine*, which contained an exhaustive profile of Newman, while also finding some rare and ancient recordings of Newman covers. Adam McCosham became an extremely supportive friend during the writing of this book. His tireless and enthusiastic search for Newman cover versions and other related matters (especially Brian Wilson's *Smile* project) added greatly to my own enthusiasm for working on *Randy Newman's American Dreams*. Andrew Scott, of Second Spin, and a massive Harry Nilsson fan, kept his eye out for essential

CDs as well as helping me add weight to the sections on Nilsson and *Smile*. Matt McLaren and Dan Corbett, of Flash and Crash Music, are not only great fans of music, they became great supporters of this book. They gave of their time generously in finding rare and out-of-print recordings. Andrew Todd, who was a big help on *Dangerous Kitchen*, provided an essential Newman CD. Special thanks to Roger Costa of Monster Records, as well, for his continued assistance. Gary Norris, Randy Newman's dedicated archivist, has been a great supporter of this project from the beginning. I hope he gets to do his own version some day. John Corcelli, at CBC archives, found some Newman interviews that I might have otherwise missed. Greig Dymond came up with Ian McDonald's essay of sharp insights into Newman's debut album. A special thanks goes to Ang, Lori, and the entire staff of Bonjour Brioche, who not only served the best espresso I've ever tasted, but also became a huge anchor of personal support for me — especially during those days when I was a zombie with little sleep. It's been said before (but bares repeating) that without Dave Downey and Anton Leo ("The Focus Brothers") none of this would have been possible.

Kevin Courrier,
April 2005

# Maybe I'm Doing it Wrong: A Reconsideration of Comedy Music

"Not *another* book about comedy music?" said a good friend in mock horror when he heard I was beginning work on a biography of American composer Randy Newman. The previous primer on "comedy music" he was referring to was my book *Dangerous Kitchen: The Subversive World of Zappa,* about the legendary, controversial composer Frank Zappa. The question struck me as oddly funny, because I had never really considered that writing about Frank Zappa, or Randy Newman, revealed some perverse predilection on my part for the genre. But, who knows? Even my publisher, Jack David, sent me an encouraging E-mail suggesting I consider yet another practitioner of the form. "After this book," he wrote, "let's do Kinky Friedman."

I suppose I never really deemed these artists part of the canon of what is generally defined as comedy music. First of all, Frank Zappa was an American composer who successfully integrated the late nineteenth century artistic revolt against Romanticism into twentieth century popular music. Mind you, he did so by treating musical history largely as a kaleidoscopic farce. Randy Newman, on the other hand, is a rather eccentric, self-deprecating composer who works more conventionally in the worlds of popular music and film scores. What makes Newman such an anomaly in that world, though, is that he writes sophisticated songs about idiosyncratic and sometimes deranged individuals. He does this rather ingeniously, too, by blending the sweeping romantic scores of Hollywood movies into his collection of ragtime shuffles, R&B, and rock & roll songs.

So then, what do I *really* mean by comedy music? Comedy music, for me, is defined largely by the novelty songs I heard while growing up — everything from the bawdy barroom tunes of Rusty Warren to "Purple People Eater" (1958), "The Monster Mash" (1962) and Napoleon XIV's deeply obnoxious 1966 single, "They're Coming to Take Me Away, Ha-Haaa!" (Side B upped the ante by playing the same tune backwards as "Aaah-Ah, Yawa Em Ekat Ot Gnimoc Er'yeht.") Parodists who perform comedy songs (Adam Sandler and "Weird Al" Yankovic come to mind) commonly trash other, more famous, artists. After all, it's been an easy way to create an instant hit record. Some, like Weird Al, have built long careers solely on the backs of those they parody, while others, like Napoleon XIV, make their dubious mark by parodying themselves and quickly disappearing forever. Novelty songs, however, almost always succeed commercially because they rely on us being in on the joke. When Weird Al demolishes Michael Jackson's "Beat It," with his own "Eat It," it is nothing more than a one-note joke, one we feel perfectly safe in sharing because we aren't the butt of it.

The work of Randy Newman, Frank Zappa, and perhaps even Kinky Friedman is cut from a different cloth. In their music, parody is not an end in itself, it's merely a means to get at something deeply resonant in American life. Where parodists like Weird Al lay waste to the work of those with larger ambitions, Newman and Zappa are people for whom artistic ambition is wrapped up in the question of what constitutes amusement and what constitutes art. Given that both take an irreverent approach to the very culture they explore, it makes sense that comedy would be a large part of their strategy.

It was Newman's particular kind of impudence, however, that convinced me it would be fascinating to write about him. Like Zappa, Newman's best songs are tinged with ambiguity and doubt, qualities not usually encountered in the songs of most musical comedians. Zappa and Newman are distinct outsiders in the American mainstream, whereas Weird Al is really a mainstream artist playing the role of the outsider. Zappa carved a niche for himself by gaining control over his own recordings and designing his own cottage industry to distribute them. Newman found a more uncommon path for himself by posing as an insider within the music industry itself. He did so by constructing his own musical Trojan Horse consistently springing surprises on unsuspecting executives and listeners.

A superficial examination of his life tells us Randy Newman is a singer-songwriter born into a musical family in Los Angeles in 1943. He started to write songs at 15, near the end of the fifties, beginning a career as a hired songwriter for artists as diverse as Judy Collins ("I Think It's Going to Rain Today"), Three Dog Night ("Mama Told Me Not To Come") and Tom Jones ("You Can Leave Your Hat On"). Before the end of the sixties, however, Randy Newman began to record his own songs, releasing a collection of albums (*Randy Newman Creates Something New Under the Sun, 12 Songs, Sail Away*) that earned him both weak sales and a devoted cult following. Then the moderate success of *Good Old Boys* (1974), a sublime and critical appraisal of the American South, had Newman, for the first time, flirting with a mass audience. Newman finally won major commercial acclaim with his largely misunderstood satirical single "Short People" in 1977. Mistrusting this sudden fame, Newman turned on those he'd just attracted with the sharply funny but acrimonious commercial failure, *Born Again,* in 1979. During the eighties and nineties, Newman began to develop a somewhat mainstream career as a film composer, scoring such earnest dramas as *The Natural* (1984) and *Awakenings* (1991), and providing orchestral music that differed radically from the distinctly personal touch he gave his songs. After numerous nominations, Newman would finally win an Academy Award for the song, "If I Didn't Have You," from the Pixar animated feature, *Monsters Inc.,* in 2002. But all of this, of course, constitutes a cursory sketch of an artist who is anything but pedestrian. In stark contrast to other popular singer-songwriters of the seventies (Carole King, James Taylor, Carly Simon), Newman didn't sing with a sweet disposition, or cry bitter tears over love affairs that went wrong. In a voice that barely registers above a drawl, Newman sings pop songs about misfits, con artists, killers and misanthropes.

"I always thought my stuff was odd, but I never thought it was difficult," Newman told *USA Today* in 2003. "It's not like physics, you know? You may not like the songs, but they're not hard to understand." They may not be hard to understand, but the mass audience often finds them hard to take. Newman might have composed accessible and melodic music, but within those harmonious chords he concealed a deeply sardonic grin.

Of course, when I started planning *Randy Newman's American Dreams,* I shouldn't have assumed there would be a large difference between Zappa and Newman. It's easy enough to see their diverse musical paths, but I also discovered they had a great deal in common. Like Zappa, Newman often writes songs, like "Davy the Fat Boy" and "Rednecks," that aren't what you would call confessional songs about love.

"Maybe people want personal confessions," Newman told *Playboy* magazine in 1987. "Maybe that's why I don't sell two million records." At his best, Newman doesn't pander to popular tastes. He presumes an intelligence and literacy in his audience, and writes assuming that listeners will ultimately grasp the obvious irony in many of his songs. "In fact, I always thought people could tell what I was like from my stuff more easily than they necessarily could tell about a confessional kind of songwriter," Newman explains.

In 1982, Frank Zappa had an inadvertent novelty hit with his daughter Moon Unit entitled "Valley Girl," just a few years after Newman's own unexpected chart-topper "Short People," a song that satirized someone who had a pathological fear of tiny folks. Although the tune was hardly representative of Newman's vast catalogue, it created a storm, and a false understanding of Newman. Everyone suddenly assumed they had a "sizist" in their midst.

"'Short People' was the worst kind of hit anyone could have," Newman later recalled bitterly. "It was like having 'Purple People Eater.'" The song led people to misunderstand Newman's work in much the same way as many had Zappa's compositions. "Audiences are unable to distinguish between a character and its author, between an argument and the unspoken, underlying reasons that a character would raise that argument," critic Stephen Leigh Morris of the *LA Weekly* once wrote about Randy Newman, in words that could easily apply to Zappa.

Newman defines himself as something of a curmudgeon, a title Zappa also wore as a badge of honor. "Randy may come across as acerbic," pianist Ralph Grierson commented in *International Musician* after Newman won his Oscar. "He's not afraid to say what he thinks about anyone or anything. There are very few people who have such a no-fear approach to life. It may well be that this is just to mask his own insecurities; but be that as it may, he is the most dedicated artist." That dedication often takes Newman to ambiguous places that bravely force the listener to confront uncomfortable emotions. "Newman deliberately stays out of his own masterfully ambiguous material," Janet Maslin once wrote in *The New York Times*. "[He forces] the listener to develop his or her own point of view."

Shortly before he died in 1993, Frank Zappa remarked that he wouldn't have had much of a chance of being signed in today's music business. Newman shared Zappa's pessimistic view. "In my opinion, an artist like me couldn't get started in the business today," Newman said in 1999. "There are few record companies now which would give you the time I was given to develop." While novelty songs have a chance at selling a million, Newman realized satirical music, which implicates the listener, certainly was unlikely to shoot to Number One with a bullet. Still, in the sixties, when both Newman and Zappa arrived on the scene, there were executives in charge ("cigar-chompers" in Zappa's words) who did take chances on unusual musicians with authentic talent with the hope that, over time, they'd develop a much larger fan base. Despite that optimism, neither Zappa nor Newman thought the ideals of the sixties could ever be realized — and they both turned out to be right.

"One thing happened out of the sixties: I was allowed to do what I do," Newman said in 1987. "There weren't singer-songwriters before then. You were allowed not to be a handsome guy; you could write your own stuff and not have a traditional voice. But the flowers aren't in anybody's hair anymore. I knew it was transitory." In general, music is now treated as a disposable commodity by a business that markets it according to its star potential rather than its musical attributes. Given that dismal scenario, Newman has accepted he'll never be an artist for popular consumption. "My taste does not correlate with the taste of the general public, for the most part," Newman admits. "There are a number of people who love my records, but there aren't enough of them to make it a booming industry. It's a very fringe kind of operation."

While Newman and Zappa shared similar views of the music business, and their role within it, there were significant differences between them. Where Zappa drew (with snide satisfaction) moustaches on the people and circumstances he mocked, Newman's ridicule is comparatively complex. Even the most depraved folks Newman sings about are embraced in a spirit that is both charitable and free of rancor. "They are portrayed without condescension, and often with outright affection," music scholar Peter Winkler writes in his essay, "Randy Newman's Americana," published in *Popular Music* in 1987. "The songs seem to ask, 'Are you and I really any better?'" Newman also doesn't turn musical history into an inspired farce the way Zappa did. No matter how preposterous the circumstances of a Randy Newman song, the music is always safely nestled within the basic formalities of pop. That's not to suggest that his work is conventional. "The music often betrays a sensuousness and romanticism that rarely surfaces in his lyrics," Winkler explains. "Though his view of American society is bleak and pessimistic, Newman's music is an affirmation and celebration of the richness and variety of American musical life."

As in *Dangerous Kitchen, Randy Newman's American Dreams* is the story of a cultural outsider on a quest to discover what America means to him. Since America is as much an idea as it is a country, its history is often veiled by legend and innuendo. This book represents a portrait of the artist as a masked man, a riverboat gambler who wisely conceals his hand. Yet even if we can only guess at the cards he's holding, Newman still provides a nuanced assessment of a country whose virtues and conflicts seem to commingle magically. Using Newman's songs as a guide, I've tried to take the reader on an equivocal voyage through the streams and tributaries of a vast and complex American domain — just as Herman Melville's *The Confidence Man* did in a fictional riverboat excursion a century ago. On the way, we encounter other masked Americans — both real and ficticious — who populate both Newman's songs and the nation he writes about. The mask changes hands; it takes different forms, sometimes concealing as much as it reveals. But it always remains a fascinating fixture that helps define the American character.

I'd like to think of *Randy Newman's American Dreams*, in part, as a sequel to *Dangerous Kitchen*. In both books I've tried to create a broader context that marries the art with the times that produced each artist. Which means, if you're one of those fans eager to fetishize the minutia of Newman's personal life, you're going to be sadly disappointed. There is also a huge difference between the two books. The fact that Zappa composed with a completely self-assured purpose made it relatively easy to elucidate his influences. Newman, on the other hand, proved a different kind of challenge. His self-doubt and musical disguises took me into a labyrinth of paradoxes — many of which I found daunting to define. But if you were to ask me whether or not, deep down, these two books are about composers who write comedy music? C'mon. You're kidding me, right?

# Inheritor of the Mask

Life is a picnic *en costume;* one must take part, assume a
character, stand ready in a sensible way to play the fool.

— Herman Melville, *The Confidence Man*

Things are seldom what they seem/
Skim milk masquerades as cream.

— Gilbert & Sullivan, *H.M.S. Pinafore*

## 1

It's safe to assume that when Frank Sinatra created Reprise Records in
1960, he didn't envision a lineup that would eventually include Tiny
Tim, Jimi Hendrix, The Mothers of Invention, Captain Beefheart &
His Magic Band, Neil Young, The Fugs and Randy Newman.
However, by 1970, there they were, not to mention a host of others
just like them — and here was Frank Sinatra situated among them.
Curiously, at that time, Sinatra was also in need of a hit song. So he
turned to an unlikely collaborator: Randy Newman.

Frank Sinatra had been a best-selling artist for Capitol Records since 1953 after a long string of sensational albums. Sinatra possessed the kind of dreamy, forlorn voice that could reach down to the very essence of tenderness in a sad song. When he interpreted such indelibly sorrowful tunes as "I Can't Get Started," on *No One Cares,* or "Willow Weep For Me," on *Frank Sinatra Sings For Only the Lonely,* he would embody the song's anguish so effortlessly it was as if the compositions were singing him. Sinatra had perfected a distinctly romantic style, a sexiness born of both heartbreak and despair. He played out the role of the lonely guy at the bar, nursing his glass of scotch, then imparting a lasting story of regret to you alone. In doing so, Sinatra could keep alive a slight flicker of romantic desire, hushed yearning or grievous moment that became more deeply intoxicating with every line he sang.

By the late fifties, however, Sinatra's real unhappiness lay with Capitol Records. Disgruntled, he wanted out of his contract, citing exhaustion with the demands of the major labels. In Reprise, what Sinatra envisioned was an independent record label which might attract folks like fellow Rat-Packer Dean Martin and jazz music's true dignitary, Duke Ellington. But while Martin and Ellington eagerly jumped on the bandwagon, the Chairman of the Board still wasn't satisfied; he just wasn't making the huge impact he had years earlier. Sinatra's subsequent Reprise recordings didn't manufacture anywhere near the number of hits his years with Capitol produced. Even still, there was an abundance of wonderful songs. Who can forget the beautiful melancholic cadences of "Summer Wind," or the unquenchable craving of "Strangers in the Night," not to mention "That's Life," with its soulful swing? But by 1968, the songs were no longer singing him. Sinatra had grown far too comfortable in the role of the romantic icon. His cover of Paul Anka's self-pitying "My Way," for example, was so overwrought that it became a self-parody of the wounded romantic Sinatra had been playing for years. When "My Way" only climbed as high as No. 27 on the pop charts in 1970, Sinatra turned to Randy Newman. When Sinatra met Newman in the studio, he found a singer-songwriter and pianist who was far from a wounded romantic, someone who shuffled shyly across the room as if trying not to be noticed. Yet Newman had already provided a nimble collection of songs for other proven performers. The song he would dream up for Sinatra had the curious title of "Lonely at the Top."

It's hard to say if Newman specifically wrote "Lonely at the Top" to take the piss out of the grandiose "My Way," but a studio session was soon arranged for Newman to play Sinatra the song. Unlike "My Way," with its phony tough-guy platitudes, "Lonely at the Top" is a biting examination of the romantically fatalistic figure Frank Sinatra had spent a career creating. Sinatra pressed himself quietly against the studio wall, while Newman crouched over the piano and slowly began to sing. As a piece of music, "Lonely at the Top" was your basic ragtime ballad, but the lyrics — spoken in the first person — were something quite peculiar. Not only did the song subtly mock Sinatra, it also caricatured the life and career of Newman himself: "I've been around the world, had my pick of any girl," sang the unworldly Newman in his customary low drawl. "You think I'd be happy, but I'm not." Ol' Blue Eyes stood attentively trying to measure the meaning of this odd little ditty, while Newman continued his sly deconstruction of the Sinatra persona: "Everybody knows my name, but it's just a crazy game. Oh, it's lonely at the top." Could this clown be serious?, Sinatra no doubt wondered. In all likelihood, Newman had already lost his big chance for a hit record, and by the song's conclusion, the jig was definitely up — "Listen all you fools out there/ Go on and love me — I don't care/ Oh, it's lonely at the top."

Without saying a word, Sinatra left the studio having made it perfectly clear there would be no new hit song coming from Randy Newman. For his part, Newman wasn't terribly surprised, as he had immediately identified one of the significant differences between the two performers. Where Newman had written a character study of a man who couldn't find solace in being on top, Sinatra was an artist who believed that solace could *only* be found there.

"It would have been real difficult," Newman told Steve Turner of *Beat Instrumental*. "[Sinatra] couldn't have played many [types of] characters in his songs." Newman recognized that his song required that Sinatra distance himself from, even parody, the image he'd helped create. "He could have [truly got] it if he had this sense of humor and he actually was leaning against a lamppost, looking forlorn," Newman told journalist David Wild years later. But if you listen carefully to Newman sing "Lonely at the Top," you immediately catch the incongruencies in the song, a caustic and clever ingredient that Sinatra surely resisted, and for good reason. Sung with a straight face, by any popular performer, Sinatra, or even Barbra Streisand (who also turned the song down), the tune would lose its character and its point. A couple of years after the fateful Sinatra session, Timothy Crouse, in *Rolling Stone*, elaborated on the discrepancy: "Although it was written for Frank Sinatra, 'Lonely' is really a parody of every self-congratulatory end-of-the-road song Sinatra has ever sung. It is also an expression of the bewildering apathy Randy [Newman] feels for his own career." Newman went even deeper into that apathy when he described the difference between his attempts at prosperity and the very burden of success for Sinatra. "*I* can do personal stuff because no one gives a shit — no one knows who the hell I am. But Sinatra can't sing 'Suzanne' [a Newman song about a rapist's fantasies] because he's *somebody*." Since Newman was a "nobody," he could be *anybody* in his songs, a luxury Frank Sinatra, with all his fame, couldn't afford.

After Sinatra's rejection, Newman sat down to write more songs and decided to keep "Lonely at the Top" for himself — as a cute joke in which the chap singing that he's lonely at the top hides a fear that he might actually be closer to the bottom. Newman added the song to live shows, and even included the track on his studio album, *Sail Away,* in 1972. Sinatra, meanwhile, abandoned recording and went into a brief retirement. But though the session did not produce a successful collaboration between these two radically different performers, it proved to be a somewhat instructive experience for Newman. He could now put his futile attempt to emulate Sinatra behind him, and in the process, finally discover his own voice.

2

"It's hard to hear a new voice, as hard as it is to listen to an unknown language," D.H. Lawrence wrote in *Studies in Classic American Literature* (1924). "We just don't listen." Lawrence wasn't just talking about something as basic as the fear of something new. New ideas, as he later suggested, can always be pigeon-holed. "The world fears a new experience more than it fears anything," Lawrence explained. "It can't pigeon-hole a real new experience. It can only dodge. The world is a great dodger, and the Americans the greatest. Because they dodge their own very selves." Lawrence, in this book, was addressing the varied works of American writers James Fenimore Cooper, Edgar Allan Poe, Nathaniel Hawthorne and Herman Melville. A panoramic and illuminating study, the polemic examined how a number of gifted writers were coming to terms with the experience of a young country still in the process of finding its identity. Lawrence's words, though, have a way of transcending time. They can easily be applied, for example, to the work of Randy Newman.

As the curious meeting with Frank Sinatra neatly illustrates, Newman is among the more paradoxical American composers, an Artful Dodger whose very self can hold a multitude of meanings. Just consider the songs. In "Davy the Fat Boy," Davy's best friend promises the boy's dying parents to take care of him, only to stick Davy in a circus freak show after they're gone. In "Suzanne," Newman's answer to Leonard Cohen's poetic tribute to a lovely and mysterious nymph, a loner finds Suzanne's name in a phone book and stalks her like a rapist. The song "Lucinda" has the poor girl accidentally chewed up by a beach-cleaning machine. "Sail Away," perhaps Newman's greatest song, features a slave trader coercing African blacks onboard his ship by promising them watermelons and wine (not to mention opportunities to sing songs about Jesus all day) if they only come to America. On the subject of God, the gospel-inspired "God's Song (That's Why I Love Mankind)" has God blithely handing down plagues, wars and famine while laughing from his home in Heaven at all the futile prayers offered him. After all, Newman chortles, that's why God loves mankind. In "A Wedding in Cherokee County," a hillbilly marries only to discover that he's impotent. In a more recent song, "The World Isn't Fair," the narrator brings Karl Marx back from the dead to show him a world so unfair that Karl wants to return quickly to his grave. Randy Newman's songs, which grapple with people and issues rarely found in chart-topping pop songs, are cleverly constructed, satirical pieces charged with ambiguity.

"My musical aesthetic is sort of romantic," Newman told Jim Macnie of the *Providence Phoenix* in 2000. "But [my] literary sensibility is different. I don't have many lyrics that I consider soppy. If I had more of a heart I'd probably have sold more records over the years." Newman has resisted writing the accessible songs that could easily attract mainstream ears — in fact, he's discovered that he can't help but fight the urge. "I don't have a record of writing hit after hit, the way Billy Joel or Paul Simon has, or Stevie Wonder had," he explained to Barney Hoskyns in *Mojo*. "Even when I set out to try, it doesn't turn out that way. If I'd written 'Just the Way You Are,' I'd have gone, 'I love you just the way you are . . . you cunt!', or something. At the end, I would have fucked it up."

What Newman has in common with many great American artists, though, is his utopianism. "Randy Newman is a typical figure in the American imagination," Greil Marcus wrote in his essay on Newman, "Every Man Is Free," from his book *Mystery Train*. "The man who does not like what he sees but is wildly attracted to it anyway, a man who keeps his sanity by rendering contradictions other people struggle to avoid." Those contradictions are torn out of the history of a country built on a dream, handed down by forefathers who fought a revolution to claim it. You can hear the ghosts of that dream in Newman's enigmatic portrait of the American South, *Good Old Boys* (1974), or in strangely quaint songs like "Love Story," in which a newly married couple wish for a child "that someday may be President, if things loosen up." Perhaps it's also there in "I Love L.A." when the narrator, cruising the city streets in his car, happily cranks up the Beach Boys at the same moment he sees a bum throwing up in the street. In almost every song I've mentioned so far, there's a delectable promise hidden behind every joke, every disaster and every dodge. It's a promise of what is commonly known as the American Dream, whereby every man is supposed to be free, but seldom is. Newman's articulation of that promise is neatly and cleverly veiled. He disguises it in satire, irony and deception. "The old American artists were hopeless liars," D.H. Lawrence also observed. "But they were artists, in spite of themselves."

More specifically, Newman subverts the established tenets of the romantic pop song by eliminating himself as a character. "Short-story writer Alice Munro doesn't have to be in her stories, why do I have to be?" he asked Sarah Hampson of the Toronto *Globe & Mail* in 2003. Hampson elaborates, saying Newman "as a songwriter is like a fiction writer with a great facility for dialogue. He inhabits a character and speaks convincingly in his or her voice. He can serve up a schmaltzy ballad that can fill an audience with Hallmark-like warmth as easily as he can write a song that will fill listeners with cynical humor and sometimes even disgust." Newman's songs can trip up his listeners, especially our expectations. "[His] best music often pulls the listener in two directions at once, against the expectations the sound sets up," wrote Sean Elder in *Salon*. Irving Howe, writing on the diabolical comedy of Lenny Bruce, said it could make you respond with the kind of laughter that suggests "convicts caught in a scheme to escape." As with Bruce, there is an antagonistic quality in Newman's songs that provokes a prurient response. "My music has a high irritation factor," Newman once remarked. "You can't put it on . . . and invite the neighbors over for a barbecue. It's got 'prick' and 'wop' in it, and 'I'm gonna take off my pants.'"

Newman's longtime producer and childhood friend, Lenny Waronker, has been a pained witness to the way Newman sacrificed the commercial potential of a song for its pure aesthetic value. "Randy would take what I thought was a potential hit and alter it if he felt that was necessary to fulfill his vision of the song," Waronker explained. "Sometimes he would remove the most accessible part of a song and replace it with something much more complex and unusual and difficult." This tactic allowed Newman the freedom to devise daring and crafty musical arrangements. But it was an approach that could upset both listeners and composers, just as Frank Zappa's did. For example, when Newman was staging his musical, *Faust,* in 1995, Stephen Sondheim asked if he could drop by the rehearsals. Newman replied that it was no problem, but he hoped Sondheim didn't mind Newman bending the rules of the musical. "I said, I hope you won't mind a few 'girl' and 'world' rhymes and things like that. He said, 'Well, I *do* mind. You don't come from that tradition.' But I *do*. I come from Frogman Henry and Fats Domino, who rhymed 'shoes' and 'New Orleans.' And I don't mind at all . . . [Sondheim's] strict about it," Newman told journalist Chris Willman. Newman isn't strict for one simple reason: he grew up in the impudent age of rock & roll. Although born in Los Angeles, Newman spent some of his early childhood in New Orleans, where his mother's family once resided. While there he absorbed a variety of influences, including the boogie-woogie sounds of pianist Fats Domino, who was a master of innuendo. The early fathers of rock helped shape part of the bedrock of Newman's actual sound. "A lot of the records I liked were from New Orleans — 'Sea Cruise,' 'Let the Good Times Roll' — although I didn't even know they were from New Orleans at the time. So maybe there was some kind of childhood osmosis going on," he recalled.

Then there is Newman's voice, which borrows liberally from the black music he heard in the South. Even here, though, he pulls a fast one on us. "What Newman has taken from black singers is not what most rock & roll singers have taken: assertiveness, aggression, melancholy, sexual power," Marcus explains. "His somnambulant personality determined his choice of a lazy, blurred sound, where words slide into each other, where syllables are not bitten off, but just wear out and dissolve." This important aspect of Newman's masquerade not only creates an illusion of helplessness, it disguises his cunning intelligence. When Fats Domino *insinuated* the thrill he got on Blueberry Hill, he was being far more subversive than if he'd been explicit. By leaving it to us, as listeners, we could imagine just about anything. Every shrewd rock singer, from Little Richard to Mick Jagger, has employed that tactic as a cagey way to seduce the teens of America.

But when Randy Newman blurs his words, he isn't out to inspire sexual mayhem among innocent adolescents. Rather it's a means for him to sneak a whole other meaning into his music. "It is as if Randy's real blues hero wasn't Howlin' Wolf, but Stepin Fetchit — as if Randy had a pretty good idea of what secrets were hidden in the shuffle," Marcus wrote. A perfect illustration of Marcus' point can be found in Newman's original version of "Mama Told Me Not To Come." In this song, the singer finds himself alone at a wild party, partly terrified at what he sees. Although Newman sings with the trembling, scaredy-cat terror of Stepin Fetchit, he insinuates that — as scared as he is — he is also *digging* this orgy going on around him. The joke that bubbles to the surface is that he doesn't know what's terrifying him more: the orgy, or his own hidden perversities, and that tension is completely missing in the better known Three Dog Night cover. Time and again, more popular singers like Tom Jones, Mariah Carey, Linda Ronstadt and Joe Cocker have recorded Newman's songs, including "I Think It's Going to Rain Today," "You Can Leave Your Hat On" and "Sail Away," and they've become hits by either making explicit what Newman merely implies, or by ducking the hidden subject matter altogether. But when Newman records these tracks, they fail to connect commercially because his voice brings out the true implications of the song. Yet even if Newman has largely failed to attract a mass audience, you can hear the impact he's had on a number of other vocal stylists.

Especially in the works of David Byrne, Elvis Costello and P.J. Harvey, you can hear how the meaning of the song is grasped by the timbre of the voice.

Critic Dave Laing, in his book, *One-Chord Wonders: Power and Meaning in Punk Rock,* explains Newman's voice another way. "Many white singers are attracted to black blues and gospel styles because of the impression of authenticity, of heartfelt soulfulness that such styles can convey," he writes. "Randy Newman seems to be appropriating black styles for precisely the opposite reason: to intensify a sense of alienation, to emphasize the gap between himself and the characters in his songs." Laing rightly observes that Newman "deliberately exploits the absurdity of a white, Jewish intellectual singing like a black from the deep South, mocking the conventions of 'white boy with the blues' even as he appropriates them. He is laughing at his own blackface act." This is no doubt why Lenny Waronker once dubbed Newman "The King of the Suburban Blues Singers." Journalist Erin Aubry Kaplan once observed that it's easier for white American performers to write songs in the first person because "the world proceeds from them." Black artists, according to Kaplan, were never historically allowed a private identity, so they embraced roles which reflected social conflict and struggle. Yet Kaplan suggests that Newman found a way to bridge both worlds. "Newman has always found intimacy and soul-baring confining and against instinct, and so has embraced emotional oblique-ness and a storyteller role — the de facto black musical tradition — by default," Kaplan wrote in the *LA Weekly.* "Despite the prevalence of the first person in his songs, he positions himself as the conscientious observer in somebody else's shoes. . . . Newman's job has always been to make things clearer, not more bearable." In that sense, Newman is subverting the traditional Jewish role in the history of minstrelsy.

At the turn of the twentieth century, Jews had become predominant in blackface entertainment, and would be for the next two decades, until the form was finally abandoned altogether. Many Jewish per-formers had become popular in blackface, including Al Jolson, Sophie Tucker and Eddie Cantor (who even used it as a form of comedy). Jeffrey Melnick, in his book, *A Right to Sing the Blues,* perceived min-strelsy as a crude form of cultural appropriation. "Jews made their first major appearance in the national marketplace of popular culture through the travesties of African-Americans." Others, like Howe, saw it quite differently. "When they took over the conventions of ethnic mimicry, the Jewish performers transformed it into something emotionally richer and more humane," he wrote in *World of Our Fathers*. "Black became a mask for Jewish expressiveness, with one woe speaking through the voice of another. Irving Berlin inserted Yiddishisms into songs deriving from 'coon song' conventions. . . . Blacking their faces seems to have enabled the Jewish performers to reach a spontaneity and assertiveness in the declaration of their Jewish selves." Melnick observed, moreover, that music provided the perfect common ground between blacks and Jews, because essentially it allowed Jews to be both white and black without losing their Jewishness. "The musical world provided a space where African-Americans and Jews could speak to, and about, each other," he wrote. "Jews in the music business, in particular, drew connections between themselves and African-Americans in order to create a narrative about the ethnic origins of the music which then became operational as a national mythology." This is why, according to Melnick, music provided an opportunity for Jews to assimilate, using the familiar black culture to connect with mainstream audiences. And, in doing so, Jews could appear less foreign and less threatening. "While leading African-Americans seemed most interested in achieving basic civil rights gains through cultural productions, Jews looked to culture as a vehicle to enter the privileged domain of whiteness, American style," Melnick explains. "African-Americans hoped their cultural contributions would convince white America that they were *people* who entertained, while Jews hoped their contributions would remind white America that they were *entertaining* people."

For his part, Newman deliberately employed a black voice, not as a means to entertain audiences, but to reveal just what lengths his antecedents would go to be accepted. It was, in short, a political act. He also wrote and performed many political songs that didn't cater to popular taste. Songs like "Sail Away," "Rednecks" and "It's Money That I Love" were vastly entertaining, yet they still found ways to cut across partisan alliances. Newman's natural audience might always have been educated white liberals, but the intricacy of his songs sometimes breaks out of the ideological straitjacket of political dogma. One such Newman fan from Chicago happened to be a Republican conservative. He wrote a review of a recent Randy Newman album on

Amazon.com that exhibited quite a clear understanding of Newman's sensibility. "Newman himself is probably a liberal, but who cares?" the fan observed. "His songs are not political screeds, they are observations on life. And they're right on target. Whether it's the devastation of 'Louisiana 1927' or using 'Rednecks' to zero in on the hypocrisy of the Northern liberal to whom integration is but a distant rumor, Randy Newman paints a picture of life in America which isn't always pretty." Which goes to prove, if indeed it ever needed to be proved, that in a Randy Newman song it's immaterial if your politics are left or right. Either way, he doesn't provide you the comfort of feeling you have the market cornered on fighting for your country's ideals.

Of course, Newman's songs *are* critical of much of American culture, but they are filled with a characteristic affection for its peculiarities, too. "How could he disdain a country that gave him so many juicy tidbits to blow out of all proportion and textbook characters to make larger than fiction?" Paul McGrath of the Toronto *Globe & Mail* asked. "In his work is a love for the flashy but clumsy giant he so loves to ridicule; but lurking underneath it is a masked horror at its possibilities." Newman describes the masked horror of his music much more simply. "I realize I have to make the uglier observations easy to swallow," he wrote in the press packet to his 1999 release, *Bad Love*. "If I made the music all spiky . . . people wouldn't hear what I'm saying. As for my intent, well, I'm not Mary Sunshine. And I'm not particularly optimistic about a lot of things. But what has been taken as nastiness in some of my songs isn't really descriptive of anything, or anyone — it's exaggeration for the sake of satire." This exaggeration puts him in good company with the writers D.H. Lawrence examined in *Studies in Classic American Literature*. "I like untrustworthy narrators and things where the audience knows stuff that the narrator doesn't know," Newman told writer Paul Zollo. "I *love* that kind of stuff. You don't see much of it in *songs*. You see it in literature a little bit." Looking for the root source of Newman's untrustworthy narrator, for example, you just might look to Herman Melville, who once wrote an unpopular, soon to be obscure novel entitled *The Confidence Man*. Although Newman never refers to Melville's novel as any kind of influence or source, it's an abstract comic masterpiece that functions as something much like an inner voice in Newman's songs.

3

When Melville's short novel, *Billy Budd,* was published in 1924, some 33 years after his death, *The Press,* a New York paper, titled a profile on Melville, "Death of a Once Popular Artist." Who would have guessed anonymity could ever swallow up an artist whose strong individual voice put such a huge stamp on American literature? "Probably, if truth were known, even his own generation thought him dead, so quiet have been the later years of his life," *The Press* declared. Melville's later years were indeed rather dormant, but he was anything but a quiet presence. "Melville is not a civilized, European writer," film critic Pauline Kael wrote in praising Peter Ustinov's 1962 film adaptation of *Billy Budd.* "He is our greatest writer because he is the American primitive struggling to say more than he knows how to say, struggling to say more than he knows."

In 1857, Melville's particular struggle took the form of his very strange and experimental novel, *The Confidence Man.* It was this book — one that well embodies Newman's idea of the untrustworthy narrator — that basically finished off the author's career, earning him some of his most scathing reviews. Critics called it "indigestible" and "baffling," and Melville was so deeply affected by the fallout he turned away from writing and started supporting his family by other means — first, in a lecture tour that ultimately failed, then in an applied for consulship that also went nowhere. Finally, in 1866, Melville landed a Customs Inspector position in the New York Customs House, which he retained until he retired in 1885. He continued to write and publish books of poetry (and ultimately *Billy Budd*) until his death in 1891.

*The Confidence Man,* published on the eve of the American Civil War, caused quite an uproar. Perhaps Americans saw the novel as inappropriate, or even an affront to the unsettling issues the nation was then confronting. A swift and satirical discourse on a variety of moral and political concerns, *The Confidence Man* was an oddly structured comic allegory about a shape-changing grifter who boards the Mississippi riverboat *Fidèle* on (of all occasions) April Fool's Day. The grifter victimizes an assortment of passengers in a series of scams on a trip that takes them from St. Louis to New Orleans. Once he wins his marks' trust, he cons them with promises of charity and virtue. But even as the con man's charm tests their resolve on a number of subjects, his ultimate goal is to reveal his fellow passengers' deeper (and often contrary) desires.

Melville introduces characters who change identities so rapidly that the reader is confronted with a portrait of the American frontier as perceived through a hall of mirrors. The novel operates on so many levels, with Melville playing clever games with both fact and fiction, it's no surprise some readers became so dizzy they desperately wanted off the boat.

The idea of *The Confidence Man* was partly inspired by Edgar Allen Poe's definition of the "diddler" in his 1843 essay, "Diddling Was Considered as One of the Exact Sciences." The term itself has its origin in the character Jeremy Diddler from James Kenney's 1803 play, *Raising the Wind*. In the play, Diddler borrows small sums of money from folks with no intention of ever paying them back. In Poe's terms, "a crow thieves; a fox cheats; a weasel outwits; a man diddles." An article in the *New York Herald* ("Arrest of the Confidence Man") in July 1849 chronicled the exploits of a con man who went by the name of "William Thompson," and that story gave Melville his title for the novel. "Thompson" had cleverly ingratiated himself into people's lives in order to swindle them. Unlike in America, Europeans had grappled for centuries with their share of tricksters and confidence men. False bishops like Adelbert and Clement were active in Germany as far back as 744, with Adelbert telling followers they needn't even confess their sins, since he could read their hearts anyway. In 1190, the death of Holy Roman Emperor Frederick Barbarossa gave rise to a whole pack of false Fredericks claiming he hadn't really died. Singer/actor Willie Nelson played a modern American variation of that character in Fred Schepisi's underrated Western, *Barbarosa* (1982).

The confidence man may have played a significant role in European history, but he would ultimately take a stronger hold on the American imagination. "There is actually a peculiarly American delight in confidence tricksters," wrote Melville scholar Stephen Matterson. "In part such affection has to do with America's emphasis on and admiration for individual enterprise and ingenuity, which are considered notably 'Yankee' qualities." Tony Tanner, another Melville scholar, describes nineteenth century America as a country in perpetual motion. "What was happening in America was not the sudden upheaval and dislocation of a previously stable and relatively settled society," Tanner wrote in his introduction to the 1989 Oxford Press edition of *The Confidence Man*. "Immigration and a moving frontier meant an endless inpouring of strangers, who in the general movement became endlessly estranged." Alexis de Tocqueville, the historian and political observer, saw Americans as a people who continuously transformed themselves, while shedding their past like dead skin. "Thus not only does democracy make every man forget his ancestors, but it hides his descendants and separates his contemporaries from him," de Tocqueville wrote in *Democracy in America*. "It throws him back forever upon himself alone and threatens in the end to confine him entirely within the solitude of his own heart." And, as Tanner would point out, a society where you can become a stranger — even to yourself — is liable to encourage the emergence of a confidence man.

The trickster, who unremittingly alters his masquerade, thus becomes a fitting metaphor for the shifting values of American life. "The very process of becoming an American is in part the making of a new self," writes Stephen Matterson. "To become American is essentially to divest oneself of a past identity, to make a radical break with the past, and so the construction of identity becomes a significant theme in American writing, present as a recognizable tradition." The grifter sees as his goal not financial reward, but the selling of confidence. "The confidence man sees more opportunity in New World fluidity, not merely to improve his lot by cleverness and technical proficiency," wrote Gary Lindberg in his 1982 polemic, *The Confidence Man in American Literature*. "But [he recasts] the self through cunning initiation." The con man depends on the trust of his victim, becoming what Stephen Matterson refers to as "a figure of covert and overt admiration." Since he flourishes best in a country where it is natural to trust people, he goes against the grain of liberal pieties such as Emerson's claim that if you trust men, they'll ultimately be true to you. The confidence man's role is much more adversarial, and it relies on our ability to be sharp and informed. The confidence man may also be the best argument against censorship in a democracy, because one needs access to as much knowledge and information as possible to match him. Yet, conversely, we need him, too. We depend on his taunts to make us stronger, smarter, and to give us a sense of community.

The con man's game, however, is also a humorous one. Absurdity plays a big hand in his success at turning the trick. "The element of social absurdity in our tall-tale jokes cannot be underestimated," wrote Jesse Bier in *The Rise and Fall of American Humor.* "That culminative production, the minstrel show, was a tall-tale joke in itself, assembling coon-hatted and overly fringed frontiersmen, white comedians putting on blackface, drawling Yankees. . . . It makes sophisticated fun of primitive powers but at the same time deflates a certain modish cynicism, which is the modern snobbery."

The con artist is a leitmotif that runs through every facet of American culture. You can find him in various guises, ranging from carny barker P.T. Barnum to the infamous Louisiana governor Huey P. Long; he's the boorish right-wing talk show host Rush Limbaugh as easily as he inhabits Limbaugh's counterpart, that shambling snake-oil salesman of the left, Michael Moore. Confidence gets put to the test everywhere in the literature and films that define and parody American culture. It's tested by Twain's Huck Finn, Sinclair Lewis's Bible-thumping fraud, Elmer Gantry, Humbert Humbert's nemesis Clare Quilty in Vladimir Nabokov/Stanley Kubrick's *Lolita* (1962), the Neal Cassady–inspired Dean Moriarty of Jack Kerouac's *On the Road,* even Ralph Ellison's pertinently titled *Invisible Man* (1952). Burt Lancaster executes his scams while bearing his Chicklets grin in *The Rainmaker* (1956), while Peter O'Toole's daredevil movie director Eli Cross plays with our perception of illusion and reality while he tests the confidence of a paranoid apprentice (Steve Railsback) — and ourselves — in Richard Rush's wonderfully exhuberant *The Stunt Man* (1980). Kurt Russell dares us to trust his brash automobile salesman, Rudy Russo, in Robert Zemeckis' outrageously funny *Used Cars* (1981). The genial huckster is alive in Michael Keaton's "idea" man, as he tests the wits of his nebbish partner (Henry Winkler), in Ron Howard's *Night Shift* (1982). *The Grifters* (1990) gives us three con artists, played by John Cusack, Angelica Huston and Annette Bening, who scam each other with tragic repercussions. We find the confidence man resurrecting himself, too, as the character of Paul (Will Smith) in Fred Schepisi's adaptation of John Guare's play, *Six Degrees of Separation* (1993). Here he becomes a catalyst for change in the lives of a number of upper-middle-class New Yorkers.

The confidence man has also found a home deep in the heart of American music. He has held court as an audacious spirit in the music and character of Bob Dylan, with his multitude of disguises and masks.

He's also played a decisive and divisive role in the insurgent rap music of Eminem (working his own devious magic through his alter ego Slim Shady). In the songs of Randy Newman, the confidence man pops up everywhere, in the slave trader in "Sail Away," or on the Senate floor, in the form of two characters who obliquely plead for both Utah and Kansas in "The Beehive State." He is the hideously expedient advisor of "Political Science," who wants "to set everybody free" while simultaneously suggesting we "drop the big one." He gets the ultimate role of God, too, testing the limits of our faith and trust while toying with our resolve in "God's Song (That's Why I Love Mankind)." Newman, like Dylan, also personally embodies the role of confidence man, and in doing so, appropriates those disguises and masks to keep us guessing at just what his songs really mean. In that sense, Newman's entire body of work could be seen as Melville's *The Confidence Man* rendered in music.

Employing the masquerade while working within the strict commercial confines of pop culture, Newman constantly questions the value of success, almost playfully testing our willingness to trust where he's taking us in each tune. In the world of pop music, however, that tactic can be a dangerous one. Pop music, by its very nature, reaches out to a broader audience. Newman's untrustworthy narrator confines him to a cult following. Thus far, that has been Randy Newman's crucible. Despite winning an Academy Award for one of his movie songs, he has not reaped the benefits of commercial success. Even so, like all American utopians, he continues to try to find a mass audience ready to take the chances that he does. "I think I wanted people who knew what they were talking about to like me almost more than I wanted a big audience," Newman recently told Greil Marcus. "For a while I did, anyway. It's kind of a snotty thing to want. I got it — and then I would rather have sold two million records." Newman's ambivalence over his own personal achievement is pivotal. Where Melville may have suffered over the fate of *The Confidence Man*, you don't sense any guilt over his career move — at least not in the way you do with Newman. That's because Newman's penitence is found behind a different disguise: his Jewishness.

4

For the confidence man to find a comfortable home in the heart of American culture, he needed a mask. "The mask was a portable heirloom handed down by the pioneer," historian Constance Rourke wrote in her 1931 study, *American Humor: A Study of the National Character*. "No doubt the mask would prove useful in a country where the puritan was still a power and the risks of pioneering were by no means over." Randy Newman's songs are often proof enough that those risks endure, but there are significant reasons why humor has become an intrinsic part of his disguise. Jesse Bier, in *The Rise and Fall of American Humor*, may have identified the root of Newman's type of waggery when he suggested the American satirist creates a form of sanctuary in order to execute his most audacious work. "Do these representative comedians throw their voices, like ventriloquists, hiding behind dummies, masks and names, because they are fearful, not of simple failure, but of too great a success?" Bier asks. "That is as much their secret motive in this country as is their desire to be two men with a sort of stereoscopic view on things. They seek safety as well as perspective."

"The mask is what in the nineteenth century came to be called the deadpan, the poker face," Greil Marcus adds in *Invisible Republic*. "The mask hides the voice no less than the face and . . . a speech made as much of silences as of words. . . ." The deadpan expression he describes would ultimately fit such diverse American figures as Buster Keaton and Clint Eastwood. But Newman's deadpan is something altogether different. He deploys the comic, self-deprecating pose of the Jewish *kvetch*, and what he veils is an underlying terror. For Jews, it could be of anti-semitism: the past pogroms, the not-so-distant Holocaust. Jews have often addressed — or sidestepped — those horrors through their use of comedy. Though he is a secular Jew, Newman's application of humor is no different. As Ian McDonald wrote in his book, *The People's Music*, "Newman's stance was that of a skeptical outsider loosely rooted in the attitudes and traditions of small-town America." Yet being an American doesn't provide for Newman any real refuge from the storied calamities that make up Jewish dread. "I know I'm American but I feel . . . they could *turn on me* at any moment," Newman told journalist Chris Bourke in 1994.

The paranoia of gentile aggression, shared by many Jewish comedians including Lenny Bruce, Woody Allen and Mel Brooks, has (to a degree) been inherited by Newman. "I'm very interested in this country," he told Erin Aubry Kaplan. "Though, I don't necessarily feel a part of it." According to Irving Howe, American Jews have adopted a number of comedic roles over the years in order to deal with that dread. "The immediate Yiddish past offered some models," Howe wrote in *World of Our Fathers.* "The *badkhn,* the jester, the fiddler, the stage comedian." In *The Haunted Smile,* Lawrence J. Epstein talks about American Jewish comics as if they were perched at the edge of an abyss. "Their stage smile is tinged with sadness," Epstein writes. "It is haunted by the Jewish past, by the deep strains in American Jewish life — the desire to be accepted and the concern for a culture disappearing — by the centuries of Jewish life too frequently interrupted by hate, and by the knowledge that too often for Jewish audiences a laugh masked a shudder." The genius of Newman's particular mask is that rather than hiding from that shudder, his humor brings us closer to it. He pokes at it, he examines it, sometimes he even falls victim to it. He makes deliberate fun of it, too.

"I have this theory I've developed about Jewish writers getting into America harder than a gentile writer would," Newman once explained to Timothy White. "Because they, or I, don't really feel like an American, exactly, I think people and even songwriters like me, we're looking at it more from the outside." The earlier generation of Jewish immigrants, especially those who would eventually become the moguls of Hollywood, weren't content looking at America from the outside — being an outsider invited annihilation. "The Jews had developed a survival instinct, an alertness bred from a fear that was almost always justified, an early warning system of the feelings of the majority culture," Epstein wrote. By inventing their own kingdom, ostensibly a film industry that introduced a beatific vision of American life, they could then feel like the Chosen People. "The Jews of Hollywood not only believed in the American Dream, [but] rather than see it fail, they tried desperately and successfully to manufacture the evidence for its survival . . . and for its existence," said screenwriter Hy Kraft. Rather than venerating that dream by drawing on their personal experiences as Jews coming to the new land, they created a fantasy America completely whitewashed of their own identity. "I could never understand how this great group of Jewish movie people had come to pick the most Waspish place in the world as the home for their industry," remarked Nik Vanet, the executive who signed the Beach Boys to their Capitol Records contract. "I mean, Warner [Brothers] was like Hitler's Aryan dream come true: do you realize that up until 1964 there wasn't anybody but *blond men* under contract? It was all Edd Byrnes and Troy Donahue — Hitler's favorite look." Louis B. Mayer, the head of MGM Studio, likely spoke for all the moguls when he remarked that they weren't there as Protestants or Jews but as *Americans*. When they traded in their *shtetlekh* past for a more dreamy pastoral America, history's most famous outsiders transformed themselves into insiders.

The Jewish mask started a process of what Howe has called "de-Semitization." But screenwriter Ben Hecht suggested that the Jew in American fiction, the stage and movies had become "the little man who isn't there" not so much out of self-hatred, but out of self-preservation. "When Hitler forced Americans to take anti-Semitism seriously, it was apparently felt that the most eloquent reply that could be made was a dead silence," Hecht explained. Turning their backs on their heritage, though, created a potential for collective guilt. The template for that remorse came long before Hitler. It took form in one of Hollywood's biggest productions: a film called *The Jazz Singer* (1927), starring Al Jolson and based on the Samson Raphaelson play *A Day of Atonement*. Warner Brothers billed *The Jazz Singer* as the first feature film with both music and dialogue. But perhaps more significant than the technical achievement itself, at least for this discussion, was the change that was made to the original material. In the play, Raphaelson depicted the story of Jack Robin (born Jackie Rabinowitz), a ragtime-singing son of a cantor. Blessed with a wonderful voice, Jack longed for a Broadway career, but he also had strong ties to the religious traditions of his father. The play ended with Jack sitting by his dying father's bedside, promising to honor him by taking his place as cantor in the Hester Street Synagogue. In the film, however, Jack ultimately opts for the secular life on Broadway, donning blackface and singing "Mammy" on one knee. As Robin's mother sits in the audience proudly beaming at her son, the dead father (and by association his cultural heritage) disappears from the story. Notably, the film had its world premiere on October 6, 1927, one day before Yom Kippur.

Where Raphaelson sentimentally honored the roots of his own

culture, the film version of *The Jazz Singer* was tantamount to embracing the Golden Calf. Its very popularity, coming at the beginning of the moguls' rule of Hollywood, set the tone for Howe's de-Semitization: if Jewish success was predicated on creating a fantasy America, it would also go hand in hand with the Jewish guilt of abandoning their own heritage. But what better way to take away the pain of that guilt, and even conceal it, than through humor?

The comedy of shame, guilt and denial has taken many forms. In one well-known story, Groucho Marx's daughter was once denied access to a gentile club where she wanted to go swimming. Groucho famously replied that he wouldn't belong to any club that would have someone like him as a member — adding that since his daughter was only half-Jewish, could she not go into the pool up to her waist? A nice illustration of the outsider predicament. His wasn't the only injustice that has translated itself into a joke. When the young Jewish teenagers in Barry Levinson's *Liberty Heights* (1999) face a sign barring them access to a public pool in mid-fifties Baltimore ("No Jews, dogs or coloreds allowed") they turn it into a gag. One of them questions how the order on the list was arrived at. Why did Jews come first, for example? On what grounds? Another poses a more logical question: What would happen if a dog showed up at the pool? Would he read the sign and then leave?

Newman himself shows that he's not above the self-deprecating gag. When Rhino Records released a CD box-set of his music in 1998, the front cover, decorated in baroque embroidery, read: "Famous Composers and Their Works." Newman then had that title scratched out and replaced with: *Guilty: 30 Years of Randy Newman*. This little joke resonates deeper when you realize just how much Newman doesn't fit the profile of the Famous Composer. "Call him typical, middle-of-the-road, middle-class," Peter Goddard wrote in the *Toronto Star*. "He doesn't even have the hero's style. He wears thick glasses. He sort of shuffles when he walks. And there's a perpetually startled look in his eyes. His grin is thin-lipped and lopsided." Newman adroitly goes against the grain of our common perception of the pop icon, just as Elliott Gould did in playing the honest gumshoe Philip Marlowe as a forlorn schlep in Robert Altman's *The Long Goodbye* (1973). Such nebbish characterizations are part of the smart guy's disguise, designed to catch you off-guard. "[Newman's] songs are sneak attacks on all that's dumb, dull — or both," Goddard concluded. It is those sneak attacks that gave Randy Newman access to the inside of the American mainstream. Once he got there, he could freely satirize the pitfalls of being successful, of being lonely at the top.

5

Through his parody of blackface vocals and his choice of subject matter, Randy Newman dries out the sentimentality of the customary pop song. The tradition he overturns is what Jeffrey Melnick called "the nostalgia-ridden Jewish productions of blackface, along with the scores of Jewish-penned Dixie songs." Newman employs the blackface persona as part of an ironic strategy that still links him to his antecedents. "I'm more in the tradition of Irving Berlin and Harold Arlen and those guys who were just doing their job. I'm just doing the job, too, with my kind of characters." But as much as Newman owes to Berlin and Arlen, he is doing more than just a job. Many contemporary Jewish songwriters besides Newman are attempting to overturn the quaint version of the American Dream that the Jewish Hollywood moguls constructed. Their goal, in the end, is to discover the deeper underpinnings of the American popular song.

"I sometimes think when I hear Paul Simon or Irving Berlin that we're more interested in America, but we're trying to just get it right," Newman explained to Timothy White in 2000. While acknowledging Berlin's artistic savvy in depicting America, Newman also recognized his attempts to avoid it: "Berlin can sing about loving Alabam', but God help him if he ever went to Alabama." Critic Stephen Holden seizes on that irony, and how it clearly separates Newman from his predecessors:

> Newman is essentially a post-Romantic composer whose musical ideas descend from Mahler, through Copland and the Copland-derived tradition of horse-opera movie-theme background music that has formed our standard musical connection to the frontier myth. Newman may use this tradition ironically, and he clearly seeks purgation from its sentimental excesses, but it is obvious that he is also in love with it. The same holds for Newman's relationship to musical Americana, whose resources he mines expansively and

with affection, paraphrasing in sketch everything from Stephen Foster, to the Charleston, to Gershwin and Kern, to the fifties' cabaret ballad. Newman's vision is, above all, a comprehensive musical and philosophical overview.

Jon Pareles, in *The New York Times,* further develops the idea of Newman's comprehensive musical overview. "[Newman] uses the nostalgic bounce of ragtime and the hymn-like chords of parlor songs to hold sentiments that would appall Stephen Foster," Pareles wrote. "He also takes a craftsman's pride as he honors or smoothly disrupts verse-chorus-bridge song forms." That "craftsman's pride," of course, is the cornerstone of Newman's musical sensibility. It's what you will find in the origins of the early Tin Pan Alley, which produced such prominent American songwriters as Rodgers and Hart, Irving Berlin, George and Ira Gershwin, Harold Arlen, Frank Loesser and Yip Harburg. Tin Pan Alley was the name given to a publishing company located on West 28th Street between Broadway and Sixth Avenue. Composers and lyricists were hired there on a permanent basis to provide an industry for popular songs. From 1880 to 1953, this block became something of an epicenter for both songwriting and music publishing in America.

European operettas may have once been the predominant influence on American songs, but by the late nineteenth century, a distinctly American ballad was starting to emerge. One such song, "After the Ball," written by Charles K. Harris in 1892, set a curious standard. "After the Ball" introduced the narrative of a short story into a song, with the same adroitness Newman would use years later in his own compositions. Although often performed today as an instrumental, the lyric tells quite a compelling fable, beginning with a young girl dancing at a ball with her fiancé. After the dance, she says she's thirsty and asks her husband-to-be to get her a glass of water. When he returns, he finds her kissing another man. Horrified, he drops the glass of water and storms out of the dance hall, never to see her again. What the fiancé doesn't realize until many years later is the man kissing his girl happened to be her brother, perhaps even congratulating her on the impending marriage. Ultimately, the young women dies of a broken heart. In the song, the story is told by the fiancé, now a gray-haired bachelor, to his young niece, looking back ruefully on the life he could have had.

The composition didn't go down well with the first singers Harris approached. Despite the strong melody, containing some of the sentimental sweetness of "Let Me Call You Sweetheart," the melodrama at the heart of the song was probably too odd, especially with its ironic twist at the end. But, in time, the tune would catch on, and as the new century approached, "After the Ball" opened the door for more American ballads because, as Philip Furia would point out in his book, *The Poets of Tin Pan Alley*, "critics who complain that the lyric is merely a 'thoroughly artificial piece of doggerel' forget that in the sentimental ballad it was the music and the story — rather than the poetic texture — that counted." As for the story, well the refrain itself could have found a home years later in any country & western song:

> *After the ball is over,*
> *After the break of morn —*
> *After the dancers' leaving;*
> *After the stars have gone;*
> *Many a heart is aching*
> *If you could read them all;*
> *Many the hopes that have vanished*
> *After the ball.*

"After the Ball" was one of the first hits from Tin Pan Alley to sell over five million copies of sheet music, thus providing a firm foundation for a publishing industry that would thrive in the coming years, especially when ragtime came along to transform the story-song ballad into what Furia calls "the urbane and vernacular love song." More than 1,800 rags were published between 1900 and 1910, beginning with "Maple Leaf Rag" by pianist Scott Joplin. By 1912, W.C. Handy had integrated the underground sound of the blues, then Louis Armstrong revolutionized jazz and led American music into the Roaring Twenties. Helped by urbanization, vaudeville and radio, song pluggers (known as "contact men") began pushing sheet music to any orchestra leader whose ear they could bend. Before long, the composers and their songs became legendary.

To paraphrase Jerome Kern, Irving Berlin didn't have a place in American music; he *was* American music. He proved it with one of Tin Pan Alley's hugest hits, "Alexander's Ragtime Band," in 1911, and followed with such exquisite romantic laments as "Blue Skies" and "All by Myself," before going on to write timeless standards like "White Christmas" and "God Bless America." Meanwhile, Kern and lyricist Dorothy Fields dreamed up "A Fine Romance" and "The Way You Look Tonight," after Kern had teamed up with Oscar Hammerstein II to write "Ol' Man River" and "Can't Help Lovin' Dat Man" for the groundbreaking musical *Show Boat* (1927). Ira and George Gershwin were a rarity as songwriting siblings. Howard Dietz, a distinguished lyricist himself, once remarked, "What George was to music, Ira was to words." They proved it with sassy romantic songs like "I Can't Be Bothered Now" from *A Damsel in Distress* (1937) and "Let's Call the Whole Thing Off," while providing the romantic pulse for the Fred Astaire and Ginger Rogers dance comedy *Shall We Dance* (1937). They composed the stirring "Swanee" (sung by Al Jolson and featured in the 1945 Gershwin biographical film, *Rhapsody in Blue*) plus the torch song, "That Man I Love" performed by Peg La Centra (providing the voice for actress Ida Lupino) in the 1947 film of the same name. Lyricist Lorenz "Larry" Hart, who found the ideal writing partner in Richard Rodgers, penned some of the most clever sexual innuendoes ever to fit snugly into a popular song. For example, "Bewitched, Bothered and Bewildered," from the 1940 musical *Pal Joey,* featured such delectible lines as, "I'll sing to him/ Each spring to him/ And worship the trousers that cling to him." The use of polysyllabic rhymes and wit in "Take Him, He's Yours" (also from *Pal Joey*) was so clever, poet W.H. Auden included it in an anthology of light verse. Rodgers and Hart's "Blue Moon" became such an enduring standard that it would live on in a marvelous doo-wop hit for the Marcels in 1961, and even survive Bob Dylan's uninspired crooning on his 1970 *Self Portrait* album.

"The history of Tin Pan Alley is a history of the United States as seen by its tunesmiths," wrote David Jansen in his book, *Tin Pan Alley.* "We can chronicle the changing musical tastes of Americans, along with our social, economic and political concerns, by the kinds of popular music we bought, played and listened to — from the tearjerker to the latest rock song." What Newman absorbed from these songwriters was the sophisticated craft involved in constructing a song, plus the lyrical humor — especially in the lyrics of Larry Hart and Frank Loesser. While many believe Tin Pan Alley officially died in the mid-fifties, with Elvis Presley and Bill Haley & the Comets storming the barricades, that's only partially true. By the early sixties, it merely took a detour to the Brill Building in Manhattan, where budding songwriters Carole King, Barry Mann, Neil Sedaka, Cynthia Weil and Neil Diamond started a second wave of narrative love songs that captivated the American teen market.

Although Newman drew no small part of his influence from the early Tin Pan Alley, by the time he started recording his own songs in 1967 he took the tradition down some very different laneways. "Tin Pan Alley composers sang about love and rain and sunshine and more love," wrote Alan Niester in the Toronto *Globe & Mail*. "Newman sings about booze, rednecks, Sigmund Freud and Albanian weddings." In essence, times had changed, and demanded an entirely different kind of song. Newman may work within a romantic tradition, but he tends to do so as a way of telling stories about folks who are not often included in that picturesque version of the American Dream. And he does so not by writing down to his public, but (to paraphrase Raymond Chandler) by finding a form that the public has come to accept. "There are very few people who are doing something so esoteric they don't hope there's an audience for it somewhere," Newman told James Keast. "Captain Beefheart wanted people to like him — and he found them. It's a prime force. The seminal fact of show business." To varying degrees, Newman has sought the same approval, but unlike Al Jolson, who donned blackface as a maudlin mask for gaining acceptance, Newman uses his mask to both express and cloak his subversion. When he does it right, the mask becomes invisible to the eye, even as it remains audible to the ear.

## 6

Where Randy Newman sheds his sardonic pose and plays it straight is in his movie music, which might explain why his scores, well-crafted and unaffecting, are also ultimately forgettable. It would be far too simple, however, to dismiss this interest in film scores as some elaborate form of sellout. After all, it was while working as a songwriter-for-hire at Metric Music in the early sixties that he was trained to write on assignment. "It's a perfectly legitimate and noble profession to be following in pop music," Greil Marcus told this author in 1991 shortly after Newman's cozy score to the somnambulant *Awakenings* could be heard droning in theaters. "Movie soundtracks pay the bills. I think the fact that Randy Newman [sometimes] makes his living composing really lifeless soundtracks for movies energizes his own songs. Just because of that contrast, his songs then have to be a lot better."

Randy Newman's active interest in movie music also follows a strong family tradition. His famous uncles in Hollywood, Alfred, Lionel and Emil Newman, were the standard-bearers at 20th Century Fox. And Randy is not alone in pursuing the family trade — Alfred's sons have also taken up the charge. "It was sort of burdensome having big guys in the family," he told Barney Hoskyns. "I'd see my Uncle Al and he'd be worried about the score for *The Greatest Story Ever Told*, and I was just a little guy — eight, ten years old — and I must have thought, if *he's* worried I'd better *really* worry." That distress may have prompted Newman's cousin, Alfred's son, Thomas Newman, to join the fray. Thomas scored a number of notable films, including *Little Women* (1994) and *American Beauty* (1999), plus the TV show *Six Feet Under*. Thomas's brother, David Newman, provided the orchestral score for the animated *Anastasia* (1997), as if to answer his father, who had scored the live-action *Anastasia* (1956), with Ingrid Bergman and Yul Brynner.

While Randy Newman's scores for *Ragtime* (1982), *Awakenings* and *The Natural* demonstrate a love for orchestration and dramatic color, the music comes across as impersonal craftsmanship. Thomas Newman's scores, especially for *Little Women*, tend to be more compelling, even haunting, because his distinct voice can be heard in his music. Randy Newman's voice tends to be invisible in his film scores, or in the case of his movie songs like "You've Got a Friend in Me" *(Toy Story)*, little more than placidly charming. Lenny Waronker, however, sees Newman's film music as a perfect extension of his work in pop. "If you listen to 'Davy the Fat Boy,' you know you're at a carnival," Waronker explains. "If you listen to *Good Old Boys*, you know you're in the South. I've seen Randy kill himself over what is basically dialogue — what a character would say — absolutely kill himself to get it right. So he has this uncanny ability to visualize a scene musically and write it from the perspective of a fully realized character. It doesn't surprise me that as his assurance as a composer grew, he began to understand that he could write for films and wanted to do so." For Newman, it was an opportunity to write a kind of music that would be completely self-less. "One good thing about movie music: You're forced by the nature of the film to write the type of things you wouldn't ordinarily get to on your own." But it's not a question of the quality of Newman's music for the movies, it's a question of what is absent in the work.

I hear Newman's voice not in his soundtracks for *Parenthood* (1989), *Awakenings* or the more recent *Seabiscuit*, but in movies that he didn't score. For example, Ron Shelton's sadly neglected master-piece, *Cobb* (1994), unfolds like one of Newman's greatest songs. It's a profoundly complex, sometimes disharmoniously funny biography of baseball's legendary bad boy, Ty Cobb (Tommy Lee Jones). In that film, Shelton taps the same turbulent undercurrents of the South Newman invoked on *Good Old Boys*. Watching Mike Nichols' intelli-gent, funny and engaging adaptation of *Primary Colors* (1998), where John Travolta transforms himself into Bill Clinton, I imagined a dozen possible Newman songs seeping from the characters' pores. It wouldn't have been out of place to hear Travolta/Clinton singing "The Girls in My Life (Part One)" shortly after Hillary (Emma Thompson) slaps him in the face for yet another marital indiscretion ("Was a little girl/ Maybe five-foot-two/ Had the cutest little feet/ Made my heart go tweet-tweet/ Quite a pleasant disposition"). And Billy Bob Thornton's portrayal of James Carville, suffering from an itch he couldn't scratch, might easily have launched into "You Can Leave Your Hat On" as he hit on some young cutie ("Baby take off your coat, real slow/ Baby take off your shoes, here I'll take your shoes/ Baby take off your dress, yes, yes, yes/ But you can leave your hat on").

What I'm suggesting here, of course, is that Newman has more in common with the sensibility at work in these movies than he does in some of the films he scores. "In his [pop] songs Newman's music is more effective because he has control of the entire work of art, and since his songs are miniature stories, this extends beyond music, words and singing to include characterization, scene-setting, and plot line," Peter Winkler explains in "Randy Newman's Americana." "The unsavoury, morally despicable characters frequently portrayed in his songs are made more real to us through his music, which reveals the continuity between the inner world and our own." Despite his love for movie scoring Newman can't provide the continuity between the inner world of the drama he's scoring, which is not of his invention, and our own. "There are people who can do both, like Sting and Billy Joel, people who write very good songs and have them be hits," Newman told Robert Wilonsky of the *Dallas Observer*. "But I think it's only when I do these Disney things and get pulled back from my natural inclinations that they are more palatable for a wider variety of people." The difference here, of course, is that Billy Joel and Sting don't usually let an untrustworthy narrator into their songs.

Without that element of subterfuge, Newman's movie tunes might be palatable for a mass audience, but they're also terribly lifeless. The use of the sardonic mask allows Newman the latitude to delve into a character drama, and give it a distinctive potency. Only once did he discard that mask successfully, but it came late in his career, and to the surprise of everyone, it also revealed a more naked emotion than anywhere in Newman's earlier work. It arrived with a record appropriately titled *Land of Dreams* (1988).

7

For many years, as a singer-songwriter, Randy Newman had avoided writing about himself. In the eighties, he was also chiefly occupying his time writing scores for motion pictures, as his uncles had decades earlier. By 1988, Newman hadn't released a new album of pop songs since *Born Again* in 1979. What prompted the return to songwriting? Perhaps it was the innocuous Hollywood scores he was writing, music that faded with the pictures they accompanied. Or perhaps it was a need for a passionate reply to the conclusion of the Reagan era. In general, the Reagan years were a reaction to the dissipated idealism of the sixties, which had given way to recession, Watergate and the Iran hostages in 1979. Ronald Reagan offered a quick remedy to America's sinking morale with eight years of cheap nostalgia. Public discourse couldn't have been more glib, poisoned by a new cynicism and cheap B-movie style dialogue that turned politics into an ugly game polarizing the saved and the damned. It was a spiritually unpleasant time concealed by a cheerful portrait of a false America that never was, and maybe never should be.

So, in 1988, after years of writing incongruently funny songs about the kind of country Reagan preferred to ignore, Newman constructed

*Land of Dreams*, a new body of work about the America he himself was part of. Only this time, his real face began to peer through the veil of ambiguity he'd created for songs like "Love Story," "Suzanne," "Sail Away," "Rednecks" and "It's Money That I Love." The opening number on *Land of Dreams*, the unassuming ballad "Dixie Flyer," begins with a beautifully lilting melody on piano and acoustic guitar that's quickly answered by the soft yearning of Mark Knopfler's electric slide. Suddenly jumping out of the mix, Newman's clearly assertive voice takes on a new authority. The cadence is especially unfamiliar and shockingly stripped of all irony. "I was born right here/ November '43," Newman sings, with the exigency of a miner staking out his first claim to a gold mine. On first listen, back in 1988, the music startled you. It made you feel that maybe the Reagan era itself, not the catalogue of satiric songs Newman had previously written, was the ironic joke that had been played on the country.

For the first time in many years, Newman wasn't kidding. As this new album played on, he continued — without fuss — to unravel his own truth, where nothing was a joke. Besides giving us an incisive portrait of a Jew living in the torpor of the deep South, Newman also addressed, much more directly than before, the lingering spectre of racism. What Newman seemed to be saying now was that all the reforms brought in to end racial inequity in the sixties were now being undermined by the Reagan eighties. In this music, Randy Newman acknowledged, by examining his own upbringing, that certain social issues some considered resolved were now in danger of returning. Forces were at work in America that aimed to push black people back to where they were before the 1954 landmark *Brown* v. *the Board of Education* ruling. Sensing this, Newman started to tap a new passion in his work, an intensity that cut deep below irony to a place where a vision of something new resided. On *Land of Dreams*, Newman asserted that whether or not he was an outsider, or a foreigner trapped in the ambiguous beauty of his own culture, he was still a huge part of it. As you listened, the music drew a delicate map of a dream — a distinctly American one in which the dreamer became an active participant. It's a dream where blacks and whites, rich and poor, took part in every pledge the country held out. At the end of "Dixie Flyer," Newman opens up the territory by inviting us on board: "On the Dixie Flyer/ Bound for New Orleans/ Across the state of Texas/ To the land of dreams."

You can hear a promise calling out to Newman, and in this song he's answering back. We'd heard a similar promise back in 1970, but that was a deliberately deceptive one voiced from a slave ship in "Sail Away." This time, in an age of diminished hopes, the promise in "Dixie Flyer" was unambiguous, and so was the dream. Newman was taking us back to a life before the mask — to his very roots. It was a candid appeal, this time, with the subversion no longer submerged. On this record, Newman asked, would we still climb on board? Sail away, he seems to be saying this time, sail away with me.

# A Life Before the Mask

Being an outsider musician isn't an aspiration. As soon as you try to make outsider music, you're not.

— Irwin Chusid, author of *Songs in the Key of Z: The Curious Universe of Outsider Music*

I'm not someone who's into self-revelatory stuff. I'm not writing about myself. Now that may be some kind of defense mechanism, but I don't think so. I think a lot of people who ostensibly write about themselves — if you know them, they're not like what their songs are. How could anyone be like what these heroic songs are?

— Randy Newman

## 1

"You can't have progress without deviation from the norm," Frank Zappa once wrote. Glancing back on the history of American popular music, it shouldn't come as any surprise that it contains a long list of deviators. Out of their time, and breaking and remaking all the rules, these innovators dauntlessly set out to change history. While gleefully altering our perceptions of the world, these artists deviate most from the norms we take for granted. American outsiders are the most compelling to watch, since they tend to transform themselves along with their work. In 1925, Louis Armstrong, already a major jazz artist, decided to turn the music on its ear with a series of masterful recordings with the Hot Five and Seven. By reconstructing jazz into a soloist's art form, Armstrong was conveying a secret to all Americans: It's more exciting to stand out from the crowd than it is to join it. A few decades later, a young saxophone player from Kansas City named Charlie Parker decided to answer Armstrong's invitation by breaking the rules of standard harmony. While riffing at lightning speed, Parker ingeniously played within the chords themselves. Soon after, a young truck driver named Elvis Presley walked into Sun Records in Memphis and made the cocky claim that he sounded like nobody else. Within a few years, he effortlessly altered the face of American music.

On the other hand, there is a whole other breed of outsider, whose talents aren't about innovation, self-transformation or changing the face of a culture. Quite the contrary: these artists live in a world shaped by their own peculiarities, and their music eagerly expresses those oddities. There is no danger that these visionary cranks will set the world aflame, but a compelling world is tucked away within their music, a world that sets them apart, too, from the bland and homogeneous conventions that mark the path to pop stardom. In the music of Jandek, for example, a reclusive young Texan who has released over 30 homemade albums, you hear a distinctly shattered performer. In a voice that sounds like Neil Young after he's been shot full of holes, Jandek seems to be reading suicide notes rather than singing songs.

Jack Mudurian is a resident of a nursing home in Boston who professes to know "as many songs as Frank Sinatra" — actually, he knows a lot more. To prove it, Mudurian once dared a hospital staff member to get his cassette recorder, then offered up an impromptu forty-five minute performance. When he was finished, Mudurian had blurted out a completely improvised and unedited 129-song medley that was eventually titled *Downloading the Repertoire*. In Fremont, New Hampshire, a trio of sisters, Dorothy, Helen and Betty Wiggin, went into a local studio in 1969 to record an album called *Philosophy of the World*. Calling themselves The Shaggs (because of their long thick locks), their music couldn't be more disharmonious, with missed beats, shredded chords and innocent, almost naive lyrics. One of their songs, "My Pal Foot Foot," was about their pet cat. Where some dismissed it as one of the worst albums ever made, others insisted *Philosophy of the World* was one of the most original and indigenous of American records. *Philosophy of the World* continues to cause serious debate some thirty years after its release; *Rolling Stone* has called it one of the most influential alternative releases ever made. Frank Zappa, who once tried to land The Shaggs as an opening act, said he thought they were better than The Beatles. Bonnie Raitt referred to them affectionately as castaways on their own musical island.

Raitt's remarks can likely be extended to outsiders in general, even if The Shaggs, Jandek and Jack Mudurian probably do prefer their oasis away from the mainstream. Randy Newman is yet another breed of outsider, something of a hybrid between the genius innovators and the eccentrics who hail from what Greil Marcus describes as "the old, weird America." Given his idiosyncratic style of composition, it's tempting to consider Newman a castaway on his own musical island, too. Yet he deeply desires to be a bridge to the mainland. Irwin Chusid, a music historian and the host of WFMU's "Incorrect Music Hour," first termed this mutant strain "outsider music," and wrote about it in a fascinating book called *Songs in the Key of Z* (2000). For more than forty years, Newman has brought Chusid's outsider aesthetic into the mainstream and confounded just about everybody with it.

"My own aesthetic I guess over the years has seemed to have developed and it's not within any sort of mainstream — in any American river," Newman explained to Scott Jordan of *OffBeat Magazine*. "I mean, the public has rendered its verdict: my thoughts are sort of odd." But Newman has tempered those unusual musings with concessions to commercial acceptance, especially in his film scores and Disney songs. While those compromises would likely terrify and alienate a Jandek, Newman sees them as a taunt, a summons to bring something discrete into the mainstream of popular music. "It still sounds like me," Newman says in defense of his movie tunes. "But it . . . keeps me closer to Hootie and the Blowfish and further away from Captain Beefheart." Yet, like Elvis, Newman doesn't sound like anybody else either. He has taken the very grain of the outsider temperament, wherein you set the terms of your own acceptance, and shaped it into an odd kind of commercial music with at least a faint hope of chart success. This daunting task, filled with American ambition, began for Newman in Los Angeles, the most likely of places for a stranger to dream — and scheme.

## 2

Randall Stuart Newman was born in Los Angeles into a musical family on November 28, 1943. He spent most of his early childhood on the move with his mother, Adele. They traveled together all across the United States, while his father, Irving George Newman, was a captain in the army overseas in Italy, serving as a doctor with General Eisenhower. But Irving was hardly the dutiful career soldier *Life Magazine* might commemorate. "I refused to salute generals, I refused to march," the elder Newman told Timothy White in 1979. "I told them I was a doctor and that was what I was there for!" Born in New Haven, Connecticut, in 1911, Irving Newman developed his own inclination for independence while growing up as one of ten children in a family of Ukrainian Jews. His father was a produce dealer with no interest in music, while his mother was a passionate connoisseur. Irving's oldest brother, Alfred, turned out to be the musical prodigy in the family, but in the end, Irving would be the only child who didn't choose a career path in music. When Alfred got a call to go to Hollywood in 1930, the whole family set out on a trek to the West Coast.

Randy Newman spent his early childhood, until he was three, in the South. He visited Mobile, Alabama, and Jackson, Mississippi, settling finally in his mother's family home in New Orleans. Compared to the urban sprawl of Los Angeles, for the young Newman the South was like traveling to Mars. "For me, [the South] was *that* other place," Newman told David Wild years later. "New Orleans was just a different place than anywhere else." Yet it wasn't just the relaxed air of the surrounding rural landscape that caught Newman's attention. There was also the great racial divide which would inspire, in the years to follow, a vivid collection of indignant songs about racism such as "Sail Away," "Rednecks" and "Christmas in Capetown." "I saw the 'Whites' and 'Colored' signs in the ice cream wagons and that sort of stuff," Newman recalled. "I don't have that sort of prejudice in my immediate family. Maybe they even pointed out to me that it was wrong."

Like Irving, Adele Fox also came from a large family — three brothers and three sisters. "They called her Dixie," Newman said, fondly recalling his mother. "But I recently learned that she was born in Brooklyn and they went to New Orleans when she was a couple of years old." Adele graduated from Sophie Newcombe High School before becoming a secretary. She would ultimately meet Irving Newman at a dance in 1937 while he was attending medical school at Louisiana State University in New Orleans. They married in 1939 and eventually had two boys, first Randy, then Alan. However, Adele and Irving exhibited quite contrary personalities — where he had a hair-trigger temper, she was softer and kindhearted. "She kept her New Orleans accent her whole life," Newman remembers. "And she didn't have anything bad to say about anybody, unlike the rest of us." Yet Newman's parents carried a certain aura of glamour, too. "My mother and father looked like movie stars — my brother and I, less so," he told a Cal Tech audience years later.

Once Newman's father's tour of duty ended in the mid-forties, the family picked up from New Orleans and moved back to Los Angeles where Randy slowly fell under the influence of the iconic texture of the city. "Los Angeles has had an enormous influence on my music," Newman remarked. According to Barney Hoskyns, in his book *Waiting for the Sun: Strange Days, Weird Scenes and the Sound of Los Angeles* (1996), Los Angeles has always had something of an ambiguous attraction. The late film producer Julia Phillips speculated about that particular allure in her 1991 exposé of Hollywood, *You'll Never Eat Lunch in This Town Again*. "I am beginning to think everyone in California is here by mistake," she lamented. But it was never a mistake, exactly. Besides the legendary gold rush of the 1840s, people were also lured west by the promise of railroads, oil, real estate and of course, the sun. But as Hoskyns clearly explains, Southern California might have been sold as an Elysian Fields with bright blue skies, but this blissful paradise hid the horrible maltreatment of indigenous Mexicans and the kind of racism against blacks which would erupt in the Watts riots of 1965. The sumptuous orange groves provided shade only to a predominantly Anglo-Saxon elite.

These inequities also helped produce an apocalyptic mindset, one that found a dour and lasting eloquence in the books of Nathanael West. In West's anti-Hollywood novel, *The Day of the Locust* (1939), the beauty of the intense sun "wasn't enough for the masqueraders who'd reached the promised land." At the end of the novel, the glamour and celebrity of Hollywood inspire a major riot which strikes with the force of divine judgment upon a licentious Eden. But Los Angeles has also been something of a Mecca for a number of artistic outsiders who came under the spell of the rich dichotomies of the city. It would attract wasted romantic jazz trumpeter Chet Baker and defiant sax player Ornette Coleman who, by the end of the fifties, would spearhead the spirited improvisation of free jazz. The city was a strangely diverse metropolis where Beach Boy Dennis Wilson could momentarily lock arms with a psychopath named Charles Manson. Los Angeles would provide deep roots for other fierce nonconformists, too, including Frank Zappa, Captain Beefheart, Brian Wilson, War, Ice Cube, Iggy Pop, Beck and, of course, Randy Newman.

In music, Southern California developed its own distinct tenor, evolving from the percolating surf sounds of the Beach Boys into the speed metal of Henry Rollins. The wide range of musical genres at play might well reflect the very geography of the place itself. Jerry Hopkins once wrote in *Rolling Stone* that Los Angeles has two often-quoted definitions: First, it is 70 suburbs in search of a city; second, it is a three-ring circus in search of a tent. Mikal Gilmore, in his book *Night Beat,* summed up the myriad pleasures of Los Angeles by saying that despite its desperate reach for romanticism, it falls ultimately for glamour and fame. "Los Angeles has stood for a measured, bright-toned sound, espousing certain romanticized truths," Gilmore wrote. "The city's music has also depended upon mass popularity (meaning accessibility) to assure its validity." As Randy Newman's music developed, it was constantly faced with those romanticized truths on the one hand, and an emphasis on mass popularity on the other. For that reason, he always stayed faithful to conventions of pop, never satirizing the harmonic textures of the music itself. All of this emerged as he observed the environment in which he was raised. "It was all more sullen and boring and small and vile," Newman remarked about Los Angeles in 1975. "There wasn't any of that fairyland stuff that I've been seeing. It was social castes, where you ate your lunch, standing around looking tough, or whatever the fuck you were supposed to do." Listening to a Newman song like "I Love L.A.," it's easy to see how it became a hit record, serving both as an anthem for the city, and a song designed to get under your skin. The bright and lively beat prepares you for "that fairyland stuff," while the subject matter turns out to be the things that are "sullen and boring and small and vile."

Apart from Los Angeles, however, the musical culture that would eventually shape the distinct pop sensibility of Randy Newman started at home. In many ways, it began with Irving Newman, a man who went his own way, contrary to the family trade. When Irving turned his back on the world of music, the legacy fell squarely on the shoulders of his oldest son. It was a heritage Randy Newman would come to reluctantly embrace.

3

In 1940, Alfred Newman, the family prodigy and patriarch, became the head of 20th Century Fox's music department, a position he would proudly hold for twenty years. Besides the numerous films he scored and musicals he arranged, Alfred Newman is probably best known as the man who composed the memorable fanfare heard before almost every 20th Century Fox picture. His brothers Emil and Lionel were part of Fox's music department as well, contributing their own scores. Lionel also conducted the studio orchestra. Younger siblings Marc and Robert didn't seek out careers in the music department, though they would become firmly entrenched in the culture of Hollywood. Marc started his career as an agent, while Robert became a studio executive. Irving Newman initially toyed with the idea of becoming a composer, writing the song, "Who Gave You the Roses?" recorded as a B-side for Bing Crosby in 1959. "I'd played clarinet and sax in pit orchestras and with Benny Goodman and Red Nichols; music came very easy to me," Irving Newman explained to Timothy White. "Then when it came time to go to college, [Alfred] asked me if I would become a doctor rather than stay in music, because we were all in music. So I said, 'Sure.' Don't matter to me. I gave up the horn and took out my microscope."

Irving may have given up on show business but show business somehow found a way to come to him. Over the years, Irving's patients included Rod Stewart, Eddie Money, Billy Joel and Jerry Lewis. Lewis wasn't a patient for long. On his first visit, the irascible Irving chased him out of the office. "He was doing all his routines," Randy recalls. "I guess my father wasn't a fan." Irving, who treated Oscar Levant's wife, didn't find her husband any more appealing than Jerry Lewis. "He *hated* Levant, chased him around the piano one day," says Newman. Even the televangelist Oral Roberts, who always claimed to have a special communion with Jesus, sampled some of Irving's vicious wit. When Roberts showed up with a bad case of hemorrhoids, Newman gave him some homespun wisdom of his own: "Why don't you stick your finger up your butt and heal yourself?"

While Irving Newman abandoned music with few regrets, he encouraged his oldest son to pursue it. "My father wanted me to take piano lessons, to be a showbiz guy, although he would deny that he pushed me into it," Randy remembered later. But his father's violent rages did little to nurture a creative climate at home. "The family got used to it," Randy explained. "It was mostly us that he got angry at." But his boyhood friend and future record producer Lenny Waronker remembers Irving's presence looming much larger. "His father was just hilarious, a terrible temper," Waronker told Timothy White. "If you've watched Jackie Gleason get mad on *The Honeymooners,* you can get the idea."

His father's temper was only the beginning of Randy's difficulties. As he was about to turn five, he discovered he was crossed-eyed. "He always had these eye problems — crossed eyes — which I think really affected him, his appearance and the way he looked and did certain things," Waronker remembered. "He was always kind of sloppy and didn't really have a good fix on himself." It took four operations, including one in his teens, to correct the condition. The final operation was conducted by the best surgeon in the field in San Francisco. The doctor not only promised Newman perfect sight, he told him his eyes would be perfectly centered. But when Newman's vision returned, he was shattered to discover his eyes were still lopsided.

"When I brought him back to see the doctor, he used terrible language to the man," Irving recalled. "The guy should have never promised . . . he didn't understand how deeply Randy gave consideration to these things. It just broke my son's heart." Randy Newman believes his skepticism and self-esteem issues developed out of that affliction. "It's always been difficult for me to look people in the face," Newman explains. "When I was a kid, they'd wonder where I was looking." His father agreed that the condition shaped his son's personality. "I think it influenced his thinking a lot, his sadness," Irving recalled shortly before his death in 1990. "He couldn't stand, as a kid, exploitation of that; being called 'four eyes' or 'cockeyed.'" This rather awkward period in Newman's young life would later be painfully observed in the song "Four Eyes," on his *Land of Dreams* album.

In high school, where it was always important to appear cool, Newman didn't even register as hot. "I had a low opinion of myself since childhood," he concedes. "I'm hard on myself." As a way to effectively interact with his peers, Newman created his first persona. "The goal when I was a teenager was to be without affect, to have a masklike face," he would tell Stephen Holden of *The New York Times*. "A lot of people I know never came out of it, and I barely did." Because of his eyes, the first mask Newman wore was that of the high school clown. But that didn't help him much in the area of dating. "I was so damned *shy* around girls," he recalled. "I really didn't have many dates. I was strange looking — and I was a bad driver." So Randy spent his time dodging classes and drinking Ripple. Because of his questionable driving skills, he would get into car wrecks — one such accident left him with a slipped disc which would cause back problems later in life. On another occasion, he got so drunk with a school friend that they smashed into a driver who was casually sitting in his parked car. The guy they ploughed into lost his teeth, while Newman, who was passed out in the back, awoke in a daze. "I climbed out of the wreck saying, 'Am I hurt? Am I hurt?' People were looking at me, going, 'No, you're all right; just lie down Randy.' I knew something was really wrong with me 'cause I could stick my tongue through my whole chin." After a trip to the hospital to get mended, Randy was whisked off to jail. "My father came down and had a few exalting moments with me." Despite his role as the class cut-up, teenage life obviously wasn't a picnic for Randy. "School was painful," Newman admits.

"What I remember about junior high is some of the questions the teachers would ask," Newman told *Rolling Stone*'s Charles M. Young. "'True or false: the Russian people are bad.'" Yet Randy's intelligence insured he would still get good marks. Also during his teenage years, Newman would become an atheist, except — according to him — when he was sick. In a way, this was totally understandable for a kid from a secular Jewish family who didn't attend synagogue. "My mother was too busy feeding us to make us go to any kind of church," Newman recalled. But the truth was, they were so non-observant that at the time

Randy had no idea he was even Jewish. When he was nine, Randy was invited by a girl he knew to the Riviera County Club for a cotillion. On the night of the ball, the girl's father phoned and told Randy he was sorry, but his daughter had no right to invite him, as the club didn't allow Jews. Newman politely told her father it wasn't a problem, then hung up. When he got off the phone, he turned to his father and asked, "Hey Dad, what's a Jew?" Irving was so dumbstruck by Randy's ignorance he suggested that his oldest son might do some reading.

Newman read everything he could find on his own Jewish heritage, including, of course, the Bible. By the time he was a teenager, the man who would later pen deeply agnostic tunes like "I Think He's Hiding," "God's Song (That's Why I Love Mankind)" and "He Gives Us All His Love," declared that he believed in nothing.

## 4

One thing Randy Newman started to believe in was music. He began to study the piano at age seven, claiming the family left the keyboard sitting there with the hope a future Mozart might emerge in their midst. But Newman wasn't quite a natural; he had to apply himself. By the age of twelve he had studied theory, by fifteen, he'd started sneaking visits to the 20th Century Fox lot. His goal was to try to grasp the skills of composition by studying Alfred Newman's film scores. "I know my Uncle Al's music the way I know Brahms," Newman says. "It's a part of me. I'd bring things to Al occasionally when I started writing. He probably had an effect on me." The music of New Orleans, including the rollicking R&B of Fats Domino, also had an indelible impact on Newman. It was also around this time he fell in love with the work of Ray Charles.

If you listen to Newman's unusual singing style you can hear the drawl of Fats, but the phrasing is right out of Charles. Newman discovered Charles in high school when he first heard the classic, *The Genius of Ray Charles* (1959). Backed by orchestral arrangements and a stellar horn section that included trumpeter Clark Terry, with David Newman and Zoot Sims on saxes, Charles redefined classic Tin Pan Alley tracks like "It Had to Be You," Irving Berlin's landmark composition "Alexander's Ragtime Band," the Johnny Mercer/Harold Arlen gem "Come Rain or Come Shine," as well as the pure New Orleans rock of "Let the Good Times Roll." Significantly, *The Genius of Ray Charles* would be Charles' last record for Atlantic, the label on which he'd begun his pop career in 1952. It put Charles into a whole new career path as one of the great musical interpreters, on a par with Frank Sinatra. The diverse New Orleans sound, with its infectious shuffles, provided a bedrock for Randy Newman's musical style; but Ray Charles became more of a kindred spirit. "I think I got it in my head and tried to sound like him," Newman explained to Andrew Male in *Mojo*. "It's like a template for what I've done all my life." What Newman perceived, particularly in songs like "Come Rain or Come Shine," was the swing in Charles' delivery. Charles could render an unaffected kick to the torch ballad: "Hearing him added something . . . in that I thought, consciously or not, that I had his voice in my head for the rest of my life."

But it would take the instigation of Lenny Waronker to get Newman going as an actual songwriter. "I've known Lenny since I was one," Newman explains. "I remember when I was four or five, he would tell me stories. I would be the audience. He would say, 'Let's ride on this tricycle.' He'd get on the back and I would pull him, and we'd fall off. I would get hurt and he wouldn't. I still have scars from that tricycle. He'd say, 'We can do this, we can do that,' and I would be the one who ended up getting smashed."

Randy and Lenny came to know each other because Lenny's father, Simon Waronker, was a violinist in Alfred Newman's 20th Century Fox orchestra. When Randy sneaked visits to the movie set to watch his uncle conduct the latest film score, Lenny often tagged along. Despite their lasting friendship, there was always a certain competitiveness between them. "He had a terrible temper as a kid," Newman remembers. "We'd play football, and he'd get mad and walk off the field." Competitiveness aside, Waronker has fond recollections of their early friendship. "From the time I was able to *have* a friend we were friends," Waronker says. "I don't know why we didn't play with other kids as much; we were basically lazy about going out and being social. [We] always have been."

According to Waronker, what attracted both to songwriting was a trip to see the MGM musical biography *Three Little Words* (1950), about the rise to fame of songwriters Bert Kalmar and Harry Ruby. The picture starred Fred Astaire, Arlene Dahl, Vera Ellen and Red

Skelton, and featured the classic songs, "Who's Sorry Now?" "Thinking of You," and "I Wanna Be Loved By You." "It really affected me, and it clearly got to Randy, too," Waronker recalled. "We were fascinated by the *idea* of writing songs — turning musical inspiration into a precise verse-chorus-bridge form." After high school, Newman enrolled at UCLA, where he studied music theory and composition. Meanwhile, Waronker decided to attend USC and study business and music. While Newman completed his course work, he never got his diploma, because he failed to have one of his pieces performed. It also didn't help that he was still having so much trouble with his eyes. "Just finding the classroom would be a big thing for him," another longtime friend, lawyer Allen Adashek, remembers. "He'd get there late, drive around unable to find a parking space, and then say 'To hell with it' and go back home."

Meanwhile, Waronker was having the time of his life. He may have begun with an appetite for jazz, but ultimately he developed a lasting interest in pop music, something he shared with his good friend. "I remember going over to Randy's house and saying, 'Why don't we figure out this arrangement for some standard?'" Waronker recalls. "And it was just amazing: He'd take any old standard song, and he'd sit down and mess with it for a while and come up with a pop arrangement!" The young friends' timing couldn't have been better, because Los Angeles was now emerging as a Shangri-la for tunesmiths.

Barney Hoskyns attributes the beginnings of the pop music industry in Los Angeles in the forties to the emergence of Capitol Records, started by songwriter Johnny Mercer, movie producer G.B. "Buddy" De Sylva and Glenn E. Wallichs, a music store owner. No one gave Capitol heavy odds outside of L.A. against such other major labels as Columbia, RCA Victor and Decca, but these three men had tremendous clout when it came to finding talent. They signed Nat King Cole, the great jazz pianist turned pop singer, in 1944, and soon followed with other jazz luminaries such as Kay Starr, Benny Carter and even Mercer himself. But it was in the early fifties, when they signed Frank Sinatra at just the time he was growing miserable at Columbia Records, that Capitol found fame and fortune. Capitol's salad days began with Sinatra's 1953 hit record, *Songs for Young Lovers,* and from there, it continued to be a feast. Capitol would go on to erect its thirteen-story complex, known as "Stack o' Records," in 1954. But despite their supremacy on the West Coast, Capitol initially underestimated the emergence of rock & roll. Besides Sinatra in the pop sphere, the label signed country acts like Tex Ritter and released soundtracks of popular musical films *(Oklahoma!)*. Rock was perceived by Capitol as something of a passing craze. It proved to be much more than a fad, leaving plenty of room for rivals to emerge.

In 1955, Capitol's chief rival would become Liberty Records, cofounded by Simon Waronker, who became the label's board chairman and saw fit to hire his son as soon as he graduated from USC. It would take time, though, for Liberty Records to catch the drift of rock's emergence on the West Coast. At first, the company had hits with such conventional songs as Julie London's "Cry Me a River" in 1955. By 1958, however, Liberty's dubious No. 1 hit was "Witch Doctor," by the novelty group Alvin & the Chipmunks. In the song, David Seville (aka Ross Bagdasarian) led a fictitious group of singing chipmunks, whose chirping voices were created by recording the vocalists at varying speeds. Turning the enterprise into one huge in-joke, Seville based the chipmunk characters on Liberty executives. Theodore was Liberty's chief recording engineer, Theodore Keep; the obstreperous Alvin was patterned on Al Bonnett, the vice-chairman and general manager; and Simon Waronker was the inspiration for the character of Simon.

Liberty Records was ultimately rescued from these corny musical critters by a Texan named Tommy "Snuff" Garrett, who'd once worked as a disc jockey in Lubbock, Texas, hometown of Buddy Holly. Garrett had been a friend of the late lamented rock star, but his tastes led him away from rock & roll towards a more streamlined pop sound. When he became the A&R head at Liberty in 1959, he immediately signed Bobby Vee, a neutered Buddy Holly whose 1960 songs "Rubber Ball" and "Devil or Angel" resembled the string-sweetened Holly of "It Doesn't Matter Anymore." Garrett continued to bring aboard aspiring artists like Johnny Burnette, a Memphis rockabilly star, having him sing dippy teen ballads like "You're Sixteen" in 1960. Similarly, he turned Gene McDaniels, a brilliant R&B singer who started his career with the Sultans in 1954, into a pop stylist. While McDaniels' chart-toppers "A Hundred Pounds of Clay" and "Tower of Strength" appealed to mainstream tastes, they didn't come close to the power of the singer's earlier work. By the early sixties, Liberty Records was such a success they'd started their own publishing subsidiary called Metric

Music, headed by Aaron Shroeder. Metric Music featured a bevy of pop writers that included P.J. Proby, Jackie DeShannon (soon to develop a career as a great pop singer), Leon Russell (who would achieve fame in the late sixties as a singer-songwriter), David Gates (a producer and the leader of the soft-rock group Bread) and — thanks to the efforts of Lenny Waronker — Randy Newman.

Beginning as a publicist for Snuff Garrett, Waronker set about finding new talent for the label. The first person he contacted was his old friend. "I would come home and say, 'I know you could do better than these guys.' And I believed it," Waronker said. "But it was very hard for him, because people like Snuff thought he was too weird. They kept saying, 'How's your weird friend?' and that's a painful thing to go through." But Newman's perceived "weirdness" didn't deter Waronker from pursuing him. "I was studying classical music, and Lenny said, 'Why don't you try writing some songs?'" Newman recalls. "We got into listening to rock & roll," Waronker explains. "We learned about the business, we learned what happened with songwriters, guys who'd write songs and get published, and the publishers would get it to whoever they could to get a record."

Metric offered songs to subsidiary labels like Dolton and Imperial Records. Metric Music became a West Coast Tin Pan Alley, or more accurately, the very shadow of the Brill Building, located at 1619 Broadway in Manhattan, the natural evolution of what was once the center of American popular music.

The Brill Building took its name from a clothing store, Brill Brothers, that was located at street level. In the early sixties, this corner would launch a whole new generation of popular songwriters, most of whom were young Jewish kids from Brooklyn. They included Carole King and Gerry Goffin ("Will You Still Love Me Tomorrow?"); Neil Sedaka and Howard Greenfield ("Breaking Up Is Hard To Do"); Jeff Barry and Ellie Greenwich ("Be My Baby"); Jerry Leiber and Mike Stoller ("Jailhouse Rock"); Barry Mann and Cynthia Weil ("You've Lost That Lovin' Feeling"); and Mort Shuman and Doc Pomus ("This Magic Moment"). As a pop music phenomenon, the Brill Building was the brain-child of an ambitious 21-year-old music publisher named Don Kirshner. Kirshner, a native New Yorker, had spent his teenage years in nearby East Orange, New Jersey, where he attended Upsala College. One summer in the mid-fifties, as a bellhop in the Catskills,

Kirshner met the boisterous pop singer Frankie Laine ("Moonlight Gambler"), who inspired him to try his hand at songwriting. Laine turned down Kirshner's first effort, but he told the young scribe how to get a demo recorded. Kirshner had nothing but hard luck in the early years, but he persevered. Eventually, in 1957, through a mutual friend, Kirshner met Walden Robert Cassotto, an aspiring songwriter who played and sang his own material. Kirshner decided to team up with him. Within a year, the duo got a record deal, and Walden Cassotto became Bobby Darin. Kirshner and Darin went door to door, offering to compose commercials, and along the way hired a young woman named Concetta Franconero to sing them. In 1955, after appearing on the *Arthur Godfrey Talent Scouts*, Franconero changed her name to Connie Francis, and began a long, successful career singing in cocktail lounges. By 1958, Don Kirshner met Al Nevins, a very successful composer with a group called The Three Suns. Kirshner convinced Nevins that by publishing songs, they could market to the booming teenage market and make a fortune. In May 1958, Aldon Music was born and set up shop in the Brill Building with an ambition to do more than make a financial killing. "No larger gap could be imagined than that between the sophisticated cocktail music of Tin Pan Alley and the rude street noise of rock & roll," wrote critic Greg Shaw. "Yet it was this very gap that Nevins and Kirshner set out to bridge."

For a brief but exciting period in American popular music, Aldon Music provided such a bridge. What helped lay the groundwork for the success of the Brill Building, and the efforts of Lenny Waronker's Metric Music, was that music publishers — as they had earlier in the century — held significant power. By contracting work to songwriters, then shopping them to a number of record companies, they could pair off songs with performers in the stables of various labels. The record companies, having quick access to Top Forty radio, could then make a bundle off releasing 45 rpm singles. From 1958 through 1963, they had astonishing and lucrative success, until The Beatles and The Rolling Stones arrived on shore to spoil the party.

"The British Invasion introduced us to the concept of the *self-contained* singing band," wrote Frank Zappa in *The Real Frank Zappa Book*. "The success of the British groups forced a change in the way new American groups were put together. They now had to be *self-contained* because every bar band that hired live music wanted its own little U.S. version of The Beatles or The Rolling Stones." Fortunately for Randy Newman, his career began in the last Golden Age of the American songwriter. One of Newman's early heroes, in fact, was Carole King — especially for her song "Take Good Care of My Baby." But Newman could not only see a direct link between the musical past of Tin Pan Alley and the present, he also saw quite clearly how the two eras differed. "The nature of things was that Carole King, as part of the line that produced Richard Rodgers and Gershwin and Harold Arlen, didn't go into writing shows," Newman told Chris Willman after staging his own first musical, *Faust*, in 1995. "She fell in love with rock & roll, and we all did. Shows went the other way . . . it wasn't for us. It was a different time. Rock & roll changed everything and then singer/songwriter stuff changed everything again."

According to Lenny Waronker, the first song Randy Newman composed (at age fifteen) was "Don't Tell on Me," written specifically for Bobby Vee. Vee turned it down gracefully, but dealing with rejection was only one of Newman's problems. A larger obstacle was his own reluctance to write. Alan Newman, who later became an oncologist in San Francisco, was brought onboard to sing demos for some of his older brother's early songs, like "Snow" and "She Doesn't Love Me." Alan immediately saw how difficult — and tormenting — composing was for Randy. "From the start, it's been agony for him," he told Timothy White. "We were living in a big house in Pacific Palisades, and Randy had this brown upright piano in his bedroom that we later replaced with a baby grand Steinway." Although Alan describes Randy as someone who was unhappily isolated, being a songwriter is by nature a solitary occupation. "He was a lonely guy, no girlfriends, was hard to get through to, and he'd work hard on those songs. But he'd also get terrible writing blocks and couldn't ever satisfy himself." By 1960, however, Newman was being pushed by Waronker to write more songs, whether he felt he could or not. They started by collaborating on a song called "Lover Doll," ultimately given to vocalist Pat Carter. Waronker produced the track while Newman provided the arrangement. Based on their satisfaction with that number, Newman was hired for about $150 a month as a songwriter at Metric Music.

The normal procedure at Metric was pretty much patterned on that of the Brill Building. Signed songwriters would do studio demos so that the label could shop the songs around to their other artists. Whenever

Newman recorded a demo of a song he published, however, he'd get someone else to sing it, because he hated his own voice. Either it would be his brother Alan, or he'd employ the vocal talents of P.J. Proby, Glen Campbell or Jackie DeShannon. "My first songs were bad rock & roll, typical Shirelles stuff," Newman told Barney Hoskyns in *Waiting for the Sun*. "At Metric, we were a kind of a poor man's Carole King and Barry Mann and Neil Sedaka." Whether Newman became the next Barry Mann, however, didn't concern Waronker. He wanted to awaken an ambition in his friend which had long been dormant. But how do you do that for someone if he's not driven by a desire for commercial success? "I never wanted anything," Newman explains. "I wasn't really hungry because I was never really poor." Thanks to Waronker's persistence, though, Newman was starting to develop an appetite for becoming a full-time songwriter.

5

One of Newman's first writing credits, at the age of seventeen, was for The Fleetwoods, one of the most stylistically engrossing crossover vocal ensembles of the time. Although basically a doo-wop trio from Olympia, Washington, The Fleetwoods exchanged the more traditional, harsh vocal style of doo-wop for a smoother, more seductive tone concentrated primarily on romantic ballads. As a result, The Fleetwoods became one of the few white vocal groups in the late fifties and early sixties to find a home on both the R&B and pop charts. Their biggest single, on the Dolphin label, was 1959's gorgeous "Come Softly to Me," which helped launch a career that lasted until 1963. They followed it up with the melancholic "Mr. Blue" and the sublimely haunting "Tragedy" in 1961. In 1962, they released a wistful new single on Dolton (formerly Dolphin) Records called "Lovers by Night, Strangers by Day." Needing a B-side, The Fleetwoods acquired a Randy Newman track that fit the gentle angst of the group's sound while being a perfect expression of Newman's early sensibility.

"They Tell Me It's Summer" begins with The Fleetwoods' trademark cooing. As Gretchen Christopher and Barbara Ellis provide a ravishing doo-wop backdrop, lead singer Gary Troxel pines over the seasonal pleasures that are eluding him:

*They tell me it's summer*
*But I know it's a lie*
*Cause summer is for laughing*
*So why do I cry?*
*They tell me it's summer*
*And the sun shines it's true*
*But it just can't be summer*
*When I'm not with you.*

As early as 1962, Newman was illustrating a gift he inherited from lyricists like Lorenz Hart, who could, as critic Raymond-Jean Frontain once put it, "assert the reality of a deeply experienced love by mocking the very conventions that other lyricists (and the record-buying public) have grown to rely on." A song like Hart's "Glad To Be Unhappy" reveals some of the same incongruous intimation that "They Tell Me It's Summer" takes off from:

*Unrequited love's a bore*
*And I've got it pretty bad*
*But for someone you adore*
*It's a pleasure to be sad.*

For Newman, "They Tell Me It's Summer" was nothing more than an uninspired song about unrequited love. "I was trying to capitalize on the season," Newman recalls. "And I kept that up. Every season I'd write, 'Oh, it's fall, look at the leaves.'" Even so, the song would reach No. 32 on the Cash Box Top 100, and impressed The Fleetwoods enough to record a number of other Newman compositions before they broke up. These would include "Who's Gonna Teach You About Love," the earnest "Ask Him If He's Got a Friend for Me" and "Lover's Lullaby," which has sampled borrowings from Johannes Brahms' Lullaby (it appeared on the *Sing For Lovers by Night* album).

That same year, surprisingly, Newman also caught the attention of singer Pat Boone, whose white bucks had already started to step all over rock & roll's blue suede shoes. Boone was the top artist at Dot Records, a major label in Los Angeles since 1956, when it moved base from Tennessee. Claiming to be a descendant of the legendary Daniel Boone, Pat Boone was first signed to Dot by owner Randy Wood in

1954. It must have seemed odd to Boone, the quintessential white Christian conservative performer, when the first song Wood offered him was Otis Williams' saucy R&B hit, "Two Hearts, Two Kisses." Yet this started a lucrative trend wherein Boone, in an era of racial segregation, was given hits from the black charts and made predominantly more bland and acceptable versions for white audiences. In 1955–56, Boone laid waste to Fats Domino's rollicking "Ain't That a Shame," The El Dorados' irresistible "At My Front Door" and Little Richard's delightfully libidinous "Tutti-Frutti." But by 1962, Boone had developed into more of a balladeer, with an amiably lazy style that suggested a sleepier Bing Crosby. However, he would rouse himself long enough to perform the affecting death ballad "Moody River" in 1961 and the goofy novelty song, "Speedy Gonzales," a year later.

Dot may have had a mainstream reputation, but that didn't stop outsiders from periodically knocking on their door. For instance, a Cucamonga misfit named Frank Zappa, operating out of his own little desert studio, one day delivered some R&B demos featuring a singer named Don Vliet (Captain Beefheart) to Dot. Rather than hand them over to the likes of Pat Boone, Dot politely rejected the tapes because "the guitars were too distorted." But Dot did take an interest in Randy Newman — and so did Boone. "He was the first person who ever liked my voice," Newman recalled. Boone was looking for a song to produce, and Lenny Waronker came up with the perfect selection. One day, he phoned up Newman to announce, "It's football season. I've got an idea!" Out of that notion came a song called "Golden Gridiron Boy." Rather than draw on the usual team of singers to do the demo, this time Newman recorded the song himself. "I was mainly reminded of Bobby Vee, but I guess it does have something a little extra," he told Robert Wilonsky of the *Dallas Observer*. "It's such an odd, anachronistic thing — a football song. The last one was, like, in the forties. It was such a weird thing to do."

Although "Golden Gridiron Boy" does resemble a high school anthem, Newman was hardly extolling the virtues of WASP beefcake. "When I went to school everyone liked the surfers, the guys who were great at pool, football players," Newman told Jonathan Cott. "I never had a hero. And I don't like them." The disdain is quite apparent in some of the song's lyrics. Anticipating the late-sixties counterculture satire of Woody Allen, Newman performs the song from the point of view of the schlep who loses his girl to the high school quarterback stud. As heard in some of the songs of the Shangri-Las, especially "Leader of the Pack," there's a call and response element built into the track. Newman is backed by a female chorus, comically acting the part of cheerleaders and occasionally answering his anguish:

> *In his football uniform*
> *He looks ten feet tall*
> *All the girls run after him*
> *And my girl's in front of 'em all.*
> *Cause he's a football hero (hero!)*
> *She's in love with him (yeah! yeah!)*
> *In every game, it's still the same*
> *She talks nothing but him (hooray!).*
> *When he makes a touchdown (touchdown!)*
> *She goes wild with joy (wow!)*
> *With every score, I lose more ground*
> *To her golden gridiron boy.*

Throughout the song, the despondently witty narrator reminds us that he's too short to play football, but he's "big enough to have a dream" (the dream's not too big, though — he plays in the school band). He also hopes his girlfriend will see that he's out for more than just fame and glory. Coproduced by Boone, it's a blissfully silly song which, in the end, says nothing significant ("'Be True to Your School' it was not," says Greil Marcus), yet it's still a pleasant hint of things to come. On the flip side, "Country Boy," Newman sang a third-person narrative about the love affair between a city girl, Chicago Mary, and a country boy from a "backwoods shack" named Jack. This familiar tale from the other side of the tracks ends predictably with Chicago Mary returning home, then deciding to come back to Jack, a more conventional romantic fantasy that echoes a simple Hollywood melodrama.

Neither song did well, but in December 1962, Newman flirted with Top 40 success when he wrote "Somebody's Waiting," a song about a Vietnam War soldier covered by Gene McDaniels as the B-side to his single "Spanish Lace." The song ultimately peaked at No. 32 on the charts. In the ensuing years, Newman became so prolific that he would draw interest from quite a diverse collection of performers.

6

As Randy Newman began to get more assignments at Metric, he couldn't help but compare himself to the East Coast scribes chalking up hits at the Brill Building. "I wasn't stunned by their greatness so much; they weren't intimidating to me," he told Barney Hoskyns. "But Carole King sorta was, because I was trying to do the same things and I knew I wasn't doing them as well." What bothered Newman most wasn't a lack of ability or a significant absence of style, it was the generic quality of what he was writing. Newman could equal Carole King and Gerry Goffin as a songwriter in every area — except that (excluding "Golden Gridiron Boy") you couldn't hear Newman's voice in his songs. No matter who sang a Goffin/King song, you could always see the songwriters' fingerprints on anything they wrote. Whether by the soft yearning of the Shirelles' "Will You Still Love Me Tomorrow?" the plaintive ache of the Everly Brothers' version of "Crying in the Rain," or the naked determination of Eric Burdon singing "Don't Let Me Down," you could always identify their work. Newman's songs, conversely, seemed adaptable to just about any voice or performer. Randy Newman was attempting to be a traditional song-writer, though his talent was anything but conventional. So the early sixties saw a collection of Newman tunes that could have been performed by anybody, and often were. Newman penned the innocuous "I Got Over You" for singer Dick Lory in 1963. In 1964, the Spike Jones Band, now far removed from their wonderfully irreverent madness — and minus Spike himself — were settling into lounge music territory. Newman provided them with a perfectly insipid ragtime shuffle called "Stoplight," which no doubt helped the martinis go down.

If his life had entered a phase of total monotony, his time occupied in writing impersonal love songs, that tedium was broken when Newman suddenly fell in love. In 1964, he met the German-born Roswitha Schmale while she was sunning herself at a friend's pool at their apartment complex. Roswitha had made the trip to Los Angeles to work for the Bank of America. When Newman saw her, he was immediately smitten. "She was real pretty," he told Christopher Connelly. "It kind of threw me when I saw her. I jumped into the pool with my glasses on." Given that slapstick introduction, it was probably fitting that Newman took her to a Peter Sellers film for their first date. They would date for three years before they married in 1967, but many considered Roswitha perfect for Randy from the start. She was a deeply grounded woman, who provided a sharp contrast to the more manic Newman. One time, after he'd knocked over a milk bottle outside their apartment stoop, Randy's six-foot-six, 280-pound neighbor backed him into a corner. Just as Newman was about to get walloped, Roswitha suddenly showed up. "She *hits* the guy in the stomach and he stops!" Newman recalls. "She saved me from getting clobbered." Allen Adashek was one friend who saw them as an excellent match. "Randy and Roswitha complement each other perfectly," Adashek told journalist Arthur Lubow. "He wouldn't know where the phone is, and she can get everything done." Roswitha's competence wasn't always perceived as a compliment by Newman. "She's friends with a lot of people in the neighborhood," he explains. "They must think I'm a little strange. It's like Boo Radley in *To Kill a Mockingbird*. There's a presence in the house."

As Newman's love life improved, so did his songs, for example, a romantic variation on "Under the Boardwalk" called "Friday Night" which was recorded by the O'Jays. It's a typical tune about a desolate chap who's lost his girl. He sits at his window and watches his pals go off on their dates:

> *It's Friday night*
> *And all my buddies are out on the town*
> *But I'm all alone and from my window*
> *I can look down on the avenue*
> *I see them go walking by with the girls that they love*
> *While I sit alone and cry as they walk down the avenue*
> *The way we used to do — Friday night.*

By 1966, just a couple of years after the British Invasion, major labels were now looking for the next Beatles or Rolling Stones. As they started to scout clubs for new talent to sign, the record companies needed A&R guys to get the process rolling. Waronker saw a ripe opportunity, and made a move that would not only change his stature in the music business, but dramatically alter Randy Newman's future as well. Waronker joined the Artist and Repertoire department of

Warner/Reprise just as Frank Sinatra, for one of the rare occasions in the sixties, was enjoying renewed success with "Strangers in the Night." As a sign that times were indeed changing, Waronker brought along with him an eccentric songwriter named Van Dyke Parks, session pianist and arranger Leon Russell and his good friend, Randy Newman.

At the helm of Warner/Reprise were two industrious executives, Mo Ostin and Joe Smith, who brought a new eclecticism to the label's roster. A few years earlier, Sinatra, founder of Reprise, had signed a four-movie contract with Warners, who in return paid him $1.5 million for his controlling interest in Warner Brothers Records. On September 3, 1963, Warner Brothers Records and Reprise merged, with Ostin running Reprise, and Smith running Warners. While both could read the growing popularity of rock, they simultaneously gave renewed power to their more established pop performers. For example, Dean Martin knocked The Beatles' "A Hard Day's Night" out of the No. 1 spot on the charts with his 1964 single, "Everybody Loves Somebody." In response to the British Invasion, Ostin signed up the Kinks, a fiercely energetic band who blasted up the Top 40 with the hard-rocking "You Really Got Me." Besides contributing heavily to the success of Sinatra's "Strangers in the Night," Smith also signed a bizarre psychedelic group whose original roots were in American traditional folk. Once known in San Francisco as the Warlocks, they were reborn in late 1966 as The Grateful Dead.

Warner/Reprise had established an exceptional business operation. The executives were music fans, and willing to take chances on some pretty unusual talent. Waronker couldn't have felt more at home. He found a freedom at Warners for the songwriter, who usually was at the mercy of the company. "In those days you had to make demos of songs, and the demos of songs had to be pretty damn close to what they should be, because record producers . . . would butcher the songs," Waronker told journalist Nick Tosches. "They wouldn't pay attention to the detail. The chords would be all wrong — all sorts of horrible stuff. That's why Randy Newman ultimately became an artist, he just couldn't stand it anymore." Recognizing that talented songwriters like Carole King and Neil Diamond sometimes had their songs butchered by poor arrangements and recordings, Waronker saw an opportunity to improve things at Warners. "I learned how to make demos, and I included the songwriters, which again wasn't something that people did," he explains. "But because of my knowledge of the struggle between producers and songwriters, all of that stuff, I decided to get it as close as you can." Warners became a label that supported the efforts of the artist over the accountant's bottom line, which is why Waronker saw it as the perfect home for Randy Newman.

Many years later, however, Newman would remark on how odd it seemed to him that Waronker became a marketing guru when he had much more of an affinity for the art of music. "He's more interested in the *content* of the Rufus Wainwright record than in necessarily trying to sell it," Newman explained to Barney Hoskyns. According to Waronker, it was those qualities that made him perfect for the job. "I work with creative people, and more often than not it was their creativity that made me look good," he told Daniel Levitin in a 1998 interview. "When you're dealing with lots of people and they're bouncing off each other, if you give them a chance to be who they are, then you have a better chance than not of coming up with something interesting and creative." One of the first groups Waronker found interesting and creative was a fey little vocal harmony ensemble called Harpers Bizarre. Led by Ted Templeman, who would later go on to produce a variety of Warners acts in the seventies, including Van Morrison, Captain Beefheart, Van Halen and the Doobie Brothers, Harpers Bizarre were originally a surf group known as the Tikis. When Autumn, their record label, went under, Warners scooped them up. After changing their name, and their image, the Harpers Bizarre became a posh Carnaby Street version of a barbershop quartet. Immediately, Waronker brought in Leon Russell to arrange and write a couple of tunes, Van Dyke Parks contributed a song called "Come to the Sunshine" and Randy Newman was recruited for the piano, as well as to provide the opening song, "The Debutante's Ball."

Arranged as a rather deranged waltz that spins madly away, "The Debutante's Ball" makes a number of casual comments about all the guests, before offering a hearty invitation to the dance:

> *Oh, come one and all*
> *To the debutante's ball*
> *It is very divine.*

Despite the overall coyness of the tune, Newman manages to provide a lovely and funny piano cadenza to end the song. On "Happyland," however, Newman provides something else that's not so pleasing — an unbearable sweetness that could bring on tooth decay. This song's vision of life turns out to be not that far from the treacly insanity of R.E.M.'s "Shiny Happy People":

> *Happyland, Happyland*
> *You can have a real nice time*
> *Any ride for just one dime.*

Perhaps Newman was being ironic here, but you wouldn't know it by the recording. Life is just one big fairground, and the Harpers Bizarre enthusiastically dig right into the cotton candy. The band's biggest hit, however, didn't come from Randy Newman, but from an East Coast songwriter named Paul Simon. "The 59th Street Bridge Song (Feelin' Groovy)" exploded into the Top 20, and provided the title for their 1967 debut record. In their follow-up album, *Anything Goes*, Harpers Bizarre included Newman's "The Biggest Night of Her Life" and "Snow." On their third album, *The Secret Life of Harpers Bizarre*, they premiered Newman's nostalgic but irreverent "Vine Street."

While helping Waronker at Warner Brothers, Newman was still providing songs to Metric. He added to the bachelor pad sounds of Martin Denny with "Scarlet Mist" for Denny's 1967 album, *Exotic Night*. Denny, a keyboard player, began as a touring musician with a combo consisting of his pals from college. The group settled in Hawaii at the Don the Beachcomber club, before moving into the Shell Bar, where they came to rival Don Ho as the voice of Hawaiian pop. *Exotic Night* has a diverse selection of tunes ranging from the theme for the exploitation flick *Mondo Cane* (1963) to the Webster/Fain standard "Love Is a Many-Splendored Thing." "Scarlet Mist," with its sonorous, lilting vibes, is styled like late-night Milt Jackson. The French-born singer Claudine Longet, a waif-like pixie with a piquant voice, had recorded one of the earlier versions of "Snow," a lovely, fatalistic track about a doomed relationship, on her 1968 album, *Love Is Blue*. Longet's album is filled with show tunes and popular hits, including "Happy Talk" from Rodgers and Hammerstein's *South Pacific* (which, coincidently, Harpers Bizarre also included on *Feelin' Groovy*), the title track (which had been done as a popular instrumental by Paul Mauriat a year earlier) and Leslie Bricusse's "When I Look into Your Eyes" from *Dr. Doolittle*. Longet's ultimate fate — she was charged with the shooting death of her lover, professional skier Spider Savich, in 1976 — makes listening to "Snow" today a creepy experience:

> *Snow fills the fields we used to know*
> *And the little park where we would go*
> *Sleeps far below*
> *In the snow.*
> *Gone*
> *It's all over*
> *And you're gone*
> *But the memory lives on*
> *Although our dreams*
> *Lie buried*
> *In the snow.*

In July 1968, at the suggestion of Andrew Wickham, a Warner Brothers producer in England, Waronker produced a concept album for the Everly Brothers called *Roots*. An ambitious undertaking, but an aesthetic and commercial failure, *Roots* was an honest attempt (before it became fashionable) to examine the common roots of rock and country. The record anticipated some of the later country experiments by bands like The Byrds, The Flying Burrito Brothers and the Eagles. The tracks included some fascinating early family radio recordings from 1952, but in the end, the album was too precious and artfully self-conscious. On *Roots*, the Everlys included Randy Newman's "Illinois," a rare, unimaginative number that gives us little of Newman's normally strong sense of place. Ultimately, it would take three dissimilar and emerging female vocalists to best interpret the early music of Randy Newman.

## 7

Most songwriters during the early sixties composed songs for other performers to sing, but Jackie DeShannon was something of an anomaly. She was one of the first composers in that era to record her own songs, joining the ranks of Carole King, Neil Sedaka and Neil

Diamond. DeShannon could write heartbreaking pop songs, although her work generally derived more from a folk tradition. Originally from Kentucky, DeShannon was the daughter of country music performers and had already had plenty of exposure, singing on Chicago radio stations from the age of six. She was so precocious, she would ultimately get her own radio show. In 1960, DeShannon moved to California, and in quick order penned hits for Brenda Lee ("Dum Dum," 1961), The Fleetwoods ("The Great Imposter," 1962) and the Searchers ("When You Walk Into the Room," 1964). By 1962, she was already a solo performer at Liberty Records, where her first chart-topper was a cover of Bob Willis's mournful "Faded Love."

It was immediately clear that Jackie DeShannon's voice could render a sharp edge to sweet ballads as well as provide an emotional intensity to more soulful numbers. In 1965, she had her biggest hit with Burt Bacharach and Hal David's anthem "What the World Needs Now Is Love," while in 1969, she recorded the similar "Put a Little Love in Your Heart." DeShannon's work with Newman began with her understated record, *You Won't Forget Me* (1965), where she also wrote in collaboration with Jack Nitzsche (who also did the arrangements) and Sharon Sheeley (who had written hits for Rick Nelson and Eddie Cochran). DeShannon and Newman did two songs for that record: "She Don't Understand Him Like I Do" and "Did He Call Today, Mama?". But their most memorable collaborations are collected on DeShannon's album *Lonely Girl* (1968). Although the record is most noted for opening with her stunning version of the Sonny Bono and Jack Nitzsche composition "Needles and Pins" (a song the Searchers had already successfully covered in 1964) it was really a hodgepodge of original compositions and covers. "Take Me Away" is a Newman ballad with a soft bossa nova arrangement that finds DeShannon whispering wish-fulfillment fantasies about the man she's just met:

> *I know one day*
> *I'll find a boy*
> *Who'll softly say,*
> *Little girl,*
> *May I take you away?*

*Then he'll say*
*That he'll love me*
*Till the end of time*
*Then he'll swear that*
*I'll never be alone.*

By contrast, "Hold Your Head High," a song they cowrote, is a cacophonous anthem with a chorus-and-string arrangement that suggests a combination of Phil Spector's Wall of Sound and Leslie Gore's "You Don't Own Me":

*Don't cry little girl*
*Hold your head high*
*When he passes you by.*

DeShannon and Newman collaborated on a number of other tracks, including the country tune "Between the Pages of My Diary (The Orchid and the Diary)" and "Why Can't You Be Loving Me?" plus the unreleased demo "There's Just No Pleasing You," in 1964. DeShannon continued to record but didn't surpass the promise of her early success until her stunning 1975 album, *New Arrangement*. Her influence was briefly felt again in 1981, when a song from that album, "Bette Davis Eyes," was covered by a young singer named Kim Carnes. Thanks to Carnes, the tune won DeShannon and cowriter Donna Weiss a Grammy for Best Song in 1982.

For most, the Queen of Soul is a label fully earned and self-declared by the Motor City's Aretha Franklin. Down in the Big Easy, though, Irma Thomas might beg to differ. She may not be quite as well known, or have the hits to back her up, but Thomas (like Franklin) is a powerhouse who can bridge both the sacred and pop worlds. When she encountered Randy Newman in the mid-sixties, Thomas had already covered a wide range of songs by a diverse selection of songwriters, from Richard Berry ("Moments to Remember") to Van McCoy ("He's My Guy," "Times Have Changed"). Essentially, Thomas recorded whatever was handed her. "I wasn't aware of who any of the writers were then," Thomas once told journalist John Morthland with a laugh. "I was the most naïve 23-year-old girl there ever was, and I did what I was told."

In fact, Thomas had grown up early and fast. She married at 14, and by the time she was 17 she had three kids and was on her third husband when bandleader Tommy Ridgley discovered her waiting on tables at a New Orleans nightclub. Thomas' only experience to that point was performing with her mother in the Marathon Baptist Church choir. But after inviting Thomas up onstage to do a couple of tunes, Ridgley was so impressed that Irma became a regular in the group. He landed her a contract with Joe Banashak's Mint label in 1960, and her first hit was Jesse Hill's "Ooh Poo Pah Doo," a gospel-inspired track with roots in Ray Charles' "What'd I Say." While at Mint, Thomas began a relationship with legendary producer Allen Toussaint, a New Orleans music icon who was taking the traditional New Orleans sound and transforming it into sophisticated commercial fare. It paid huge dividends for Thomas, whose most significant work included the 1962 "Ruler of My Heart" (a near-miss hit for her but a huge song for Otis Redding when it was rewritten as "Pain in My Heart" in 1964).

When Toussaint went into the army late in 1963, Mint started to falter and Thomas ultimately ended up at Imperial Records. There she began recording some of Randy Newman's best early songs. One of the first was "Anyone Who Knows What Love Is (Will Understand)," the B-side to her sublime "Time Is On My Side" (a song that would become the first Top 10 hit for The Rolling Stones). "Anyone Who Knows What Love Is (Will Understand)" borrows some of its arrangement from the Flamingos' 1959 version of "I Only Have Eyes for You." It's a song that comfortably sits in that long pop — and blues — tradition of the sacrificial good woman who stands by her no-good man:

> *You can blame me*
> *Try to shame me*
> *And still I'll care for you.*
> *You can run around*
> *Even put me down*
> *Still I'll be there for you.*
> *The world may think I'm foolish*
> *They can't see you like I can*
> *Oh, but anyone who knows what love is*
> *Will understand.*

Thomas takes this familiar story and gives it an immaculate conviction that is both defiant and pained. Newman's jaunty "While the City Sleeps" (from Thomas' debut album, *Wish Someone Would Care*) turns the tables on "Anyone Who Knows . . ." spinning a darker tale of an affair between two lovers in which the woman is cheating on another man. Thomas rides on a naked desperation underneath the tune that seems to say no one can truly understand the real mysteries of love:

> *The stars grow dim*
> *And the moon sinks low*
> *It's getting kind of late*
> *And soon I'll have to go*
> *So hold me now*
> *And maybe you'll hear*
> *The secret my heart keeps*
> *As we stand here in the shadow*
> *While the city sleeps.*

Thomas also recorded Newman's soulful "Baby Don't Look Down," which she included on her 1966 record, *Take a Look*. After doing some sizzling tracks for Chess Records in 1967, Thomas took a long break from music, before finally coming back in 1995 to honor her early gospel roots with the roof-raising *Walk Around Heaven*. One listen proves once and for all that the bridge Irma Thomas built between the pop and sacred worlds was a sturdy one.

One of the finest white soul singers to emerge in the sixties was Dusty Springfield. Rob Hoerburger, in his illuminating liner notes for *The Dusty Springfield Anthology* (1997), described this husky-voiced artist's impact on pop music: "Dionne Warwick was more polished and Diana Ross sexier and Martha Reeves tougher and Aretha, well, Aretha. But Dusty Springfield, the beehived Brit, was always the smartest, the most literate, the *wisest*." Born Mary O'Brien, Springfield had a career that spanned more than 35 years. She covered, in the most sophisticated and delicate way, the gamut of soul, lushly orchestrated pop, disco and R&B. She not only could mine the emotions buried within a song, she would sometimes find emotions that weren't planted there. Like Jackie DeShannon, Springfield's roots were also in folk. The folk trio she began with her brother, called The Springfields, made an early success of "Silver Threads and Golden Needles" in 1962. But Dusty left the band early in 1963 to pursue a solo career. It wasn't long before she quickly climbed the charts with the exquisite "I Only Want to Be With You" in 1964, quickly followed by the majestic "Wishin' and Hopin'."

When she was recording her R&B album, *You Don't Have To Say You Love Me,* in 1966, Springfield made a decision to include tracks by Burt Bacharach ("Long After Tonight Is Over"), Goffin/King ("I Can't Hear You," "Oh No! Not My Baby") and a new song by Randy Newman called "I've Been Wrong Before." Although Newman never thought much of it, "I've Been Wrong Before" is one of his best early pop songs, an elusive track that gets at the desperation and romantic ambivalence merely hinted at in "While the City Sleeps." It opens with a mournful melody played on the piano, where the keyboard invokes a haunted sense of loss even before Springfield has opened her mouth to sing. When she does, we realize she is singing about a new man in her life:

> *The night we met*
> *The night that I won't forget*
> *You seem to be what I've been waiting for*
> *But, baby, I've been wrong before.*

Under the lyrics, the piano chords are played cautiously, as if afraid to find the next note, while the melody floods the song with sadness. Having made a horrible mistake once, Springfield sings, what's stopping her from repeating it? When it comes to love, she seems to be saying, we sometimes fear what our instincts are telling us. Springfield plays off that fear, too, with a voice that fills us with both the tingling anticipation of what love can bring, and the dread of its possible consequences. By the time she hits the bridge, with the string section supporting her like a satin net, Springfield is wrestling with the fragile hope this new love holds out for her. She performs the song with the fragile conviction that exorcising the pain of the past will free her for the future:

*He used to smile at me*
*And hold my hand*
*Like you do*
*Then he left me*
*And broke my heart in two.*

When she reaches the end of the bridge, Springfield painfully pulls the song back into the present:

*I see your face*
*And feel your warm embrace*
*You're all that I adore*
*But, baby, I've been wrong before.*
*Oh, baby, I've been wrong before.*

The last word dissolves on a whisper which leaves no sense of resolution. "I've Been Wrong Before" is a love song that defies the conventions of most romantic tunes. Rather than presenting a lover's world divided into victims and victimizers, Newman suggests victim and victimizer can coexist in the same person. It's a powerful piece, and Springfield's beautifully nuanced performance helps it achieve greatness.

"I've Been Wrong Before" has been covered by a variety of artists, but oddly enough, Dusty Springfield's version has gone largely unnoticed. Most people, including Newman, point to Cilla Black's interpretation as the definitive one. But Black, a loud and overdramatic singer, squashes the ambiguity in the song. You don't believe for a second that this woman has *any* doubts that she's been wrong before. Black's brassy style is far better suited to boldly optimistic material like "You're My World" and Paul McCartney's "Step Inside Love." The most bizarre version was recorded by the Chicago psychedelic band H.P. Lovecraft in 1967. Taking their name from the famous horror writer, H.P. Lovecraft mixed originals with covers on their self-titled debut album. Their rendition of "I've Been Wrong Before" comes complete with a darkly exotic arrangement. Vocalists Dave Michaels and George Edwards perform the track as if they've just risen from the crypt. Their affected droning turns "I've Been Wrong Before" into a tale of Count Dracula scorned.

The scant attention Springfield received for her recording of "I've Been Wrong Before" changed in 1969 with her masterpiece, *Dusty in Memphis*, which included two other Newman songs, "I Don't Want To Hear It Anymore" and "Just One Smile," that were far too strong to resist. For that matter, so was the album. It was Ahmet Ertegun, the head of Atlantic Records, who brought Springfield to Memphis. Ertegun had heard her compelling version of Carole King and Gerry Goffin's "Some of Your Lovin'," and sensed she had some of what Aretha Franklin had — a voice that could reach out and deeply stir listeners. So Springfield came to Tennessee to record what would amount to her first soul album, including songs by Goffin/King and Burt Bacharach/Hal David, as well as the pair by Newman.

In "I Don't Want To Hear It Anymore," Newman wrote a pop song in the same class as the best of Carole King or Barry Mann. Like "I've Been Wrong Before," "I Don't Want To Hear It Anymore" is a track about the ambiguities of romance, only this time, the singer is in an ill-fated love affair. She lives in a poor neighborhood in an apartment block where the walls are so thin she can hear right through them. What she hears is people talking about her love affair with a man who lives in the same building. Then, one day, she overhears them talking about another woman in his life. The irony of the song, and the title, comes from the fact the singer keeps hearing from everyone else not only about her own life, but about his life with the other woman:

> *I don't want to hear it anymore*
> *Cause the talk just never ends*
> *And the heartaches soon begin*
> *The talk is so loud*
> *And the walls are much too thin.*

As usual, Springfield drys out the moist melodrama of the material in her beautifully understated performance. When she cries out that she doesn't want to hear it anymore, what hurts in her voice is the recognition that she hears it all too well. "I don't know *how* we arrived at that one," Springfield told Jim Feldman, when the album was re-released as a deluxe edition on CD in 1992. "But it's my favorite song on the album, genuinely. It has a really great atmosphere to it." The song had such appeal that Jerry Butler, the Walker Brothers and

Melissa Manchester would also record it. The track "Just One Smile"
— already covered in 1966 by Gene Pitney ("It Hurts To Be in Love")
and rather tastefully by Blood, Sweat & Tears on their 1967 debut,
*Child Is Father to the Man* — is a masterpiece that opens with a gentle acoustic guitar. Springfield makes a plea for love and understanding
that seems as natural as breathing:

> *Just one smile*
> *Pain's forgiven*
> *Just one kiss*
> *The hurt's all gone*
> *Just one smile*
> *Will make my life worth livin'*
> *A little dream*
> *To build my world upon.*

Springfield's plea doesn't become shrill, as did Sheena Easton's in her
version on *Best Kept Secret* (1983). While Springfield recognizes a
smile can bring you joy, she keeps you aware of the heartache a smile
can hide. "[Newman] comes up with some good stuff," Springfield
recalled. "It's from way left field — and anything from left field is
going to fascinate me." "Just One Smile" would also fascinate many
others: Karla De Vito, the Tokens and Lenny Welch all went on to
cover it.

As for *Dusty in Memphis*, the album was a huge hit, reaching No.
10 on the Billboard Charts in November 1968. ("Son of a Preacher
Man," a Top 10 single from the album, would be resurrected by
Quentin Tarantino for his film *Pulp Fiction* in 1994.) Springfield fol-
lowed the album up with the equally fine *A Brand New Me* in 1970.
But by the seventies, with the exception of the critically acclaimed
*Cameo* (1973), Springfield was battling substance abuse problems that
severely damaged her career. She made a comeback in 1987 thanks to
the Pet Shop Boys, who collaborated with her on the aptly titled
"What Have I Done to Deserve This?" The single was a hit worldwide,
peaking at No. 2 on the Billboard chart. A best-selling album,
*Reputation* (1990), followed and Springfield was back into the pop
mainstream. While recording *A Very Fine Love* in 1995, however, she
was diagnosed with the breast cancer that would take her life in 1999.

On March 12, ten days after her death, she was honored with a well-deserved place in the Rock & Roll Hall of Fame.

8

As innovative as Jackie DeShannon, Irma Thomas and Dusty Springfield were in interpreting Randy Newman's early compositions, it would take a 1966 recording of a new song, "I Think It's Going to Rain Today," to convince Newman to finally become his own interpreter. "I don't like 'I Think It's Going to Rain Today,' never have," Newman admitted to Margaret Daly of the *Toronto Star* in 1977. "I don't like its image-laden quality [with] broken windows and empty hallways. I'm not that kind of writer. I like to create a character — not myself — and tell a story." Yet ironically it was this track that would be recorded more than any other song in Newman's repertoire (some might even identify it as a Randy Newman signature song). Yet it was largely misinterpreted each time it was covered. The first notably misguided version came from a likely source — a young folk singer originally from Seattle named Judy Collins — who never could catch the correct nuance of a song.

Judy Collins hailed from a musical family; her father, Chuck Collins, was both a bandleader and DJ in Denver. Although she studied classical piano with Antonia Brica, Collins was more swept up by the burgeoning folk scene in the mid-fifties. She possessed a very fine soprano voice, which caught the attention of Jac Holzman of Elektra Records, then in the process of signing a stable of folk singers that would include Tom Rush, Phil Ochs and Tim Buckley. Collins' first two records, *A Maid of Constant Sorrow* (1961) and *Golden Apples of the Sun* (1962), were steeped in traditional folk. By 1963, modern songwriters like Bob Dylan, Fred Neil and Tom Paxton were having an impact, and Collins recorded albums featuring Dylan and Paxton covers. In 1966, she sought even more variety. With producer Joshua Rifkin, Collins recorded a pop album featuring songs by both contemporary and classic songwriters. Recorded in England, *In My Life* included solemn versions of Dylan's "Just Like Tom Thumb's Blues," Richard Fariña's "Hard Lovin' Loser," Leonard Cohen's "Suzanne" and "Dress Rehearsal Rag," Brecht and Weill's "Pirate Jenny" and even Richard Peaslee's music for the play "Marat/Sade." And, of course, the Lennon/McCartney title track.

Yet what caught everyone's attention was a Randy Newman tune called "I Think It's Going to Rain Today." Despite his own distaste for it, this was his first composition that truly revealed signs of his sardonic mask. Yet every singer who has tackled the song, including Judy Collins, hasn't seemed to realize that ambiguity was even there. "I Think It's Going to Rain Today" is Newman's first stab at clever irony. On the surface, it appears to be a poetic song about loneliness. Yet on closer inspection, the lyrics parody the popular folk imagery of the time — especially in songs like Paul Simon's "The Sounds of Silence":

> *Broken windows and empty hallways*
> *A pale dead moon in a sky streaked with gray*
> *Human kindness is overflowing*
> *And I think it's going to rain today.*

When Newman recorded the song for his first album, *Randy Newman Creates Something New Under the Sun* (1968), he tweaked the pretentious quality of the lyrics by singing it in a voice that sounded completely dissipated. Collins, Joe Cocker, Neil Diamond, Claudine Longet and Bette Midler, however, took the high road.

"I Think It's Going to Rain Today" has a melodic structure not unlike classic Anglo- and Afro-American folk songs, plus a largo arrangement that calls up any number of American gospel songs. There's even a suggestion here of Jerome Kern's "Ol' Man River." But music scholar Peter Winkler, in the article "Randy Newman's Americana," finds a significant difference. "Newman's appropriation of these associations is entirely ironic," Winkler explains. "Newman's vocal sound and inflections express the sad, bitter, withdrawn mood of the words, and the agitated, tonally disoriented music of the bridge lends an air of despair and anguish to the cry, 'lonely, lonely'. On the other hand, the music does not support the verbal discontinuity we found in the verse."

Collins' performance, by contrast, is dour and sentimental. "Her vocal timbre is clear; every note is precisely in tune, with little variation in pitch except a slight, controlled vibrato . . . her style seems inappropriate," Winkler observes. "Aside from a certain dolefulness, the expression is rather deadpan. It doesn't do the song justice. The melody fares better in the hands of less technically skilled singers . . . singers who don't approach every note straight on, whose pitch intonation is highly variable, whose vocal qualities have a certain amount of 'dirt' (impurities such as raspiness or growliness) in them." One singer who did possess some of that dirt and raspiness was Joe Cocker. Yet even Cocker, according to Winkler, didn't quite grasp the meaning of the song. "Joe Cocker bawls 'Lonely! Lonely!' as though he were Charlton Heston suffering the wrath of God," he writes. In Newman's view, the singer realizes he's as much a participant in his state of disaffection as he is a victim of it. Cocker, employing an ersatz gospel sound coupled with a hodgepodge of American pop musical styles, interprets the song as a maudlin tale of woe — especially in the final verse:

> *Bright before me the signs implore me*
> *Help the needy and show them the way*
> *Human kindness is overflowing*
> *And I think it's going to rain today.*

"The intention is to put the song in a more positive light and give it a Hollywood happy ending, turning the bitter irony of Newman's last verse into a hymn to human brotherhood," remarks Winkler of Cocker's version. Bette Midler commits the same sin with her rendition, recorded for the dreadfully lachrymose film *Beaches* (1988). Today, in hindsight, Newman has developed a more generous view of the song — as if he, too, was finally let in on the joke. "I used to think it was just sophomore, college-boy romantic misery somehow," he told Barney Hoskyns. "But it's not bad. . . . Just the fact that the song uses the word 'implore,' it's almost outside the vocabulary you use for pop music nowadays."

If "I Think It's Going to Rain Today" represents the first use of Newman's satirical mask, his next, "Simon Smith and the Amazing Dancing Bear," was about the pose itself. "It's the first song I wrote where I wasn't trying to be Carole King," Newman recalls. "It was the first song I wrote that sounds like me." The idea for the song came about quite innocently while Newman was working on assignment. "[The song] had a girl's name [like] 'Su-zy! Da da da da,'" Newman told Sarah Hampson of the Toronto *Globe & Mail*. "I said to myself, 'I know more words than that. I've read more books and everything. I can't stand what I'm doing here.' It was also that the song was really bad." Out of that dissatisfaction grew a song about a young man, Simon Smith, who by donning a disguise gets to be the most entertaining character in town:

> *Oh, who would think a boy and bear*
> *Could be well accepted everywhere*
> *It's just amazing how fair people can be.*

This song is the first hint of Newman the outsider looking to entertain the world, and could have easily served as the model for John Irving's novel *The Hotel New Hampshire,* where a sidekick bear helps define a whole family of outsiders. Although Smith is hardly a Jewish name, Newman has alluded in interviews to Simon's partner as a "gentile" bear. The "insider" bear becomes a gimmick employed to "get you in anywhere," to a place where they will love and feed you. You may not get rich, but you'll surely become a fully assimilated headliner:

> *Who needs money when you're funny*
> *The big attraction everywhere will be*
> *Simon Smith and his Amazing Dancing Bear.*

Harpers Bizarre were the first to record "Simon Smith and the Amazing Dancing Bear," on *Feelin' Groovy,* but their version comes off as merely a goof. It was Alan Price, the former organist with The Animals, who first developed a serious interest in this odd little song. Price released "Simon Smith" as a single in March 1967 with another Newman composition, "Tickle Me," as the B-side, and included it with three other Newman tracks on his wonderful solo debut, *The Price Is Right,* in January 1968. Newman has called these some of the best interpretations of his work, and as it turned out, "Simon Smith and the Amazing Dancing Bear" was deemed just idiosyncratic enough to get him a record deal.

At this point in his career, Newman was already frustrated by hearing cover versions that missed the essence of the songs. "What got me to start recording was, I was complaining so much, I was just wearing myself out," he recalled. Lenny Waronker underlined his friend's disappointment. "Those who understood the songs were frightened," he told Robert Wilonsky of the *Dallas Observer*. "Others who didn't give a shit sang right through them." Those "others" would later include the King Singers. The British vocal group's pompously titled *America* album (1989) airbrushed out all the edges in "Simon Smith" and overemphasized the ironies of "Lonely at the Top." Both songs seemed horribly out of place among dreary renditions of Paul Simon's "Homeward Bound," Don Maclean's "Vincent" and Peter Cetera's "If You Leave Me Now." The King Singers' attempt to give a "classical" touch to American pop merely demonstrated how out of touch they were with what it actually was. The rebellious undercurrent that takes off like the breeze in the best of American pop is given the tasteful, stiff-upper-lip treatment here.

Waronker understood Newman's sensibility as a songwriter could be more clearly expressed if he started recording his own songs. "I had a much clearer picture of his potential than he did," Waronker recalls. "It was much easier for me to see his work as a building process. Each song, each record, was better than the last. I knew it was only a matter of time before his work found an audience." Yet as eager as Newman was to find that audience, he wasn't entirely pleased with the deal he got from Warner Brothers. "Lenny tried to get me to sign with Warner Brothers for no money," Newman recalls. "I said, 'I can't believe that. You're my friend. A&M is offering me $10,000 and Warners is offering me nothing? Fuck you.'" Waronker, however, stood firm; He understood how hard he'd had to push Newman just to get him to perform his own material. "[Lenny] got so pissed off at me," Newman recalls. "Of course, I do remember [finally] getting the $10,000 from Warners." Based on the hit version of "Simon Smith" recorded by Harpers Bizarre, Waronker signed up Newman on August 15, 1967.

With "Simon Smith," it was clear Newman was changing his style of songwriting to suit his own temperament. "I reached a point where I was writing relatively conventional songs," he told David Kligman of the Associated Press. "Musically, they were all right, but it wasn't what I was responding to in literature and television and comedy." Meanwhile, Irving Newman was pleased his son had finally become a successful songwriter. "It's so hard to get him to talk about himself," Randy's father recalled. "I think he would have flipped his cork if he didn't have his own words to sing back." Newman had finally found a better voice to accompany his songs — his own.

# A Life Behind the Mask

The humorous story depends for its effect upon the manner of telling.

— Mark Twain, *How to Tell a Story*

Perhaps I'm a short-story writer who got stuck with being a musician.

— Randy Newman

## 1

By the time Randy Newman wrote "I Think It's Going to Rain Today" and "Simon Smith and the Amazing Dancing Bear," he'd discovered the true value of the mask. By creating an unreliable narrator for his songs, Newman could deliberately set himself apart from other pop composers — he'd developed an astute way to obscure his identity. The intent wasn't to confuse people, exactly; still it seemed to have that effect. Each song begged the question: Just who is the real Randy Newman? What does he really think?

"When you write a song for yourself, people sort of tend to expect the 'I' in the song to be yourself," he explained. "That's not the case in my songs. I embody in myself the sort of narrow, bigoted, stupid, cowardly, untrustworthy people I portray in my songs, but I like to think I'm a bigger person than that."

The urge to embody in himself a variety of unflattering roles is Newman's elaborate twist on the grinning American con man offering us paradise on Earth. Melville scholar Tony Tanner calls this particular desire to don a disguise as "a fidelity to the actual radical discontinuity and plurality of the self." As a role model for Newman, there was probably no popular musical figure more devoted to that radical discontinuity than Bob Dylan. "Dylan . . . made it all right for your voice not to be *bel canto,* to be full of character," he explained to Barney Hoskyns. Dylan's impact on Newman, though, is much more significant. If Randy Newman unwittingly took on the strategy of Melville's confidence man, Bob Dylan had swallowed the confidence man whole. For more than forty years, Dylan had transformed himself into any number of incongruent characters keeping his fans both baffled and infuriated in the process.

Before Dylan turned 22, he had already abandoned his real name of Robert Zimmerman and become a folk-singing enigma. Arriving in New York with the emblem of Brando's corduroy cap from *The Wild One* on his head, Dylan had the cunning of a vaudevillian troubadour. He slung an acoustic guitar over his shoulder and sang as if he were the second coming of Woody Guthrie. Like Guthrie, Dylan set out initially to be a man of the people, leading a charge against social injustice. Yet just as audiences and fans were starting to embrace the acoustic "Blowin' In the Wind" and "The Times They Are a-Changin'" as anthems for storming the barricades, Dylan started a-changin' himself. Abandoning the cap and donning a leather jacket, Dylan altered his repertoire, picked up an electric guitar and plugged in. In response, a loud and unhappy throng expressed their displeasure during the 1965 Newport Folk Festival. Simultaneously, Dylan began tearing up the charts with the electrifying six-minute single, "Like a Rolling Stone," boldly announcing to his followers that, yes, maybe rock & roll was folk music, too. Then, just as people caught on to the urban blues of *Highway 61 Revisited* and *Blonde on Blonde,* Dylan once again started having other ideas. While folks tripped out to the heavy rock of Cream and Jimi Hendrix in 1967, Dylan put out a stripped-down and staggering country folk record *(John Wesley Harding)* that couldn't have appeared more archaic next to something like Cream's *Disraeli Gears.*

In 1970, Dylan pulled the ultimate fast one by releasing an album called *Self Portrait.* What may have appeared, by its title alone, to reveal the man behind the mask, in fact, did the exact opposite. How could *this* record be considered a self-portrait when 95 percent of the songs were written by other people? What were we to make of a Bob Dylan who sang Rodgers & Hart's "Blue Moon," Gordon Lightfoot's "Early Morning Rain" and performed a duet with himself (playing both Simon and Garfunkel) on "The Boxer"? When he did sing his own material, like the desultory "Wigwam," the man behind the mask became even more obscured. On "Wigwam," Dylan hummed his way indifferently through a bed of Muzak that might have been dreamed up by James Last. (Compounding the joke, Dylan released "Wigwam" as the album's single.) *Self Portrait* opened with the lovely little opus "All the Tired Horses," yet even that became a gag, as Dylan's voice wasn't heard on the track. It didn't even sound like a Bob Dylan song: a female choir repeating, over and over, "All the tired horses in the sun/ How am I going to get any riding done?" This was the same man who five years earlier had opened a record with the explosive "Like a Rolling Stone." The counterculture became so perplexed by *Self Portrait*'s hodgepodge of musical styles that Dylan earned some of his worst reviews. When *Rolling Stone* delivered its verdict, critic Greil Marcus' famous first words were: "What is this shit?"

What *was* this shit? Well, basically, it was Bob Dylan donning another disguise, and in doing so, once again dodging the urgent desire in his fans to know who the *real* Dylan was. A few years later, Dylan deepened the riddle by playing the enigmatic character Alias in Sam Peckinpah's inchoate Western, *Pat Garrett and Billy the Kid* (1973). When James Coburn's Pat Garrett turns to Alias and asks, "Who are you, anyway?" Dylan answers, "That's a good question." Bob Dylan has kept that question front and center for the last thirty years. Whether he was doing a reversal of minstrelsy, wearing a whiteface mask on his Rolling Thunder Revue Tour in 1975, or adopting the pose of a Vegas lounge lizard in 1979 on *Bob Dylan at Budokan,* the question of who Dylan was developed into a deeply unresolved matter. Dylan's elusiveness reached its apogee that same year when this crafty

Jewish-American poet became a born-again Christian. Naturally, for many fans, this was perceived as the ultimate act of apostasy.

The paradoxical consideration of Bob Dylan, and the role of the mask, became the subject of the movie *Masked and Anonymous* in 2003. The story centers on Jack Fate (Dylan), an aging cult singer pulled from prison to headline a benefit concert in an alternate America torn by civil war and corruption. The film posed more questions than it ultimately answered, but the questions were at least intriguing. For example, in the opening moments, we're startled to hear Dylan's "My Back Pages" sung in Japanese by the Magokoro Brothers, while scenes of chaos and world war flash by. At another juncture, a young black girl performs an *a cappella* interpretation of "The Times They Are a-Changin'." From loudspeakers in the distance, we hear fragments of an Italian version of the regretful "If You See Her, Say Hello," sung by Italy's folk hero, Francesco de Gregori. In another sequence, Turkish pop star Sertab Erener contributes a version of "One More Cup of Coffee" that suggests the song's roots might be found in Sufi trance ceremonies. In short, *Masked and Anonymous* offered a view of Dylan as an everchanging, undefinable force in the world. He's everywhere, in every language, and yet he's also masked and anonymous. "But looking at the mask is the way to understand him," *Masked and Anonymous* director Larry Charles told *Uncut*.

While presenting Dylan as an omnipresent figure, the film also asks the question: What does Dylan mean to American culture? Perhaps, as an American, he's a performer who is merely a sum of the masks he wears. But maybe it's something more — a hidden history lurks behind each face, and behind each recorded album. Like Melville's confidence man, Bob Dylan may be only what we want him to be. In *Masked and Anonymous,* Jack Fate declares, "I was always a singer, maybe no more than that." But history and Dylan's music assert otherwise. When he took the stage on Halloween (no less) in 1964, in one of his last concerts as the folk troubadour, he told New York's Philharmonic Hall, "I have my Bob Dylan mask on. I'm masquerading." Film critic Roger Ebert, who rarely meets a movie he doesn't like, dismissed *Masked and Anonymous* as "a vanity production." But isn't the purpose of a vanity production usually to make us fully aware of the person behind the work? Dylan is as much a puzzle at the end of *Masked and Anonymous* as he was before it. "His masks hidden by other masks, Dylan is the celebrity stalker's ultimate antagonist," former *Village Voice* music critic Ellen Willis wrote in her book of essays on the sixties, *Beginning to See the Light: Pieces of a Decade* (1981). "Dylan's refusal to be known is not simply a celebrity's ploy, but a passion that has shaped his work. As his songs have become more introspective, the introspections have become more impersonal, the confidences of a no-man without past or future. Bob Dylan as an identifiable persona has been disappearing into his songs, which is what he wants."

From Dylan, Newman learned how to disappear into his compositions by creating an elaborate front. His face and voice would be familiar, like Dylan's, but the meaning of his songs would be continually elusive and hidden by a self-deprecating veil. Dylan would later acknowledge the subtlety of Newman's brilliant disguise. "Randy might not go out onstage and knock you out, or knock your socks off," Dylan once remarked. "But he's gonna write a better song than most people who can do it." On the eve of recording his first solo album in 1968, Newman was about to put his brilliant disguise in place.

## 2

"There is nothing new under the sun but there are lots of old things we don't know," Ambrose Bierce wrote in *The Devil's Dictionary*. In 1968, Randy Newman was about to prove the exception to Bierce's rule. Since they had worked together so harmoniously on Harpers Bizarre's *Feelin' Groovy*, Lenny Waronker teamed Van Dyke Parks and Newman on a project that would be one of the most ambitious pop records Warner had ever released — one of their biggest commercial flops. Waronker realized right away that Parks could be a kindred spirit to Newman.

Born on January 3, 1941, Van Dyke Parks was Hollywood incarnate. He began his career as a child actor, his most notable credit being a small role in Grace Kelly's final picture, *The Swan* (1956). In his adult years, Parks developed into an iconoclast who ultimately wound his way into the orbit of the Beach Boys' recalcitrant genius Brian Wilson. They met at producer Terry Melcher's place in 1965, where Wilson suggested bringing Parks into the Beach Boys as a possible writing partner. "Brian was a revolutionary, a participant of the sixties," Parks told Sylvie Simmons in *Mojo*. "I can't say that for all the band members. . . . But Brian decided to grow up." Parks lived in a small apartment above a garage on Melrose Avenue, where he'd hold forth with amphetamine-fueled discourses on American culture. Wilson, whose own drug intake was starting to give him similar aspiring visions, was completely taken with Parks. "I knew that I could write some lyrics and that [Brian] was looking for a lyricist," Parks told Barney Hoskyns in *Waiting for the Sun*. "What I had to offer was the diligence I associated with the crafting of lyrics from what I thought were the halcyon days of the pop song in America . . . the days of Cole Porter and great musical theater. I was interested in the thoughtfulness of cadence that had preceded rock & roll."

This drug-induced gaze back on the early frontier spirit of the American past became the exceptional characteristic Parks brought to Wilson's beach party. In February 1966, Parks worked his way into the band by playing some piano and marimba on the Beach Boys' exuberant hit, "Good Vibrations." Wilson's miniature symphony wasn't released to American radio until the following autumn, and he and Parks spent the rest of the winter entertaining ideas of collaborating on some songs. Their budding friendship, though, was starting to infuriate the rest of the band — especially Wilson's usual writing partner, Mike Love. Parks and Wilson cooked up a series of songs for a concept album the 24-year-old Wilson had already been considering for the Beach Boys called *Dumb Angel. Dumb Angel,* the eagerly anticipated follow-up to the Beach Boys' staggering *Pet Sounds* (1966), was to be a teenage symphony to God. Since, in Wilson's mind, God had a healthy sense of humor, the pairing of "dumb" and "angel" seemed quite natural. With the assistance of hashish and speed, Wilson and Parks began to assemble a musical collage designed to be both enchanting and spiritual. Before long, the incongruous *Dumb Angel* title would be dumped, replaced with something more modest: *Smile*.

The tunes written for *Smile* were some of the most abstract pieces ever constructed for a pop record. On this project, Wilson set out to abandon his long celebration of Southern California youth culture and its amiable hedonism — even though it had been the Beach Boys who depicted this world so well, and so generously. Wilson and Parks instead concocted an American pastiche that was meant to move the Beach Boys into adulthood. *Smile* was to open with "Our Prayer," a wordless, *a cappella* benediction with cascading harmonies immediately invoking antecedents like the Four Freshmen. An elliptical allegory, "Heroes and Villains," would follow, pointing a way out of the teen wilderness the Beach Boys had occupied for so long:

> *I've been in this town so long*
> *That back in the city*
> *I've been taken for lost and gone*
> *And unknown for a long, long time.*

"Heroes and Villains" was intended to be a getaway car exuberantly gunning out of town, an adult love story playfully adorned with whistles, a honky-tonk piano serenading a cantina, and those familiar Beach Boy voices decorating the song like colored lights on a Christmas tree. But as a whole, *Smile* seems less a collection of songs than a madly inspired soundscape, a wildly ambitious series of components with faint echoes of America's pop past. Included were wistfully contemplative tracks like the exquisite "Surf's Up," the heavenly "Cabinessence," "Wind Chimes" and an experimental suite known as "The Elements."

Capitol Records eagerly anticipated the record and began promoting it as a January 1967 release. But by the fall, something started to go terribly wrong. For one thing, the *Smile* sessions were starting to leave the rest of the Beach Boys grumbling rather than grinning. Mike Love, who had been quite content singing, "She'll have fun, fun, fun, 'til her daddy takes the T-bird away," wasn't pleased at having to wrap his tongue around lyrics like, "Dove-nested towers — the hour was strike the street, quicksilver moon." In effect, Parks had become the equivalent of The Beatles' Yoko Ono — a loquacious outsider who, before long, had everyone but Brian searching for the right words to get rid of him. The calamitous collision of personalities ultimately collapsed Brian Wilson's already fragile state of mind. By the new year, *Smile* had been shelved. To fulfill their contractual obligations, however, a few of the songs formed a shadow project called *Smiley Smile*. Released later that year, the new album was more a work of oddball chamber pop. While featuring some rerecorded versions of *Smile* songs like "Wind Chimes," "Wonderful" and "Vegetables," it lacked the thematic unity Wilson and Parks envisioned for their original project. Other *Smile* tracks would be scattered like crumbs over the next few Beach Boys' albums.

Time, though, has a way of changing our perspective on failure. Within a year after it was shelved, *Smile* started to take on a rather curious status in the American pop underground. Although incomplete and unreleased, it became oddly influential. While functioning mostly as a rumor, when some bootlegged tracks confirmed its existence, *Smile* became a catalyst for records that followed in its wake. It was the ultimate ghost project, a masterpiece of ambition, an idea that found a significant home. Looking back now, it's hard to consider The Beatles' *Sgt. Pepper's Lonely Hearts Club Band* (1967), Love's *Forever Changes* (1967), The Monkees' pop experiments on *Head* (1968), The Byrds' *The Notorious Byrd Brothers* (1968), Jimi Hendrix's sprawling masterpiece *Electric Ladyland* (1968), Al Kooper's *You Never Really Know Who Your Friends Are* (1968), Spirit's *The Twelve Dreams of Dr. Sardonicus* (1970), Shuggy Otis' *Inspiration Information* (1974) or Fleetwood Mac's *Tusk* (1979) without thinking of *Smile*.

The reach of this phantom record would go beyond the music world. In 1991, author Lewis Shiner wrote *Glimpses,* a contemporary novel offering readers the appetizing fantasy of going back in time to complete lost and abandoned albums. The main character, Ray Shackleford, is a sixties idealist and the veteran of various failed garage bands. His countercultural ideals, however, have been dashed just as succinctly as his current marriage. When his father dies tragically, Ray starts to think about a number of unreleased records that left their creators' hopes dashed. A strange and unique power enables him to record the lost albums he hears only in his head, which he then magically burns onto a CD. Besides The Beatles' original *Get Back* sessions and the Doors' lost *Celebration of the Lizard* project, Shackleford reconstructs *Smile* for the sole purpose of having Brian Wilson complete it and fulfill his dream. In 2004, fiction would become fact when Wilson, with the help of a young band called the Wondermints (a group whose very sound is an homage to the Beach Boys), finally went back into the studio to resurrect *Smile* and release it to the public years after it was declared dead. But back in 1968, *Smile* was no more than a transitory object, a subterranean voice in the pop unconscious, yet a voice that coincidently opened countless doors for other artists to walk through.

The first two artists to scamper through the portal were Van Dyke Parks and Randy Newman. The failed aspiration of *Smile* served as a guiding spirit that year for both Parks' *Song Cycle* and Newman's debut, *Randy Newman Creates Something New Under the Sun. Song Cycle* satisfied Lenny Waronker's desire for Parks to record a solo album inspired by his creative partnership with Wilson. "He never admitted that to me, but it's no offence to him to say that," Parks explained. "If it wasn't his ulterior motive it should have been, because I'd learned a lot from Brian — among other things, a balance between rationality and instinct and play." The contract Waronker offered Parks stipulated that the twenty-two-year-old would be an arranger with the label, plus a leader and pianist on all his own solo sessions. "This indicates the degree of reliability that Lenny placed on my studio savvy," Parks told Matthew Greenwald of *The Tracking Angle*. Taking only a piano, Parks rented a house out in Palm Desert and started putting together *Song Cycle*. His idea was to develop a concept album about the utopian promise Southern California — and more specifically, Hollywood — held out to people.

*Song Cycle* opens with "Vine Street," a song Newman wrote for Parks describing the desperate aspirations of songwriters in Los Angeles. "In 1960, the record business was contained between the intersection of Selma and Argyle and the parking lot at Hollywood and Vine," songwriter and Hollywood hustler Kim Fowley once remarked. "You could sell any tape for $100, and there was no playing clubs for guys in suits. We were kids running amok in studios like rappers do now. . . . We were all thieves — there was no bullshit about art or integrity or sensitivity. People were willing to pay us to do shit and keep doing it, and we were addicted to the process." Before "Vine Street" begins, we are introduced to what sounds like an ancient demo tape of Parks singing the fatalistic folk standard "Black Jack Davey." So he gives us a nostalgic look back before thrusting us into the present:

> *That's a tape that we made*
> *But I'm sad to say it never made the grade.*

By plunging us into a timeless void where the tunes could emerge from any period, Parks lays claim to the belief that American music — past and present — is intrinsically linked. When it was released, however, *Song Cycle* didn't lay claim to much of an audience. In fact, it sold so poorly Stan Cornyn, of Warner's creative marketing division, took out an ad in the music press that promoted *Song Cycle* by playing off its commercial failure: "How we lost $35,509 on the album of the year (Damn it)."

Parks was somewhat philosophical about the album's failure to connect with the counterculture. "A novelist would have gotten away with it, but in music if something doesn't satisfy the libido it's taboo," he recalled. Perhaps it is worth considering that Parks' version of the American musical landscape was an integration of Richard Rodgers, Charles Ives and George Gershwin, hardly a musical brew for people who, at that time, were weaned on the Doors. "[Song Cycle] was condemned to the safety of some white southern nursery," Parks said bitterly. "You listen to it and you think, 'Isn't this effete?' or 'Nice parlor music,' but there's nothing but sorrow attached to it." What audiences missed was a bold experiment, an emulous attempt to complement Smile, while establishing a continuity between the musical pop of the past and the present. On Song Cycle, Parks examines the American past, with its faintly romantic aspirations, but he reenvisions it in the pop panorama of the sixties. And it did succeed in forming a link between Smile and Randy Newman's first album. During the recording of Song Cycle, Newman wandered into the studio as Parks was finishing a keyboard part for "Donovan's Colors." He became so fascinated with what was going on, he called Waronker to tell him he wanted Parks onboard for his own record.

The title, Randy Newman Creates Something New Under the Sun, wasn't exactly Newman's idea. "I intended it to be called Randy Newman," he recalled. "Naturally, I would never say 'creates something new under the sun.'" Stan Cornyn was — again — the culprit here. And the record not only lived up to its title, it surpassed what Parks had tried to accomplish with Song Cycle. As bold as Parks' effort was, it was weak in dramatic structure. Newman, on the other hand, created an album of sharply focused pop songs which resembled a series of short films. In each song the orchestrated melodies alone functioned like a film score embellishing the story. Newman drew on older material, including "Bet No One Ever Hurt This Bad" from 1965, "I Think It's Going to Rain Today" from 1966 and "So Long Dad" and "Love Story" from earlier in 1967. He abandoned the original pop arrangements, and scored each song for a seventy-five-piece orchestra. "I figured an orchestra could move things along rather than a rock & roll beat," Newman explained. While Newman did all the arrangements himself, Waronker brought in Parks to help produce the record.

The first song was "Love Story," a simple tale of a young couple, how they meet, get married, have kids — and eventually get shipped off to Florida by their offspring to retire and die. "We'll play checkers all day/ Until we pass away," the husband remarks in the matter-of-fact tone of someone checking off purchases on a shopping list.

"It's about someone with a dream so modest that it hardly counts as a dream," Newman remarked some thirty years after he recorded it. As modest as they sound, the dreams in "Love Story" have huge consequences. The desires expressed by Newman's couple have their roots in earlier standards like "For Me and My Gal" and "Makin' Whoopee!" which playfully took us through the rituals of romance and marriage. But in "Love Story," Newman pulls the rug out from under those rituals. Opening with a quaint piano melody, Newman begins with a plaintive observation:

> *I like your mother*
> *I like your brother*
> *I like you*
> *And you like me, too.*

As the singer promises to find a preacher and get a ring, Newman's lovely string arrangement, straight out of Aaron Copland, emphasizes the couple's simple yearnings. However, in the orchestration, Newman parodies the Hollywood movie-music convention of "mickey-mousing." This crude style of writing, put to use most notably in Max Steiner's score for *King Kong* (1933), has the music parroting every action on the screen; for example, when King Kong is thumping his way through the jungle, the music echoes every footstep. So as Newman describes his suitor hiring a band with an accordion and a violin, we hear accordion and violin in the mix.

By the time we get to the chorus of "You and me/ You and me, baby," we can imagine the singer dancing the Charleston, since the orchestra is swinging madly behind him. But while the music calls up romantic values of the past, when the couple start talking about having kids, we're immediately thrust back into the present with a very odd set of lyrics:

*We'll have a kid*
*Or maybe we'll rent one*
*He's got to be straight*
*We don't want no bent one.*

By then, the couple have settled into a rather bland domesticity, except that Newman sings it as if it's wildly romantic:

*Some nights we'll go out dancin'*
*If I am not too tired*
*Some nights we'll sit romancin'*
*Watching the Late Show by the fire.*

Before long, the kids are grown up with their own families, and this rather banal romantic couple we've followed from the altar are mere steps from the grave, and Newman scores his dire conclusion with a delicately melancholic string coda.

A couple of years after Newman's exquisitely unsentimental song, Arthur Hiller made the grossly sentimental hit film *Love Story* (1970), starring Ryan O'Neal and Ali McGraw as a young couple whose love affair is doomed by her cancer. The film approached death in a sanctimonious manner and spawned the famous tag line, "Love means never having to say you're sorry." Film critic Pauline Kael provided an intuitive observation of the primitive appeal of the picture at the time in *The New Yorker*: "An audience that's swimming in tears, drowning in a sea of virtue, can be a very self-righteous audience. Sentimentality and repression have a natural affinity; they're two sides of one counterfeit coin." Newman deliberately works against that mawkishness in *his* "Love Story." As Susan Lydon wrote in *The New York Times*, "[Newman] creates a real world inhabited by real people whose lives and loves are, as he says, 'spectacularly unromantic.'" The composition would have some resonance for Newman, in any case, as his first son, Amos, was also born in 1968.

Newman's second song, "Bet No One Ever Hurt This Bad," a song Linda Ronstadt faithfully covered the following year on her *Home Grown* album, is a ballad with a blues-based melody. David Clayton-Thomas would later borrow it for Blood, Sweat & Tears' "Spinning Wheel." The story has some resemblance to "Friday Night," a song

Newman wrote for the O'Jays. The singer sits by his window watching the rain, as Dee Clark did in "Raindrops," because his girl has left him:

> *My baby left me and now I'm alone*
> *Wait for a letter and I sit by the phone*
> *Oh, the troubles I've had*
> *Bet no one ever hurt this bad.*

The next track, "Living Without You," also deals with loneliness, but the opening lines set such a dramatic sense of place and detail, it goes beyond establishing a mood. "The economy of such scene-setting is better than mere atmospherics," Clive James wrote in *Creem*. "The song dawns like a day."

> *The milk truck hauls the sun up*
> *And the paper hits the door*
> *The subway shakes my floor*
> *And I think about you.*

The melody is so straightforwardly beautiful that when Newman reaches the chorus, "It's so hard, baby/ It's so hard/ Living Without You," his phrasing of the word "hard" raised rather odd questions as to what the song was about. In particular, writers Scott Montgomery, Kevin Walsh and Gary Norris projected a hidden motive when they wrote their exhaustive Randy Newman profile for *Goldmine* magazine in 1995. "Could the emphatic chorus 'It's so hard/ Living Without You' really be endorsing separation as a cure for impotence?" they asked. Their interpretation is (no pun intended) something of a stretch. But because of his use of the untrustworthy narrator, the interpretation of a Newman song is always up for grabs — no matter how apparently absurd the interpretation. "Newman approaches pop [by] subverting songs from within," Montgomery writes. "It is his deliberate use of the simplest words and Moon-In-June rhyme schemes that makes his narrator's intentions suspect, simply because they're too easily understood." "Living Without You" would later be handsomely recorded by Manfred Mann's Earth Band on their debut album in 1972, and by The Nitty Gritty Dirt Band on *Uncle Charlie & His Dog Teddy* (1970).

"So Long Dad" is "Love Story" told from the point of view of the kids — just before the parents get carted off to the nursing home in Florida. A string quartet arrangement contributes a charming intimacy to a tale about a son coming home to impress his parents with his new girlfriend. There's a slight nod to Lorenz Hart, too, in the way Newman pushes the rhyme of the opening line: "Home again/ And the streets are not much cleaner/ And the quaint old South side scener-y/ Is quaint no more." Besides the forced rhyme, the song itself is disharmoniously funny. The son, in an effort to appease his father, glides over any objections his dad might possibly have:

> I think you'll like her Dad
> I hope you do
> But if you don't
> That's all right, too.

Soon enough, the son starts to chat with his father, and their partial estrangement is a comical crosscurrent downplayed by the pleasant shuffle arrangement of the song:

> Come and see us, Poppa, when you can
> There'll always be a place for my old man
> Just drop by when it's convenient to
> Be sure and call before you do
> So Long Dad.

"I Think He's Hiding" is the first song that clearly expresses Newman's rather complicated agnostic views. He rejects the idea of God, as Herman Broder — a Polish Jew who survived the Holocaust — did in Isaac Bashevis Singer's novel *Enemies, A Love Story* (1972). Newman (like Herman) needs God to exist in order to defy both him and our desperate need to have faith in a benign deity. Newman's argumentative views would be no less complex in the years to come, in tunes like "He Gives Us All His Love," the portentous "God's Song (That's Why I Love Mankind)" on *Sail Away* (1972), and his musical, *Faust* (1995). Called "Big Boy," Newman's God in "I Think He's Hiding" is a cross between Santa Claus and Big Brother:

*Have you been good?*
*Have you been bad?*
*If you haven't lived the way you should*
*You'll wish you had.*

Newman demonstrates his astuteness by suggesting, in an era when God was pronounced dead and John Lennon declared The Beatles more popular than Jesus, that He's merely hiding.

In the love song "Linda," Parks encouraged Newman to draw on some of the movie-score arrangements he learned from watching his uncle Alfred — especially his film version of the Rodgers and Hammerstein musical *Carousel* (1956). Newman augments his composition with an accordion to recreate the carnival music as he describes a distinctly painful tale of heartbreak:

*Linda, the carousel's playing*
*But that merry-go-round*
*Is bringing me down*
*'Cause I remember what it meant to you.*

Ian McDonald, in *The People's Music* (2003), accurately describes Newman as an artist who "bluffs like a poker player" and "Linda" as a composition that "mocks the facile pseudo-symbolism of Newman's urban 'folk singer' contemporaries, but so lightly that the dig almost constitutes a private joke." "Laughing Boy" may also represent something of a private joke. Coming on like gangbusters, as if it were the opening number in a revue, the song contains perhaps Newman's most self-deprecating view of the satire in his own work:

*Find a clown and grind him down.*
*He may just be laughing at you*
*An unprincipled and uncommitted*
*Clown can hardly be permitted to*
*Sit around and laugh at what*
*The decent people try to do.*

"Cowboy" is inspired by the film *Lonely Are the Brave* (1962), in which Kirk Douglas plays a misfit cowboy — the last noble man of the wilderness — who has just escaped from jail and enters contemporary urban life. Ultimately, the modern world destroys him. This self-righteous civics lesson (written by Dalton Trumbo) was seen at the time as a bold critique of contemporary America, but Newman's song isn't out to deliver lectures. Rather, "Cowboy" is a quiet lament for a man who longs to return to the wilderness:

> *Wind that once blew free*
> *Now scatters dust to the sky*
> *Cowboy, cowboy — can't run, can't hide*
> *Too late to fight now — too tired to try.*

Here, the character's isolation is emphasized by the sparse melody. Newman's piano is absent throughout, replaced by an exquisite horn coda in the bridge. The lonely sound it calls forth is a haunting elegy for the American West.

"The Beehive State," which along with "I Think It's Going to Rain Today" was released as a single, moves so swiftly it barely gives you time to absorb the story. It's a deceptively obscure song, too, that recalls Constance Rourke's observation that Americans are "a people unacquainted with themselves, strange to the land, unshaped as a nation." Despite the urgency of Newman's performance, a slight vagueness permeates "The Beehive State." It begins with a delegate from Kansas taking the Senate floor, where he is asked to describe what his state is all about. But we don't find out very much. First, we discover that Kansas is for the farmer and "the little man." The representative then tells the senators gathered that they need a firehouse in Topeka. Next, the Senate calls to the floor a delegate from Utah. He steps forward with a desperate plea that is also rather opaque: he insists Utah needs water to irrigate their desert, but mostly he just urges everyone to tell this country about his state, "'cause nobody seems to know." We don't even have a clue as to what time period is being depicted in the song, but for all this uncertainty, "The Beehive State" has all the immediacy of historical fact and portentous events. "It should be longer," Newman once said of the song. "But I couldn't think of any more to say."

As short and as simple as Newman's tale remains, the real meaning of "The Beehive State" may lie between the lines of what the delegates are urgently saying. Keith Reid, the lyricist of the British rock band Procol Harum, decided to peer into the slim narrative of Newman's "The Beehive State" and imagine just what might lurk deep inside. Many people know Procol Harum only for their Bach-inspired 1967 hit "A Whiter Shade of Pale," but the group continued to record albums of varying quality leading up to *The Well's On Fire* (2004). Like Newman, Reid preferred writing songs that were character dramas. For their third (and best) album, *A Salty Dog* (1969), singer/keyboardist Gary Brooker and Keith Reid concocted a series of cryptic compositions about haunted sailors ("A Salty Dog," "Wreck of the Hesperus"), death ("Juicy John Pink"), martyrdom ("Crucifiction Lane"), salvation ("Pilgrim's Progress"), betrayal ("The Milk of Human Kindness") and the portentous "The Devil Came From Kansas."

"It came about because I've always liked Randy Newman," Reid told *Beat Instrumental*. "I bought his first album, which featured a song called 'The Beehive State.' It had a line about a senator from somewhere. That inspired the song." "The Devil Came from Kansas" fleshes out Newman's brief bulletin. It's a song about a spiritual test of faith, in a land that was settled by puritans. "The puritans came [to America] with a utopian vision they could not maintain," Greil Marcus wrote in *Mystery Train*. "Their idea was to do God's work, and they knew that if they failed, it would mean that their work had been the devil's." This anxiety is at the heart of the Procol Harum track, about a pilgrim who has what he describes as "a monkey riding on his back." The Devil claims to know this pilgrim so well that the piety of his faith can no longer protect him:

> *The Devil came from Kansas*
> *Where he went to, I can't say*
> *If you really are my brother*
> *You'd better start to pray*
> *For the sins of those departed*
> *And the ones about to go*
> *There's a dark cloud just above us*
> *Don't tell me 'cause I know.*

In "The Devil Came from Kansas," the battle for the pilgrim's soul leaves no possibility for redemption. His struggle with the Devil leads him eventually "to that pool inside the forest/ In whose waters I should drown." It's an exciting yet harrowing story, told as a solid rock & roll dirge. While B.J. Wilson's persistent drum beat relentlessly stalks Gary Brooker's apprehensive voice, Robin Trower's stinging guitar notes shriek and snap, trapping the singer in a snare. Trower rips into the strings with such intensity, the sounds he calls forth suggest a banshee let loose from the depths of Hell. "The Devil Came from Kansas" presents a larger historical context for the veiled pronouncements made by the delegate in Newman's "The Beehive State." Given the prophetic quality of "The Devil Came from Kansas," it's intriguing to know that just outside of Topeka there is a small town called Stull, Kansas, where locals claim the remains of a church, on top of a hill overlooking the town, is one of two places in the world where the Devil could exit Hell and walk freely upon the Earth. In 2002, the church was finally torn down, leaving a small village in Germany as the last of the Devil's portals.

Procol Harum's harrowing tale about Kansas is paralleled by the dark history of Utah. "They're a very prosperous kind of state," Newman says coyly. "The Mormons have done well by it." Doing well by it is one thing, the story of how the Mormons got there is quite another. Utah's history is a blood-stained affair filled with the kind of violence and dread usually reserved for late-night horror stories. Its origins date back to 1820, when fourteen-year-old Joseph Smith, from Sharon, Vermont, wanted to know which religion he should join. Retreating to a secluded section of the woods, to petition God, Smith was visited by two "personages" who identified themselves as God the Father and Jesus Christ and dissuaded him from joining any Church. Then in 1823, Smith was visited by an angel of God called Moroni, who revealed to him an ancient record chronicling God's dealings with the former inhabitants of the American continent. In 1827, Smith began translating the record (purported to be printed on gold plates) that would eventually become *The Book of Mormon*, published in March 1830. A month later, Smith organized what was called The Church of Jesus Christ of Latter-Day Saints, and became its first president.

What Smith said he found through the translation of these plates was an ancient record that amounted to the discovery of a lost text to complement the Old and New Testaments. He told followers the story of a prophet named Lehi, who fled Jerusalem in the year 600 B.C. God had Lehi and his sons build a boat to sail to the New Land in America, where Lehi was to teach one important lesson — the redemption of the soul by dutifully following the laws of God. Since rivalry existed within the family clan, God's laws were difficult to adhere to. When Lehi appointed one of his youngest sons, Nephi, as the spiritual leader, his oldest sons, Laman and Lemuel, rebelled against their father's choice. Nephi was then forced to remove his tribe from his brothers' rule. But God took issue with their insurgence, and struck Laman and Lemuel with red skin, telling them that all their descendants would carry this imperfection as a reminder of His disapproval.

The historical arc of the Mormon faith started with this breach between the Lamanites and the Nephites. For a millennium, these two families were caught in an eternal vendetta like the Hatfields and the McCoys, a bloody battle that never abated — even after Christ visited following his crucifixion and resurrection. The mission of peace he preached was short-lived. By the end of the *Book of Mormon*, Moroni is the last living soul of the Nephites, having witnessed such carnage all around him that he calmly waits for the Lamanites — descendants of his estranged brothers — to kill him and release him from his misery.

Author Mikal Gilmore traced the Mormons' troubling legacy of murder in his haunting book *Shot in the Heart* (1994). By examining his own Mormon family, Gilmore uncovered the effect of this brutally unresolved heritage on the life of his brother Gary Gilmore, who was executed for murder in Draper, Utah, in 1977. In his illuminating memoir, Gilmore writes, "God is the hidden architect of all the killing at the heart of America's greatest mystery novel, the angry father who demands that countless offspring pay for his rules and honor, even at the cost of generations of endless ruin." In 1844, following the inevitable murder of Joseph Smith in Illinois for polygamy, the bloody tale of this book would continue in Utah, where Brigham Young delivered the flock in 1846. The Mormons' tumultuous and violent mythology is not only analogous to the allegory of Procol Harum's "The Devil Came from Kansas," it underlies the ambiguous exhortations of Newman's Senate delegate from Utah in "The Beehive State."

"'The Beehive State' is mainly about the obscurity of some parts of this country, to which attention isn't paid," Newman said of the song. "That was just about Utah. To us out here [in Los Angeles] it's like

Delaware. . . . People's reaction to the song are like, 'I'm glad you noticed us,' and they're glad I knew the nickname, the Beehive State." The nickname comes from the state's emblem, a beehive, an important icon in the Mormon religion also depicted on the state flag, standing for thrift and industry. So what do people today know about the Beehive State? Not much, apparently. For one thing, Newman's song is so unrenowned it didn't even earn a place in the promotion of the 2002 Winter Olympics in Salt Lake City. According to Greil Marcus, in his Real Life Top 10 column in *Salon,* John Crumpacker, a writer for *The San Francisco Chronicle,* proved just how ignorant the country still remains about Utah. In a piece he wrote about the state, Crumpacker failed to mention the Mormon Church, Brigham College or even that Utah was named after the Ute tribe, a name that translates as "people of the mountains." Instead, Crumpacker wrote that "Utah is known as the Beehive State for the archaic hairdos worn by waitresses in time-warp coffee shops." We gotta tell this country about Utah, Randy Newman sang back in 1968, 'cause nobody seems to know.

Although much of Newman's catalogue has been covered by other performers, very few have ever touched "Davy the Fat Boy." It's not hard to understand why. This deeply unsettling final song on *Randy Newman Creates Something New Under the Sun* is one of the most audacious bits of satire Newman ever committed to vinyl. It tells the story of Davy, a lonely fat boy, whose only friend gives a deathbed promise to his parents that he'll take good care of their only son. It turns out his idea of care-giving involves sticking Davy in a freak show so that people can pay to see how "round" he is. Newman cleverly composes carousal music to accompany the deathbed verse as if to augur what's coming. According to Waronker, it was something of a chore for Newman to even complete that opening verse, and it took him three weeks to perfect it. "He had this beautiful piano part that I happened to love, but he decided to scrap it and do something much more challenging," he recalled. "Randy literally spent the better part of a month conceiving and then writing the intro." Newman invokes the spirit of the freak show by drawing on the technique of film composer Nino Rota, whose carnival band music adorned many of Fellini's outlandish pageants, including *La Dolce Vita* (1960) and *Juliet of the Spirits* (1965). When Newman gets to the circus scene, he dramatically alters the arrangement to suggest a cruel carnival barker rather than a carousel ride:

*Davy the Fat Boy, Davy the Fat Boy,*
*Isn't he round? Isn't he round?*
*What do he weigh, folks?*
*Can you guess what he weigh?*

If "Davy" suggests the spirit of Brecht and Weill, it's only natural it would strike a strong resemblance to a movie made in the time of their collaboration. "It reminded me of that unbearable climactic scene in von Sternberg's *Blue Angel*, where Emil Jannings — the fallen professor forced to stand before his ex-students imitating a chicken — holds his body like one enormous clubfoot, his face a frozen mask of terror and madness, and produces a squawk that can shrivel the soul," Marcus wrote in *Mystery Train*. The orchestration in "Davy" is also so extraordinarily dense that it's easy to forget just how vicious the humor is here:

*It's only a quarter*
*Win a teddy bear for the girlfriend*
*Or something for the wife*
*You've got to let this fat boy in your life.*

"Newman had asked for requests, and I had yelled out for 'Davy' because I had vaguely remembered being moved by it some years before," Marcus said, recalling a Newman performance he attended a few years after the song was released. "If I had remembered it better I probably would have kept my mouth shut." Newman didn't go for easy laughs in "Davy the Fat Boy." It was an equivocally shrewd song, the first in a series of compositions, including "Sail Away," "Rednecks," "It's Money That I Love" and "My Life Is Good," which implicated the educated and tolerant liberal listener in abhorrent behavior. In "Davy the Fat Boy," Newman reminds us not only of our own cruel childhoods, but also of the cruelty we sometimes abet. "That person singing in 'Fat Boy' is so callous that it's almost kind of funny," Newman said. "In 'Fat Boy,' I wanted people to recognize what a bastard that guy singing that song is." It's not hard to see why. Many cover artists, eager for a Top 40 hit, wouldn't want to get pulled into the emotional life of such an appalling character. But in a

Newman composition, characters often lead lives we don't want to lead. Most songs invite us to identify with the performer, even encourage us to sing along with him. But Newman goes against the grain, to the point where we have to ask ourselves just what we are saying when we sing a Randy Newman song. Newman demands that we ask that question, and acknowledge that he's situated us in an uneasy place. In "Davy the Fat Boy," he suggests the only way we can truly confront brutality is to get inside the head of the actual tormentor.

Reluctant to appear callous, singers didn't exactly line up to cover "Davy the Fat Boy" (as they did for "I Think It's Going to Rain Today"). The same year "Davy" came out, only one artist did take the chance. British rocker Joe Brown released it as a single in England for MCA Records. In the early sixties, Brown was a popular singer who had a huge hit with "A Picture of You." In the United Kingdom, Brown was a headliner; even The Beatles were his warm-up band on tours before they became famous. Apparently, Brown heard "Davy the Fat Boy" in demo form; his producer Mike Leander (who also produced Gary Glitter) played it for him.

In the age of psychedelic rock, the idea of a solo piano accompanying an orchestra, with the singer performing in a voice *Variety* critic William Tusher compared to "a frightened bison," was an outrageous thing to consider. Thirty-six years after it was recorded, *Randy Newman Creates Something New Under the Sun* still holds up as an audacious, masterful piece of work. The album is not only surprisingly inventive; it still has the power to shock you, make you laugh and then shock you again for having laughed. Unlike so much of today's music, the record makes no concessions to marketing concerns. Instead, there's a single-minded purpose to execute perfectly the artist's vision, without succumbing to mere indulgence. The distinctive and uncompromising flavor of *Randy Newman Creates Something New Under the Sun* continues to make fresh demands on a listener. The length of the record — a brisk twenty-eight minutes — provides a different kind of jolt when we realize that, despite its brevity, the breadth of the material creates a lasting impression long after the album's over.

Following the failed experiment of Brian Wilson's *Smile*, Newman, like Van Dyke Parks, set out to transform the tenor of late-sixties pop. In a sense, they were playing against the self-loathing that had crept into the dissonant political music of the time, which depicted America, in the heat of the Vietnam War, as an agent of Satan. Newman and Parks tried to connect to something larger and more complex in the American spirit. They reached into the deeper roots of the country, to an immeasurable love for a place that could bear both criticism and respect. They likely shared the same view of America as The Band, a group of mostly expatriate Canadians, who that same year, in *Music from Big Pink*, expressed an affinity for a richer American tradition. "It's like we never heard The Rolling Stones," says Newman today of his first album. "That's what that first record sounds like to me. . . . It's like, 'What the fuck?' Didn't I know that 'Satisfaction' had been out already? It really was an ambitious thing to have done for a twenty-three-year-old." Lenny Waronker couldn't agree more. "[Randy] felt — and I believe rightly so — that his approach to orchestration was unique," he explained. "He was intrigued by the idea of building an album around it. People were taking big chances in making records. The Beach Boys had done *Pet Sounds*. The Beatles had done *Sgt. Pepper's*. It was a natural inclination for Randy to go in that direction."

Comparable to both *Pet Sounds* and *Sgt. Pepper's Lonely Hearts Club Band*, *Randy Newman Creates Something New Under the Sun* is Newman's own kind of song cycle. "I tried to use the orchestra to accompany myself," Newman recalls. "Like it was cheating to use sit-down drums, bass or guitar. . . . Like [I was] emulating Mahler and his hit song cycle, *kindertotenlieder,* a shimmery confection of hilarious songs about dead children." And Newman's album did have its fans. Robert Wilonsky, in the *Dallas Observer,* called it "a soundtrack without a film" and a love letter to equal Gordon Jenkins' epic ode to New York, *Manhattan Tower* (1945). "[Newman's album is] as grand and sumptuous as a Broadway musical — and as intimate and disturbing as any short story," he wrote. Parks is still stunned at Newman's bold decision to record a pop album that broke with the rules of pop. "What amazed me with that first album was his faculty for distancing himself from the person who is singing the song," Parks remarks. "That was a revelation to me, and I think that became his greatest asset, that he could develop perspective and a character beyond his own field of vision. He could put himself in another's point of view, and he did that to mixed emotional reaction."

Yet the record didn't really elicit a mixed reaction: it garnered almost no response at all. Released in March 1968, the album might have been something new under the sun, but as far as sales were concerned, it would sell a paltry 4,700 copies in its first release. The front cover certainly didn't help. There, standing against a backdrop of sheet music and wearing a cheesy bachelor-pad suit, was Randy Newman looking like a misanthropic Paul Anka. The Warners publicity staff thought reissuing the record with a new cover, featuring a hipper shot of their new star, might help boost album sales. But the second cover wasn't much of an improvement: now he bore a misleading resemblance to Neil Sedaka. Warners eventually placed an ad in the papers priming listeners for a unique experience. A full-page spread featured Newman's face and the cutline, "Once You Get Used To It, His Voice Is Really Something." They might have done better offering free swampland in Florida.

Parks and Newman continued their collaborative work after *Something New Under the Sun.* Parks assisted on Newman's next album, *12 Songs,* and they would come together in the eighties for Shelley Duvall's *Tall Tales and Legends* TV series. Newman adapted "Darlin' Clementine," based on Barker Bradford's 1885 song, for the show, with Newman serving as the narrator and Parks accompanying him. Although the traditional song deals with a diligent miner looking for his daughter lost in a mining accident, Newman adds a few new verses to supply some badly needed pungency. A sample: "Though in life I used to hug her/ Now she's dead/ I draw the line."

As if to hint where he was heading on his second album, Newman decided to record a tune called "The Goat," an old blues track he liked by Sonny Boy Williamson, which ultimately didn't make an appearance until Rhino's *Guilty* box-set years later. "It's a very bad and white recording of it," Newman told Amazon.com. "It makes me suspect drugs were at the bottom of it somewhere — that it was very late when we did it." Newman also recorded his own version of the R&B ballad "Love Is Blind," which Erma Franklin had covered definitively a few years earlier. For his second record, Newman decided to abandon the orchestra in favor of some boogie-woogie.

3

When Randy Newman first delved into the R&B of the Deep South, his natural starting place was the music of pianist Fats Domino, whose boogie-woogie shuffle style was the biggest influence on his own technique. Antoine "Fats" Domino, born February 26, 1928, was the most popular exponent of boogie-woogie in New Orleans in the fifties, selling more than 65 million records worldwide. Although he was an astonishing pianist, he was the son of a violinist. He had to learn piano from Harrison Verrett, an uncle who was an accomplished jazz banjo player. He taught Fats by marking the keys and showing him all the progressions. A quick study at the keyboards, by the age of fourteen Domino had abandoned school and committed himself strictly to music. There was likely no better place in America to have such a consuming passion than New Orleans. Its richness as a musical capital was due largely to the diversity of cultural elements feeding the city since 1718, when it was a French colony. The city finally became part of the United States as a result of the Louisiana Purchase in 1803.

In the ensuing years, New Orleans became home to people of disparate origins — African, French, Cajun and Creole — who created an exotic mix of language, food and entertainment. In this sumptuous environment, devoted to sensual delight and ritual (acted out each year in the Mardi Gras), grew the most joyous music in the country. The merging of rhythm, ethnic folk and Southern blues created an extravagant gumbo that nourished jazz, R&B and rock & roll. In time, Fats Domino would share center stage with the best in all those musical genres, including Professor Longhair, Huey "Piano" Smith, Clarence "Frogman" Henry, Little Richard, Lee Dorsey, Ernie K-Doe, Shirley & Lee and Lloyd Price. Seeped in this fertile milieu, Domino drew on an abundance of musical eclecticism. In the early fifties, he played clubs at night after working all day in a factory. One evening, in a club called The Hideaway, a local trumpet player, bandleader and A&R man named Dave Bartholomew heard him and arranged a recording session with Liberty Records. Using Bartholomew's group as his backing band, the twenty-one-year-old Domino recorded his first hit, "The Fat Man," in 1949, on the Imperial label. This signature song would become a million-seller in 1953. "The Fat Man" was a loosely disguised version of Champion Jack Dupree's happily sodden 1940 blues standard, "Junker's Blues":

> *Some people call me a junker*
> *Because I'm loaded all the time.*

Domino altered the lyrics:

> *They call me the fat man*
> *Because I weigh two hundred pounds.*

There was a sweet self-deprecation in Fats Domino's delivery of "The Fat Man" that made him instantly appealing. He also tripled the tempo of the original arrangement, while adding riffing saxes and a boogie-woogie piano. The resulting warmth and emotional intensity made the song irresistible. In 1952, he had his first No. 1 hit on the R&B charts with "Goin' Home," a rollicking number that inadvertently assisted the success of Lloyd Price's "Lawdy Miss Clawdy." Apparently, Price was having problems in the studio with the opening bars of the song, so Domino (who was recording "Goin' Home" down the hall) dropped by and laid down a few piano triplets. Ironically, inside a few weeks, "Lawdy Miss Clawdy" knocked "Goin' Home" off the top of the charts.

In 1955, after Domino had already built a strong rapport with black audiences, he infiltrated the white charts with "Ain't That a Shame." In the coming years, he would follow with a succession of crossover hits including, "Blue Monday," "Whole Lotta Loving," "Blueberry Hill," "My Blue Heaven," "Walking to New Orleans" and "Let the Four Winds Blow." Beyond the charismatic charm of his songs, Domino had a wider appeal than just about any R&B artist from New Orleans, partly due to a voice with the kind of sex appeal subtly couched in innuendo. But Fats didn't possess the raw sensuality of singers like Howlin' Wolf or Muddy Waters; he preferred seduction to aggression. Dave Bartholomew always thought of Fats as more of a country singer. "I loved country music," Domino told Michael Hurtt in *Mojo*. "Just like rhythm and blues, it's a feeling." It was this ability to convey the pure pleasure and feeling of a song that enabled Domino to sneak some pretty racy content into his music and onto the radio.

Throughout the sixties, Domino played to packed houses across the country, even as his record sales began to diminish. Until 1969, at least, when he did a cover of The Beatles' "Lady Madonna" — a song written as a tribute to him. It became Domino's first smash since "Let the Four Winds Blow" in 1961, and was included on a comeback album called *Fats Is Back!* on which Newman and Domino had the opportunity to collaborate. Newman arranged the horns for "Lady Madonna" and eight of the eleven tracks. Domino would continue to record and perform without losing any of his allure. "Removed from the trumped-up hysteria of the rock & roll revival, his live shows continued to be a series of genial reunions, in which with a twist of his body, a flash of his chubby jewelled pinky, a shy winsome smile, or a discreet upward rolling of the eyes, Fats could evoke the charm of an era, convey his simple pleasure simply to be there and entertain," critic Peter Guralnick wrote in what is perhaps the finest tribute to him.

Newman could not approach Fats' warmth, or his magnetism, but that slow drawl in his voice is certainly unthinkable without Domino. Besides his style of playing, Newman also learned, by listening to Fats, how to use his voice to disguise the meaning of what he was singing. One clear example was on Newman's wily vocal for the Jack Nitzsche/Russ Titelman rocker "Gone Dead Train." It was included in the soundtrack to Donald Cammell and Nicolas Roeg's *Performance* (1970), a garishly psychedelic gangster film starring Mick Jagger and James Fox, in which the music was the strongest element. If The Beatles' "Please Please Me" is perhaps the craftiest plea for a blow job ever to become a No. 1 hit, "Gone Dead Train" is the most cunning song ever written about penile dysfunction. With Newman pounding feverishly on the organ, and Ry Cooder's snapping slide guitar cracking along beside him, Newman spits out the lyrics so frantically you barely have time to grasp the meaning of what he's saying:

> *My engine was pumping steam*
> *And I was grinding at you hard and fast*
> *And I laughed at the conductor*
> *Who was telling me my coal wouldn't last*
> *When the fire in my boiler up and quit*
> *Before I came*
> *There ain't no end to selling me*
> *A gone dead train.*

That same year, Newman arranged a lovely orchestral section for Peggy Lee's sublimely funny "Is That All There Is?", a Leiber and Stoller tribute to dashed expectations. In the same session, Lee recorded a faithful interpretation of Newman's "Love Story." Waronker also brought Newman in to provide some orchestral arrangements for Gordon Lightfoot, one of his new artists at Reprise. Newman conducted the orchestra and composed a gorgeous string section for "Minstrel of the Dawn" and "Approaching Lavender" on Lightfoot's *Sit Down Young Stranger* (1970).

All of this work put Newman in gear for a completely different recording experience for his second album. *12 Songs* abandoned the seventy-five-piece orchestra used on *Randy Newman Creates Something New Under the Sun* for a rock combo featuring Ry Cooder and Clarence White (of The Byrds) on guitar, Al McKibbon and Lyle Ritz alternating bass and Gene Parsons (also of the Byrds) and session drummer Jim Gordon on percussion. Initially assisted by Van Dyke Parks, Waronker soon took full command as Newman's producer. The new album was recorded in a single session at United, a sixteen-track studio, with some assistance from Jack Nitzsche, who handled some of the arrangements. Recording engineer Lee Herschberg felt the sessions were not only dramatically different from those for *Randy Newman Creates Something New Under the Sun,* but they also set a pattern for how Newman would record future albums. "It was still more like a demo session than a record session," Herschberg told Dan Daley of *Mix.* "He would come in and sit at the piano and play a song, and the musicians would start to add parts as they heard them. But mostly, we were recording piano-and-vocal demos, which became the core of the records." Waronker supported this approach, but suggested that while they sped through the recordings, they should take time to pull the album together as a whole. "Of course, the approach to *12 Songs* was totally different from the one we'd taken with *Randy Newman . . .*" he remarked. "Each one of those songs was an *idea,* and it can take time to bring an abstraction to fruition, to flesh it out in a concise way. A lot of time was spent *thinking* about those songs." The thought that went into this second record had a lot to do with Newman — with increasing confidence — adjusting his sardonic mask.

"Have You Seen My Baby," which opens the album, is Newman's tribute to Fats Domino, who would acknowledge the compliment later by recording it himself. But *12 Songs,* on the whole, wasn't simply a loving tribute to Fats or New Orleans R&B. As Scott Montgomery wrote, "It's still hard to imagine how the Fat Man would have handled [other] songs about sex and arson, a genteel rapist, suicide (by way of a beach cleaning truck), or the joys of inbreeding." Yet that's pretty much the sweep of Newman's subject matter on his second record. "Have You Seen My Baby" takes its title from the opening line of Ernie K-Doe's "$10,000 Reward." The song is a playful romp that could have appeared anywhere in the canon of Southern R&B, but for one verse, which is pure Randy Newman:

> *She's always been unfaithful to me*
> *She ain't never been no good*
> *I say, "Please don't talk to strangers, baby"*
> *But she always do*
> *She say, "I'll talk to strangers if I want to*
> *'Cause I'm a stranger, too."*

"Have You Seen My Baby" has been covered successfully by a variety of performers, including Ringo Starr on his third solo record, *Ringo!* (1973). Ringo's lively version has real verve, and bolts along aided by some great boogie guitar from T-Rex's Marc Bolan and some deft honky-tonk piano work by James Booker. The San Francisco proto-punk band, The Flamin' Groovies, also did a straightforward rave on *Teenage Head* (1971), their boyishly enthusiastic response to The Rolling Stones' *Sticky Fingers* from that same year.

Newman's second track, "Let's Burn Down the Cornfield," crawls ominously out of the silence — just congas and Ry Cooder's sinous bottleneck slide — to tell a tale of pyromania and lust. In the style of a tranquil Howlin' Wolf, Newman quietly whispers the lyrics as if he were letting us in on the dirtiest of secrets:

> *Let's burn down the cornfield*
> *Let's burn down the cornfield*
> *And we can listen to it burn.*
> *You hide behind the oak tree*
> *You hide behind the oak tree*
> *Stay out of danger 'til I return.*

Part of the song's effectiveness lies in that deadly hush — a submerged eroticism percolates just beneath the deceptively calm surface. That kind of tension and heat likely had a strong influence on Elton John when he wrote his deliciously steamy "Amoreena," featured on *Tumbleweed Connection* (1971). And since, that same year, Elton also produced the second side of Long John Baldry's *It Ain't Easy,* it's also possible he had a hand in Baldry's choice of "Let's Burn Down the Cornfield." Baldry, a tall, dynamic British singer who switched from folk to blues in 1961, had a dramatic influence on Rod Stewart and Elton himself (who, born Reg Dwight, took the "John" from Baldry). Both singers produced Baldry's solo effort for Warner Brothers, each taking charge of one side. On the whole, it's a marvellous album which opens with Baldry's now legendary "Don't Try to Lay No Boogie-Woogie on the King of Rock & Roll." Highlights also include a beautiful duet rendition of Leadbelly's "Where Did You Sleep Last Night?" (called "Black Girl") with Maggie Bell; the dreamy "Morning, Morning," from Tuli Kupferberg of The Fugs; and a tear-down-the-house version of Willie Dixon's "I'm Ready," with Ron Wood playing a nasty slide guitar. Unfortunately, despite John's delectable playing and Caleb Quaye and Joshuah M'Bopo's appetizing guitar solos, "Let's Burn Down the Cornfield" is so overwrought it becomes a parody of the blues style. Baldry grunts and snarls his way through the tune with such obvious lascivious intent, he inadvertently douses the eroticism.

The great blues singer Etta James made a similar mistake when she recorded the song in 1974. James performs "Let's Burn Down the Cornfield" as such earnest blues she lays bare the clichés in the song. In the process, she unwittingly turns it into a reverse minstrel number: she sounds like a black artist performing in the style of a white woman trying to sing the blues. Newman's performance buries, even disguises, the blues clichés with that drawling delivery of his, so the sensuality of the song sneaks up on you. As straight-ahead blues, "Let's Burn Down the Cornfield" sounds utterly fake, even ridiculous, but the ambiguity of Newman's untrustworthy narrator supplies the primal power — and humor — until (by the end) we can't tell if the singer is more turned on by the fire or the girl.

The same interpretive confusion arose over "Mama Told Me Not to Come." The bastard offspring of "One Night of Sin," a 1955 hit for New Orleans R&B singer Smiley Lewis, "Mama Told Me Not to Come" is a hilarious tale of unbridled debauchery. In "One Night of Sin," Smiley gleefully takes in a local orgy. He sees all kinds of stuff, he claims, things that "would make the earth stand still." But where

Lewis candidly revels in his carnal pleasures, in "Mama Told Me Not to Come" (with its cheeky double-entendre title) Newman shrewdly downplays any boasting, providing instead a strange sense of how sex, in inspiring desire, can also inspire fear:

> *The radio is blasting*
> *Someone's beating on the door*
> *Our hostess is not lasting*
> *She's out on the floor.*
> *I've seen so many things here*
> *I ain't never seen before*
> *I don't know what it is*
> *But I don't want to see no more.*
> *Mama told me not to come.*

In the end, "Mama Told Me Not to Come" is such a delightful mix of desire and dread that it becomes desperately funny. The joke, however, was lost on a number of artists, including Odetta, The Jackson Five and even Wilson Pickett (whose version sounds like he's happily revisiting the midnight hour). At least the people responsible for the cheesy horror film *April Fool's Day* (1986) recognized the spooky underbelly of the tune when they included it on the soundtrack.

By going well beyond simple misinterpretation, Three Dog Night, however, turned "Mama Told Me Not to Come" into a monster hit in June 1970. Their rendition gave us a fundamental blackface version of events which reduced the song to little more than a catchy curio. Chuck Negron, for one, had his doubts about the group's take on this song: "For whatever reasons, the politics of the band, we didn't believe [singer] Cory [Wells] understood the tune. We kept it off for one or two albums." When the track finally hit No. 1 on the charts, Wells felt vindicated — "My credibility went up."

Credibility of the commercial variety, though, is dubious at best. And Newman wasn't impressed — even if he expressed his displeasure in a manner that thanked the band while simultaneously putting them down. "At first I didn't really like the way they did the song," Newman explained to Susan Lydon. "But when the royalty cheques started drifting in, I figured they might be able to send my son to Harvard." Newman understood the ambiguities at work in his composition, the very equivocations that Three Dog Night avoided. After all, this is a comic story of a man reluctantly getting in touch with some secret and forbidden desires. When Newman sings, "Mama said, 'That ain't no way to have fun'," you're very much aware of how far his idea of fun might go. Writing about "Mama Told Me Not to Come" in *Rolling Stone,* critic Timothy Crouse made an apt comparison to Bob Dylan in discussing the way certain cover versions deliberately misinterpret the original song's intent. "If you heard nothing but Joan Baez's rendition of 'Don't Think Twice,' you might think the song was a heartbreaking, darkling ballad," Crouse writes. "Dylan's snarl tells you that it is a scathing put-down." What's missing in Three Dog Night's recording of Newman's song is a skepticism that would implicate the audience's prurient fascination with the excesses the singer is observing.

No one could make that mistake, however, with "Suzanne," a song Newman aptly describes as an answer to Leonard Cohen's poetic ode to a nymph, on "a somewhat lower moral plane." "Suzanne" is an unnerving track about a potential rapist who stalks a woman from a name he picks out of a phone book. Like "Let's Burn Down the Cornfield," the meaning sneaks up out of the quiet. A country melody, with steel guitar punctuating each line, strolls along while in the background, a dissonant organ slithers into the mix in the way ominous noises do in David Lynch's films:

> *I took down your number*
> *Looked up your address, Sue*
> *And I was hopin' that maybe*
> *You could love me, too*

Once the stalker obtains the number, he waits in the shadows, where he promises to run his fingers through her hair, while reminding her, "I don't want to get too romantic/ That's just not my way." Greil Marcus has pointed out that what made this song so chilling to its first listeners was the fact we were "caught up in the woman's terror and the rapist's crime. Both were real, both mattered." As listeners, we're drawn into the same deviant mind that Sting took on years later in The Police's "Every Breath You Take" and Kurt Cobain portrayed in Nirvana's "Polly."

There's an element of delirious peril embroidered into "Suzanne." Moreover, Newman tests our confidence in him — that he knows where he is going, and why he's going there. He isn't playing it safe.

Newman lets "Suzanne" loose into the world trusting his audience will work out what it means. The danger, of course, is that the private obsessions of the pop fan might somehow lead to a real act of rape and murder. Marcus raised the issue when he alluded to how Charles Manson's interpretation of The Beatles' "good old rock & roll fuck song 'Helter Skelter'" ultimately led to the murder of Sharon Tate and six other people. "It's not just a matter of what people will think of Newman," Marcus wrote. "What if someone heard the song and went looking for a woman to rape?" But Newman figures the forlorn desperation of the character makes it clear that "Suzanne" could hardly be considered an endorsement of rape.

"It's a weird song," Newman told Jonathan Cott. "The guy singing says, 'I don't mean to get too romantic' after he's said all this horrible stuff. There's something funny in his type of desperation, something pathetic, too. He wouldn't get far as a rapist." Peter Winkler, concurring with Newman, writes that it's the music itself that takes us inside the rapist's desires, as if we were privy to the soundtrack music playing in his head: "The music reveals his seductiveness (the relaxed country beat and lyrical steel guitar fills) as well as his menace (the dissonant organ harmonies)." "Suzanne" has the beguiling creepiness of a comic nightmare.

Newman's "Suzanne" is also likely the precursor to David Byrne's "Psycho Killer." Recorded by Talking Heads on their 1977 debut album, "Psycho Killer" is also a song about a rather pathetic and desperate loner:

> *I passed out hours ago*
> *I'm sadder than you'll ever know*
> *I close my eyes on this sunny day*
> *Say something once, why say it again?*
> *Psycho killer, q'est-ce que c'est?*
> *fa fa fa fa fa*
> *fa fa fa fa fa.*
> *Better run run run run run run run away.*

Also like "Suzanne," "Psycho Killer" deals quite humorously with the banality of a character's obsessions ("We are vain and we are blind/ I hate people when they're not polite"), the "fa fa fa's" quote from Otis Redding's "Fa-Fa-Fa-Fa-Fa (Sad Song)," with all the soul drained out of them. By song's end, Byrne buries the character's rage in a strangled yelp that leaves "Psycho Killer" equally funny and disturbing.

"Suzanne" was a song Newman had originally hoped to record with Jimi Hendrix. "I kind of wrote it with him in mind, playing the guitar part," Newman told Paul Zollo. "He said, 'I'm not a real musician. I can't read music'. . . . But then he went to Hawaii, and he was going to come back to do it, but it never happened." Clarence White of The Byrds filled in just fine.

Continuing *12 Songs*' theme of desperate men, "Lover's Prayer" is a satirical love song for the hopeless, an up-tempo ballad about someone who's grown tired both of young girls ("Don't send me no hand-holdin' baby/ 'Cause I been with babies before"), as well as the sophisticated, politically aware kind ("She started talking to me about the War, Lord/ I said, 'I don't want to talk about the War'"). In the end, he's become about as desperate as the poor sap Frank Zappa parodied in "Jewish Princess":

> *Don't send me nobody with glasses*
> *Don't want no one above me*
> *Don't send me nobody takin' night-classes*
> *Send me somebody to love me.*

Newman would often introduce "Lover's Prayer" in concert by reminding audiences that "this song hopefully represents a new low in rock & roll bad taste."

In "Lucinda," Newman writes a dazzling parody of the rock soap opera. Throughout the sixties, tragic teen ballads dominated the charts. Some were obvious and conventional melodramas, like the Shangri-Las' "Leader of the Pack," where the rejected biker/lover dies proudly on his wheels; others included Frank J. Wilson's "Last Kiss," where Frank's girl dies not-so-proudly because of her boyfriend's faulty wheels. Other pop sagas appeared, too, but these were downright perverse. Mark Dinning's "Teen Angel" got the sixties off to a fiendishly grim start. The bizarre story concerns the singer's girlfriend, who gets leveled by a train after she rushes back to her stalled car to rescue her high school ring. In the wake of "Teen Angel" came Johnny Cymbal's "The Water Was Red," where the singer's girl gets torn apart by a shark while swimming at the beach. The boyfriend bravely wades through the bloodied waters, not just to gather up her remains, but to take on (with his pocketknife, no less) this early progenitor of the killer shark in *Jaws*. Warren Zevon would ultimately deliver an affectionate shot at these macabre tales with his hilarious "Excitable Boy" (1978), but Newman fired the first salvo with "Lucinda."

Sung as a slow blues in the style of Ray Charles, it's a song about a woman who accidentally gets chewed up by a beach-cleaning machine, a harrowingly funny story that, in its own peculiar way, tops "Teen Angel." Lying on the sand in her graduation gown with some boy she just met that night, Lucinda seems to have fallen asleep just as the mechanical contraption starts chugging along. Her companion tries vainly to wake her up, but to no avail, 'cause Lucinda is doomed to lie under the sand:

> *Put under by the beach-cleaning man*
> *Lucinda, Lucinda, Lucinda — why'd you have to go?*
> *They sent her to high school*
> *They sent her to low school*
> *She just wouldn't go no further.*

Blues lyrics are usually expressed dynamically, in the first person, but in "Lucinda," Newman cleverly makes the first person dull-witted and inert. "Lucinda is apparently paralyzed with ennui, possibly even unconscious, but the narrator doesn't appear to notice this, nor does it occur to him to move Lucinda or stop the truck," Peter Winkler explains in "Randy Newman's Americana." He also notes how Joe Cocker, in his cover version, imbued the song with such theatrics that "nothing in his singing establishes any distance between himself and the character portrayed in the song." Did he even notice, Winkler wondered, that it was supposed to be funny? The Canadian band The Corndogs did get the gag when they recorded "Lucinda" on their album *Tell Your Friends There's Friends Around* (1989).

"Underneath the Harlem Moon" stands out on *12 Songs* because, unlike the rest of the record, it's an early jazz standard. But does this

mean Newman has a secret love for jazz? "I don't like those chords
that much, to be honest," Newman explained to Jim Macnie. "I'm not
into twenty-minute solos. The ensemble stuff, Fletcher Henderson,
Ellington, when they had tubas. I like that era." "Underneath the
Harlem Moon" is from that era, a Fletcher Henderson favorite that he
recorded in 1932, with Katherine Handy aptly handling the vocal.
Originally a Cotton Club song, written by Mack Gordon and Harry
Revel, it is included here for possibly two reasons. Placed among the
R&B tracks, it's a song that reminds listeners of Newman's Tin Pan
Alley roots. But more important, on a contemporary album influenced
by black music, it has something to say about race relations:

> Creole ladies walk along with rhythm in their thighs
> Rhythm in their feet and in their lips and in their eyes
> Where do highbrows find the kind of love that satisfies?
> Underneath the Harlem moon!

Listening to those lyrics today, filled with racial stereotypes, it would
be easy to dismiss "Underneath the Harlem Moon" altogether, just as
many of the songs from the musical *Show Boat* are today, but it would
also be absurd. Despite its declarations against racism, *Show Boat* is
routinely attacked because, as Toronto film and theater critic Martin
Knelman once remarked, the direct descendants of slaves don't speak
like Harvard graduates. "It's a great song," Newman told Jonathan
Cott. "[But] you have to know the historical context."

The historical context Newman makes reference to is the Cotton
Club, the famous late-night dinner club in Harlem, located over a
theater on the corner of 142nd Street and Lenox Avenue. From 1923
to 1936, it was the most popular speakeasy in New York, with a sensational floor show featuring black entertainers engaged in racial
hyperbole for the pleasure of white audiences. The club earned its
name through its advertising, which described the establishment as a
"window on the jungle" and "a cabin in the cotton." Movie stars,
politicians and gangsters — from Fred Astaire to Lucky Luciano —
would frequent the establishment, especially after 1927, when Duke
Ellington became the house bandleader. The club's popularity continued after Ellington left to tour, when Cab Calloway took over, with the
entertainers including Josephine Baker, the Nicholas Brothers, Bessie

Smith and Ethel Waters. Financed by white mob syndicates, these performers were among the highest paid in Harlem. However, the Cotton Club also had strict segregationist rules, though on occasion, they were conveniently bent. For example, twelve seats were put aside for notable black figures, including politicians, relatives of performers and black gangsters.

The night spot became a showcase for black art and entertainment — of the kind captured in Gordon and Revel's "Underneath the Harlem Moon" — while remaining, nevertheless, a racist establishment. But, as Pauline Kael would point out in her review of the botched Francis Coppola musical, *The Cotton Club* (1985), it was also something more. "It was part of a liberating social upheaval — not the most creative part but the most conspicuous part," Kael wrote in *The New Yorker*. "And if some of those white swells were slumming when they went up to Harlem to watch 'the coloreds' they put on their evening clothes to do it." Kael was also quick to point out that the performers were not simply the victims of white exploitation. "There was joy in those black entertainers, and there was heat. That was what the white audience recognized; that was what the radio listeners responded to. It's what the Jazz Age was about: the emergence of black music — hot jazz — and the thrill that white artists and white audiences felt as black artists began to enter the cultural mainstream, moving from Harlem to Broadway and across the country." This emergence and integration into white culture were the very things Newman responded to in "Underneath the Harlem Moon," and likely the reason he included it on *12 Songs*. Despite its language, the song remains a celebration of the emergence of black music, and a repudiation of slavery:

> *There's no fields of cotton*
> *Picking cotton is taboo*
> *They don't live in cabins*
> *Like the old folks used to*
> *Their cabin is a penthouse*
> *Up on Lenox Avenue*
> *Underneath the Harlem moon!*

Notably, in 1959, Randy Newman cowrote a rock song, "Laurie (Come Back To Me)," with Mack Gordon's son, Roger. Although it was never recorded, Newman archivist Gary Norris uncovered some of the handwritten lyrics:

> *When you walked out*
> *Without a goodbye*
> *All — I could do was cry, oh, oh, oh, oh, oh, oh, oh*
> *Please listen to me*
> *I didn't know how it would be*
> *Oh, oh, Laurie, come back to me*

Norris was quite accurate in describing "Laurie (Come Back to Me)" as a poor man's answer to Neil Sedaka's "Carol." Newman and Gordon never again pushed their luck and wrote another song.

If "Underneath the Harlem Moon" was about what Greil Marcus called "the charms of racism," "Yellow Man" indulged those charms to create a deceptively clever indictment of racism. Lyrically, both songs feature stereotypes, but "Yellow Man" has a satirical purpose:

> *Very far away in a foreign land*
> *Live the yellow woman and the yellow man*
> *He's been around for many-a-year*
> *They say they were there before we were here.*

Later in the year, at his Bitter End concerts, Newman would introduce "Yellow Man" as "a pinhead's view of China," but it's probably more accurately described as an inside view of China as seen maybe by Busby Berkeley:

> *Eatin' rice all day*
> *While the children play*
> *You see he believes*
> *In the family*
> *Just like you and me.*

The idea apparently came about when Newman read Will Durant's exhaustive history of civilization, *Our Oriental Heritage*. "It's consigning, you know, six thousand years of Chinese history into *our* oriental heritage," Newman laughs. The direct influence for "Yellow

Man," though, was Busby Berkeley's "Shanghai Lil" production number in *Footlight Parade* (1933).

Although "My Old Kentucky Home" reaches further back into the American musical past, to Stephen Foster, Newman's song was initially about Adolph Rupp, the legendary basketball coach at the University of Kentucky who, from 1930 to 1970, won 875 games and four NCAA championships. Once called the "Baron of Bluegrass" because he took more than 80 percent of his players from the hills of Kentucky, Rupp was driven by an uncompromising desire to win. Newman might have seen Rupp as a sketch for what he would later do with Huey P. Long on *Good Old Boys,* but he abandoned the idea and instead created an ode to Stephen Foster. Born in Lawrenceville, Pennsylvania, in 1826, Foster is one of Newman's true antecedents. Besides being one of America's great popular songwriters, and probably its first truly professional one, Foster was the earliest white musician to explore the deeper current of black music and culture. W.C. Handy, the black bandleader, once wrote perceptively of Foster: "The well of sorrow from which Negro music is drawn is also a well of mystery. I suspect that Stephen Foster owed something to this well, this mystery, this sorrow."

Whether it was the deceptively simple folk song "Oh! Susannah" (1848), or the nostalgic portrait of "Old Folks at Home" (1851), Foster crafted handsomely arranged, mysterious and dignified compositions of a country caught in the throes of slavery and racial injustice. Foster also made a successful living from songwriting, composing over 200 tunes before his death in 1864. While his lyrics may have inherited the patronizing attitudes of their time, Foster also brought a complexity — both technical and emotional — to American popular music. In "My Old Kentucky Home" (1853), Foster depicted a pastoral America, but one without the nostalgic gloss popularized in the 20th century by Norman Rockwell. Instead, Foster's sensibility reveals a detailed love of place, an impressionistic celebration of roots and, in "My Old Kentucky Home," the stark voice of a black slave. Inspired by Harriet Beecher Stowe's *Uncle Tom's Cabin* (1852), a powerful indictment of slavery, Foster's song is ultimately lamenting the loss of a slave's home:

> *The day goes by like a shadow o'er the heart*
> *With sorrow where all was delight*

> *The time has come when the darkies have to part*
> *Then my old Kentucky home, good-night!*

In *Uncle Tom's Cabin,* the slave Tom is forced to vacate his cabin in Kentucky when the owner, Mr. Shelby, goes into debt and must liquidate his assets, including Tom. In "My Old Kentucky Home," Foster provides words for Tom that, at first, harken back to the quaint dwelling he's been forced to abandon. Newman's "Old Kentucky Home" is an updated, booze-soaked portrait of that idyllic abode. "The funniest part of the song is taken from Stephen Foster — 'The sun shines bright on my old Kentucky home/ And the "young folks" roll on the floor,'" Newman explains. "Now it was probably originally 'piccaninnies' or 'darkies' at some point. It's about mountain people's ignorance, or making fun of people who think that's funny. It's a good song because Stephen Foster wrote the hook, that's why."

If Foster's song was a compassionate ode to a homesick slave, Newman's is a sardonic, slapstick lampoon of hayseed behavior. The protagonist in Newman's home likes drinking dandelion wine and shooting birds off his telephone line, but he's always quick to remind us he's doin' fine. His sister, Sue, is "short and stout," although their mother thinks she is simply plain. Brother Gene is "big and mean" and has little to say. When he does express himself, it's usually through beating his wife. When she finally leaves him, Gene gets drunk and kicks his mother down the stairs. Newman paints such a ridiculous picture of family dysfunction that when he gets to the chorus, Foster's words are not only stripped of their longing for home, they're transformed ironically into a denial of one:

> *Oh, the sun shines bright on My Old Kentucky Home*
> *And the young folks roll on the floor*
> *Oh, the sun shines bright on My Old Kentucky Home*
> *Keep them hard times away from my door.*

Newman's version of "My Old Kentucky Home" is ingenious in that, unlike Foster, he doesn't give you a clue as to where his sympathies lie. Newman puts the uncertainties of his confidence-man persona up front, as Dylan often has, so that the listener can't be sure just what he's taking in. To achieve that effect, Newman sings as if in a drunken stupor, regaling other lushes in some bar. Just as in "Suzanne," "Underneath the Harlem Moon" and "Yellow Man," Newman taunts us to work out the paradoxes. Not surprisingly, the ironies of "My Old Kentucky Home" breezed right over the heads of groups like the Beau Brummells. Tennessee Ernie Ford and Johnny Cash took it to be just another down-home country song. Even Ry Cooder, who played on Newman's version, offered only a respectably dull cover later that year on his eponymously named solo record.

Newman's "Rosemary" is a straightforward love song that quotes from Fats Domino, while "If You Need Oil" offers up the kind of precious sexual innuendo that "Let's Burn Down the Cornfield" thankfully undermines. However, "Uncle Bob's Midnight Blues," which concludes the album, is a terrific ragtime number that Newman performs solo on piano. Originally titled "In Defense of Alcohol," Newman conceived it as a celebration of the enduring appeal of booze over the centuries. But the song also referred to Bob Krasnow, hired in 1966 to the Warner's A&R department to help them shed their image as the whitest label in Burbank. In the fifties, Krasnow had developed a fine ear for R&B working for King Records, and had a long association with singer James Brown. The plan was to have Krasnow head up a new subsidiary label, Loma, which would concentrate specifically on soul records. But the label stiffed, mostly due to bad luck. First, Krasnow signed the Olympics, a great fifties black vocal group, best remembered for "Western Movies," to record a song called "Good Lovin'" — only to see a new white soul group called The Young Rascals, at rival Atlantic Records, beat them to the punch and take the same song to Number One. Krasnow also signed Ike and Tina Turner, and even lewd comic Redd Foxx, but to no great effect. Hence, Bob's midnight blues.

Newman randomly loaded "Uncle Bob's Midnight Blues" with stock phrases from best-selling counterculture books like Richard Fariña's *Been Down So Long It Looks Like Up To Me* (1966). "When the blue of the night meets the gold of the day" was included as a tribute to Bing Crosby, and the chorus of "we love you" at the end was a nod to The Rolling Stones. The Stones had recorded a psychedelic B-side single in 1967, with John Lennon and Paul McCartney singing back-up, called "We Love You." Their song was a fabulous, wildly experimental track recorded to show support for their fans after the

Stones survived a major drug bust. In his song, Newman was poking fun at the idea that the very popular Beatles would actually help out their rivals. "The fantasy was that the Stones were in their decline and McCartney and The Beatles were singing on the record, which they were, and saying: 'Sure, man, we'll sing with you, so long!'," Newman recalled with a laugh. "Uncle Bob's Midnight Blues" is such a patchwork of anecdotal vignettes, it's hard to see where Bob Krasnow figures in it. But since Krasnow's search for the ingredients of a hit at Warners was futile, perhaps Newman, in "Uncle Bob's Midnight Blues," was showing Bob that he had a stockpile of lyric clichés right here in his song.

During the sessions for *12 Songs,* Newman recorded duets with Cooder, including "Don't Ruin Our Happy Home," "Magic in the Moonlight" (which led Newman to proclaim that he'd "record it someday Viennese style") and "Beat Me Baby," an obvious precursor to "You Can Leave Your Hat On." Released in February 1970, *12 Songs* is a deviously satirical contemporary twist on the panoramic tradition of American music. Singing here with a bold confidence lacking on his first record, Newman also adjusts his mask with less self-consciousness. The ironies and riddles are also executed so effortlessly they seem to go down before you even notice them. Essentially, *12 Songs* is a rock & roll album, but one that draws attention to questions about what constitutes pop entertainment. "Newman can only be called a rocker in the way Andy Kaufman was a comedian," Sean Elder once noted in *Salon.* Which is to say, Newman writes songs that bring a complex awareness to questions regarding their meaning, just as Kaufman's routines were as much commentaries on the spectacle of doing stand-up comedy as they were routines themselves. With this new album now behind him, Newman had started to gather a devoted cult following. His next challenge was to win over a mass audience and keep them. In the decade ahead, Newman would discover just how difficult that task would prove to be.

# Claiming the Mask

It is a good thing, and speaks well for human nature,
that men *can be swindled*.

— Evert Duyckinck, *The Merchant's Lodger*

I don't think there's a part of me in every character. . . .
It's like in the movies — when you see a bad guy who's
strictly bad, the character appears cartoonish and in
some ways is easily dismissed. Human beings are much
more complex than that.

— Randy Newman

## 1

When singer/songwriter Harry Nilsson died of a stroke on January 15,
1994, composer Al Kooper and producer Danny Kapilian were hard at
work on a tribute album to the veteran performer. A year earlier, there
had been some urgency about getting the project off the ground.
Nilsson had already been ill with diabetes and complications from a
Valentine's Day stroke. Kooper immediately contacted Kapilian, a
longtime fan, and they started to discuss the possibilities of a record.

"We decided to round up a bunch of Harry's friends and fans and record an album of his songs, not only to cheer him up, but to remind the world about one of its great treasures," Kooper recalled. And indeed, the world had largely forgotten this notable singer. If Nilsson still registered in anyone's consciousness, it was as a vague remembrance at best. If anything, pop music fans recalled his rather touching version of Fred Neil's "Everybody's Talkin'," from the hit film *Midnight Cowboy* (1969); or maybe the Badfinger song, "Without You," which Nilsson's emotionally overpowering cover helped top the U.S. charts for more than four weeks in late 1971. But the last time Nilsson had made anything resembling news was on one memorable evening in 1974, when he and John Lennon got tossed out of a nightclub after getting violently drunk and heckling the Smothers Brothers. Within a matter of days, Nilsson became notorious as the lush who contributed to Lennon's lost weekend.

But if the public was no longer cognizant of Nilsson in 1994, his contemporaries certainly were. When Kooper and Kapilian sent out the call, artists immediately expressed keen interest, including Aimee Mann, Fred Schneider of the B52s, Victoria Williams, Brian Wilson, Marshall Crenshaw and Ron Sexsmith. The other performer on whom both Kooper and Kapilian were strongly counting on to join them was Randy Newman.

Back in the sixties, Nilsson and Newman were two sides of the same coin. Journalist Curtis Armstrong, who wrote a commemorative piece on Nilsson, explained quite persuasively what the pair had in common: "They shared much: a fierce intelligence, occasionally caustic cynicism, an encyclopedic knowledge and affection for American music in all its forms, extraordinary powers of observation, and the uncanny ability to write whole novels into a three-minute popular song structure." And not only were they both eager composers, launching parallel careers in Los Angeles, they were also largely songwriters-for-hire. Yet both Nilsson and Newman were determined to record their own material one day. After idly watching while others took their best songs to the top of the charts (usually with inferior performances), they were both convinced that they could do much better.

Harry Nilsson was born Harry Edward Nelson III on Father's Day, June 15, 1941, in the Bushwick section of Brooklyn, New York. His father abandoned the family soon after the war, leaving Nilsson, his mother, Betty, and a half-sister to pack up and move to California. They settled in San Bernadino, until the family encountered more difficulties due to Betty's drinking and financial woes. For years, this family instability forced Nilsson to move constantly between the East and West coasts, staying with various relatives. However, it was through his mother that he developed an eager interest in music. "She wrote a couple of songs and I eventually recorded them," Nilsson said. "One was 'Marchin' Down Broadway.' I found out that Irving Berlin offered her a thousand bucks for it." If Nilsson's active interest in songwriting came from his mother, he became equally fascinated with becoming a vocalist thanks to his Uncle John. A gifted singer himself, John taught Harry how to sing harmony. Within a few years, Nilsson had studied some piano, played a ukulele, and like many his age, became fascinated with rock & roll. His first exposure to this music, besides the radio, was working at the Paramount Theater in Los Angeles, where rock bands performed on a regular basis. It gave Nilsson the bug for songwriting. It was while he was working night shift at a bank that he first entertained the idea of being a composer for a living.

At the beginning, Nilsson spent his days making calls to various music companies, then in the early fall of 1960 he began singing demos for songwriter/producer Scott Turner at Capitol Records. Within a few years, Nilsson had hooked up with Phil Spector, who was hitting his stride with his Wall of Sound productions featuring The Crystals, The Ronettes and Ike and Tina Turner. Spector and Nilsson composed three songs together, "This Could Be the Night" (covered by the Modern Folk Quartet), "Here I Sit" and "Paradise," which they wrote for the Ronettes. "Here I Sit" shows the playful sense of humor Nilsson would display later in his career, taking its title from perhaps the most infamous piece of public toilet graffiti:

> *Here I sit, broken-hearted*
> *Paid a dime*
> *And only farted.*

The lyric, though, goes beyond being a clever variation on a scatological theme — it shows a tickling wit:

*Here I sit, broken-hearted*
*Fell in love but now we've parted*
*Couldn't see the writing on the wall.*

Nilsson continued to write colorful songs, like "Ten Little Indians" and "Cuddly Toy," which showed both a childlike innocence and a street-smart buffoonery. When The Monkees recorded "Cuddly Toy" for their *Pisces, Aquarius, Capricorn & Jones* (1967) album, the song secured a recording contract for Nilsson at RCA Records. His first album, *Pandemonium Shadow Show* (1967), contained a couple of Beatles covers, "You Can't Do That" (which became a sparkling medley of several Beatles tunes), "She's Leaving Home" and a powerhouse performance of "River Deep, Mountain High" in the style of Spector's Wall of Sound. The album opened with the autobiographical track, "1941," which expressed Nilsson's grief at losing his father.

What set Nilsson apart from other pop singers was his ability to use his light tenor voice, with its divergent range, to replicate an entire vocal group by overdubbing his own harmony and lead vocals. The first real attempt he made to expand his range came on his next record, *Aerial Ballet* (1968), an exquisitely crafted collection of introspective pop songs. "Good Old Desk," for example, was a lovely childlike lament about the strong affinity a writer can have for his desk. "Mr. Richland's Favorite Song" is a disarming requiem for an old vaudevillian. "One" (a song Three Dog Night would turn into a million-seller in 1969) is a desolate tale of abandonment. The inclusion of "Everybody's Talkin'," which became Nilsson's first Top 10 hit in 1969, would draw enormous attention to *Aerial Ballet*. That included the interest of four lads from Liverpool who started describing Harry as their "favorite American group." Thanks to The Beatles' valuable praise, Nilsson started to achieve some modicum of commercial recognition.

Nilsson's next album, *Harry* (1970), included yet another Beatles cover, "Mother Nature's Son," and concluded with Randy Newman's "Simon Smith and the Amazing Dancing Bear." "At the time he was writing a lot of songs," Nilsson told Paul Zollo years later. "I thought they were better songs than what I was writing." Nilsson's first wife, Diane, confirmed this admiration. "Harry was in awe of Randy and his music," she told Curtis Armstrong. The recording of "Simon Smith," where Harry's pristine performance intensified the song's ironic intent, immediately caught Newman's ear. Inspired by his interest, Nilsson released *Nilsson Sings Newman,* a serendipitous collaboration between two unflappable talents. The record was executed with utter simplicity. While Newman played the piano, Nilsson added a vast number of voices (according to the singer, there were over 118 overdubs). The result was an ingeniously crafted masterpiece of chamber pop. With the exception of one track Newman wrote specifically for the record ("Caroline"), the album contained previously released material ("Love Story," "Vine Street," "Yellow Man").

*Nilsson Sings Newman* may have been partly inspired by Rick Nelson's concept approach to Randy Newman on his *Perspective* album in 1968 (where he also covered songs by Nilsson). In the age of psychedelic rock, Nelson was perceived as an anachronism. A superior rockabilly performer, Nelson nevertheless didn't see himself merely as a washed-up oldies act, so with *Perspective,* he consciously began deconstructing his rockabilly image. Produced by John Boylen and featuring arrangements by Jimmy Haskell, the record contains a wide breadth of what were then contemporary songs. Besides Newman and Nilsson, Nelson covered tunes by Paul Simon ("For Emily, Wherever I May Find Her") and Richie Havens ("Three Day Eternity"). He also does a lovely rendition of "I Think It's Going to Rain Today" and creates an ambitious medley out of Newman's previously unreleased "Wait Till Next Year," "Love Story" and "So Long Dad/ Love Story (reprise)." Nelson's idea for *Perspective* was to tell a story about a famous family by connecting a series of songs. In many ways, the record was shaped by Nelson's own memories of his show-biz clan, depicted on TV's *The Ozzie and Harriet Show,* which painted a serene picture of old-fashioned fifties suburban life. As if emulating Brian Wilson, Nelson incorporated a playful mix of sound effects, which included splashing in the bathtub, cars driving and phones ringing, giving the record the flavor of a radio drama.

Beginning on August 20, 1969, Nilsson and Newman began laying down tracks for their own concept recording. However, the process of doing the album became somewhat laborious — especially since Nilsson went over each song painstakingly to be certain he properly comprehended them. "I needed to learn the songs inside out the way he knew them," he explained. "I needed that practice . . . [to] do it my way so that it [stylistically] matched both of us."

The record opens with "Vine Street," the same tune Van Dyke Parks used to begin *Song Cycle*. But where Parks adopted it as a key to open the door to the American musical past, Nilsson used it to bring us into the present. This was an appropriate choice, after all, since Harry's career as a songwriter began at Capitol, near the corner of Hollywood and Vine. "Vine Street" is about an artist reflecting on his demo tape — the one "that never made the grade" — so Nilsson (like Parks) begins the actual track with a segment from another song. Parks chose "Black Jack Davey" because of its link to an earlier folk era, but Nilsson includes a Newman original, an unreleased modern rock number called "Anita." Surprisingly, this subtly composed chamber album begins with a rocking and twanging electric guitar. As the melody establishes itself, with the inclusion of Newman's piano and maracas, Nilsson jumps in to perform a song that bears some resemblance to Newman's "Have You Seen My Baby":

> *My baby left this morning*
> *With everything I had*
> *She didn't give me no warning*
> *That's why I feel so bad.*

As Nilsson marshals his bevy of harmony vocals, his lead voice adds a comical chorus filled with clever wordplay:

> *Oh, Anita*
> *Anita*
> *I need some sympathy*
> *Anita*
> *I love ya*
> *Come and sit by me.*

Then, in less than a minute, "Anita" comes to an abrupt stop. Newman's piano and Nilsson's solo voice now settle into the parlor to reminisce. Throughout the record, the two musicians continuously remind us we're listening to the recording of an album. On several songs, we even hear a voice (presumably Nilsson's) telling the engineer to add more harmony vocals, or simply to drop a vocal part. As Frank Zappa did on many of his own records, Nilsson and Newman continually break up the act of listening to a song by drawing listeners into the very process of how the song is recorded.

Nilsson and Newman follow "Vine Street" with a straightforward performance of "Love Story." Stripped of the quirky orchestration that adorned the version on *Randy Newman Creates Something New Under the Sun,* the composition has a distilled charm. Nilsson's voice, which has the flexibility Newman's lacks, gives it an entirely different emotional weight. Newman makes you more aware of the irony because his voice distances you from the pain in the story, whereas Nilsson's takes you to the very heart of the sorrow. For evidence, just listen to the way Nilsson clips the phrasing near the end. When he sings the lyric, "They'll send us to a little home in Florida," he chokes deeply on "Florida." "Yellow Man" has the same arrangement featured in *12 Songs,* but Nilsson provides a harmony chorus of "oohs" for his lead vocal, eliciting something of the feeling of a barbershop quartet. Once again, Nilsson draws us into the recording process. In the concluding verse, thanks to overdubbing, we hear his voice in the control room reading the lyrics to his voice in the studio. Given the lyrics ("Eating rice all day/ While the children play"), the impact of hearing Nilsson sing "Yellow Man" is reminiscent of listening to the Canadian Mounties in Monty Python's "The Lumberjack Song" — especially when they suddenly comprehend the meaning of what they're singing.

"Caroline" is an exquisite Newman original which seems perfectly suited to Nilsson. By Newman's standards, it's a simple love song of the kind he might have written for Metric Music in the early sixties. Nilsson's melodious harmonies compete with each other in a way that makes the pining in the composition seem bottomless:

> *And when it's springtime*
> *And daylight surrounds you*
> *And there's no one around you*
> *But me.*

Nilsson's version would eventually become the inspiration for the animated short *Caroline* (1993), directed by Patrick Ahearn. The film premiered at an Animation Society screening at the Palace of Fine Arts/Exploratorium's McBean Theater in San Francisco.

"Cowboy" on *Nilsson Sings Newman* is even starker than

Newman's original. As in "Love Story," the orchestration (including the haunting horn coda) is stripped bare, enhancing the desolate atmosphere. With the sound of a cold wind blowing in, Nilsson slowly describes Newman's cowboy's sad fate. When he reaches the chorus, Nilsson turns the bleakness into a piercing cry for acceptance:

> *Cowboy*
> *Can't run*
> *Can't hide*
> *It's too late to fight now*
> *Too tired to try.*

The "can't run" and "can't hide" pleas are rendered so intensely the singer seems cornered by his own desperation. As if to directly address the cowboy's fate as both misfit and outsider, Nilsson (at the urging of Diane) concluded "Cowboy" with a harpsichord, playing John Barry's theme from *Midnight Cowboy,* a clever inside joke that referenced his hit version of "Everybody's Talkin'" from the same picture.

"The Beehive State" has more urgency than Newman's take, without losing any of the song's paradoxes. The Mates of State, a punchy rock duo from San Francisco consisting of Jason Hammel on drums and Kori Gardner on organ, released a wonderfully buoyant version of the song as a single in 2001. A careful listen to their staccato arrangement suggests they based their interpretation on Nilsson's cover rather than Newman's original.

"I'll Be Home" is probably the best song on *Nilsson Sings Newman,* despite the fact Newman cared little for it. While he would perform it in concert, and eventually include a studio recording on *Little Criminals* (1977), the song was originally written at the request of Derek Taylor, press secretary for The Beatles and Apple Records. Paul McCartney apparently needed a song for singer Mary Hopkin ("Those Were the Days"), but she would never record it. Perhaps because it was done on assignment, the composition lacked Newman's usual capriciousness, but Nilsson transforms "I'll Be Home" into a stirring affirmation of devoted love:

> *I'll be home*
> *When your nights are troubled*
> *And you're all alone.*

When Nilsson reaches the chorus, "I'll be home," he adds a gospel call-and-response ("Oh yes, he will!"), and when he repeats the line, he does a Beatlesque harmony response ("Leaving in the morning, yeah!"). It's a stunningly economical performance that establishes it as the best interpretation of that song. In "Living Without You," Nilsson provides the kind of intricate harmonies that might make Brian Wilson sick with envy. When Nilsson reaches the last line, "It's so hard," he emphasizes the singer's anguish with a prolonged, heartfelt "haaaaaar-rrrd" that fades off into the distance.

"Dayton, Ohio 1903" was a recent Newman song, later included on his *Sail Away* album in 1972. It's about a couple lounging on their porch on "a lazy Sunday afternoon," and there's a nostalgic feel that would almost be too maudlin if it weren't for Nilsson humorously humming Glenn Miller's "Moonlight Serenade" under the middle verse. The record concludes with "So Long Dad," which, given that "Vine Street" opens the album, is bookended with "Love Story." This is fitting, since "So Long Dad" has always felt part of the same story. As it concludes, Nilsson's control-room voice starts asking for "more first voice," while another Nilsson voice answers back, "Actually I need more current voice. Forget the voice that's saying more first voice." All the while, the full chorus of Nilsson voices happily croons, "So long Dad!" right down to the final fade. Both Newman and Nilsson recorded a version of "Snow," and "Linda" as well, but neither was included on the original album. "Snow" would turn up as a bonus track on the thirtieth anniversary rerelease of the record on CD.

While Nilsson spent more than six weeks happily overdubbing all of his vocals in preparation for the album's release in February 1970, Newman begged off. "Randy was tired of the album when we were finishing making it," Nilsson remarked. "For him it was just doing piano and voice . . . over and over. . . . Once I got the take down, I knew what I was going to do with it later. He didn't." But that didn't diminish the overall experience for Newman. "I was honored that a writer with Harry's talent would choose to do an album of someone else's songs," he explained. "He was such a great singer, a virtuoso singer really, and he could do so many things as a vocalist that I couldn't do — like hold a note." *Stereo Review* magazine named *Nilsson Sings Newman* their album of the year for 1970, but it failed to receive many other good reviews until years later. Ben Wener remarked in his 2000 appraisal of the rereleased album for *The Orange County Register,* "Newman's sly, dramatically structured impressionistic pop was ideally suited for Nilsson's theatrical tone." In fact, Nilsson's voice gave a whole different meaning to Newman's songs, without losing any of their sardonic wit. "It's not so much that Nilsson's takes are better than Newman's," Wener continued. "[It's] just refreshingly different — less wicked and vicious, more melancholy."

Nilsson recognized the singularity of the project: "It was one of the first albums where an artist recognized another artist. I think they used to do that in the forties a lot." This may account for the faintly nostalgic air of the record, reflected also in the cover art (created by Dean Torrence, formerly of Jan & Dean, who had become a graphic artist shortly after Jan Berry's car crash ended the duo's career). On the front of the album, in sepia tones, Nilsson is seen driving Newman in an old jalopy across the American countryside. Oddly enough, while Nilsson is quite identifiable as the driver, Newman sitting in the backseat bears more of a resemblance to Kurt Vonnegut Jr.

It may well have been the idiosyncratic quality of the record that ultimately doomed it to oblivion with the mass audience. "I went into a shop to see how the album was selling in L.A.," Newman explained to Keith Altham of the *New Musical Express.* "This assistant comes up and asks if he can help. 'Sure,' I say. 'Do you have any Nilsson albums?' He goes through 'em all, one by one, saying how well they are selling and how he can recommend this one and that one. Then he comes to *Nilsson Sings Newman* and says, 'And this is the one that nearly finished him off. . . .'" Yet, by 1994, this unfettered collaboration had finally found acclaim among a whole new generation of musical performers, including Rufus Wainwright, Ron Sexsmith, the Jellyfish and Adrian Belew.

"[In 1970], Randy was an up and coming songwriter when . . . Nilsson recorded an *entire album of his songs,*" Danny Kapilian explained with unbridled enthusiasm. "To my knowledge, Randy had never recorded a Nilsson tune." In 1994, almost twenty-five years since Nilsson honored him, Newman was about to return the favor. The homage, which sadly became a memorial, was titled *For the Love of Harry: Everybody Sings Nilsson* (1995). When Newman agreed to come aboard, he selected three possible songs to record. They were all intriguing choices. One was "1941," the distinctly autobiographical song about a father who leaves his son. Perhaps what made the song appealing for him was its resemblance to the whimsical familial tone of his own "Love Story" and "So Long, Dad":

> *In 1941*
> *A happy father had a son*
> *But by 1944*
> *The father walked right out the door.*
> *In '45, the mom and son were still alive*
> *But who would know by '46*
> *If the two were to survive?*

In Nilsson's song, the son runs away to join the circus, gets married, has a child and ends up committing the same sins as the father. The sadness is submerged in a carnival melody that carries with it the faint reverberation of a childhood lost. Innocence is not only irreclaimable here, it can't even be recalled. The wistful mood cast over "1941" saves it from becoming as treacly and self-conscious as Harry Chapin's comparable "Cat's in the Cradle." The second selection Newman considered was the vociferous anthem, "I'd Rather Be Dead," written (and performed) as a protest song for geriatrics tired of being helpless participants in life. It might have been a fitting tribute, too, since "I'd Rather Be Dead" has a perspicacity worthy of Newman's own clever eye:

> *I'd rather be dead*
> *Than wet my bed*
> *I'll tie my tie*
> *Until the day I die*
> *But if I have to be fed*
> *Then I'd rather be dead.*

Nilsson originally recorded the song in a nursing home with an amateur choir, and it has a cutting sarcasm that probably appealed to Newman. Yet there was a tempered optimism, too, that had more in common with the other work of Nilsson than with Newman's:

*Oh, it's nice to be alive*
*When the dream comes true*
*But you'd be better off dead*
*It can happen to you.*

Newman ultimately decided against both of these songs and settled instead on "Remember (Christmas)," a sad yet dreamy song about looking back on a life and realizing that, in the end, "love is but a dream." Nilsson once wrote in an earlier composition ("The Puppy Song") that dreams are nothing more than wishes, and a wish is just a dream you wish to come true. "Remember (Christmas)" is a reply to that deeply romantic song, only this time, those aspirations have been stripped of nostalgia:

*Remember — is a place from long ago*
*Remember — think of everything you know*
*Remember — when you're sad and feeling down*
*Remember — turn around.*

In Newman's hands, "Remember (Christmas)" became an affectionate eulogy for a lost friend. "The first time I heard it, I called Al Kooper and said, 'No matter what other tracks come in, Al, this must be the opening song on the album,'" Danny Kapilian recalled. There's a fragile intimacy in Newman's performance, quite unlike any other recording he's made, as if, with silence punctuating each line, Newman is left waiting for one of Harry's many voices to reply. But there's nothing; only silence. As "Remember (Christmas)" begins, Newman sings "Long ago . . . far away . . . life was clear . . . close your eyes. . . ," and finally a great treasure, once forgotten, is suddenly made vivid again.

## 2

In June 1970, Randy Newman started to make a series of live appearances, beginning with NBC's *Liza Minnelli Special*. Minnelli had already recorded a number of Newman songs on her eponymous 1968 debut album, including "The Debutante's Ball," "Happyland" and "So Long Dad." On the show, which aired Monday, June 29th, Newman did a solo rendition of "Love Story," then performed a duet with Liza on "So Long Dad." *The Hollywood Reporter,* with its tongue planted firmly in its cheek, claimed Newman's Minnelli appearance was only his third in front of a live audience, "if you don't count a dance he once did for Douglas Aircraft Plant workers while he was still in high school which so put him off that he didn't reappear for years." Indeed, until 1970, Newman wasn't much of a road rat. But that year he began making a habit of doing concerts, especially in support of his first two records. Beginning in September with a ten-night stand at New York's popular Bitter End Club, Newman launched his career on the road.

If he was going to tour, Newman wanted to create a different stage persona from that of most popular singer-songwriters. For one thing, instead of proselytizing on the sensitivity of his soul, in the manner of Cat Stevens, Newman provided self-deprecating patter. Introducing "Lonely at the Top," for example, Newman played off his status as a cult figure. "All combined, my records have sold as many copies as James Taylor's last album sold in Des Moines," he remarked. After a pause for laughter, he added, "But I'm fantastically wealthy, so nothing matters." Then he'd perform the ridiculously obsessive "Lover's Prayer." When he yelled, "Take it!" to his imaginary band as he got to the instrumental bridge, he'd have a ready-made explanation. "I have to do that because it gets kind of lonely up here," he told the audience. Likewise, when he introduced his new song "God's Song (That's Why I Love Mankind)," he'd remark, "I consider it a great honor to be God's spokesman." He'd follow with a few bars of music, then (as an afterthought) add, "I'll try to sit up straighter when I sing His part."

Newman, of course, wanted popular success, but the mask he donned to create his artistic persona far from guaranteed huge album sales. Jokes and asides riddled Newman's performances, as if they emerged organically from the compositions themselves. But these digressions were part of a self-protective instinct highly intelligent Jewish-American artists have often developed to make themselves appear harmless and helplessly docile when, in fact, they are wickedly smart.

Sometimes, Newman faced audiences who were baffled by his disguise. He didn't exactly look like your average rock & roller, and it wasn't a straightforward rock & roll show he was performing, so the reaction to his concerts was often mixed. A Newman performance was usually sneaky and satiric, biting and funny, and if you weren't paying attention, you'd be utterly lost. In October 1970, at the Revolution Club in London, England, Newman took the stage in an environment usually reserved for the latest in psychedelic fashion and entertainment. The shuffling Newman sat at the piano and opened with "Lover's Prayer." Immediately, he found the crowd utterly uninterested and chattering. He sped into "Yellow Man," before announcing a quick "good night" after a section of "I Think It's Going to Rain Today." Critic Richard Williams, who attended this truncated set, was appalled at the crowd's behavior. Reporting in *Melody Maker*, he wrote, with some embarrassment, that the crowd didn't truly deserve Newman, and applauded Newman's manner of handling the indifference. "Instead of making a big production out of [it], he just split in the most eloquent way," Williams wrote. "Those two-and-a-quarter songs were unforgettable, the brevity of the set illuminating the quality of the songs, which have the miniaturist beauty of Japanese haiku."

As for the Bitter End concerts, producers Russ Titelman and Lenny Waronker decided to record them. The idea was to have just Newman and his piano running through his songbook in front of a small yet enthusiastic audience, the same folks who had eagerly embraced the *12 Songs* album. "I was playing at the Bitter End in front of about twelve people at a 1 a.m. show, the third show on Saturday," Newman recalls. "It still amuses me that [the] live version of 'Lonely at the Top' [has] six people clapping." Nevertheless, the fervor generated by these intimate concerts excited Titelman and Waronker enough that they released the album as a promo to radio stations in May 1971. *Randy Newman Live,* which featured fourteen tracks from three of those shows, had a plain white bootleg-style sleeve with Newman's name, the titles and scant other information. Newman was also hard at work on his newest studio record, and Titelman and Waronker were trying to create some anticipation for it.

They issued *Randy Newman Live* to the general public in June. Surprisingly, the disk cracked the Top 200 at No. 191, though it barely caught the sardonic quality of Newman's work onstage. For one thing, it included very few of Newman's comic asides, just a rapid run-through of his songs. Like his first two studio records, it was also horribly short, barely lasting a half-hour. The selections, which generally came from his first two albums, included "Mama Told Me Not to Come," "So Long Dad," "I Think It's Going to Rain Today," "Old

Kentucky Home" and "Yellow Man." And a number of tracks didn't make the album, like "Vine Street," a cover of Fats Domino's fabulous "Blue Monday," a hilarious tribute to masochistic romance, "Beat Me Baby," "Maybe I'm Doing it Wrong" and "Tickle Me" — yet another track about hidden perversities. That particular song would be covered by Alan Price on *A Price on His Head* (1970).

*Randy Newman Live* represented a lull in the action, although Waronker, who would become vice president of Warner/Reprise in 1971, saw it as a significant album that set up the one that followed. "People loved him in that setting," Waronker said, describing Newman's minimalist presentation on stage. "We pressed a limited number of records and — surprise — the live set sold better than Randy's studio albums. It went a long way in establishing him as an artist in his own right." Newman's live performances were idiosyncratic and distinct, personal without being solipsistic and harsh without being grating. On his new album, *Sail Away,* Newman would produce a compelling hybrid of everything he'd accomplished on his first two releases. He combined the orchestral strains of early Americana that seeped through *Randy Newman Creates Something New Under the Sun,* with the rollicking R&B of *12 Songs,* and he did it with a new authority. Unlike the first two records, *Sail Away* wasn't a concept album. "It was song to song," Newman explained to David Wild. "There was no thought that it would cohere into a whole, and it doesn't." Yet, even as a collection of songs, *Sail Away* does cohere into a powerfully complex delineation of the American experience. Once again, the cast of characters is diverse — a slave trader, a meek pervert and God playing nasty practical jokes — and there's a range of subject matter (rivers on fire, atomic war, an old man's death and an admonition to a young son) that reveals something of Newman's restless intelligence.

Besides fulfilling the promise of his previous albums, *Sail Away* cut an epic path through the American pop terrain, transcending the nascent narcissism of seventies popular songwriters like James Taylor, Carly Simon and Cat Stevens. The collapse of the sixties counterculture, heralded by the election of Richard Nixon in 1968 and culminating in the shootings at Kent State in 1970, had led many people to turn inward for enlightenment. Newman, however, still saw a country out there he was definitely part of, and felt obliged to address it in his own inimitable way. Whether or not he saw the record as a loose collection of disparate songs, a thematic unity still emerges within it. *Sail Away* offers listeners a deep and lasting pleasure — even if it doesn't provide much in the way of easy comfort. The title song came rather innocently out of a movie project on which a number of rock artists, including Van Morrison and Neil Young, were each given ten minutes to do whatever they wished. While the aborted movie project never came to fruition, Newman still composed his song, an account of the slave trade told from the point of view of the slave trader on his ship. "I also wrote this little sea shanty, this Irish kind of song ["The Ballad of Pat O'Reilly"] for the [voyage]," he recalled. "But the guy never made the movie." Instead, Newman created his *own* idea for a movie.

One of the most ingenious and ambiguous tales in American popular music, "Sail Away" tells the story of a trader arriving in Africa to entice black Africans to climb onboard his huge ship to travel to the new land. "I wrote 'Sail Away' because the slave trade is our main imperialist crime, our insoluble problem," Newman told Susan Lydon. The horrible paradox is that without the slave trade there is also no contemporary black American culture — no Bessie Smith, Louis Armstrong, Charlie Parker, Muddy Waters, Koko Taylor, Booker T. Washington, Aretha Franklin, Ray Charles, Martin Luther King, Malcolm X, Denzel Washington, Dr. Dre or Condoleeza Rice. When he wrote about "Sail Away," that irony wasn't lost on Greil Marcus. "Scary, astonishing, Newman has presented an American temptation," he wrote in *Mystery Train*. "[He's] tempting not only the Africans, who became Negroes and went on to create the music that finally tossed up Elvis Presley, rock & roll, Newman, and his audience, but tempting America to believe that this image of itself might be true . . . the song transcends its irony." "Sail Away" transcends its irony because it is a disturbingly unresolvable work rather than a polemic about the evils of slavery.

The song opens with a hideous joke. Newman (as the slave trader) sings, "In America, you'll get food to eat," as if the Africans must somehow be starving. Meanwhile, a beguiling horn ostinato forms behind him to create a luscious portrait of the new land awaiting them. The trader then confronts the Africans with the very stereotypes that await them — far in their future:

*You'll just sing about Jesus*
*And drink wine all day*
*It's great to be an American.*

What makes "Sail Away" so effective is the manner in which Newman portrays this flesh merchant. So eager is he to introduce his captives to his idea of America, he furnishes them with the horrible fruits of his sales pitch just as the string arrangement soars in anticipation:

*Ain't no lions or tigers*
*Ain't no mamba snake*
*Just the sweet watermelon*
*And the buckwheat cake*
*Everybody is as happy as a man could be*
*Climb aboard, little wog —*
*Sail away with me.*

The orchestral arrangement is so majestic, it arouses an eagerness to jump onboard in spite of the words you're hearing. By providing a diverting piano melody that runs counterpoint to the sad yearning of the strings, Newman fools you into believing in a false promise, an assurance that can't possibly be fulfilled.

Never before had a song about the slave trade been told in such a paradoxical manner. Lee Herschberg, Newman's recording engineer through *Trouble in Paradise* (1983), fully recognized the song's uniqueness. "At a time when people were making pop records, Randy was making social commentary, and I enjoyed working with people who actually had something to say," he told Dan Daley of *Mix*. In describing the ambiguity of "Sail Away," Gary Mairs, a reviewer on Amazon.com, said that Newman holds us with "a vision of the America that awaits them [as] so sweet, so Edenic, that you forget, for a moment, the horrors they'll really face."

Many of the other singers who chose to cover "Sail Away" didn't want to face the horrors described in the song, preferring instead to just skirt the subject matter. Linda Ronstadt, for instance, on her 1973 album *Don't Cry Now,* displays a complete misunderstanding of the composition, singing so majestically, her voice riding on the soaring gospel chorus, that she sounds completely unaware the song is a con.

Newman's vocal, on the other hand, makes that dimension perfectly clear. "In part, that's why his vocals were so unprocessed," Herschberg explained. "We hardly ever put reverb on them. He didn't want to highlight the vocal as much as he did the message he was singing. I always knew what Randy was trying to do and say in the studio." Ronstadt wasn't alone; very few seemed to grasp what Newman accomplished in this song. According to Marcus, a group called Salvation even changed the term "little wog" to "little child." Others, including Bobby Darin, Joe Cocker, Etta James and Gladys Knight and the Pips, performed "Sail Away" as if it were "God Bless America." Given the liberal views of these performers, perhaps they felt uncomfortable with the self-incriminating aspect of adopting such an adversarial role in a pop song.

Their trepidation is reminiscent of Joan Baez's in her recording of The Band's "The Night They Drove Old Dixie Down," a powerfully moving song told from the point of view of Virgil Cane, a defeated Southerner at the end of the American Civil War. Baez, a Northern liberal, could hardly place herself comfortably in the character of a white Southerner, so she changes a couple of lyrics, and in doing so, alters the song's meaning. First, she amends Virgil's exhaltant vision of the arrival of Robert E. Lee into "the Robert E. Lee," reducing Virgil's startling vision of the famous General to that of a boat arriving pointlessly at some nonexistent port. Next, when Virgil defiantly asserts that, like his father before him, "I will work the land," Baez modifies the line to, "I'm a working man." That particular phrase recalls the rallying cry of the migrants of John Steinbeck and the noble countrymen Woody Guthrie sang about in "This Land is Your Land." It is associated with left-wing revolts against capitalist exploitation, not with a defeated Confederacy vainly attempting to till the land that is its very heritage. In the case of both "Sail Away" and "The Night They Drove Old Dixie Down," cover artists took huge liberties in changing inconvenient aspects of the lyrics to present a more affirmative view. But in doing so, they also rendered both songs completely meaningless.

In the case of Etta James and Gladys Knight, could the fact they were black have added to their difficulty in achieving ironic distance from the disconcerting material in "Sail Away"? Possibly. Yet the best cover version of the song came from two veteran black performers who understood the material all too well — Sonny Terry and Brownie

McGhee — who had played the blues together for many years, and probably saw the song as a great opportunity to connect to the source of the bitter legacy that made their best music possible. In 1973, after years of recording on a variety of independent labels, they made an album for A&M Records entitled *Sonny & Brownie*. This gorgeous, handsomely crafted record features an assortment of pop, R&B and blues tracks. It tells a genuinely charming story of two old men, looking back on their storied career and taking solace from the many pleasures gathered during their partnership. *Sonny & Brownie* is also filled with good humor and randy anecdotes. Including sturdy covers of Curtis Mayfield's gospel affirmation "People Get Ready" and Sam Cooke's sumptuous "Bring It On Home to Me," the album tackles episodes of good, raunchy sex ("You Bring Out the Boogie in Me"), cultural appropriation ("White Boy Lost in the Blues"), salvation ("Jesus Gonna Make It Alright") and the immeasurable satisfaction of friendship ("On the Road Again").

In their version of "Sail Away," Terry and McGhee decided to tell Newman's story from the point of view of two old slaves, looking back on the long trip that brought them to America. It opens with Maurice Rogers playing an African melody on a thumb piano (doubling for the kalimba), taking us back to the so-called Dark Continent. When Sonny's harmonica is first heard over the opening notes of the thumb piano, we're brought into the American plantation fields where the lonely sound of that harp was first born. At this point, Brownie starts to sing the words of the slave trader, but in the voice of a slave remembering what he once heard. He gives us the sense, as he tells this story, that he's still trying to remember why he found the slave trader's words so enticing. The clever addition of a banjo at this point has the effect of summoning the early nineteenth-century American folk music of Stephen Foster. In Sonny and Brownie's hands, "Sail Away" calls up the whole history of the nation, especially when Brownie (with the help of Arlo Guthrie) starts to sing the chorus, urging one and all to sail away.

The next verse is taken by Terry. If McGhee sings with a resigned satisfaction, Sonny brings a righteous defiance to his version of the story. When he cries, "In America, every man is free," you know he recognizes the fib buried in that declaration. His life on the road, often in segregated states, has told him it's a whopper, and now, finally, he gets to state his truth. "Be American, sail away with me," Sonny proclaims with the satisfaction of one who has survived all the indignities of America's racial injustice. By the end, Sonny and Brownie initiate a call and response with Arlo Guthrie that firmly links the traditions of blues, folk, R&B, and black gospel. "Sail Away" is movingly captured in its full incongruous glory:

> *Sail away — Sail away*
> *We will cross the mighty ocean*
> *Into Charleston Bay*
> *Sail away — Sail away.*

Newman's version of "Sail Away" was released as a single, but not surprisingly, the record failed to chart. And thirty-odd years after its recording, the song still proves troubling for some. In an interview with Newman on the National Public Radio show *Morning Edition* in the fall of 2003, Bob Edwards questioned his motivation for composing such a beautiful song about such a horrid subject. "What am I supposed to say," Newman replied, "'Slavery is bad?' It's like falling out of an airplane and hitting the ground. It's just too easy. And it has no effect." Edwards, though, continued to press. "But the contrast is so strong," he implored. "That beautiful melody . . ." Newman, reaching for a larger contradiction, summed up just how little impact a pop song can have on reality. "It worked out well," he remarked sarcastically. "It ended racism in this country. Kids today don't remember, now that it's gone away."

Newman followed "Sail Away" on the album with the Sinatra-inspired "Lonely at the Top." But Newman sings this ragtime shuffle as if he sees himself as someone hovering near the bottom. "I wasn't at the bottom," Newman insisted to journalist David Wild on the thirtieth anniversary rerelease of the album. "I *did* get noticed, if only in the press and by some people who were into music. *They* liked me — they liked my music better than I did." Newman may have grown up in the secure environment of a Hollywood family where he was never alone, but he still wears the mask of the loner, of a deeply dissatisfied man who perceives himself as an outsider. Shortly after the release of *Sail Away*, he expressed as much to Susan Lydon of *The New York Times*. "I achieved what I thought I wanted, critical acclaim and all that," Newman explained. "But it wasn't enough. It didn't make me happy."

The inner turmoil, shared by such Jewish-American artists as Woody Allen, Groucho Marx, Jackie Mason and Rodney Dangerfield, feeds their zeal for self-expression. When Dangerfield said, "I get no respect," it was his particular way of *getting* respect. When Newman sings he's lonely at the top, it clearly conveys the conflict of a misunderstood artist who fears he'll pay dearly if he ever gets anywhere *near* the top.

Of all the groups who covered "Lonely at the Top," The Bobs actually caught its peculiarities. On their 1994 record, *The Bobs Cover the Songs Of. . .* , they defined their take on "Lonely at the Top" succinctly in their liner notes: "Yes, it's lonely when you're the best there is at what you do, but it's even lonelier when you're the only one who does whatever it is you do . . ." In 1998, Newman's version of "Lonely at the Top" and Nilsson's "The Puppy Song" were both included in *You've Got Mail,* the tepid Tom Hanks/Meg Ryan remake of the classic Ernst Lubitsch comedy, *The Shop Around the Corner* (1940).

The next track on *Sail Away,* "He Gives Us All His Love," is another wry shot at God based on Laurie London's "He's Got the Whole World in His Hands." In Newman's universe, though, God is having a mighty laugh:

> *He knows how hard we're trying*
> *He hears the babies crying*
> *He sees the old folks dying*
> *And he gives us all his love.*

"Last Night I Had a Dream" is a ballad, augmented with congas and Ry Cooder's slide guitar, which was first recorded with a rock arrangement in 1968. The song has some of the comic paranoia of "Mama Told Me Not to Come," as Newman tells us of a dream in which the least obvious thing horrifies him:

> *I saw a vampire*
> *I saw a ghost*
> *Everybody scared me*
> *But you scared me the most.*

After a brisk ride through "Simon Smith and the Amazing Dancing Bear," Newman introduces another new song, "Old Man," quite removed from Neil Young's sentimental ode to a farm hand. Some believed Newman's "Old Man" was a song written for his own father, but it wasn't. "I was inspired by the astronaut in *2001: A Space Odyssey*, when they sing 'Happy Birthday' to him," Newman told Jim Macnie of the *Providence Phoenix*. "I like the idea of a father raising his son with no emotion. No God, no nothing. And then that's what he gets back when he's dying." It's not a song Newman performs in concert very often. "It's one of my best songs, but I never play it because it's so depressing," he explained to Scott Jordan of *OffBeat Magazine*. "I got a little carried away and made it too pretty for what the song is about in that case. It should have been a little colder." But despite the colorful orchestral arrangement, the sentiments in "Old Man" are cold enough. Newman doesn't offer much room for emotional reconciliation:

> *Won't be no God to comfort you*
> *You taught me not to believe that lie*
> *You don't need anybody*
> *Nobody needs you*
> *Don't cry, old man, don't cry*
> *Everybody dies.*

Not surprisingly, Art Garfunkel's version, on his first solo album *Angel Claire* (1973), was so tepid in tone he managed to distort the song into an expression of human compassion.

With "Political Science," you could be listening to Mort Saul dressed as Phil Ochs performing a Tom Lehrer song. While many regard "Political Science" as a song that tackles easy targets, when heard today it seems to address the anti-American spirit lingering in the air. "It's closer to reality today than it's ever been," Newman recently told Alex Mulcahy. Although "Political Science" was written at the height of the Vietnam War it now resonates with the Iraq War and its international consequences. The song begins with the main character, perhaps a state official, realizing that nobody likes America, and he just doesn't know why. He admits America isn't perfect, but "heaven knows we try." Despondent because even America's friends put them down, he decides that the U.S. should just "drop the big one and see what happens." Through the course of "Political Science" America grows tired of being, in the eyes of this official, the great protector. Feeling unappreciated, America turns on its critics, deciding to wipe out almost everybody. The official does make concessions for Australia ("Don't wanna hurt no Kangaroo"), but London, Paris, they are all gone — and besides, "Europe's too old."

"[Politicians] are almost that dumb," Newman explains. "[Secretary of Defense Donald] Rumsfeld did say 'Old Europe.' Who would have ever thought anyone would do that? We may have been doing bad things for thirty years, but not as clumsy as this stuff." The song's paranoid view of America as dangerously solipsistic was common (and often justified) among leftists during the Cold War years, but as many of them today feel George W. Bush is an embodiment of American fascism, "Political Science" continues to hit a nerve.

Even if Newman never intended it, "Political Science" has an edge that cuts both ways. Whether or not one agrees with Bush, or the war in Iraq, it's true that some of the hatred and envy currently fired at the United States is as pathological as the opinions expressed by the narrator in the song. Despite his rampant suspicions, his description of the world view of America isn't far off, because probably no nation on Earth has divided its allies and enemies more consistently than the United States. "I am reminded by my journey how exceedingly new this country still is," Henry David Thoreau observed in 1848. In comparison to most nations, after all, America is still the new kid on the block. It's that newness, and the bold arrogance that often comes with it, that rankles the Old Guard. And as young as the United States remains relative to Europe and Asia, their democratic ideals have served as a larger beacon to all parts of the world.

America has had a compelling history that seems to invite dreamers to take root, producing writers as boldly distinctive as Mark Twain, Walt Whitman and Jack Kerouac, and painters as uniquely gifted as Georgia O'Keeffe and Jackson Pollock. It's a country that finds a place for the blatantly patriotic anthems of John Philip Sousa, just as it freely opens a door for the dissonant melodies of Charles Ives. The Beatles and The Rolling Stones may have conquered America in the sixties, but they did it with American music. America can create the mindless diversion of Disneyland, but it can also prepare a corner for the

Smithsonian Institute. Yet as they reach out to the troubled regions of the world, they can just as easily behave like a school yard bully. When a nation built on a dream becomes a world leader, it's potentially hazardous if they believe their dream is the only valid one. It's this very quality that Newman addresses in "Political Science." British poet and scholar Christopher Ricks also addressed America's dual impact in his literary anthology, *America*. "Great disappointment has to be proportionate to greatness," Ricks wrote. "What America promised, and fulfilled for many people, is implied in what is criticized: its failures to be all it promised." Educated liberals can still laugh at the Dr. Strangelove figure Newman creates in "Political Science," because his jingoism turns him into a convenient villain. But beneath the song's twisted vision of America's role in the world is a pathological resentment towards America's failed promise which, in turn, fuels the narrator's America-centric paranoia.

Randy Newman loves to create paradoxes in his songs, and America is riddled with them. It's a nation founded on slavery, yet it ultimately helped send Soviet communism to its grave. It saved Europe after the Second World War by refinancing it through the Marshall Plan, but has also wantonly (with self-interest) toppled governments by supporting coups. America's promises and its failures are an unresolvable part of what makes "Political Science" such an unsettling song.

"Burn On" is the one track on *Sail Away* that could be defined as an easy target, even though the bizarre subject matter is right up Newman's alley. Ostensibly, "Burn On" is a folk song about how the Cuyahoga River in Cleveland, Ohio, polluted to the point of being flammable, suddenly burst into flames back in 1969. "I saw it on television," he told Timothy White. "That's what gave me the idea, and I just wrote it. And the idea of saying, 'Cleveland, city of light,' I mean, I've been to Cleveland, and I'd stayed in Swingos [on The Lake, in Lakewood, Ohio], and I heard eight car wrecks outside my door on a Saturday night." "Burn On" is a lovely shuffle that satirizes the theme of "Ol' Man River." Instead of a mighty river that just keeps rolling along, Cuyahoga just "burn[s] on, big river, burn[s] on." "Burn On" would later serve as an inspiration for the R.E.M. song "Cuyahoga" from *Life's Rich Pageant* (1986), and as background commentary on the hapless Cleveland Indians in the baseball film comedy *Major League* (1989).

While Newman was recording *Sail Away,* he had recently become the father of two sons. His oldest, Amos, had just turned two, while his second son, Eric, had been born a year later. In "Memo to My Son," directed at Amos, parenthood becomes a sport like football, with the singer as the coach:

> *A quitter never wins*
> *A winner never quits*
> *When the going gets tough*
> *The tough get going.*

This father spends more time studying the playbook of Vince Lombardi than Dr. Spock. "The big idea of the song — if there *is* a big idea — was about fathers who weren't interested in kids until they could laugh at their jokes," Newman explains. "In fact, my father was kind of like that. They weren't interested in the 'coo-coo-coo' stuff and the physicality of picking up a baby, all of which I love. Some people don't know how to deal with human beings." That's exactly the predicament for the father here:

> *I know you don't think much of me*
> *But someday you'll understand*
> *Wait'll you learn to talk, baby*
> *I'll show you how smart I am.*

Although "Memo to My Son" is an amusing ballad, it reveals some of Newman's doubts about his own ability to be a good father. "I'm just not up to it, I believe," he told Timothy White in 1979. "Giving the kids lots of love is not enough. . . . Dealing with the fact that they're people and you can't tease them — I mean, you've got to think about it all. . . . I'm not a bad father, but I'm not a first-rate one. . . . I don't bring work home in any way. My wife [Roswitha] is not interested in my work and neither are the kids."

Newman also included his interpretation of "Dayton, Ohio, 1903," quite similar to the version on *Nilsson Sings Newman*. But in retrospect he admits it's probably out of place on *Sail Away*. "I wasn't crazy about that song," Newman told Paul Zollo. "It's got kind of a false nostalgia that I don't like. I don't *believe*, necessarily, that 1903 in

Dayton, Ohio is much better than now." If "Dayton, Ohio, 1903" carries a quaint fakeness, "You Can Leave Your Hat On" takes us back to the familiar perversities of "Suzanne." Like "Sail Away" and "I Think It's Going to Rain Today," this is a tune that has been widely covered and just as wildly misunderstood. "You Can Leave Your Hat On" is a mockingly sultry track about a nebbish who, suddenly finding himself alone with a delectable female, proceeds to share his private fantasy with her:

> *Baby take off your coat . . . (real slow)*
> *Baby take off your shoes . . . (here I'll take your shoes)*
> *Baby take off your dress*
> *Yes, Yes, Yes*
> *You can leave your hat on.*

Artists from Tom Jones to Joe Cocker have made the song's kinkiness overt, as if this were some hot stud having the time of his life. But the story is about a joker with a hat comfortably in his lap, getting his jollies from a woman with one on her head. And like the character in "Mama Told Me Not to Come," he's both tickled and terrified by his desires. While Newman is slyly suggesting what he wants the girl to do, Cocker and Jones are *ordering* her to disrobe. "It's mainly just sort of low-grade sleaze, but you know sex is something people don't laugh at much," Newman explains. Although Cocker and Jones put their own stamp on the song, it deviates from Newman's intent. The most striking deviation is in the portrayal of the speaker. Where Newman doesn't mind occupying the persona of a middling pervert, Cocker and Jones show their discomfort by turning macho. "The guy is not a sexual guy and it's not a sexy song, really, because what the guy has the girl doing is so lame," Newman told *Rolling Stone*. "It's really about a bully."

"You Can Leave Your Hat On" became a hit single for Cocker (whose version garnished Kim Basinger's striptease in Adrian Lynne's 1986 debacle *9 1/2 Weeks*). Cocker would revisit it in 1996 on his album *Organic*, also including a version of "Sail Away" featuring Newman on piano. Jones recorded "You Can Leave Your Hat On" in 1996 (a remixed version appearing in the hit 1997 British film *The Full Monty*). Singer Mary Coughlan treated it in an inappropriately raunchy blues style, as did Etta James on her 2002 album, *Red Blues*.

The sixties Toronto rock band Robbie Lane & the Disciples did a memorable version in their 1995 reunion concert. Their live interpretation of "You Can Leave Your Hat On," released in 1996 on their appropriately titled *Ain't Dead Yet,* stayed true to Newman's original arrangement and intent.

*Sail Away* begins with a song promising African blacks a new land where they can sing about Jesus all day. In the concluding track, "God's Song (That's Why I Love Mankind)," Newman demonstrates just how futile an act that ultimately is. Faced with a world searching for answers to plagues, murder and destruction, God merely sits in Heaven and laughs. This cruel, merciless patriarch loves mankind because we have so much blind faith in Him — no matter what horrors He inflicts on us. The composition that confronts Newman's agnosticism most directly, "God's Song" not only completes the album, it drops a huge dark curtain on the world around it. It might also be the only song refuting God that has the emotional punch of great gospel music.

Newman prepared the ground for "God's Song" with an earlier unreleased demo (which eventually turned up on the Rhino box-set called "Jesus in the Summertime.") As two lovers begin an affair, the Lord takes a special place in their lives:

> *We may not know all the answers*
> *After all we're so very young*
> *I only know that I go crazy*
> *When I love my baby*
> *Jesus, can such a love be wrong?*

The singer has become so happy with this new relationship he assumes Jesus must have died for it. Before long, he's so flushed with the sunshine of his love that he wants Jesus to come back — in the summertime. "I think I was trying to write something about easy, comfortable faith," Newman recalls. "I do know that it offended almost everyone who heard it — one of the musicians walked out." The strangely comical idea of a man who believes his faith in Jesus is equalled by the purity of his love for his girl gets tested by one crucial question:

*Lord, why did you let your son die?*
*Jesus died for you.*

How can love last eternally when One so mighty sacrifices His only son — a son He supposedly loves? In "God's Song," Newman goes further inside that question and pulls out some amusing and deeply uncomfortable answers. While Newman is agnostic, he's also Jewish, which likely accounts for his tendency to question God's authority. With the possible exception of Jesuits, most Christians accept God on faith alone, whereas debate and commentary are intrinsic to Judaism. This need to question goes all the way back to that pivotal moment when Abraham argues with God about His request to sacrifice his son, Isaac, a query so primal Bob Dylan felt the need to give it a modern voice. In "Highway 61 Revisited," Dylan conjured up this fundamental episode as a proverbial legend out of the blues:

*Oh, God said to Abraham, "Kill me a son"*
*Abe say, "Man, you must be puttin' me on"*
*God say, "No." Abe say, "What?"*
*God say, "You can do what you want Abe, but*
*The next time you see me comin' you better run"*
*Well Abe says, "Where do you want this killin' done?"*
*God says, "Out on Highway 61."*

The thought of God's asking a man to sacrifice his own son as an act of servitude is a chilling one. Author and film director Michael Tolkin, also Jewish, felt that chill, too, when he wrote and directed his provocative 1991 film, *The Rapture*. In the film, a promiscuous woman turned born-again Christian (Mimi Rogers) is ultimately jailed for a sacrificial murder. When another follower tells her to ask forgiveness from God, Rogers calmly responds, "But who forgives God?"

Newman also begins his song with a simple question to God, and it concerns Cain's slaying of Abel. The singer wonders: If the children of Israel are to multiply, why should any of God's children die? Instead of offering a reasonable explanation to justify this horrific sacrifice, God gives him an answer that collapses the underpinnings of his faith:

*Man means nothing*
*He means less to me*
*Than the lowliest flower*
*Or the humblest Yucca tree*
*He chases round this desert*
*'Cause he thinks that's where I'll be*
*That's why I love mankind.*

In Newman's world, mankind is a joke. After all, God burns down our houses while we praise Him; He takes away our children while we bless Him. "You all must be crazy to put your faith in me," God chortles. Yet He adds that this is why He loves mankind: We may be fools, but we're His fools. "You *really* need me," God needles at the end.

In part, "God's Song" is a retelling of Dostoevsky's Grand Inquisitor story from *The Brothers Karamazov* (1880). Ivan Karamazov, an agnostic scribe, composes a poem called "The Grand Inquisitor," a tale of horror during the Spanish Inquisition, which he reads to his brother, Alyosha, a religious novice. In his poem, Jesus returns to Earth to perform miracles, but witnesses the slaughter being inflicted in his name. Once he confronts the Grand Inquisitor, he's soon incarcerated, and the Inquisitor then admonishes Jesus for giving mankind free will. He explains to Jesus that rather than the responsibility of freedom, mankind wants miracles, food and most important, the security of an institution like the Church to be obedient to. The Inquisitor asks Christ: "Did you forget that peace and even death are dearer to man than free choice in the knowledge of good and evil? There is nothing more seductive for man than the freedom of his conscience, but there is nothing more tormenting, either." He reminds Christ "the mystery of man's being is not only in living, but in what one lives for." Mankind doesn't really want what Christ offers them, but what the Inquisitor delivers. At the end of Dostoevsky's story, a speechless Christ is told to leave the city and never return. He kisses the Inquisitor gently on the lips and disappears into the night.

"God's Song" is about the abdication of free will that permits Newman's deity to inflict whatever chaos He wishes on a mankind that will praise Him anyway. The song has its roots, too, in the mordant satire of Kurt Weill and Bertolt Brecht's *The Threepenny Opera* (1928), in particular the song, "What Keeps Mankind Alive?" The source of the musical play is John Gay's 1728 *The Beggar's Opera*, which set out to parody not only the politics of the time, but also the shrill romanticism of Italian opera. Gay's larger target, however, was the corruption and hypocrisy of mankind. The drama was filled with thieves, whores and informers rather than the usual chaste heroines and noble heroes. Reconceived by Brecht and Weill as *The Threepenny Opera*, it became an open attack on the heroic bombast of Wagnerian opera, as well as a parody of the bourgeois society of Germany's Weimar Republic. In this musical cabaret, "What Keeps Mankind Alive?" is sung by the bandit Macheath (also known as Mack the Knife) and Celia Peachum, wife of the proprietor of "Beggar's Friend," a store that employs London's beggars and supplies their dishevelled disguises. At the end of the second act, Macheath addresses the self-important, judgmental bourgeoisie:

> *You gentlemen who think you have a mission*
> *To purge us of the seven deadly sins*
> *Should first sort out the basic food position*
> *Then start your preaching.*

When a voice from the gathered throng asks him, "What keeps mankind alive?" Macheath has a ready answer:

> *What keeps mankind alive?*
> *The fact that millions are daily tortured,*
> *Stifled, punished, silenced, oppressed*
> *Mankind can keep alive thanks to its brilliance*
> *In keeping its humanity repressed.*

The theme of greed and avarice winning out over mankind's more noble inclinations is part of what links "What Keeps Mankind Alive?" and Newman's "God's Song." As he demonstrated in "I Think He's Hiding," Newman (despite being agnostic) needs God to exist in order to defy Him. To borrow a pithy but offhand comment once made by Pauline Kael about Ivan Karamazov in her review of Kon Ichikawa's *Fires on the Plain* (1959), Newman is obsessed with evil in the world because it stands in the way of his believing in God. Newman *wants* to believe, but his disgust with God's indifference to human suffering brushes aside the hypocrisy of phony proselytizing.

Whatever hostility Newman may have towards God is complemented by the love he feels for gospel music. "You can't compete with it, the power of gospel music," he once told Paul Zollo. "It almost makes you wonder. Not quite, but almost. You can combat it with reason, which is dry. It's not musical. Music's not reasonable." So rather than compete with it, Newman opens up to gospel music's power. Sister Rosetta Tharpe, a fiery gospel singer who could play a steel-bodied guitar like Chuck Berry and swing her hips like Elvis Presley, understood the depth of that power. "There's something about the gospel blues that's so deep the world can't stand it," she told gospel music authority Tony Heilbut. Which means that if you can never fully comprehend its essence, you still need to submit willingly to its force. In 1944, Tharpe, herself wavering between the sins of the secular world and the promise of God's kingdom, gave voice to that force in her rollicking single, "Strange Things Happening Everyday":

> *On that last great Judgment Day*
> *When they drive them all away*
> *There are strange things happening every day.*

The view offered here is no less apocalyptic than that of "God's Song" — except Tharpe sounds ecstatic. She accepts the mystery of miracles and salvation because strange things *do* happen to mankind every day:

> *If you want to view the crime*
> *You must learn to quit your lyin'*
> *There are strange things happening every day.*

On the B-side of "Strange Things Happening Everyday" Tharpe included a gospel standard, "Two Little Fishes and Five Loaves of Bread," a slow gospel blues that more closely fit the pattern of Newman's song. It tells the tale of Jesus instructing the disciples as to how to feed the hungry. He first advises them to bring all the bread and fish:

> *A crowd of people went out in the desert*
> *To listen to what the good Lord said*

*All day long, they heard the good Lord's word*
*And they got hungry and had to be fed*
*I've got only two little fishes and five loaves of bread.*

In Tharpe's song, she submits to the transcendence faith offers her ("If we love one another/ We can live on this little fish"), whereas Newman, the skeptic, is interested only in the idea of transcendence. "I am *interested* in it," Newman told David Wild. "It's a *gigantic* idea. It's the biggest hit in history — the invention of God, because you know you're going to die." Yet "God's Song" is not an expression of one man's cynicism any more than it's an absurdist knock at organized religion like Frank Zappa's "The Meek Shall Inherit Nothing" and "Heavenly Bank Account." Instead, "God's Song" is a powerful riddle, an enigma wrapped in satirical garb. Newman attacks the idea of God with the zeal of a man still in search of the values that created the idea of a God — which makes him really not unlike Dostoevsky's Ivan Karamazov.

It would take another four years before the agnostic passion of "God's Song" could be answered. An angry young singer-songwriter from Surrey, England, named Graham Parker responded with a tune called "Don't Ask Me Questions." Parker wrote and performed romantically tough R&B in an era that spawned punk. Partly inspired by Van Morrison's fiery work with Them, Parker married the fury of punk with the black soul music that ran in his veins. Unfortunately, Parker would be eclipsed by Elvis Costello, and he never found the commercial success he truly deserved. "Don't Ask Me Questions" was the concluding track of his phenomenal debut album, *Howlin' Wind* (1976), and it brought his collection of heart-on-the-sleeve barbed-wire rock & roll songs to a menacing conclusion.

Unlike "God's Song," Parker's composition isn't told from God's point of view. It is about one fervent believer railing at God's handiwork. "Don't Ask Me Questions" opens with Parker's band, the Rumour, establishing a dramatic blues rhythm so startling, you're almost relieved when they shift into a bouncing and catchy ska arrangement. Punctuated by Brinsley Schwarz's stinging guitar lines, the sound the band creates doesn't allow any relief, though it is both awesome and arresting. While Parker rants his displeasure at God's handiwork, the music tells us Armageddon is not far behind. Schwarz's guitar notes are so sharp, they sweep the singer along like a broom with teeth. The speaker is disgusted because his faith in God has brought him into a hideous collusion with evil:

> *Well, I stand up for liberty*
> *But I can't liberate*
> *Pent up agony I see you take first place*
> *Well, who does this treachery?*
> *I shout with bleeding hands*
> *Is it you, or is it me*
> *Well, I never will understand*
> *Hey Lord, don't ask me questions.*

Parker's speaker's complicity makes it painfully difficult for him to make sense of God's plan, to the extent that when he finally sees Judgment Day, he wishes he could avoid it:

> *Well, I see the thousands screaming*
> *Rushing for the cliffs*
> *Just like lemmings into the sea*
> *Who waves his mighty hand and breaks the precious rules*
> *The same one must understand who wasted all these fools*
> *Hey Lord, don't ask me questions*
> *There ain't no answer in me.*

Parker sings "Don't Ask Me Questions" like a man trapped under the moral weight of each line. He twists the vowels, even spits them out, but never finds comfort. By the conclusion, Parker grunts and growls, periodically shouting disbelief, as the rhythm section carries his bleeding carcass off into the next life. "Don't Ask Me Questions" comes at you with the force of a tidal wave. In Parker's expression of total horror, he (like Newman) also raises questions about what constitutes faith. Although both songs feature a laconic deity who laughs in the face of mankind, "God's Song" and "Don't Ask Me Questions" raise bigger questions about why faith matters, and why the question is often etched in torment and human iniquity.

Because of the sophistication of the required orchestrations, *Sail Away* took a year to finish, and did not come out until May 1972.

During the recording, Lee Herschberg had to hook up microphones on either side of Newman's head because — like Ray Charles — he tends to move his head from side to side when he sings. "The two microphones were about six inches apart on his vocal to catch him," Herschberg recalls. "The vocals were always live; he rarely overdubbed them, so they had to be recorded well and consistently every time." Newman felt he had ample assistance from the other musicians at the time, too. "First, of course, there was Lenny [Waronker] and Russ [Titelman] sitting in the booth," he recalled. "There was [also] Jim Keltner and Ry Cooder." Given Newman's style of playing, he had a special appreciation for his drummer, Keltner. "Someone once asked him how he follows me, because you know I *can't* keep time," Newman explained to David Wild. "I'm not used to it, because I never played in a band for any length of time. Jim said that he watches my hands, which is kind of pathetic, really."

In *Sail Away*, Newman and his production team created a beautiful melding of his first two records. Unfortunately, the album would peak at No. 163 on the *Billboard* album chart, though it has consistently been one of Newman's most highly regarded records. Stephen Holden, writing in *Rolling Stone*, saw *Sail Away* as a milestone in American songwriting. "In the popular arts we have moved into an era of tragic realism," he wrote with particular prescience. "I think that this is an inevitable outcome of the sixties apocalyptic sensibility and the growing up of the rock & roll generation. *Sail Away* is a major achievement of this new era." The tragic realism expressed in *Sail Away*, however, was also an instinctive celebration of America's promise. From the cabaret setting of "Lonely at the Top" and "Simon Smith and the Amazing Dancing Bear," to the stark gospel piano of "God's Song (That's Why I Love Mankind)," the R&B tinged "You Can Leave Your Hat On" and the sweeping orchestral color of the title song, *Sail Away* paints a lush, ambiguous picture of the American character. It embraces the country's stark beauty by taking in its most enigmatic aspects.

*Sail Away* brought critical acclaim to Newman, even if he remained a virtual nobody in the mind of the mass audience. Newman's music provided a perplexing riddle: How do you create a popular music that both satirizes and celebrates a country of oddballs, misfits and carny hustlers? Since Newman's gift was to create paradoxes, he could hardly expect a simple, or conventional, relationship with a listening audience. The use of the untrustworthy narrator, especially in pop, guarantees neither clarity nor understanding. Instead of telling audiences what to think, Newman simply invites us to experience fully the stories in his songs, giving us the freedom to make our own judgments. Newman's fans generally understand, and welcome, this approach, but they are a relatively small faction.

But when an unorthodox artist sets out to gain a wide fan base, as Newman did with *Sail Away,* it can create another set of problems. For example, it automatically changes the relationship between the artist and his listeners. Newman had led a small group of followers into uncharted waters, but if he was to become popular would he then be compelled to play to the expectations of those fans? Would they start to lead him rather than it being the other way around? Newman had flirted with pop success without realizing his achievement could jeopardize the very effectiveness of his brilliant disguise. Newman's mask had always purposely and cleverly cloaked the true essence of his work. Soon it would be mistaken for his real face.

# The Success of the Mask

Never trust the artist. Trust the tale. The proper function
of a critic is to save the tale from the artist who created it.

— D.H. Lawrence

A man may build himself a throne of bayonets, but he
cannot sit upon it.

— William Inge

## 1

In the period following the critical success of *Sail Away,* Randy
Newman didn't immediately start work on a new project. Instead, he
spent his days at home watching television, hanging out with his kids
— and procrastinating. "He's not your normal everyday artist who
likes to groove around in the studio," Lenny Waronker explains.
"Randy needs to have a lot of pressure on him to produce. If it's loose,
and it's all left up to him, there may not ever be another record. It's
hard to get him into the studio; I have to beg, threaten, drag him out

of bed sometimes. If I book the studio time and the musicians for the orchestra, then he knows we can't cancel, and he'll show up. But he never approaches anything optimistically; he'll drag himself in here and say, 'This is going to be really rotten.'" For Newman, songwriting has always been defined as hard work, and he's never drawn much pleasure from it. "It's not like I love what I do," he told Elysa Gardner of USA Today. "I have to force myself to do it. I love having written something, but I don't love the writing process."

Fortunately for both his fans and Waronker, Newman did get out on the road and perform. Between gigs one evening in 1972, Newman happened to catch The Dick Cavett Show, a sophisticated TV talk show out of New York. On this night, Cavett's guest was Lester Maddox, the segregationist governor of Georgia. Born in the working-class district of Atlanta, Maddox was a high school dropout who found himself embroiled in one of the most contentious periods in American history. It was Maddox, the day after the 1964 Civil Rights Act had been signed into law in Washington, who chased blacks from his Pickrick fried chicken restaurant. Not long after his defiant stand against integration, Maddox became even more obstinate, choosing to sell his restaurant rather than be forced to serve blacks. Adopting a pick handle as a symbol, Maddox entered politics, where he made two unsuccessful bids for mayor. In 1966, however, he captured the Democratic nomination for governor after an odd fluke of circumstance. During the general election, Maddox trailed Republican Howard H. "Bo" Callaway, but write-in voters ensured that neither got the majority vote. As a result, the election was thrown to the Democratic-dominated Georgia legislature, which threw its support behind Maddox.

To the surprise of just about everyone, a newly elected Maddox urged peace, declaring that there would be no place in Georgia "for those who advocate extremism and violence." He also confounded critics by appointing more blacks to key positions in government than had any of his predecessors. In 1968, however, Maddox reverted back to his old form, stirring up resentment when he refused to close the state capitol for the funeral of the assassinated Martin Luther King Jr., and raised hell over the state flags being set at half-staff. Despite his often odious behavior, Lester Maddox was clearly a complex figure usually portrayed as a caricature possessed of a slick pate, thick glasses and a folksy humor. Maddox was an easy target for jokes, as he would be that night on *The Dick Cavett Show*. The guests, besides Maddox, included the highly opinionated novelist and polemicist Gore Vidal and the black football player and actor Jim Brown. Mere moments after Maddox sat down, both started to mock him. When Cavett did nothing to discourage them, the Georgia governor walked out.

"Cavett had an ultraliberal show on PBS that reeked of snob appeal," Waronker recalled. "And Randy, who's a true liberal, was always able to see through that and had a certain amount of resentment toward the program." Newman's resentment took the form of a new song, "Rednecks," which set out to provide a more balanced view of America's racist legacy. "Randy had very little sympathy for Lester Maddox," Waronker explained. "But he always responded to the underdog." In particular, Newman was perturbed by the condescension expressed by Northern liberals towards the crazed segregationist. "The audience hooted and howled, and Maddox was never given a chance to speak," Newman said. "So I wrote the song, and Northerners have recognized ever since that they are as guilty of prejudice as the people of the South." As Cavett had already judged Maddox a clown, the governor never had a chance to present himself in any other light. Newman recognized this as the worst kind of double standard, and that it exemplified Northern arrogance. "He wasn't even given a chance to prove what an idiot he was," Newman said. "It was like, they sat Jim Brown next to him, and the crowd was razzin' him. . . . He didn't get a chance to do anything, and they had just elected him Governor, in a state of six million or whatever, and if I were a Georgian, I would have been offended, irrespective of the fact that he was a bigot and a fool."

"Rednecks" was written from the point of view of one, and started Newman thinking about a larger conceptual album about the South. In early February 1973, he and producer Russ Titelman went into the studio to tape some informal demos for a project Newman tentatively titled *Johnny Cutler's Birthday*. It was to be a song cycle that focused on a steel worker from Birmingham, Alabama, and how his relationship with his family comes to a head on his thirtieth birthday. "Because of the nature of the language in 'Rednecks,' which made me nervous, I felt like I had to explain this guy in the song more," Newman told David Wild. "You know, give him a job and a wife. So that's what I did." But in the end, *Johnny Cutler's Birthday* was never officially released, morphing instead into *Good Old Boys*. The *Johnny Cutler's Birthday* sessions, however, were finally included in a special edition CD rerelease of *Good Old Boys* in 2002. While many of the *Johnny Cutler* songs were eventually fleshed out and rerecorded for *Good Old Boys*, others were left off and new tracks were written for the new record. In retrospect, listening to *Johnny Cutler's Birthday* today provides an illuminating contrast to *Good Old Boys*. Even if Johnny Cutler was no longer the subject of what became *Good Old Boys,* he's a spectral presence who haunts the record.

2

*Johnny Cutler's Birthday* opens in a small park in Birmingham, where Cutler has taken his young daughter, Suzie, to play. As she scampers off to join the other kids, Johnny begins to assess his life and define exactly who he is. He begins by singing "Rednecks." The song opens with Cutler describing the Dick Cavett debacle where Lester Maddox was humiliated. After identifying Cavett as a "smart-ass New York Jew," Cutler turns on the TV audience sharing laughs at Maddox's expense:

> *Well, he may be a fool*
> *But he's our fool*
> *And if they think they're better than him*
> *They're wrong.*

After thus setting the scene, Cutler launches into a hilariously self-deprecating appraisal of his Southern heritage. In the manner of "Sail Away," "Rednecks" is deliberately riddled with identifiable stereotypes — only this time, instead of a catalogue of black clichés, we're witness to a honky burlesque:

> *We talk real funny down here*
> *We drink too much and we laugh too loud*
> *We're too dumb to make it in no Northern town*
> *And we're keepin' the niggers down.*

The chorus, cleverly designed to get Northern white liberals on

Newman's side, appears — at least initially — to be a smug put-down of Johnny Cutler and his ilk:

*We're rednecks, we're rednecks*
*We don't know our ass from a hole in the ground*
*We're rednecks, we're rednecks*
*And we're keepin' the niggers down.*

But before we can draw any satisfaction from this putdown of Southern crackers, Newman plays an eloquent piano bridge, in the manner of Stephen Foster, which puts us in the spirit of the Old South. Then we're rudely thrust into Johnny Cutler's view of the North. The effect is to pull the rug out from under Northern liberal conceit. While claiming "the Northern nigger's a Negro" who has been set free, Cutler names the ghettos outside the South where blacks are anything but liberated, including Harlem, the Hough in Cleveland, the east side of St. Louis, the Fillmore district in San Francisco and Roxbury in Boston. Taken together, they tell a woeful story of criminal neglect and urban squalor that has the effect of putting the North on the same playing field as Johnny Cutler's Southern racists. This hideous irony has a longstanding history according to Mark Royden Winchell, a professor of English at Clemson University. In his essay "The Dream of the South," a study of the role of Stephen Foster in American music, Winchell explains that the double standard Newman sings about was argued long before the Civil War. "Throughout the 1850s, Southern apologists argued that slaves in the South enjoyed more social and economic security than the typical factory worker in the North," Winchell wrote. "Even in the debates over slavery immediately prior to the War Between the States, honest Northern liberals such as Orestes Brownson noted the hypocrisy of Yankee abolitionists decrying slavery in the South while turning a blind eye to the plight of factory workers in their own backyard."

Although "Rednecks" is shrewdly sarcastic, Newman believes he strayed from the character of the narrator. "So the guy does this song, and the one thing wrong with it is he wouldn't know the names of all the ghettos, he wouldn't know Hough in Cleveland and all that stuff," he told Paul Zollo. Yet Newman needed Cutler to step out of character to provide a larger truth. The song would have been simply a cheap put-down of Cutler had Newman failed to provide the historical conditions that created him. In the end the real controversy that surrounded "Rednecks" wasn't the character, but the use of the word "nigger," which kept it from getting any radio airplay. Stations likely saw the word, even in a satirical song, as exploitative. Newman, though, was returning to this word the very power it has to hurt and shame blacks.

In "Rednecks," Newman gives the lie to one of Lenny Bruce's most celebrated routines of the early sixties, "Are There Any Niggers Here Tonight?" After a short preamble on integration, Bruce asked the crowd, "Are there any niggers here tonight?" The audience, usually consisting of both blacks and whites, became restless and uneasy. Bruce proceeded undaunted, pointing at the audience and calling out to the "kikes," "niggers," "spics" and "micks." By the end, he was parodying a gambler at a poker game ("I pass with six niggers and eight micks and four spics") and finally arrived at his point:

> The point? That the word's suppression gives it the power, the violence, the viciousness. If President Kennedy got on television and said, "Tonight, I'd like to introduce all the niggers in my cabinet," and he yelled "niggerniggerniggerniggerniggerniggernigger" at every nigger he saw . . . till nigger didn't mean anything anymore, till nigger lost its meaning — you'd never make any four-year-old nigger cry when he came home from school.

At its best, Lenny Bruce's art combined satire with shock. Here he dips into phony moralizing, and his solution, terribly naïve and maudlin, would hardly end racial intolerance, or inure four-year-old black children from the pain associated with the slur. Moreover if "nigger" lost its meaning, it would also lose its tragic historical significance, and as a consequence, give comfort to racists everywhere.

Today, of course, the word is hardly repressed; it's been uttered quite freely by both black and white rappers, as well as other hipsters. Yet it still has the capacity to cause anger and pain. Newman makes us aware of that pain. "It always bothered me when that word went by," he told Barney Hoskyns. "But I needed the word in those songs. And I do the song everywhere, and people get it. It's kind of complicated, in that when you've got a big word like that, you gotta be careful it doesn't blast out the next minute and a half." Sometimes it still does. Despite Newman's care, "Rednecks" was banned in Boston during the desegregated bussing riots in 1975. The word still hasn't lost the ability to offend. "There was a black kid in Louisiana who was offended because he was sitting in an audience of fifteen-hundred white people who were *roaring* at the fact they were rednecks," Newman told Paul Zollo.

Although "Rednecks" was set in the South, boldly addressing racism in the North, Newman likely drew his feelings about racial discord from what he witnessed in Los Angeles. He just may have observed the same prejudice black novelist Walter Mosley would recall years later. "Black L.A. is a place where people came to realize their dreams," Mosley wrote in his 1990 novel, *Devil in a Blue Dress*. "Many people did realize them, but many were trapped in the image they brought with them from the South, and all that was informed by the racism of whites, or of blacks towards themselves." On *Good Old Boys*, "Rednecks" featured a ragtime arrangement and some tasty pedal-steel guitar fills by Al Perkins. Glenn Frey, Don Henley and Bernie Leadon, all of the Eagles, would also contribute background vocals as fellow rednecks.

After "Rednecks," the scene of *Johnny Cutler's Birthday* shifts to a white Baptist church, where we hear the gospel song "If We Didn't Have Jesus." Newman hadn't planned to sing this himself on the final album, but the song's there to create a sense of place, and perhaps, provide an elegy for the American South:

> *If we didn't have Jesus*
> *We wouldn't have no one at all*
> *God gonna set this world on fire*
> *One of these days*
> *All the sinners are gonna turn up missing*
> *One of these days.*

Unlike "God's Song" and "He Gives Us All His Love," this is a sincere gospel track, but it didn't make the final cut for *Good Old Boys*.

*Johnny Cutler's Birthday* returns to the park, where Cutler continues to ponder his life. He sings "Birmingham," a coarse but dignified song about his hometown. "I like that guy being proud of where he's from, even if the city has a bad reputation, even in the South, for being ugly," Newman told Timothy White. "Now it's entrepreneurial and a second Atlanta, but when I wrote it, it wasn't thought of as anything but sorta dirty and low." What Cutler expresses in "Birmingham" is a sense of feeling distinguished by both his family and his surroundings. We also discover that, though his father was a barber from Tuscaloosa, he ultimately died in Birmingham. At the conclusion of the *Johnny Cutler* version of "Birmingham," the family takes a holiday to Seattle, where all it ever does is rain. But Newman provided a stronger ending for the revised version on *Good Old Boys*. Instead of the innocuous trip to Seattle, we get introduced to the meaner side of this admiring view of Birmingham:

> *Got a big black dog*
> *And his name is Dan*
> *Who lives in my backyard in Birmingham*
> *He is the meanest dog in Alabam'*
> *Get 'em Dan.*

Newman follows "Birmingham" with a track originally written in 1966 called "The Joke." For a short while, he'd toyed with the idea of including it on *Sail Away,* but found it fit more neatly into the *Johnny Cutler* narrative. The full title of the song is "A Joke by Cecil Baker," and it's based on an anecdotal story told at the Jones County Country Store in Greencreek, Georgia, in the summer of 1959. The tune is a variation on one of those anthropomorphic shaggy-dog morality tales, like Chubby Parker's 1928 "King Kong Kitchie Kitchie Ki-Me-O," itself a version of the folk standard "Froggie Went a-Courtin'." On the album, "The Joke" is sung by the MC at Johnny Cutler's birthday party. The anecdote, however, originated with a traveling salesman who took great pleasure in regaling customers with tall tales every time he popped into town. On this occasion, he imparts an allegory about two dogs and a rabbit. The bunny is being chased by a black hound, while the dog's brother, who is as white as snow, stands idly by. When the black dog comes upon his chalky sibling, he asks him to continue chasing the hare so they can have some rabbit stew. His brother eagerly takes up the chase because he "hates to see a rabbit smile." Meanwhile, the bunny assumes there is only one dog — that the white mutt is the black brother with his jacket removed. The moral of the story is that any rabbit who thinks a dog wears a jacket should "get out of the rabbit racket." In the studio, between songs, Newman acknowledged the lameness of the joke to Russ Titelman.

The joke also receives groans from the guests at Johnny Cutler's birthday. One of them, David Williams, is asked to follow up with a song about the great 1927 Louisiana flood. Apparently, it's something he sings every year, as if he's afraid that everyone would somehow forget this cataclysmic event otherwise. It earns about as many complaints from the invited guests as "The Joke" did. Still, this is a tale that gives everyone pause — since the events in "Louisiana 1927," for Southerners, were very real.

The great flood of the Mississippi River took place on Good Friday, April 15, 1927, and when the levee broke, just above Clarksdale, water inundated the state. New Orleans in particular was hit with 14 inches of rain in 24 hours, although the city survived. What is most significant about the calamity is the transformative effect it had on the culture of Louisiana. Racial strife was exacerbated when the flood caused over 300,000 blacks to live in refugee camps for many months. Ultimately, hundreds of thousands headed North. It didn't help matters that in the late twenties, Louisiana was a compromised state mortgaged to Standard Oil and under the boot of the Old Bourbons, wealthy city fathers who controlled the political fortune of the Big Easy. As far as Newman was concerned, the Bourbons had a hand in bringing about the catastrophe. "The Bosses in New Orleans probably were behind the decision to let it flood up there, diverting the water away from their city," Newman explained. "Anyway, the cotton fields were wiped out, changing America forever, disemploying hundreds of thousands of black field workers, most of whom held executive positions in the cotton industry, meaning that they were permitted to wear gloves while picking." It also meant they were forced out of the South. "They all moved North and were greeted with open arms right across America," Newman added sarcastically.

In 1927, New Orleans was a dynamic, economically vital place, a city that dwarfed all others in the South, thanks to its prosperous investors, who hailed mostly from Boston and New York. The Old Bourbons, however, were afraid of what a flood might do to the city, not to mention the confidence of their investors. Therefore, they attempted to make sure no flood could ever reach New Orleans. When the great deluge happened, they dynamited a levee 13 miles below the city, completely flooding out their neighbors and destroying the livelihood of many poor whites. To understand the full enormity of the Louisiana flood, we have to remember the population of the United States, at that time, was 120 million, close to one percent of whom were just trying to stay afloat.

"The 1927 flood is a big deal in the history down there," Newman explained. "The flood of the Mississippi [causing $300 million — in pre-Depression dollars — worth of damage] wiped out the cotton fields and the sugar, too. People left, and that's when blacks started to move out of there — the flood was almost the proximate cause. Although none of that's in the song, that's why it interested me." While the river destroyed the homes of over one million people in Louisiana, it also gave birth to the political career of Huey P. Long, who became governor a year later. During his term, Long boldly challenged the corruption that had brought much of the destruction. The disaster also influenced the political ambitions of Herbert Hoover, then U.S. Secretary of Commerce, who acted as flood relief director. Hoover's efforts, which included decentralizing government bureaucracies so that no red tape would prevent rescue efforts, helped catapult him into the White House in 1928.

The flood aroused such popular interest that there was no shortage of songs depicting the tragedy, and not surprisingly, most of them were rooted in the blues. They included Bessie Smith's "Muddy Water (A Mississippi Moan)," Blind Lemon Jefferson's "Rising High Water Blues," Memphis Minnie's "When the Levee Breaks" (which Led Zeppelin would cover years later, amplified to the pitch of an apocalypse) and Vernon Dalhart's "The Mississippi Flood." One of the strongest recordings, "High Water Everywhere," was by blues singer Charley Patton. Described at one time as the father of the Mississippi Delta blues, Patton generally straddled the fence between sacred and blues music. As a result, he performed blues under the pseudonym "the Masked Marvel," while when he sang church music he became Elder J.J. Hadley. In his blues, Patton developed a pivotal style of whooping and hollering, as if he were gleefully sharing episodes of lewd abandon and drunken revelry. But in "High Water Everywhere," recorded in two parts in 1929, Patton isn't in much of a party mood. He performs the song like an urgent dispatch of breaking news, shouting over his guitar lines, too, as if afraid he could be cut short at any second:

*Oh, Lordy, women and grown men drown*
*Oh, women and children sinkin' down*
*Lord, have mercy*
*I couldn't see nobody's home*
*And wasn't no one to be found.*

"High Water Everywhere" had such lasting power that Bob Dylan would answer Patton's urgent appeal, some seventy years later, in "High Water (For Charley Patton)." In typical fashion, Dylan presents a masked ball featuring archetypal blues figures like Big Joe Turner, while dropping quotes from Elmore James' "Dust My Broom." Then we hear the faint echo of Clarence Ashley's forebidding "The Coo Coo Bird" ("The cuckoo is a pretty bird/ She warbles as she cries"), recorded by Ashley two years after the flood and carrying within it a symbol of homelessness — the cuckoo, which lays its eggs in the nests of others. Somehow, in the middle of this revelatory jamboree, in which Dylan also captures a number of American artists and their work, he creates a formidable image that seizes forcefully on the calamitous event:

*High water risin', six inches 'bove my head*
*Coffins droppin' in the street*
*Like balloons made out of lead*
*Water pourin' into Vicksburg, don't know*
*What I'm gonna do*
*"Don't reach out for me," she said*
*"Can't you see I'm drownin' too?"*
*It's rough out there*
*High water everywhere.*

However memorable these recorded accounts are, Newman's "Louisiana 1927" transcends them all. The song has a majestic emotional sweep wherein Newman digs deep beneath the tragic consequences of the flood and plunges us into the wounded soul of the South. His performance has both passion and empathy, yet also helps us understand why the roots of the South are so durable. Newman begins "Louisiana 1927" by recycling the opening melody of "Sail Away," deliberately tying the two songs together. "Louisiana 1927" may, on one level, simply be revealing the details of that horrible day, but those details are charged with a deeper metaphorical meaning — that the transgressions of the South, and the unresolved issues emanating from the Civil War, have invited this calamity. The winds (significantly from the North) dramatically change and transform the countryside, until the town of Evangeline has six feet of water flowing in its streets. In the chorus, Newman reaches the essence of the retribution suffered by Southerners:

> *Louisiana, Louisiana*
> *They're trying to wash us away.*

"Louisiana 1927" also offers up some memorable minutiae like President Coolidge standing at the front of a train, along with his aide, "a little fat man with a notepad in his hand." Observing the devastation, Coolidge turns to him to ask, "Little fat man, isn't it a shame/ What the river has done to this poor cracker's land?" Far from a simple question, Coolidge's comment underlines the South's fear — and resentment — of the North's indifference to their plight. "The storm comes from the North," Newman reminded Timothy White. "There's a feeling down there, definitely, of anti-Yankee animus toward the North, toward government, toward people trying to tell them what to do. And that's what it's about to me." On *Good Old Boys*, "Louisiana 1927" opens with an elegiac string section worthy of one of Alfred Newman's finer film scores. This striking final version also features one of Newman's more passionate vocals. We are never distanced from the pain in the material; Newman wants us to feel the tidal pull of the song's power.

Of all the compositions written about the flood, "Louisiana 1927" has had the strongest influence on other musicians. Aaron Neville, who hails from New Orleans, did full justice to this staggeringly beautiful song in 1991. The song was included in the closing credits of Ron Shelton's film, *Blaze* (1989), which dramatized the life of Huey P. Long's brother, Governor Earl Long (Paul Newman) and his relationship with the stripper Blaze Starr (Lolita Davidovich). Percival Everett also borrowed President Coolidge's little fat aide for his 1999 novel, *Grand Canyon, Inc.* In the book, the flood takes place in Iowa, and it's President Truman who comes to visit the devastated state. As a father and son watch "pigs, cows, barns and a sleigh bed floating away," the son seems surprisingly nonplussed by it all. The youngster is, however, impressed by "the idea of [President Truman] having a little fat man with a notepad by his side."

On *Johnny Cutler's Birthday,* after David Williams performs "Louisiana 1927," the crowd joins in to sing "Happy Birthday" to Johnny, who then performs a song titled, "My Daddy Knew Dixie Howell." Although the tune suggests Howell was a football player, he was actually a catcher for the Pittsburgh Pirates from 1947 to 1952, later traded to the Brooklyn Dodgers, where he played until he retired in 1956. The song serves as an introduction to the bitterly contentious relationship between Cutler and his father. When his dad dies, Johnny remembers how his father put a football, and later a football helmet, in his cradle. However, Cutler, drunk at the funeral, places a razor in the coffin and rubs Vaseline on the corpse's head. His last words to his father before they lower the coffin bring out the animosity between them:

> *Daddy, don't you wish it was me*
> *Laying there instead*
> *But tomorrow I'll be sober, Daddy*
> *And you will still be dead.*

After "My Daddy Knew Dixie Howell," the story shifts to the Cutler home for the beguiling "Shining." While Johnny's wife, Marie, watches wrestling on television, his mother phones to impart her birthday greetings. Since he's not home, Marie shares a "cold and empty" conversation with her. Although it unfortunately wasn't included on *Good Old Boys,* "Shining," about living in a spiritually empty marriage, is one of the most shattering songs Newman has ever written. During the phone conversation, Marie remembers being a sixteen-year-old with long flowing hair that was always shining. As she slowly follows the tracks of her years, Marie realizes time hasn't been kind and life has been quickly slipping away from her. Looking back enables her to confront the barrenness of her life:

*And there wasn't no baby cryin'*
*And there wasn't no laundry waitin' for me on the line*
*If I didn't want to be alone, I didn't have to be alone*
*All I had to do was shine.*

Newman follows "Shining" with another song about the wife simply called "Marie," sung this time by her drunken husband. "Marie" may be one of Newman's most endearing compositions — though it's one he says he could not care less about, because it is not his style of song. Still, coming on the heels of "Shining," the track has a poignancy it doesn't have standing alone, as it does on *Good Old Boys*. When Cutler comes home, hammered from the festivities, he finds his wife asleep. Being drunk allows him to tell her how much he loves her. Just as Marie became lost in her memories in "Shining," Johnny gets wistfully lost in his:

*You looked like a princess*
*The night we met*
*With your hair piled up high*
*I will never forget.*

Perhaps what Newman dislikes about "Marie" is its naked romantic sentiment. There's little room here for the untrustworthy narrator in a song about a man's deep regret over the failure of his marriage. Like "Shining," it's a love song about bereavement. Not surprisingly, many artists have tried to cover "Marie," including Brent Spiner, the artist formerly known as Data from *Star Trek: The Next Generation*. (Spiner tried — but failed — to rouse the ghost of Sinatra on his album of Tin Pan Alley standards called *Ol' Yellow Eyes Is Back* [1992].) In 1989, Mandy Patinkin recorded a rather pallid version of "Marie" as part of an eponymous concept album. The album bore some resemblance to Harry Nilsson's captivating *A Little Touch of Schmilsson in the Night* (1973), where the singer strung together a series of famous standards to detail the struggles of one couple's love affair. But where Nilsson's effort distils the essence of the songs he included, Patinkin's record is so self-conscious it suggests an eager singer performing in front of a mirror.

The next morning at breakfast, Marie sings "Good Morning" to Suzie, as Johnny, hung over from the previous night, sits belligerently at the kitchen table. As Marie serenades her daughter, she quietly reveals her barely repressed anger at Johnny. Meanwhile, Johnny responds gruffly to each line ("Now, Daddy may not spend much time with us/ [Johnny]: Fuck off!/ But I'm sure he loves you a lot/ Suzie, sing 'Happy Birthday' to Daddy/ He's the only Daddy you've got/ [Johnny]: Fuck off!"). Although "Good Morning" wasn't included on *Good Old Boys*, it's one of the rare examples of Newman writing conflicting character parts into a song, creating a tension that's both startling and funny. He follows "Good Morning" with the rather uncertain "Birmingham Redux," a reprise of "Birmingham" (featuring different lyrics), in which, later in the day, Johnny confronts one of his coworkers after they literally collide at the Steel Mill. Newman wasn't wild about the piece, probably because he hadn't added anything significant to it.

"Doctor, Doctor" is an early take of "Back on My Feet Again" (included on *Good Old Boys*). Here Johnny discovers his brother has been institutionalized. Since his physician has very little information to impart, Johnny decides, in his brusque manner, to enlighten him. He tells the doctor his brother was a machinist in a textile mill ("and he probably makes more money than you ever will"), that he's married to a Polish girl ("with a space between her teeth") and that once, as a kid, he worked in their father's barber shop sweeping up hair. As he sings, it becomes more and more obvious that Johnny's plea for his brother's release is a cry for deliverance from the torment of his own life:

> *Doctor, Doctor*
> *What you say?*
> *How about letting him out today?*
> *I can promise you he'll be okay*
> *There ain't no reason for him to stay*
> *Get him back on his feet again.*

Johnny's desire to get his brother back on his feet again is also a projection of Cutler's desire to become his own man. He explains to the doctor that, one day, his sibling knocked over a set of cologne bottles with the handle of his broom, an accident that made him cry with remorse. To cheer him up, their father took him to a baseball game, but to no avail. Then they went to the zoo; still the same tears. Finally, the father turns towards Johnny's brother and harshly admonishes him:

> *Daddy says, Son, I ain't angry*
> *But I'm so disappointed in you.*

Disappointment is a theme that runs right through *Johnny Cutler's Birthday*. Johnny has had to live with disappointment. So has Marie. So has the South.

The action switches back to the Cutler household, where the whole family is watching television. *The Glen Campbell Variety Show* is featuring, for some reason, the West Point Glee Club performing the Albanian National Anthem. "I was real interested in Albania at the time," Newman recalls. "Four thousand people and eight thousand goats, real vitriolic. I wanted to write them an anthem: 'Albania, Albania,' but it didn't work out, so I wrote this Albanian wedding song. But I didn't have any idea of plot in mind at all." "Albanian Anthem" doesn't have a plot, but its spirit is right out of Irving Berlin. The lyrics Newman provides, on the other hand, are not typical Berlin fare:

> *The white moon shines on the goatherd*
> *And the snow lies yet on the ground*
> *In the forest deep*
> *Where the grey wolf sleeps*
> *Comes a wonderful, wonderful sound*
> *Albania, Albania*
> *We pledge our faith in thee.*

After "Albanian Anthem," Cutler tells Marie of his visit to his brother and the reason for his brother's hospitalization. The story, which would ultimately become the basis for "Naked Man" on *Good Old Boys*, is based on a real legal case. Apparently, a public defender whom Newman knew in New Orleans was representing a thief accused of stealing a woman's purse — while naked. The swindler's alibi placed him in a married woman's bedroom. When her husband came home, he says he jumped out the window without his clothes. The story was that as he ran down the street, he ran into another naked man with a purse in his hand, who handed it off to the accused and escaped down an alley. In Johnny's story, his brother is the naked man who fled his lover's apartment, only to later find himself innocently in possession of a stolen purse.

As the recording session for *Johnny Cutler's Birthday* neared its conclusion, Newman still wasn't sure how Cutler's story should end. A temporary final track was called "Rolling," which Newman described as a song about the joys of boozing. Shrouded in a Stephen Foster-styled melody, "Rolling," which would also end *Good Old Boys*, suggests that Cutler, like the South, endures with all his faults and virtues. In many ways, it presages the finale of Robert Altman's *Nashville* (1975), also set in the South. In Altman's film, after the assassination of a country performer at a benefit concert, another singer with aspirations to be a star takes to the stage to calm down the anxious crowd with "It Don't Worry Me":

> *It don't worry me*
> *You can say that I ain't free*
> *But it don't worry me.*

In "Rolling," having inherited the legacy of a defeated people, Cutler resigns himself to it:

> *Rollin', rollin'*
> *Ain't gonna worry no more*
> *Rollin', rollin'*
> *Ain't gonna worry no more.*

Once Newman finished the demos for *Johnny Cutler's Birthday,* he realized he hadn't delved as far into the tragic realism of the South as he'd wanted. He needed to seize on a stronger theme, so he dropped the character of Johnny Cutler and focused instead on one of the South's legendary controversial figures: Huey P. Long. The decision to depict Long, whose political star had risen after the events described in "Louisiana 1927," couldn't have been more timely. The recording of *Good Old Boys* happened to coincide with the downfall of President Richard Nixon, a more contemporary American demagogue on the verge of leaving office after the Watergate scandal.

3

In the history of the Southern States, no figure could be more immense or more mythic than Huey Pierce Long. If Johnny Cutler was an average Southerner coming to terms with his lot in life, Huey Long was the Southerner-as-avenger, a man who refused to accept the fate of the South. In describing his life and career, Long would modestly summarize, "I am *sui generis,* just leave it at that." Yet Long was more than just one of a kind. A living example of the worst of what American demagogic populism could produce, Long became an embodiment of the simmering rage of the South. He also took on the role of the confidence man. In Long's early days working as a traveling salesman, as he once remarked, he "could sell anybody anything," and he spent his short but turbulent political career doing just that. Long was a character who could have walked right out of Melville, and his life ultimately inspired a powerful work of fiction, *All the King's Men,* by Robert Penn Warren. All of these ingredients made him a perfect subject for Randy Newman.

Elected governor of Louisiana in 1928, Huey P. Long would be the only governor of that state whose effect on the political and social landscape lasted far beyond his death, inspiring as many people as he infuriated. The Black Panther Party cofounder, Huey P. Newton, was named after Long. Newton, who was black and born in Monroe, Louisiana, in 1942, lived as complex and as contradictory a political life as his namesake, ending in his murder in 1989. He wrote about the significance of inheriting Long's name in his chillingly prophetic 1973 memoir, *Revolutionary Suicide:* "Governor Long had impressed [my father] by his ability to talk one philosophy while carrying out programs that moved Louisiana in exactly the opposite direction. While most whites were blinded by Long's outwardly racist philosophy, many blacks found their lives significantly improved."

Not only did Long put forth radical alternatives to the paternal rule of the Bourbons in New Orleans, he also transcended the progressive wing of the Democratic Party he represented. Until 1928, Louisiana had been dominated by fiscal conservatives who were opposed to increasing severance tax on natural resources, to the paving of roads and the building of a new state capitol, and to increasing literacy among the poor by providing free textbooks. Long and his supporters pushed for an unprecedented expansion of government services in education, transportation and health. He told his adversaries he would make the United States regret it had ever purchased Louisiana, and he followed through on that threat. Long increased political participation for blacks and poor whites by removing a poll tax as a voting qualification. His reconstruction of the state involved paving more than 13,000 miles of its roads. Besides ensuring all schoolchildren would receive free textbooks, he expanded the Charity Hospital System, built the Louisiana State University Medical School and brought natural gas to New Orleans, threatening the exclusive power of Standard Oil.

Long did all this, however, at a price to the very principles of participatory democracy. He ignored the basic tenets of the rule of law. In a democracy, every citizen has a special interest in his or her country's affairs. Since those interests seldom exist in a state of harmony, debate settles disputes through political compromise and accommodation. Long disparaged the diversity of the American electorate, becoming instead a flamboyant dictator disguised as an American utopian. He also provided his new services without full financial accountability, strong-arming the legislature and attempting to silence all who opposed him.

Long maintained political power over Louisiana even after he was elected to the U.S. Senate in 1930; his slate of candidates took over the state government in 1932. But in trying to bring his social reform platform to the national stage, Long posed a serious threat to President Roosevelt's reelection hopes just before the 1936 election campaign. But on September 8, 1935, an assassin's bullet prevented that threat from ever being realized. On that night, Long arrived at the Louisiana capitol building — a monument built with pilfered funds — to convene an emergency session of the state legislature. On the agenda was a bill to rearrange the boundaries of the district of one of his biggest political enemies, Judge Benjamin Pavy. Pavy's son-in-law, Carl Weiss, a physician from Baton Rouge, fired a pistol at Long's abdomen from close range. While his bodyguards fired 30 bullets into Weiss, Long scampered away wounded. He sent for two of the best surgeons in New Orleans to perform emergency surgery, but they were delayed in a traffic jam, so it fell to the local doctor to stop Long from bleeding to death. The doctor's failure to complete all the tests required to assess the wounds caused him to miss damage to the kidneys, an oversight that led to Long's death two days later. His widow, Rose, would end up completing her husband's Senate term.

Huey Long's violent death added to the mythology of his incendiary life. Whatever one thought of him, Long's impact on American politics and culture took on a legendary stature. Exploring that myth in *All the King's Men* (1946), Robert Penn Warren created a fictional governor named Willie Stark. The novel was a study of an American style of fascism, and would ultimately be adapted for an Academy Award-winning film in 1949. Directed by Robert Rossen, and starring the formidable Broderick Crawford in the role of Stark, the movie dramatized the ambiguous and vivid portrait Warren painted in his book. Warren's novel brought to light, in a compressed melodramatic form, the deeply convoluted history of the South:

> If you were living in Louisiana you knew you were living in history defining itself before your eyes and you knew that you were not seeing a half-drunk hick buffoon performing an old routine; but witnessing a drama which was a version of the world's drama, and the drama of history, too: the old drama of power and ethics.

The idea of living in a history defining itself is what Newman attempted to create in *Johnny Cutler's Birthday*, and succeeded in capturing on *Good Old Boys*. Arriving in the fall of 1974, *Good Old Boys* offers a broader perspective on the South than *Johnny Cutler's Birthday* did. Newman's portrait of Long is stretched over four songs in the middle of the album. He begins with "Louisiana 1927," fully orchestrated, setting the stage for the emergence of Long as a political force in the state. Newman follows with Long's own composition, "Every Man a King." Cowritten in 1935 with Castro Carazo, this is Long's quixotic manifesto put to music:

> *Why weep or slumber America*
> *Land of the brave and true*
> *With castles and clothing and food for all*
> *All belongs to you*
> *Every man a king.*

"We were hoping to find a recording of Huey Long singing 'Every Man a King' but weren't able to," producer Lenny Waronker explained. "So [coproducer] Russ Titelman and I ended up singing it with Randy on the record." Although no actual recording exists of Long and Carazo performing this song, there is film footage of them at the piano, looking every bit like a famous lounge duo. The presence of "Every Man a King" on Newman's album underlines the paradox that nobody in the South was allowed to be royalty *except* Long. Years later, Newman's version was heard over the opening credits of Michael Ritchie's cutting satire *The Survivors* (1983), in which Robin Williams and Walter Matthau play two desperate men who lose their jobs in Reagan's recession-plagued America. When Williams decides to become a survivalist, Matthau desperately tries to rescue him from the militia movement he's joined. At the same time, they're both trying to escape the clutches of a hit man (Jerry Reed), whom they witnessed robbing a diner (even he's in a pinch due to the economic slump). *The Survivors* is a story about two disparate middle-aged characters who become unlikely soulmates. Ritchie's inclusion of "Every Man a King" illustrates just how far removed from the reality of America Huey Long's song really was — some fifty years later.

Newman's next track, "Kingfish," is titled after Long's nickname, which some claim was inspired by a character of the same name in the radio comedy *Amos and Andy*. But Long insisted the name had another meaning: "I'm small fry here in Washington. But I'm the Kingfish to the folks down in Louisiana." Here Newman explores — and parodies — Long's paternal leadership:

> *Who took on the Standard Oil men*
> *And whipped their ass*
> *Just like he promised he'd do?*
> *Ain't no Standard Oil men*
> *Gonna run this state*
> *Gonna be run by little folks*
> *Like me and you.*

In the chorus, where Newman identifies the Kingfish, the strings soar in mock triumph as he announces that "the Kingfish gonna save this land."

It's significant that just before Newman launched into the Long tetralogy on *Good Old Boys*, he first dealt with Richard M. Nixon.

"Mr. President (Have Pity on the Working Man)" was recorded on August 9, the same night Nixon, in an effort to stave off impeachment hearings, gave his resignation speech. Although the song is a simple plea for compassion from America's leader, Newman also addresses Nixon, who has some very familiar attributes:

> *Maybe you're cheatin'*
> *Maybe you're lyin'*
> *Maybe you have lost your mind*
> *Maybe you're only thinking 'bout yourself.*

Newman portrays Nixon, like Long, as a dreamer caught up in a quest for absolute power, and sets out on *Good Old Boys* to illustrate how both dreamers represent both the promise and failure of their country's largest ambitions. To frame "Mr. President (Have Pity on the Working Man)," Newman draws partly from the well of lyricist E.Y. "Yip" Harburg, who cowrote "Brother, Can You Spare a Dime?" with Jay Gorney during the early part of the Depression. Their song focused on an everyman who is the victim of broken promises:

> *Once I built a railroad*
> *I made it run*
> *Made it race against time*
> *Once I built a railroad*
> *Now it's done*
> *Brother, can you spare a dime?*

In "Mr. President (Have Pity on the Working Man)," Newman borrows some of Yip's outrage to express his own disgust at a man who made a travesty of his own presidency:

> *We're not asking you to love us*
> *You may place yourself high above us*
> *Mr. President have pity on the working man.*

Harburg once insisted the character he wrote about in "Brother, Can You Spare a Dime?" was anything but bitter. "He's bewildered," Harburg explained. "Here is a man who had built his faith and hope in this country . . . then came the crash. . . . He still has faith. He just doesn't understand what could have happened to make everything go so wrong." That bewilderment is also at the heart of Newman's narrator in "Mr. President (Have Pity on the Working Man)":

> *I know it may sound funny*
> *But people ev'rywhere are runnin' out of money*
> *We just can't make it by ourself.*
> *It is cold and the wind is blowing*
> *We need something to keep us going*
> *Mr. President have pity on the working man.*

*Good Old Boys* opens with three rerecorded songs originally part of *Johnny Cutler's Birthday*. The beautifully orchestrated "Rednecks" is followed by "Birmingham" with its amended last verse. The record continues with "Marie," which is given an ethereal string arrangement. The new material includes "Guilty," a slow blues song about self-loathing, in which the narrator is sodden with booze and drugs. Newman couldn't resist altering the orchestration ever so slightly, even if it might jeopardize commercial airplay. "During playbacks, Lenny [Waronker] used to pretend he was dancing with someone — enjoying it — until the woodwind-and-organ dissonance comes in on the second verse, after which he'd stop dancing and look puzzled and confused," Newman recalled with relish. "It is sort of a groove killer." Bonnie Raitt heard Newman's demo of "Guilty" and recorded it before he did; her rather tepid rendition appears on her third album, *Takin' My Time* (1973). Years later, Joe Cocker set out to prove the song still had a groove to kill — actually, he massacred it, indulging his masochistic tendencies with his version on *I Can Stand a Little Rain* (1988). "Naked Man," the story told to Marie by Johnny Cutler about his brother, features an elegant calypso arrangement. "A Wedding in Cherokee County" is a touching tale about impotence. A painfully shy local falls in love with an equally awkward woman. He believes marrying her will finally give him "the strength to carry on." She comes from a family of freaks ("Her papa was a midget/ Her mama was a whore/ Her granddad was a newsboy 'til he was eighty-four") and as this odd contingent gathers for the wedding, all the narrator can think about is the consummation of the marriage:

*I will attempt to spend my love with her*
*But though I try with my might*
*She will laugh at my mighty sword.*

The melody of "A Wedding in Cherokee County" evolved out of "Albanian Anthem" from *Johnny Cutler's Birthday*. "I moved it to Cherokee County, to fit in with the theme of *Good Old Boys*," Newman explained. "I didn't have to change it much." Unlike "Davy the Fat Boy," where our horror at Davy's fate comes from Newman's putting us inside the mind of his tormentor, this song takes us inside the mind of the victim. The song is far from solemn, however, with a looping pedal steel guitar consistently undermining the romantic allusions in the story. Despite the parodic elements, Newman doesn't score easy laughs from what might have been a hillbilly caricature. He also plays with the point of view on "Back on My Feet Again." Where it was once about the early life of Johnny Cutler's brother ("Doctor, Doctor") the song now has a completely different framework. Newman adds a compelling final verse about a sister who marries "a Negro from the Eastern shore" and runs off to Mobile, Alabama. When they get there, she discovers her intended was really a white man done up in blackface:

*He said, Girl, I ain't a Negro*
*I'm a millionaire*
*As you can plainly see*
*So many women were after my money*
*But I'm proud to say that you were only after me.*

Here the metaphor of the blackface disguise is embroidered exquisitely into an album that has already offered up so many disguises. Whether it's Huey P. Long's utopianism, which eventually becomes a facade for tyranny, or Newman tipping the tables on the hypocrisy of the North's attitudes towards racism in the South, *Good Old Boys* is about the cost of gaining acceptance. It's also about the lengths people will go to achieve acceptance, and what we stand to lose in trying.

"There's this wanting to be part, wanting to be accepted in America," Newman explains. "I think sometimes it's why I glom onto whatever Southern background I have so hard." In "Back on My Feet

*Randy Newman's uncle, the formidable and gifted Hollywood composer Alfred Newman* (Wuthering Heights, The Song of Bernadette), *inspired in his nephew an active interest in music. (Bob Landry/GETTY IMAGES)*

*In a pose evoking his Uncle Alfred, Randy Newman does some studio recording of one of his songs in the early '70s.*
*(Bill Eppridge/GETTY IMAGES)*

*In the early '80s, now delving deeply into the family tradition of composing movie music, Randy Newman prepares some score sheets for the orchestra.*
(Photo courtesy of Gary Norris)

*Randy Newman conducts the orchestra for a scoring session of* Ragtime *(1982).*
(Photo courtesy of Gary Norris)

*Singer/songwriter Harry Nilsson ("Everybody's Talkin'," "Without You")*
*collaborated with Randy Newman to record* Nilsson Sings Newman *(1970).*

*Randy Newman wears out another pencil as he struggles to write another song.*

Randy Newman's satirical hit song, "I Love L.A.," inadvertently became a celebratory anthem for the city. Newman performs the song prior to an L.A. Lakers' basketball game. (Jeff Gross/GETTY IMAGES)

After enduring sixteen Academy Award nominations without a victory, Randy Newman finally captures the prize in 2002 for his song, "If I Didn't Have You," from the Pixar animated feature, Monsters Inc. (©Kevin Sullivan/ Orange County Register/CORBIS)

Again," the minstrel's face is given a whole new connotation. Newman offers us a well-established white man who feels that only by faking miscegenation can he fully trust the woman he hopes will marry him. Here the role of black man, the common victim of racial abuse, is elevated to a preferred status. "I'm very interested in how weird 'Back On My Feet Again' is," Newman told David Wild. ". . . [A]nd that is a genuinely *strange* song." Strange as it is, the tale is not out of the ordinary. After all, the United States is a country in which it's totally credible that a black man could successfully pass as white or Jewish (as professor Coleman Silk does in Philip Roth's bold and brilliant novel *The Human Stain*). Like Melville's *The Confidence Man*, *Good Old Boys* reminds us America is filled with people who change identities.

*Good Old Boys* was Newman's most commercially successful album to date. Released in September 1974, the record eventually reached No. 36 on the North American charts. It also won a Gold Record in Holland, though for the most dubious of reasons. According to Newman, the album was loved there because the Dutch believed Newman hated America. "How depressing," he would later comment. *Good Old Boys* is, of course, a far more complex vision of the American South than the Dutch response to it would suggest. In fact, it resembles the first two records by The Band *(Music from Big Pink, The Band)* in its celebrating the rich dualities within the American character. To paraphrase journalist Pete Hamill on the work of Bob Dylan: If totalitarian art tells us what to feel, Newman's art *feels*, and invites us to join him. Since doctrinaire thinking is as popular today on the left as it is on the right, Newman's work on *Good Old Boys* comes across now as refreshingly nuanced, music that engages us with ideas and challenges our prejudices and assumptions. *Rolling Stone* music critic David Wild recognized this the first time he heard the album in 1974. "Growing up in a lily-white small town, among a family of McGovern liberals, I'd probably never even heard the N-word then," Wild wrote in his liner notes to the 2002 CD reissue of *Good Old Boys*. "Yet on this album . . . I encountered the intimate spectacle of a great artist exploring race, regionalism, love and death with a brutal honesty and an eye for telling detail unlike anything I'd ever heard before. Here there were no easy slogans, no easy answers and no easy listening. This wasn't easy liberalism but hard truths, hard feelings — high art that exposed and examined prejudices on all sides."

*Good Old Boys* was Newman's bid to come to grips with an evolving South. It was, as Greil Marcus wrote, an "elegant album about the white South in a time of confusion: Martin Luther King was dead and Richard Nixon was President." But there was more. "People could still convince themselves nothing would ever change," Marcus continued, "even though they understood nothing would ever change back." *Good Old Boys* went right to the bleeding heart of that quandary, and it earned for Newman an opportunity to open his work up to a larger audience. Its world premiere at Atlanta's Symphony Hall, a month after its commercial release on October 5, 1974, featured Newman accompanied by guitarist Ry Cooder and the Atlanta Symphony Orchestra.

Around this time, however, Newman's mask began to have a peculiar effect on his status as a cult star and outsider. It started to become its own persona, rather than a disguise. For one thing, Newman began pandering to a very appreciative audience, one which was generally as educated and liberal-minded as he was. His humor, which usually left no one unscathed (including himself), was no longer implicating the audience in the joke. He began using comedy (as filmmaker Michael Moore does now) as a way to make his audience feel morally superior because of their leftist values. *Salon*'s Sean Elder has written about this particular change in Newman's performance of "Yellow Man." "[Newman] was hit with a yellow spotlight," Elder wrote of a performance in the seventies. "'Very sensitive,' he wisecracked, and the audience howled. Nearly ten years later, I saw him again, and when he introduced the number he *again* got the yellow spotlight and made the same crack. . . . [But] the gag seemed studied and cruel the second time; *he* wasn't the insensitive one, mind you, and neither were you for laughing. It was that imaginary oaf of a stagehand." Even the oddly compassionate "A Wedding from Cherokee County" now presented what Greil Marcus called, "a postcard of an old Kentucky moonshiner with flies buzzing around his head." Marcus pointed out in *Mystery Train* that when Newman finally won over his cult audience with *Good Old Boys*, the fans became part of an exclusive Randy Newman Fan Club. As reassuring as that might be to fans claiming Newman as their totem of nonconformity, it would momentarily hinder his ability as an artist to continue to test that loyalty. For a short time, Newman simply catered to it.

# 4

The triumph of *Good Old Boys* had another unusual effect on Newman. Rather than set him off on a prolific course of writing hit records, it seemed to paralyze him. Most artistic outsiders simply continue adding rooms to their ever-expanding palaces in the sky. Newman, however, spent his days with his head in the clouds. While appearing in the Lyrics and Lyricists concert series in New York in 1975, Newman started to get desperate. He told the audience he wanted to do a concept album which showed the human side of Hitler, using Mahleresque melodies and Bachman Turner Overdrive arrangements. Thankfully, this dubious project never got off the ground.

Newman had hit a creative wall. Where he once joked about James Taylor selling more records than he did, he was now appearing on those albums — in 1975, playing the horn organ on "Lighthouse," from Taylor's *Gorilla*. Yet even his new rank as a cult artist didn't earn Newman membership in the rock elite. "If there was a club of rock people, I wasn't in it," Newman told *Playboy*. "When the Troubadour was open, I'd go there occasionally. But I'd go there by myself and see if I could pick up a disease."

By 1977, Warner Brothers was rolling in cash. Album sales had risen rapidly and the company had more gold and platinum records than any of its competitors. Recent LPs by Fleetwood Mac *(Rumours)* and the Eagles *(Hotel California)* had sold more than five million each. In 1976 alone, more than seventy Warners artists had sold in excess of one million units in the United States. But Newman was suffering from a bad case of writer's block. Most days, he sat around the house watching TV and playing with the kids. "I was afraid I'd never write again," he told Charles M. Young. "I came to dread the thought of returning." The only composing he'd done was a jingle for a Dr. Pepper ad. That popular commercial might have proven lucrative if Newman had agreed to sing it, but when he refused, he got a flat fee rather than royalties every time it was broadcast.

His manager at that time, Elliott Abbott, eventually found a way to light a fire under Newman. In April, he booked an August concert for Newman at the L.A. Amphitheatre. The thought of having to produce new material for a show got Newman writing quickly. In May, he even rented an office rather than scribbling at home, and the new daily routine gave Newman a fresh outlook. "I almost felt like I was part of the community," he said. "I'd never been able to establish a rhythm for working before." It was in this little office that Newman started writing the songs that would comprise *Little Criminals*. By June, he was recording at the Amigo/Warner Brothers Recording Studios in North Hollywood. He began by putting on tape piano demos of music that would eventually appear in the movie *Ragtime* (1981). But there were new songs as well, one of them a lament about World War One called "Going Home (1918)," which Newman would rerecord and include on his 1999 release, *Bad Love*. The demos of "Going Home (1918)" and another song called "Interiors" would eventually turn up on the box-set *Guilty: 30 Years of Randy Newman*. In "Interiors" Newman poked fun at his tendency to turn every song into a parody. But it was also an attempt to peer out from behind his disguise and express regret to a woman he loved. "'Interiors' surprised me," Newman told Amazon.com years later. "It's really honest and autobiographical, like I actually *am* going to talk about evading emotion through comedy." But then, after apologizing for turning every heartfelt moment into a joke, Newman couldn't resist following up his confession *with* a joke.

*Little Criminals* kicked off with the song "Short People." Conceived as a harmless satirical ditty, it ended up both epitomizing Newman's brand of satire and working against it. An obvious broadside attack on the absurdity of prejudice, few, in the end, read it that way. While his new listeners made "Short People" a hit, and Randy Newman briefly a household name, others were pissed off by what they heard. But who else but Newman could express paranoia about tiny folks? The film *Freaks* did so unintentionally back in 1932, but that movie was hardly a satire; there was a weird sentimentality in the way the picture played on our sympathies for circus dwarfs and pinheads. "Short People" was at the other end of the spectrum. The character Newman created here was pathetic, much like the stalker in "Suzanne" or the voyeur in "You Can Leave Your Hat On."

The idea for the song began when Titelman and Waronker urged Newman to write an up-tempo song for the album. At first, Newman responded with "Hard Hat Blues," an ode to a member of Nixon's silent majority, but he never get around to completing it. "With Randy, if he said he couldn't finish something, there was no way you were going to get him to do it," Waronker complained. One evening, he called up Waronker to play "Short People" for him over the phone. "My initial response was, 'Shit, there goes our up song,'" he recalled. But Titelman thought it was one of the funniest Newman songs he'd ever heard. Even then, Waronker balked about having it open the record. Still needing to be persuaded, he decided to ask Newman to perform it — in the days before MTV — as part of a promotional film featuring a number of Warner Brothers artists to be presented at a Warners' convention in Miami. Lenny figured that with an audience comprised primarily of promoters, they could safely gauge whether or not the song was a potential hit. The film shoot began with Newman setting up in the studio to lip-sync the basic track without any over-dubs. As he concluded, Newman offered a small coda for the camera that wasn't in the song. "He turned and looked straight into the camera and flipped the bird with real attitude," Waronker said. Even so, the executives went crazy for "Short People," and Waronker finally had his confirmation.

Driving back from Miami, Lenny came upon a song on the radio that gave him a idea for an arrangement they could use when they were tidying up the track for the album. "[I] heard 'Love Will Keep Us Together' by Captain & Tennille on the radio," he explained. "I called Randy and said, 'Here's what we should do: use some of their arrange-ment.' And he was fine with that because he likes pop music." Perhaps it was the smooth conventional pop sound of Captain & Tennille that hid Newman's untrustworthy narrator, but many listeners wrongly believed the song was performed with utter sincerity. "It surprised me that anyone took it seriously," Newman recalled. "It was obvious to me the narrator of the song was a lunatic, no one I know of has a con-spiracy against short people. And I always liked them — until I wrote the song!" The narrow-minded protagonist of "Short People" begins his outlandish manifesto over a galloping piano:

> *Short people got no reason*
> *Short people got no reason*
> *Short people got no reason*
> *To live.*

He proceeds to explain his reasons for holding this view by listing every ridiculous cliché imaginable. For example:

*They got little hands*
*And little eyes*
*And they walk around telling great big lies.*

"Short People" consciously copies the style of a school yard rhyme sung by nasty kids. The trick for Newman is to inhabit the part of the nasty kid without becoming one. The problem is solved partly by the bridge. With the help of Glenn Frey and Tim Schmit of the Eagles, plus singer-songwriter J.D. Souther, Newman mocks the use of pop songs in the chorus by citing the standards "A Fool Such as I" and "What a Wonderful World" as if they were endorsements for world brotherhood. In doing so, the clichés of the popular romantic song become inseparable from the blather coming out of the narrator's mouth. Of course, little of this was picked up by a listening public. Some embraced "Short People" as a novelty song; others were deeply offended. "I had no idea that anything that silly would be taken seriously," Newman told journalist Arthur Lubow. "It was a fad, like goldfish-swallowing, and I couldn't get away from it. I was glad when it ended."

Before it ended, though, the song started a furor that prompted two Boston radio stations to take it off the air. "We had some letters and calls from people who thought it was insensitive," said one FM station programmer. "We had one schoolteacher who . . . said that children are short people, and they're very worried about their self-image." Newman even received death threats, including one in Memphis while he was on tour supporting the *Little Criminals* album. The fact that he stands over six feet tall likely didn't help his cause; Newman had to hunch over his piano to make himself a smaller target. Asked by journalists to answer for the song, Newman brought his usual irreverence to the table. "A short person?" he'd ask. "Let's say three feet, seven inches. No. That'd mean some little karate guy is likely to kick the shit out of me. . . . Actually I don't expect this record to be a big commercial success in Japan." A commercial success it was, at least in the U.S., selling 750,000 copies and climbing to No. 2 on the *Billboard* chart. Bob Merlis, the Warner's publicity director at the time, didn't understand the fuss. "You've got to have a sense of humor to appreciate it," he said. "But you don't have to have a very well-developed sense of humor to realize how ridiculous it is. The song is ridiculous. People who get upset about it are ridiculous."

Critic Robert Christgau saw something more. "[People] didn't understand that what made the song worthy of censorship was also what made it a masterstroke," he wrote in *Grown Up Wrong* (1998). In the end, Christgau saw the protests as proof of the song's truth and power. "If you enjoyed the song, you had to do so in the certain knowledge that your pleasure was someone else's pain — no doubt a hypersensitive crank, and a pushy one at that, but since [as Newman wrote sarcastically in the bridge] all men are brothers until the day they die, a fellow human nonetheless. Then again, some of your best friends were short, and they thought the song was pretty funny, right?" It all came down to an audience's willingness to be the butt of and the participant in an ironic joke. "But the nature of irony is that not everyone understands it," Christgau argues. "Dumb people — or smart people with a little touch of dumbness where the issue of height arises — don't necessarily get the joke. With Randy Newman, they rarely do." The producers of the picture *Harry and the Hendersons* (1987) obviously did when they featured "Short People" on the soundtrack. In the film, an American family encounters a large Bigfoot-style monster. *The Little Rascals* (1994) also included the tune. Perhaps its most inauspicious appearance came in the John Irving short story, "The Old Friends," in the anthology *Wonders: Writings and Drawing For the Child in Us All*, published by Rolling Stone Press in 1980. There's a moment in the narrative when one of the children plays "Short People" incessantly, much to the narrator's annoyance. Apparently, when the diminutive John Irving found out the composer of "Short People" was six-foot-four, he was not amused.

Compared to the brilliance of "Short People," the rest of *Little Criminals* was disappointingly short on imagination. The details in the songs seemed to lack their usual edge. "You Can't Fool the Fat Man" was a generic Fats Domino shuffle hiding a thin story about a grifter who attempts to dupe a scam master. Despite some tasty slide-guitar work from Joe Walsh, "Little Criminals" was a conventional rock song about the leader of a gang who has big dreams of knocking over a gas station in his neighborhood. "It's about a junkie who wants to go with these guys on a robbery and they don't want him to go," Newman told Richard Cromelin. "Kids who are going to rob a gas station generally try not to have a junkie along. It's a point of honor — no junkies." Yet there's little more to this story than you'd find today in an episode of *Trailer Park Boys*. Likewise, "Baltimore" lacked the detailed precision of a comparable social commentary piece like "Louisiana 1927." When Newman describes the downward spiral of life in Baltimore, his observations are no more than a collection of banalities:

> *Hooker on the corner*
> *Waitin' for a train*
> *Drunk lyin' on the sidewalk*
> *Sleepin' in the rain.*

Still, "Baltimore" created almost as much furor as "Short People," because Newman was barely familiar with the city. "I'd only been through it on a train when I wrote it," he told Timothy White. "And then I saw a *National Geographic* article that had all these white marble steps, rows and rows of them, and fences with people talking over the backs of them. It was famous in the news as a tough, hard, low-income city and a bad-looking city. And when I saw it, I thought it was." The citizens of Baltimore decided to strike back. One local politician, Hyman Pressman, in the spirit of Lynyrd Skynyrd's retort ("Sweet Home Alabama") to Neil Young's scabrous "Southern Man," wrote a poem about the ingrate who slandered his fair city:

> *There is no need for us to fret*
> *For we all know that Randy is all wet*
> *He doesn't seem to know the score*
> *When he downgrades our Baltimore.*
> *We caught old Randy with the goods*
> *He hasn't seen our neighborhoods*
> *We speak of love but he can't hear it*
> *He knows not our great city's spirit.*
> *He cannot feel, he's made of leather*
> *He wonders why we work together*
> *He slides down banisters every day*
> *And all the splinters point his way.*
> *We have a city that is bloomin'*
> *But Randy Newman isn't human.*

The controversy seemed to divide the city. When Newman played the city's Lyric Theatre even Miss Baltimore showed up to deliver a wad of letters both denouncing and praising him. "A lot of my songs are about places I've sort of never been to or don't know well," Newman explains. "They have a kind of romance to me, just the names of them, American names." But the real problem with "Baltimore" is that Newman doesn't commit himself emotionally in the song. The sense of place — so vivid in "Louisiana 1927" and "Old Kentucky Home" — is far too vague here. Nina Simone turned the song into a dirge, with an arrangement loosely based on "St. James Infirmary," for her 1978 album, *Nina*. On his first solo album, Nils Lofgren also gave "Baltimore" some of the gritty passion the original lacked. In 1979, the reggae group The Tamlins decided to strip "Baltimore" of Newman's lackluster arrangement and put a spring in its step. They sound like a band of explorers attempting to bring the city back to life.

"Jolly Coppers on Parade" takes its title from a Swedish mystery novel, but the song itself holds no suspense, essentially describing a child's view of a police cavalcade. "My kids are really into uniforms lately," Newman told Margaret Daly of the *Toronto Star* in 1977. "Maybe I was trying to set them straight." The arrangement has an appealing bounce, what Janet Maslin called "the sleepy, soulful rhythm of Marvin Gaye's 'Let's Get it On.'" Otherwise, it's insignificant. "In Germany Before the War" is inspired by Fritz Lang's powerful 1931 film *M*, about a child murderer in Dusseldorf (Peter Lorre), but the track fails to haunt you the way the film does. Although Newman creates a creepy mood with a Kurt Weill-style horn melody, the spookiness is too obvious, too fully thought-out. A song like "Suzanne" crept up on you, pulling you inside the mind of the stalker. But in "In Germany Before the War," Newman cautiously stays outside the character, singing most of it in the third person. He does compose some evocative lyrics in the chorus; while they don't illuminate the pathology of the killer, they have more poetic power than the story itself:

> *I'm looking at the river*
> *But I'm thinking of the sea.*

"Rider in the Rain," one of the more popular tracks on *Little Criminals,* is a faux-cowboy ballad done (with the help of the Eagles) in a style that Margaret Daly of the *Toronto Star* called "pure Sons of the Pioneers." "Rider in the Rain" is about a cowboy who is anything but macho, and who is running away from all the women in his life ("My mother's in St. Louis/ My bride's in Tennessee/ So I'm going to Arizona/ I'm just a rider in the rain."). Critic Charles M. Young suggested that Newman's cowpoke resembled "Chaucer's pansy knight, Sir Thopas." Newman agreed. "I thought it would be funny to make him a sissy," he explained to Young. "The Eagles had a good sense of humor, so they knew what the song was about." According to Newman, guitarist Joe Walsh drove more than 180 miles a day round-trip to be at the studio. Hearing the harmonies of the Eagles surround his own slow drawl was a strange experience for Newman. "You remember the fat kid at the pool when you were little whose mother made him wear nose plugs and earplugs and goggles and he'd have to hold them all when he jumped in?" Newman asked. "I felt like him when the Eagles sang." Although Newman plays against the myth of the cowboy hero, "Rider in the Rain" lacks the surreal absurdism of a tune like Frank Zappa's "Montana." As for the beautiful "I'll Be Home," Newman treats it as an afterthought. "I didn't want to record it," he said. "People like it. And I've made more money off of it than off of 'Davy the Fat Boy' by about a hundred times, and it doesn't even interest me except for the arrangement." "Old Man on the Farm" is a barren track about a farmer living a very barren life. Featuring Newman on solo piano, the ending has one of his typical vagaries — but that's about all that can be said for it:

> *Goodnight ladies*
> *Sorry if I stayed too long*
> *So long it's been good to know you*
> *I love the way I sing that song.*

*Little Criminals* isn't without its high points. "Texas Girl at the Funeral of Her Father" — a pretty song from the point of view of the girl — represents the first time Newman sang in the voice of a female character. The musical arrangement is borrowed from Alfred Newman's lovely score for *How Green Was My Valley* (1941). Written as if it were a musical postcard, "Texas Girl at the Funeral of Her Father" has a richness of detail and emotion that's missing elsewhere on the album.

"The inspiration was the idea of someone never having seen the sea, living away from it," Newman told Timothy White. "It's about some-one who's read about it or yearns for it — someone from Pampa, up near Amarillo — and it's just inaccessible to them, they never got there." You can hear that lasting sadness in the final lyric — especially when Rickie Lee Jones performs it at one of her live shows:

> *Here I am alone on the plain*
> *Sun's going down*
> *It's starting to rain*
> *Papa, we'll go sailing.*

"Sigmund Freud's Impersonation of Albert Einstein in America" is the album's sole masterpiece, playing the same frisky games with historical figures novelist E.L. Doctorow already tried with *Ragtime* (1974). (Freud and Jung, for instance, made a memorable appearance there, with Freud suffering a fainting spell.) All of Newman's strengths come out in this song: his sense of irony, the counterpointing of melody and content and the use of the untrustworthy narrator. "Sigmund Freud's Impersonation of Albert Einstein in America" revolves around Einstein's leaving Germany to come to "the land of the brave and free." Newman is telling us the archetypal story of the Jewish immi-grant coming to America, only here, Einstein is impersonated by Sigmund Freud, another Jew, who provides a psychological interpreta-tion of a dream — the American Dream:

> *America, America*
> *God shed his grace on thee*
> *You have whipped the Filipino*
> *Now you rule the Western Sea.*

"I was making fun of Freud," Newman told Brian Case of *New Musical Express*. "I've heard Freud criticized [for being] a product of the Vienna of the late nineteenth century." Newman supplies a sharp analysis of the outsider with his anticipation of how America — the land of dreams — will transform his character's life. But Newman has Freud getting the details of American culture wrong, when he starts referring to America's dreams of gypsies, "gypsy thighs" and long

"African appendages" reaching for the ground. "Freud in the song, because of his lack of knowledge of America, gets the dream mostly wrong," Newman explained. "[My wife, Roswitha] is German and to scare her, her father would tell her that the gypsies would get her. It's a European thing. You couldn't scare an American with that." Newman ultimately contributed a perfect American punchline to this tale about blending in, quoting Irving Berlin:

> *America, America*
> *Step out into the light*
> *You're the best dream man has ever dreamed*
> *And may all your Christmasses be white.*

"Kathleen (Catholicism Made Easier)" is about a groom who is so hopped up to marry his Irish sweetheart, he gets the Mass confused with various lyrics to Italian pop songs — including the famous "Volare." Newman supplies a catchy blues arrangement that is comically engaging.

On first listen, *Little Criminals,* released September 27, 1977, seems like the most accessible of Newman's recordings. It had the glossy sound of some of the more popular late-seventies L.A. rock — like Fleetwood Mac or Linda Ronstadt. The cover art, at first glance, was pretty basic, featuring a photo of Randy on a bridge standing over a highway that, for Newman, became highly suggestive. "The photograph makes it look like I have two penises," he recalled. "It's a hell of a way to sell records." While Waronker and Newman felt they had a good record on their hands, they weren't entirely confident it would be a hit. "I remember it so clearly, being in the studio and suddenly saying, 'Oh my God, it's not working. This record doesn't feel right. What are we thinking?'" Waronker recalled. "While we were sequencing it, we sat down and made all these little lists and then tore them up. We put all the song titles in a wastepaper basket and then spilled them out on the floor, hoping the perfect sequence would magically appear. It was insane." For Waronker, *Little Criminals* represented "the difficulty of trying to make a great record." That year, with a new record contract on the Warner Brothers label (instead of its subsidiary, Reprise Records, now consolidated with Warners), Newman found he had finally reached a mass audience.

When *Little Criminals* was released, the label seized on the controversy surrounding "Short People" to promote the record. This meant producing T-shirts, posters and buttons (one that read "Short People Power" publicized a concert in Berkeley in November). No previous Newman offering had ever been pushed so strongly. A big Foster and Kleiser billboard of the album cover overlooked Sunset Blvd. To push sales Newman set out on a massive tour of North America and Europe, giving a hundred shows between the release date and August 1978. But although the album scored big commercially, reaching No. 9 on the *Billboard* chart and going gold, it was an artistic disappointment. This time, Newman's disguise felt more like an affectation than a masquerade. And the reviews, save for that of Mark Kernis of *The Washington Post,* who heard thematic links to both *Sail Away* and *Good Old Boys,* were either lukewarm or completely indifferent. Robert Christgau, in his 1981 *Christgau's Record Guide,* said that Newman didn't "[write] one song that ranks with his best" on *Little Criminals.* In the 1995 edition of *The All-Music Guide to Rock,* Rick Clark called *Little Criminals* "relatively tame by Newman standards."

One of the first critics to express dissatisfaction with the new record was Greil Marcus. Marcus had been one of Newman's strongest and earliest supporters, yet he also found the album vague and mediocre. "*Little Criminals* offers all the minor charms of Randy Newman's music and none of the major ones," he wrote in *Rolling Stone.* "[There's] craft without vision, which means the craft is uninspired. The songs aren't even funny; they lack bite." Marcus once described rock & roll at its best as a music that could "provoke as well as delight, disturb as well as comfort, create as well as sustain. If it doesn't, it lies, and there is only so much comfort you can take in a lie before it all falls apart." *Little Criminals* was, for Marcus, that sort of lie. He singled out "Baltimore," a song "meant to be about The Death Of An American City, but there isn't a detail in it that has anything to do with Baltimore." Interestingly, Marcus used the Newman pan as an opportunity to praise a new, angry young artist out of England named Elvis Costello, whose acerbic voice was almost unthinkable without Newman. "I was very impressed by Randy Newman and wrote a lot of songs with that ragtime feel," Costello told *Rolling Stone* about his 1977 debut album, *My Aim Is True.* "I was very impressed with those very funny chord changes that he used to play and I was emulating that on guitar." Unlike the tunes on *Little Criminals*, Marcus said Costello's best songs "are anything but timid . . . they're as intelligent as some of Newman's finest, as endearingly elusive in their meanings, and funny in the same bitter, self-deprecating manner."

Although it's hard to hear Newman's stylistic influence on Costello's early albums, Costello's approach to his material certainly had that same piercing cleverness. In a song like "Watching the Detectives," where a man grows so tired of his girlfriend getting engrossed in her detective shows that he shoots her dead, or in "Oliver's Army," where he depicts British imperialism plundering the world with a musical arrangement right out of Abba, Costello shares Newman's sense of the absurd. Stylistically, however, Costello didn't match Newman until much later, once he started using his voice for more than just barking out his wickedly bright lyrics. Around the time of *King of America* (1986) and *Spike* (1989), Costello began to dig more deeply into the words, drawing out their meaning, and he borrowed much of his phrasing from those great early Dusty Springfield recordings. He became much more emotionally expressive in the songs from this period, as, for example, on "Let Him Dangle" from *Spike*. It tells the story of Derek Bentley, a slow-witted British lad sentenced to death for a murder committed by his younger partner. Rather than just sing it in protest for the injustice committed against Bentley, Costello gets inside the mindset of the accusers. By pulling us into the blood lust of the mob, Costello seizes on the same incongruities you find in Newman's best songs:

> *Well it's hard to imagine*
> *It's the times that have changed*
> *When there's a murder in the kitchen*
> *That is brutal and strange*
> *If killing anybody is a terrible crime*
> *Why does this bloodthirsty chorus come round*
> *From time to time*
> *Let him dangle.*

In 1995, Costello would pay full tribute to Newman with an emotionally convincing interpretation of "I've Been Wrong Before" on his *Kojak Variety* cover album.

With the commercial success of *Little Criminals,* and the controversy over "Short People" dying down, Newman's third son, John, was born in 1978. Shortly after, Newman started to concentrate on what he would call "his broader insult," a record that would lay waste to all the public support — and controversy — he had just received. In other words, Randy Newman's punk album.

5

In August 1979, Bob Dylan once again confounded his fans with *Slow Train Coming,* a full-blown announcement of his coming out as a born-again Christian. That same month, another Jewish performer would also be born again — only not as a Christian. *Born Again* was the title of Randy Newman's new album, but rather than worshipping at the feet of Jesus, Newman was featured on the cover sitting at a desk in an executive's suit, wearing Kiss-style whiteface make-up decorated with green dollar signs around his eyes. Partly an affectionate shot at his kids, who were massive Kiss fans, the cover was also a hint that *Born Again* would be Newman's most savagely satirical record to date, taking aim at all the attention he'd just attracted with *Little Criminals.* While Newman was disguised on the cover, he left nothing hidden in the songs. "I just thought it was kind of funny to be born-again, not as a Christian but as a moneygrubbing Kiss kind of guy," he told Timothy White.

Since 1974, Kiss had built a huge empire by shrewdly combining the macabre theatrics of Alice Cooper with the glam punk of the New York Dolls. Eventually, thanks to crafty marketing, the group turned into a billion-dollar franchise. The image they projected from the stage was of masked, Kabuki-style cartoon warriors fitted with huge shit-kicker boots. This storm-trooper outfit didn't invite you to rock along with them; rather, the band aggressively set out to rock *you.* The idea of a group like Kiss is a rather odd conception, especially coming from someone named Chaim Witz, an Israeli Jew and the son of Hungarian immigrants and Holocaust survivors. When he was nine, Witz's parents divorced and he moved to the United States with his mother. One night in 1964, watching the legendary Beatles appearance on *The Ed Sullivan Show,* he envisioned his own supergroup. Within ten years, Witz would learn to play the bass and change his name to Gene Simmons. Simmons and his pal, singer and guitarist Paul Stanley, picked up drummer Peter Criss and lead guitarist Ace Frehley, dressed themselves in proto-fascist costumes and dubbed themselves Kiss (could the emblazoned SS in their name be something of an ironic gesture?) Like Newman, Kiss had their masks, but theirs served a different purpose, as Sarah Hampson was quick to point out in her Toronto *Globe & Mail* profile of Simmons in 2004. When she tried to get behind the disguise to find the *real* Gene Simmons, she found just another facade. "Unmasked, he is still masked," Hampson wrote. "He wears a kind of psychic grease paint. Under it all, he is a guy called Chaim Witz . . ." Through the clever merchandising of Gene Simmons, Kiss became fantasy macho superheroes prevailing over the pretensions of artistic ability. Stanley, an accomplished vocalist, clearly defined the Kiss ethos. "We're the McDonald's of rock," he said proudly. "We're always there to satisfy, and a billion served." For a songwriter like Randy Newman, a group like Kiss was fair game — corporate rockers who disguised themselves as rebels.

*Born Again* began as a vicious attack on the emergence of the yuppie class which Kiss, in its heavy metal way, personified. Frank Zappa was one of the first American artists to recognize that behind the noble hippie of the sixties was the cash-grabbing yuppie-in-waiting, boldly skewering flower-power values in his prescient *We're Only in It for the Money* (1967). On his own new record, Newman quickly caught up to Zappa's long-range prediction. *Born Again* opens with the perfect anthem to usher in the junk-bond eighties: "It's Money That I Love." Performed as a glorious boogie-woogie shuffle, in full tribute to Fats Domino, "It's Money That I Love" zealously attacks yuppie entitlement, a subject Newman would return to in the eighties with "My Life Is Good" and "It's Money That Matters." Yet rather than spell out his outrage at the acquisitiveness of the American middle class, Newman gleefully personifies the role of the liberal hippie who renounces his past and is born again into the religion of commerce:

> *Used to worry about the poor*
> *But I don't worry anymore*
> *Used to worry about the black man*
> *Now I don't worry about the black man*
> *Used to worry about the starving children of India*
> *You know what I say now about the starving children of India?*

*I say, "Oh, mama!"*
*It's money that I love.*

Newman's dramatic commitment to the lyric gives the tune a powerful jolt; otherwise we would simply laugh at the character's scandalous point of view. "It's Money That I Love" is a triumphant song about the most dubious of triumphs.

After torpedoing liberals in "It's Money That I Love," Newman goes for rock & rollers in "The Story of a Rock & Roll Band." It's a hilarious parody of Electric Light Orchestra, an ersatz Beatles outfit that married pop with overwrought, futuristic synthesized classical themes. Although extremely talented, the band often crossed the line into pretension — and they were as massively successful in the seventies as Kiss. Formed in England in 1970 by Jeff Lynne and Roy Wood (formerly of the art-rock band, The Move), they announced their lofty intentions were to "pick up where 'I Am the Walrus' left off." ELO's second Top 10 hit in 1973 was "Roll Over Beethoven," which included a clever marriage of Beethoven's Fifth Symphony and Chuck Berry's fifties chestnut. In "The Story of a Rock & Roll Band," Newman borrows Berry's "Johnny B Goode" and presents it as if ELO had arranged it. The results are riotous, with some nifty shots at ELO's trademark chorus fills and synthesized string arrangements. Life, of course, is full of poetic ironies: One of the producers at the helm of Newman's 1988 *Land of Dreams* album turned out to be none other than ELO founder Jeff Lynne.

On the surface, "Pretty Boy" is a brutal swipe at Italian machismo. Although that swagger is embodied here in both Bruce Springsteen ("All the way from Jersey City/ And you look pretty as a picture") and John Travolta ("And he looks like that dancing wop/ In those movies that we've seen/ With his cute little chicken shit boots on"), the song is a parody of the tough-guy stance in rock music. "Musicians aren't tough," Newman told Barney Hoskyns. "It's artifice. . . . There haven't been five tough musicians in history, and they're doing all this posturing and sneering and snarling. . . . 'Street Fighting Man,' 'Under My Thumb,' I mean, how long would it take you to get out from under Mick Jagger's thumb?!" "Pretty Boy" begins as an intricately arranged, ominous blues, with Newman's piano rumbling out of the silence. It's eventually joined by the bass strings and a huge pipe organ. Oddly enough, the music sounds more threatening than Newman's voice. In his essay "Randy Newman's Americana," Peter Winkler wrote: "[Newman] uses blues idioms to express scorn and contempt, but the anger is more veiled, more impersonal and therefore more menacing." While he unmasks the macho pose of the rock star using tough-guy language, Newman deftly adjusts his own disguise.

"Mr. Sheep" tweaks the hipster satire of straight society (Bob Dylan's putdown of the square Mr. Jones in "Ballad of a Thin Man" is just one famous example). Mr. Sheep is the conformist clone who bumbles his way to work every morning:

> *Maybe you got a little girlfriend*
> *Stashed somewhere in town*
> *Maybe you ain't got a little girlfriend*
> *Ha ha ha ha ha*
> *Poor Mr. Sheep.*

Reading the lyrics, it may sound as if Newman is getting easy laughs out of the corporate clown, but (if you listen to the exaggerated aggression in his performance) he is actually putting down the put-down artist — as David Byrne would also do when he lamented the sad fate of the straight in "Mr. Jones," on Talking Heads' *Naked* (1988). Unfortunately in Newman's case, once again nobody got the joke. Stephen Holden in *Rolling Stone* called "Mr. Sheep" "the cheapest shot" where "a seventies hippie lashes out at the briefcase-toting square." Holden judged the moral irony "appallingly smug" because "both characters are such ciphers that they're impossible to care about."

Newman was baffled by the charge. "I must have done it badly, 'cause the real intelligent people thought I was making fun of the guy with the briefcase, the Mr. Sheep guy himself," he told Paul Zollo. "But I was making fun of that rock & roll voice. That sort of big, whiny, heavy metal kind of bullying voice," in fact, the voice of Kiss itself, which Newman had already explicitly parodied on the album cover. The generic symbol of Mr. Sheep has a firm basis in pop history, playing off familiar song titles like The Fleetwoods' "Mr. Blue" and Johnny Cymbal's "Mr. Bass Man." Newman may have also got the idea from a radio dispatcher he heard in a cab, sounding quite juiced, announcing to the driver that he was about to give an award for Rookie of the Year to "Mr. Quiet."

"Ghosts" is a dark, minimalist track featuring only Newman on piano. In interviews, Newman later compared the song's sombre air to cuts like Clarence Carter's "Patches" (1970) and Jody Reynolds' eloquent ode to death, "Endless Sleep" (1958). It's about an elderly man who has been deserted by his family and shrinks into the corner of a room. It's a desolate tale, like the story of the couple in "Love Story":

> *Once I flew in a plane*
> *And I fought in a war*
> *We lived in a castle*
> *And slept on the floor*
> *And I don't want to be*
> *All alone anymore.*

Canadian singer Holly Cole included a lamentable version on *Romantically Helpless* [2000]. "They Just Got Married" is also a variation on the theme Newman explored in "Love Story." This time, a young couple from Boston go off to get married in California. He gets a job working in a car wash in Santa Cruz, while she teaches nursery school. Two years after they have their first child, his wife thinks she's pregnant again — but tragedy strikes: what she really has is a fatal malignancy. After her death, her husband picks up, moves to L.A., meets a new girlfriend ("A foolish young girl with lots of money"), and gets married again. If "Love Story" was a comic horror story about how a married couple's traditional values are undermined by their offspring, the horror in "They Just Got Married" is in the fact that the couple's values have already been compromised.

In "Spies," where the melody is based on a Waddy Wachtel guitar riff rather than Newman's piano, Newman returns to the xenophobic nightmare of "Yellow Man," by way of the paranoia expressed in "Short People." He creates a noir-ish mood with the synth strings as he rails comically against a secret invasion:

> *If you love this country*
> *And I hope you do*
> *Then listen closely*

*To what I say to you*
*They're in the shipyard*
*They're in the factory*
*And they might look just like you*
*Or they might look just like me*
*But they're . . . spies.*

The slow blues shuffle of "The Girls in My Life (Part One)" lists all the dubious romantic encounters in the narrator's life. Here Newman relates even the most outrageous episodes in a matter-of-fact manner:

*Met a girl at the bakery*
*She wanted to borrow my car from me*
*She took it down to Mexico*
*Ran over a man named Juan.*

"Half a Man," partially inspired by a story Irving Newman told Randy and Lenny Waronker when they were kids, is a bold and daring satire of homophobia. Largely misunderstood, the song garnered numerous letters of protest. One day, Dr. Newman treated an elderly gentleman who had been beaten up in a gym shower because he refused to give another man a blow job. "Randy's father was saying, 'It could happen to you boys. Better watch it.' So you could imagine how terrified and mortified we were," Waronker recalls. The episode haunted Newman and Waronker the way Hitchcock's *Psycho* haunts many viewers. "It killed us," Newman added. "Every time I was in the shower I'd literally try to get the hell out as soon as possible." Unlike Waronker's story which is about the fear of being attacked by a predatory homosexual, Newman's song plays off a perverse heterosexual fear that homosexuality might be a disease you might catch. In "Half a Man," a drag queen is standing on a corner looking for company. As he waves his hanky at a passing truck driver, the infuriated motorist gets out of his vehicle to beat him up. But as the drag queen begs for his life ("I am but half a man/ I'd like to be a dancer/ But I'm much too large"), the trucker begins to transform into a homosexual himself. "Girl, it happens all the time," the queen comments. The trucker's own response takes the form of a pun: "Holy Jesus, what a drag." Here Newman is playing off some very unpopular notions of what it means to be gay, but clearly, he is making fun of those ideas.

Newman described the song "William Brown," about a tobacco farmer who moves from North Carolina to Omaha, in very basic terms in the liner notes to *Guilty: 30 Years of Randy Newman:* "I wanted to write something flat in which nothing happens emotionally." Judging by the results, he succeeded. The record concludes disappointingly with "Pants." Despite the colorful synthesizer fills, which arrive with all the pomp and circumstance of E. Power Biggs blasting forth Bach on the pipe organ, the song is basically a one-note retread of the sexual perversities better expressed on "You Can Leave Your Hat On." Newman threatens to take off his pants and "your mama can't stop me, your papa can't stop me" — hell, even the President of the United States can't stop him. By the end, in typical Newman fashion, the bark is bigger than the bite: "Will you take my pants off?" he pleads. But though the storyline is familiar, Newman demonstrates a new gift here for orchestrating on the synthesizer. In fact, the album as a whole has some of the most intricate and extraordinary synthesizer arrangements ever heard on a pop record. "I use synths when I need a sound that the orchestra can't give me," Newman explained in an on-line chat in 2001.

Originally, Newman's idea was to close *Born Again* with a cover of Kiss's "Great Expectations," but he opted instead for his original, "Pants." "Great Expectations," which concluded Kiss's 1976 album, *Destroyer,* would not only have matched perfectly with the theme of *Born Again,* it would also have been an interesting song for Newman to cover. Written by Gene Simmons and producer Bob Ezrin, it's an inflated ode to the group's fans with the explicit goal of stoking their own overblown egos as rock stars. The song even has the gall to stick in a segment from Beethoven's *Pathétique* sonata. Lead singer Paul Stanley proclaims to his audience, "You wish you were the one I was doing it to/ You've got great expectations." Newman might have taken the bloated self-interest right out of the song — as he did with "Lonely at the Top" — and satirized the pop narcissism at work in the Kiss persona. In a sense, "Pants" is also a fantasy rock stars dream about when playing to their audience, but it's an obvious joke next to "Great Expectations." That same year, Newman recommended to the Eagles that they do their own version of "Great Expectations," but they balked at the idea. "They looked at me like I was nuts," Newman told Timothy White. "[It's] like when you tell someone you like Andy Gibb's stuff."

Although *Born Again* was an acrid response to the commercial success of *Little Criminals,* especially the song "Short People," it was also a searing commentary on the arrival of the eighties. It also demonstrated much more inventiveness and guile than *Little Criminals.* Unfortunately, it climbed no higher than No. 41 on the *Billboard* chart. When Newman released the album on August 3, 1979, he decided not to give any interviews to support it, or even tour, perhaps hoping the audience would be there for it anyway. But they were nowhere in sight. Moreover, the record also acquired its share of bad reviews. Stephen Holden, in *Rolling Stone,* put his finger on what bothered him most about the record. *"Born Again* sounds less like a coherent song cycle than a sloppy nightclub act whipped up at the last minute in a fit of pique and 'produced' in a studio," he wrote. "How dismaying that the Mark Twain of American pop should have shrunk to the size of Martin Mull!" Holden compared Newman's effort unfavorably to Stephen Sondheim's misanthropic musical, *Sweeney Todd.*

Newman wasn't bothered when some critics missed the joke, but he took issue with being compared unfavorably to Sondheim. "Why compare *me* with *Sweeney Todd?"* he asked Steve Pond in *Rolling Stone* a few years later. *"[Born Again]* was a comedy record." Newman considered it one of his best. "I run into a lot of people who like my old, sensitive, issue-orientated albums better than that kind of nihilistic, no-human-feeling album, but I like it best." Europe responded to the record; *Born Again* even won some awards, including Foreign Album of the Year from the German television show *Stars From Many Lands.*

The success of *Little Criminals* was likely the result of Newman pandering to the audience he'd won after the release of *Good Old Boys.* After *Little Criminals, Born Again* came as a pleasant shock to the senses. Newman's untrustworthy narrator had returned with a whole new authority because he's posing a damn good question: Is the audience responding for the right reasons? It was the same question that had crossed the mind of John Lennon when he made his Primal Scream record in 1970, repudiating The Beatles myth he'd helped create. Sly Stone asked it again in 1971, after creating some of the finest and most racially inclusive soul music with the Family Stone. When he turned around and made the powerfully bleak (and distopian) *There's a Riot Goin' On* (1971), in the long shadow of Martin Luther King's assassination, Stone was implicitly asking if there was any point in working towards this kind of inclusiveness. Kurt Cobain pondered the same question in 1992, after Nirvana's State of the Nation single "Smells Like Teen Spirit" took the group to the top of the charts. Cobain's rejection of the band's success ended tragically in his suicide in 1994, as did the hopes of the audience who had come to identify with that song.

When Newman asked the question, his record tanked, but *Born Again*'s commercial failure wasn't a tragedy. It only cleared the decks of those who thought of Newman as a quirky oddball who liked putting down short people. Rather than head back to the drawing board to plan his next assault, Newman took a sudden and surprising turn away from making records. In 1980, he entered the family trade, vanishing from the world of pop and immersing himself in another world, the one that had once sustained his uncles — film music.

# The Celluloid Mask

I'm terrified every time I undertake a new film score. I sit and stare at the blank manuscript paper, pondering the unfathomable depth of my dry well. Finally, in pure desperation, before I can run and hide, I reach out and jab a quarter-note onto the page. It is not that necessity is the mother of invention, but more like insecurity being the father of action.

— Alfred Newman

One of my uncles, who didn't write [film] music, would say . . . that it was better than threading pipe. It is — but the gap is closing.

— Randy Newman

## 1

There's an old Hollywood story about movie music that has been repeated so often it's almost an urban myth. In 1944, while Alfred

Hitchcock was making *Lifeboat* for 20th Century Fox, he made the decision to jettison the score. After being informed of the bad news, composer David Raksin asked how this rather unusual decision was reached. "Well, Hitchcock feels that since the entire action in the film takes place in a lifeboat on the open ocean, where would the music come from?" a studio bureaucrat replied. Raksin paused for a moment before making a logical retort of his own: "Ask Mr. Hitchcock to explain where the cameras come from, and I'll tell him where the music comes from."

As funny as that story remains, it still touches a raw nerve in every Hollywood composer. All of them could justly lay claim to the aphorism made famous by Rodney Dangerfield: They get no respect — at least, nowhere near the respect that other film craftsmen do. Even classical composers, who should be their most obvious peers, generally dismiss film music as hack work. It's a thankless job, many say, especially since it's commonly believed a good score can never save a bad picture, and a bad score can't damage a good one. "It's kind of a low job," Randy Newman laments. "I've watched it since my uncles did it over forty years and there's been progressively less respect given to music people. Progressively less autonomy, trust and less time — yet more money. So you're a well-paid farmer's mule and the scores are worse because of this."

How could an art form British composer Ralph Vaughn Williams once described as "containing potentialities for the combination of the arts such as Wagner never dreamed of" end up so demeaned? For that matter, why would Newman, a songwriter who had already struggled long and hard to forge his identity in the pop world, opt to enter a world where anonymity and disrespect were bound to be his fate? "Before I did movies, I did whatever I wanted all of my life," he explained. "When you do movies, you have a boss. It's not a democratic system. It's an autocratic system." With a boss and a deadline, Newman could no longer afford to procrastinate the way he often did between pop albums.

Newman's celluloid mask would prove to be a trickier disguise than the one he donned when he wrote popular music. Newman was now entering the family business, once practiced by his esteemed uncles — most famously Alfred Newman — and the demands of film required that he abandon the use of the untrustworthy narrator. In scoring movies, Randy Newman, the pesky satirist, basically disappeared to accommodate the needs of the picture. "The main challenge for me is to write for orchestra," he told *The Economist* in 1996. "You have to subdue your ego because you're supposed to serve the picture. You don't want someone coming out of the film saying the music was good and the picture stunk. You're entirely in the service of the picture and not yourself." Newman was now adapting his skills to serve a vision created by someone else, and his own dramatic and comic voices would have to be stifled.

Still, many Hollywood composers, including Newman's own cousins, found their sensibility came through, even in the background music they made for a film. In *Music for the Movies* (1973), critic Tony Thomas described how, by underscoring the dramatic meaning of the picture and heightening the characters' motives, the individual identity of each composer could be fully expressed. "[It's] Erich Korngold persuading you that Errol Flynn was really Robin Hood in a previous life," Thomas wrote, "Max Steiner telling you what it was like to be a Southern aristocrat and lose the war and a way of life *[Gone with the Wind]*, Miklos Rozsa letting you know how Ray Milland felt on a lost weekend when he craved a drink, or Bernard Herrmann helping you to die of fright as some weirdo butchers Janet Leigh in the shower. If you believed Dana Andrews really loved Laura, thank David Raksin, or if you shared Dana's mind wanderings as he sat in the nose of a wrecked B-36 and mused on the best years of his life, you might tip your hat to Hugo Friedhofer." But can we say the same about Randy Newman? Scores like *The Natural* and *Awakenings* lack the distinctiveness of his best songs. Unlike Max Steiner and Erich Korngold, Newman had already discovered the best way to use his own voice — through dramatic characters invented for his songs. In a sense, these ingeniously crafted and orchestrated compositions were already Newman movies — scripted for and acted by himself. When he submerged himself into an art form that demanded a certain kind of anonymity, it came at great cost to one aspect of his art.

When Alfred Newman, born March 17, 1901, in New Haven, Connecticut, became a film composer, he paid a different price than his nephew. His first love — like Randy's — was the piano. "As a child I was fascinated by the piano," he once told Tony Thomas. "[Then] I became that most offensive of creatures — a boy prodigy." By the time he was eight, he was effortlessly performing Beethoven piano sonatas. He began earning money playing clubs and organizations in the New Haven area, making enough to allow him to study with one of New York's finest music teachers, Sigismond Stojowski, who had also taught Oscar Levant. Fortunately for the Newmans, Stojowski was not only a highly acclaimed educator, but he was also generous, and took Alfred on for a nominal fee. Unfortunately, when he was twelve, Alfred Newman's parents divorced. His mother was given custody of the whole brood, including Randy's father, Irving. But it was Alfred — at the tender age of twelve — who had to assume the economic responsibility for the family.

When he turned thirteen, Alfred Newman took off for New York and joined a vaudeville tour, performing as Little Lord Fauntleroy and providing piano accompaniment for singer Grace La Rue. By the age of seventeen, he was giving recitals so that he could send money home. These were so successful, he was soon doing five shows a day at the Harlem Opera House. While touring with musical comedy road companies, Newman had learned how to conduct an orchestra. "I was always happiest as a conductor," he once remarked. "I studied music composition and counterpoint because I wanted to be a good conductor." Alfred's major conducting assignments included many of Broadway's biggest hits, including *George White's Scandals of 1920, Funny Face* and *Treasure Girl*, all of which featured the music of George Gershwin. Alfred's gifts didn't escape the eye of the musical elite in New York. Irving Berlin took special notice of his dexterity, and it was Berlin who provided the opportunity for the Newman family to head west to Hollywood when he asked Alfred to conduct his score for the 1930 film musical *Reaching for the Moon*.

In the thirties, film music was an art form still in its infancy — even though music and movies had been intrinsically linked since the silent era. Hanns Eisler, in his book *Composing for the Films* (1947), suggests that silent films needed music because their ghostly quality strongly resembled that of a shadow play: "The magic function of music . . . consisted in appeasing the evil spirits unconsciously dreaded. Music was introduced as a kind of antidote against the picture. The need was felt to spare the spectator the unpleasantness involved in seeing effigies of living, acting and even speaking persons, who were at the same time silent." This appeasement would first take the form of a piano player in a pit situated below the screen. He might perhaps play Beethoven's Minuet No. 2 for the opening credits. Then he'd accompany a chase with a scherzo, or provide an andante for the customary love scene. As movies began to multiply with their increased popularity, producers raided the sheet music of the classical repertoire — as most of it wasn't protected by copyright. Bach's chorales could now be heard accompanying scenes of profound sadness, while hacked fragments of Tchaikovsky's symphonies would turn up as sinister mysterioso music to highlight intense moments. Wedding marches by Wagner and Mendelsohn would underscore not only scenes of marriage, but marital discord and divorce, too. But by the end of the twenties, with the arrival of talking pictures, the sheet music business became obsolete.

After the success of Al Jolson's *The Jazz Singer* in 1927, Hollywood became determined to make a full transition to talkies. The sound era was inaugurated — naturally — with more musicals. Warner Brothers followed *The Jazz Singer* with *The Singing Fool* (1928), where Jolson once again played an aspiring vocalist, this time with an unfaithful wife and a terminally ill child. The film boasted even more singing and dialogue — and it went on to gross $5.9 million worldwide. MGM took the concept further in *The Broadway Melody* (1929), which included talking, singing and dancing, as well as a backstage drama that would serve as a template for future productions built around the staging of a musical show. As sound grew more sophisticated, scripted dialogue between actors became more prominent. But producers were still confused about how best to use music to intensify a drama, where action was no longer the predominant force. They found their answer partly in the romantic music established in the mid- to late-nineteenth century by Puccini, Wagner and Richard Strauss. When four inheritors of this style — Erich Wolfgang Korngold, Max Steiner, Franz Waxman and Dimitri Tiomkin — immigrated to Hollywood, they brought with them a great knowledge of the relationship between music and drama. What they also recognized (Korngold especially) were the similarities between screen drama and opera.

Wagner, according to Donald Jay Grout in his book, *A History of Western Music* (1965), saw the function of music as an instrument to "serve the ends of dramatic expression." The early pioneers of screen music saw cinematic drama as a further evolution of the opera. "If we equate the dialogue in a film to the 'sung words' of opera, we can see there is little difference between opera and film," Roy Prendergast writes in *Film Music: A Neglected Art* (1977). "In opera, the stage is the most visible element and, like the screen in a film, it draws most of our attention. . . . In opera, like film, when the action onstage is the most important element, the orchestra disassociates itself from the action and becomes a commentary on it." So when Errol Flynn and Olivia de Havilland exchange love vows in *The Adventures of Robin Hood* (1938), Erich Korngold composes a love theme that treats their dialogue as a series of operatic arias. When the female creature is being created in James Whale's *The Bride of Frankenstein* (1935), Franz Waxman doesn't write the typical scare music that accompanied a silent horror film; instead he composes a romantic rhapsody expressing the longings of the monster, eagerly anticipating the birth of his intended. In *Casablanca* (1943), Max Steiner took the popular song "As Time Goes By" (sung in the movie by Dooley Wilson) and developed variations based on its theme. Running like a leitmotif throughout the film, "As Time Goes By" comments on the turbulent romance between characters played by Humphrey Bogart and Ingrid Bergman.

Alfred Newman would also put his personal stamp on the art of motion picture scoring. Newman's career in film music, however, was a serendipitous accident. While working on *Reaching for the Moon,* the film became delayed, and the producer, Joseph Schenck of United Artists, lent Alfred out to Sam Goldwyn so he wouldn't have to put him on salary. Goldwyn was producing the romantic comedy *One Heavenly Night,* with Evelyn Laye, featuring songs by Bruno Granichstaden, Nacio Herb Brown and Edward Eliscu, and he was so impressed with Newman's abilities he immediately recommended him to other producers. After *Reaching for the Moon* was completed, Goldwyn hired Newman to arrange the music for several films, including the largely forgotten *The Devil to Pay* and *The Unholy Garden.* Alfred was so busy arranging and composing for movies he had no time to consider a career on Broadway, let alone fulfill his dream of being a full-time conductor. Newman was also establishing himself as a film composer at a time many consider to be its Golden Age. In 1933, when Darryl F. Zanuck and Schenck formed 20th Century Pictures, sharing the United Artists studios with Samuel Goldwyn, Alfred Newman became its musical director and when 20th Century Pictures merged with Fox Films to become 20th Century Fox in 1935, he remained the head of the music department.

Like those of his colleagues, Newman's style of composition borrowed heavily from the nineteenth-century European romantics. But in some scores, like *How to Marry a Millionaire* (1953), he demonstrated his own unique grasp of the twentieth-century American school of George Gershwin, Aaron Copland and Virgil Thomson, for example in the jazz-inflected music he had already written for King Vidor's *Street Scene* (1931). In this adaptation of Elmer Rice's Pulitzer Prize-winning play about hardship in the New York tenements and a younger generation's desperate attempts to escape it, Newman showed he was as deeply rooted in American jazz motifs and rhythm as Gershwin was in *Rhapsody in Blue* (1924). Newman also drew stylistically from the French impressionists. In *Captain from Castille* (1947), a swashbuckling adventure with Tyrone Power and Jean Peters, he evoked some of the vivid orchestral color of Claude Debussy and Jules Massenet. The score featured a riveting love theme augmented with the quivering sound of *misterioso* strings. There was also a rousing march featuring over 128 musicians, to accompany Cortez's conquest of Montezuma's empire. One of the most haunting scores Newman ever wrote was for William Wyler's *Wuthering Heights* (1939). This satisfying adaptation of Emily Brontë's novel featured a theme for the tempestuous Cathy that was charged with romantic longing.

Alfred Newman won his sole Academy Award as a composer (he won eight as an arranger) for *The Song of Bernadette* (1943), based on a novel by Franz Werfel. Set in the 1800s, the story follows a deeply religious woman in France who witnesses a vision of the Virgin Mary, and ultimately attracts the wrath of the locals. The actual "miracle" posed problems for Newman musically. At first, he wanted to compose something in the spirit of Wagner's "Grail" music from *Parsifal,* or perhaps adapt Schubert's *Ave Maria,* but when he read the book, he discovered the Virgin Mary was referred to merely as a "beautiful lady." The discovery liberated Newman's muse. "I now wrote music I thought would describe the extraordinary experience of a young girl who was neither sophisticated enough nor knowledgeable enough to evaluate it as anything more than a lovely vision," he told Gerald Pratley of the Canadian Broadcasting Corporation (CBC). "With this in mind, I thought the music should not be pious or austere or even mystical, or suggest that the girl was on the first step to sainthood. She was, at that point, simply an innocent, pure-minded peasant girl, and I took my musical cues from the little gusts of wind and the rustling bushes that accompanied the vision, letting it all grow into a swelling harmony that would express the girl's emotional reaction. And it was important that it express *her* reaction, not *ours*." By creating a more secular motif with strings, Newman connected more strongly with the tender emotions Bernadette (Jennifer Jones) experienced while witnessing this vision.

Newman would compose music for a variety of genres — Biblical epics *(The Robe, The Greatest Story Ever Told)*, costume dramas *(Anastasia)*, sophisticated comedies *(All About Eve)*, overblown Westerns *(How the West Was Won)* and finally, in 1970, the first disaster melodrama, *Airport*. Yet Newman brought to everything he wrote the same strong sensitivity to the material and professional dedication to craft. "Newman achieved this by approximating the human element with truth, holding that knowledge, musical and otherwise, is preferable to ignorance and human sympathy more valuable than ideology," wrote film critic Page Cook. "His understanding of and appreciation for the heart of the matter caused him to 'take pains,' which some people identify as the hallmarks of humanity." Those pains, however, came at a price. Though nominated for fifty Oscars, more than any other Hollywood composer, and awarded nine (eight of them for his arrangements), Newman remained deeply unhappy, a perfectionist who made inhuman demands on himself. "Composing is a very lonely life," he remarked. "One sits in a room . . . wearing out pencils."

It was in this basic dissatisfaction that Alfred Newman most resembled his nephew. Randy also wore out pencils, struggling for each note, suffering as he pushed himself to scribble something on the page. And the results brought neither man much pleasure. "Randy's Uncle Alfred was a major influence on the Newman family," remembers Lenny Waronker. "A very powerful man. People who worked for him really respected him, and I guess, quite frankly, they feared him." Alfred was a formidable patriarch, a role he had been forced into before he'd even reached adulthood. For Randy, his uncle's ear for music became deeply intimidating. "[Uncle Alfred] would hear some music and go, 'Ahh, that's shitty,'" he told Robert Wilonsky of the *Dallas Observer*. "I'd think, 'Oh Jesus, I thought that was good.' It's tough having a family in the field." Randy, of course, recognized the quality of his uncle's work, and that left a lasting impact on him. "I was about four or five when I had my first memories of my uncles. Uncle Alfred did *All About Eve* in 1951," he recalled. "I can remember having to be very quiet while he conducted the big orchestra on the soundstage for *The Robe.* I realized it was something I wanted to do, and I was lucky because it was such a great orchestra, and I had the sound in my ear very early."

In 1962, Randy Newman started responding to that sound. He wrote his first score for an episode of the *Dobie Gillis* TV show called "Northern Comfort." By 1964 it had become pretty much standard procedure to compose pop songs specifically for movies, and Newman cowrote "Look at Me" with Bobby Darin for *The Lively Set.* In 1966, he moonlighted part-time at Fox, working an old copy machine and acting as gofer for other film and television composers. "I'd see Jerry Goldsmith doing *Voyage to the Bottom of the Sea,* John Williams doing *Lost in Space* and Arthur Morton doing *Peyton Place,* and I learned an enormous amount watching them," he recalled. Early in 1965, Newman composed the music for several episodes of *Peyton Place,* with the score recorded by an innocuous group called the Randy Newman Orchestra. "That was some tax scam my uncle was running," Newman explained. "Some of that I wrote, some of that I didn't write. And, of course, it wasn't the Randy Newman Orchestra. That was some kind of malicious fantasy joke." Most of the score was a joke, too, featuring slick lounge pop or hipster-cool rock, definitely unrecognizable as the music we'd come to identify with Newman. In 1966, he cowrote the song "Galaxy a Go-Go! — Or Leave It to Flint," with Jerry Goldsmith for the Bond-spoof *In Like Flint,* which starred James Coburn as yet another sexy super-spy. The tune opens with a solid drumbeat, reminiscent of The Ronettes' "Be My Baby," but once the congas, theremin and electric guitar kick in, it quickly devolves into bachelor-pad Muzak by way of Ennio Morricone. Newman would go on to provide small contributions to TV shows like *Lost in Space* (1966) and *Voyage to the Bottom of the Sea* (1967), and worked with his uncle Lionel on the song "Blue Skies, Green Meadows," sung by Ed Ames in an episode of the TV show *Daniel Boone* (1967). In the middle verse, you can hear a little of Newman's capriciousness:

*The robin sings its song in the summer*
*The bluebird sings its song in the fall*
*The blackbird only sings in the early spring*
*If he's gonna sing at all.*

Between 1967 and 1969, Newman contributed to the legal drama *Judd for the Defense*, featuring Clinton Judd (Carl Betz), a high-powered criminal attorney who crossed the country each week to defend everyone from rich tycoons to flower children.

In the early days, Newman brought to film scoring the same work-for-hire approach he used when writing pop songs for Metric Music. But given the family legacy in the symphonic score, he soon started to think in terms of writing for an orchestra. Newman's first taste of that came with *Cold Turkey* (1971). Directed by Norman Lear (who created TV's *All in the Family* the same year), the film featured Dick Van Dyke as Reverend Clayton Brooks, a small-town American minister who makes a wager that he could quit smoking for the sole purpose of winning a bundle of cash in a local contest. Newman's music was a droll blend of Copland and his Uncle Alfred, but he dismissed the effort later, saying it wasn't a real score because he merely sketched it out and left the rest to Jerry Goldsmith's regular orchestrator, Arthur Morton. "It's always scared me to write for orchestra," Newman remarked. "With experience, I've gotten better about it. This job, being the first, really got to me." *Cold Turkey* did feature the debut of Newman's song "He Gives Us All His Love," later included on *Sail Away*. The movie bombed at the box office and the soundtrack remains unreleased — although one cue, "Rev Running," a lovely pastoral arrangement with a touch of Stephen Foster, appears on the *Guilty* CD box-set.

Newman also composed the song "Let Me Go," a quirky track about romantic ambivalence ("Maybe I'll drop you a line/ When I'm feeling better/ Maybe I won't at all") included in Robert Mulligan's *The Pursuit of Happiness* (1971), a drama about a young man sentenced to a long prison term because of the bad attitude he displayed in court. Aside from theme music Newman wrote for a remake of the 1950s animated children's series *Crusader Rabbit* (the last two chords came from his song "Linda"), he never fully committed himself to writing film music until 1979. His career as a film composer would begin with a couple of projects that promised to be up to Randy Newman's best pop albums.

## 2

There couldn't have been two assignments more perfectly suited to Randy Newman than adaptations of E.L. Doctorow's 1975 novel *Ragtime* and Bernard Malamud's *The Natural* (1952). Both novels are richly textured parables of American lore in which the authors played masterful tricks with the history we thought we knew. Some historical figures were disguised, others merely alluded to, while a few others were used by name — popping up in both narratives in the same colorful ways they're used in Newman's best songs. In *Ragtime*, Doctorow captured the spirit of America in the era between the turn of the twentieth century and World War One. But rather than write a realistic account of the period, he created a sumptuous pastiche, a visual flipbook that was, in many ways, already a movie. "[It was] an extravaganza about the cardboard cutouts in our minds — figures from the movies, newsreels, the popular press, dreams and history, all tossed together," wrote Pauline Kael in *The New Yorker*. "Doctorow played virtuoso games with this mixture — games that depended on the reader's having roughly the same store of imagery in his head that the author did." In calling the novel an "elegant gagster's book," Kael underlined how Doctorow cleverly portrayed American history as a confidence game that tested our ability to separate fact from fiction.

The novel opens in 1906 in New Rochelle, New York, with escape artist Harry Houdini swerving his car into a telephone post outside the home of a white affluent family. As the story advances, seemingly random events pop up. J.P. Morgan and Henry Ford meet to exchange thoughts on the subject of reincarnation. Architect Stanford White is assassinated while his mistress, Evelyn Nesbit, becomes political ammunition for anarchist Emma Goldman. Sigmund Freud and Carl Jung, bickering over the role of the unconscious, turn up on the Lower East Side, with Freud desperate to find a public toilet. After visiting Niagara Falls, the fifty-three-year-old father of modern psychoanalysis has "had enough of America," and sails back to Germany. "He believed the trip had ruined both his stomach and his bladder," Doctorow wrote. All through *Ragtime*, Doctorow mixes historical icons like J.D. Rockefeller and Booker T. Washington with created characters like Younger Brother and black ragtime pianist Coalhouse Walker Jr. (based on the hero of Heinrich von Kleist's 1810 literary classic, *Michael Kohlhaas*), who becomes a victim of a racist practical joke.

The key figure in the novel is an immigrant Jewish merchant referred to as Tateh (Yiddish for "Father"), who lives in a tenement on Hester Street with his young daughter. Tateh cuts out paper portraits of people he meets in the street, an act that develops into flip-page movie books. Eventually he creates a new identity for himself as the Baron, a film producer. His silhouettes — metaphors for the ongoing assimilation of the immigrant — become Doctorow's key American emblem. The other, of course, is the ragtime music that gives the novel its title. As a musical form, ragtime appeared in the mid 1890s, piano music defined by Irving Berlin as "virtually any Negro dialect song with medium to lively tempo, or a syncopated rhythm." In other words, it was a musical hybrid, a symbol of the American melting pot. Ragtime music may have had an African-American rhythmic style, but it also drew on the European emphasis on written-out compositions.

By the end of the novel, the Baron sheds his disguise to reveal himself as "a Jewish socialist from Latvia" and proposes marriage to the woman from New Rochelle whose telephone pole had been clobbered by Houdini. They head to Hollywood to produce the *Our Gang* comedies, which featured an ethnically mixed cast of characters. Drawing the ragtime era to a close just as the First World War emerges, Doctorow declares that "history was no more than a tune on a player piano."

Newman had already played some of the same historical games in "Sigmund Freud's Impersonation of Albert Einstein in America," so he found the book quite appealing. "I was a big fan of the way the book took those historical characters and treated them so shabbily," he told journalist Steve Pond. "And the period interested me historically: the *belle époque*, before World War One. That kind of romantic ideal that we have of the period — it's not true, there was horseshit in the streets." Doctorow understood America was a culture in flux, a land where the American identity was never static. Literary critic Leslie Fiedler once wrote that being an American "is precisely to *imagine* a destiny rather than to inherit one." So Doctorow imagined a country that was like a lively card game running long into the night, where wild stories were traded, jokes shared and anecdotes laid down with the assurance of a flush hand. His pen dipped in the well of the tall tale, Doctorow took what he knew of historical fact and imagined the outcome.

If *Ragtime* was perfectly suited to the sensibility of Randy Newman, it couldn't have been more removed from that of emigré film director Milos Forman. In his Czech films, especially *Loves of a Blonde* (1967) and *The Fireman's Ball* (1971), Forman had developed a politically charged neorealistic comic style, but it had huge shortcomings. Whether he wanted audiences to identify with or laugh at the follies of ordinary people, the tone often came across as churlish. It wasn't that Forman hated his characters exactly, but he didn't trust the transformative magic of movie art to make human absurdity engaging. This may be one reason why Forman's movies are not only visually drab, but his characters always seem to be pinioned in front of the camera. When Forman came to the United States, his movies developed another problem — they appeared to be largely out of touch with the culture. With the exception of his superb adaptation of Ken Kesey's *One Flew Over the Cuckoo's Nest* (1975), in which he eliminated some of the excesses of Kesey's parable, Forman's American films are hollow and shrill. His adaptation of the musical *Hair* (1979), despite its energy, completely missed the childlike spontaneity of the stage version. As Pauline Kael commented, "Forman didn't seem to understand that the great achievement of the hippies was that they loosened up the middle classes; he had them shocking rich stiffs who lived in a style that might have come out of editorial denunciations in *Pravda*." Like other Eastern European artists who lived under communism, what Forman truly lacked was an appreciation for the vulgar juices that propel American popular culture — exactly what Doctorow celebrates in *Ragtime*.

Milos Forman wasn't the first choice to direct the film. After *Ragtime* was published, four things looked certain: Dino De Laurentiis would produce the movie, E.L. Doctorow would write the script, Robert Altman would direct it and Randy Newman would compose the score. In the end, only De Laurentiis and Newman would survive. Altman already had a string of films, *McCabe and Mrs. Miller* (1971), *The Long Goodbye* (1973), *Thieves Like Us* (1974) and *Nashville* (1975) demonstrating quite convincingly why he was ideal for the project. He had an amazing aptitude for mixing genres, he worked brilliantly with large casts and he had an unparalleled intuitive grasp of American popular culture. Not surprisingly, he was excited about the possibilities of directing *Ragtime*. Maybe a little too excited; he started doing his own version of *Ragtime* while still directing *Buffalo Bill and the Indians* (1976), mixing and matching historical and fictional figures. But somehow Altman wasn't able to bring the Buffalo Bill myth to life and the film bombed at the box office. This was unfortunate, since De Laurentiis, who owned the rights to *Ragtime*, also had money invested in *Buffalo Bill*. When it failed, he took *Ragtime* out of Altman's hands and gave it to Milos Forman. Doctorow was originally wedded to the Altman deal, so Forman had a new script written by Michael Weller, the screenwriter who had worked with him on *Hair*.

It's hard to say just what Forman and Weller thought they were aiming for in their version of *Ragtime*, since the movie misses the mark in just about every conceivable way. The film doesn't even begin to approximate the themes in Doctorow's novel. Many of the historical figures — Houdini, J. P. Morgan, Booker T. Washington and Stanford White — are either tangential to the story, relegated to a newsreel or given graceless cameos. Emma Goldman, Sigmund Freud, Carl Jung and Emiliano Zapata don't even appear in the film. Despite the elegant casting of James Cagney (emerging from a twenty-year retirement to play Police Commissioner Waldo), Pat O'Brien as a lawyer and Donald O'Connor as — what else? — a choreographer, Forman doesn't develop their scenes; his only apparent purpose in casting the characters is simply to have them appear on screen. *Ragtime* is reduced essentially to one story: Coalhouse Walker Jr.'s. Forman saw *Ragtime*, with its emotionally scarred black piano player, as a solemn civil rights story rather than a wildly playful jamboree. "*[Ragtime]* would have been the one project you do give Robert Altman to do," Newman explains. "The picture was supposed to be all over the place just like the book — that's what was so great about it." In the end, Newman was disappointed the picture didn't play the same clever games that the novel did. "The movie did less of that," he said. "Rather than focus on Coalhouse Walker, I would rather have seen the story go all over the map."

In July 1981, Newman started the recording sessions for *Ragtime* at the Evergreen Studios in Hollywood. Rather than drawing primarily on the ragtime styles of Jelly Roll Morton and Scott Joplin, Newman peppered the score with waltzes and polkas. The main title theme, for instance, was a beautiful waltz for piano and orchestra that had some of the same haunting luminescence as John Morris' opening music for

David Lynch's *The Elephant Man* (1980). But Newman's score, unfortunately, never acquires thematic unity, partly because the film itself doesn't build any lyrical momentum. The first scene, which shows Coalhouse Walker Jr. (Howard E. Rollins Jr.) at the piano in an orchestra pit playing to a film newsreel, could have established atmosphere, but fails. The movie is so badly structured the score ends up plugging holes rather than commenting on the story. Newman did manage to get some input into the placement of the music in the picture, but his overall involvement was minimal. For example, when Coalhouse Walker comes to visit Younger Brother's home in New Rochelle for the first time, he plays the Chopin A major Prelude (Opus 28 No. 7) for his family before slipping into Newman's own paraphrasing of the same piece. When the song "I Could Love a Million Girls" is sung in the dinner club where Stanford White was assassinated, what we hear isn't exactly the original song; Newman changed some of the lyrics because he thought the original words were dreadful.

Newman also wrote a couple of original tunes for the picture. "One More Hour," sung by Jennifer Warnes, had an arrangement based on a lovely turn-of-the-century ballad, and it ended up being nominated for an Academy Award. He also composed "Change Your Way," intended to be performed by actor Scatman Crothers in the film's opening scene, but the Crothers sequence was never shot. The song later appeared, with Newman performing it, on the *Guilty* CD box-set.

Given the apparent potential of the material, Newman was disappointed his score wasn't as well served in *Ragtime* as it could have been. "It's funny that the music isn't showcased, because the central character is an excellent black piano player," he told *Rolling Stone*. "Hell, I guess if they really wanted the piano playing to be believable, they would have hired Billy Joel." Doctorow wasn't well served by Forman's and Weller's adaptation either; Newman's score would at least earn him his first of many Academy Award nominations. At the 1982 presentation, however, Vangelis's synthesized sludge for the mawkish *Chariots of Fire* won for Best Original Score. The evening was nerve-wracking for Newman, because he always felt weighed down by the expectations of his uncles. "Standards are high in the family," he told Arthur Lubow. Conducting an orchestra in his film scores was something Newman found particularly petrifying. "The scariest thing in the world," he explained. "[Before one orchestra date]

Roswitha woke me up in the middle of the night — I was trying to crawl under her back to hide."

If *Ragtime* was a case of the wrong man hired for the wrong job, *The Natural* (1984) was an example of smart and talented people just dropping the ball. Bernard Malamud's first novel was a canny parable written with true American gusto in which the author digs into the spirit of one of Ted Williams' famous declarations. Looking back on his storied career, the baseball great once remarked, "All I want out of life is that when I walk down the street folks will say, 'There goes the greatest hitter who ever lived.'" Malamud asks the question: If you *were* the greatest ball player who ever lived, blessed with extraordinary athletic gifts, could you just as easily piss it all away? *The Natural* is a vivaciously entertaining story of a thirty-four-year-old rookie named Roy Hobbs who gets a second shot at becoming a baseball star — and blows it. Fifteen years earlier, as a can't-miss prospect, Hobbs is almost killed by Harriett Bird, a disturbed groupie who seduces and shoots him. Years later, and recovered from his injuries, Hobbs gets a new contract and arrives at the dugout of New York Knights' manager Pop Fisher to join the team. Given Hobbs' age, Pop is initially reluctant to bring him onboard. His corrupt partner, Judge Goodwill Banner, has been dumping lousy players on him all year with the purpose of decimating the team; he figures if the team finishes last, Pop will give up and sell him his share of the franchise. Hobbs changes all that by leading the Knights to a league pennant. But he's also an unbridled hedonist. When he gets involved with Pop's niece, Memo, he's distracted from his quest to be the best, as he was by Harriett, once again betraying his natural gifts. He may be a natural, but he's only human.

As Doctorow did in *Ragtime*, Malamud adroitly weaves fact and fiction. For instance, as a player, Pop Fisher once committed a blunder ("Fisher's Flop") that cost his team the World Series, a faux pas loosely based on the story of the New York Giants' first baseman Fred Merkle, whose error cost his team the pennant in 1908. Malamud's sportswriter, Max Mercy, is obviously based on Ring Lardner, and Walter "Whammer" Wambold, a lumbering slugger Hobbs strikes out as a brash nineteen-year-old in the book's opening moments, is most certainly Babe Ruth. Judge Goodwill Banner has shades of former Chicago White Sox owner Charles A. Comiskey, who treated his players so badly they went into cahoots with gamblers and threw the 1919 World

Series in the famous "Black Sox" scandal. These rich associations seemed to make Malamud's novel perfect for the movies, and as it happened the plot was already loosely based on one: *Elmer the Great* (1933), an adaption of a play by Ring Lardner and George M. Cohan and the second in a baseball trilogy starring Joe E. Brown. Directed by Mervyn LeRoy, *Elmer the Great* featured Brown as a loudmouthed rookie who attempts to break in with the Chicago Cubs.

Once again, Newman had promising dramatic material to work with, and as an added bonus, he was a baseball fan who had supported the Los Angeles Dodgers since childhood. Brought in to direct *The Natural* was Barry Levinson, a career screenwriter who had only recently turned to making movies. Levinson's directorial debut was *Diner* (1982), a beautifully written and directed autobiographical comedy about a group of friends in Baltimore at the end of the fifties. The movie was remarkably perceptive, a fresh and honest view of the sexual relations between men and woman on the cusp of the sexual revolution. *Diner* launched the careers of talented actors like Ellen Barkin, Mickey Rourke and Kevin Bacon, and featured the lone great performance by Steve Guttenberg. So with Levinson in charge, a script written by Roger Towne and Phil Dusenberry, and shot by acclaimed cinematographer Caleb Deschanel *(The Black Stallion, The Right Stuff)*, the picture seemed ripe with possibilities. But instead of being a hip, funny American yarn, *The Natural* became an overripe and gauzy piece of nostalgic whimsy. The film changed the meaning of the book, turning it into a hollow piece of hero worship.

Their horrible reworking of the story, in which Roy Hobbs fulfills his destiny rather than flubbing it, had everything to do with the casting of Robert Redford as Hobbs. By the 1980s, Redford, as an actor, was indistinguishable from a baby-kissing politician running for office. Rather than portray Hobbs as a man who could not resist temptation, he plays him as a hero triumphing over adversity. Hobbs is mythic in the novel, yet we never forget that he's human. But Redford's Hobbs is a Golden Boy beyond temptation, an innocent country lad whom city folks try to corrupt. Redford's plaster-saint performance turns Malamud's pointed prose into movie corn, and Newman's music is as hollow as the canned Americana of the picture.

Approaching Levinson's now black-and-white morality tale, Newman fills *The Natural* with the kind of pompous fanfares and inspirational surges he'd normally satirize in his songs. Occasionally, as in the prologue, Newman employs some of the American rural folk arrangements Copland adapted effectively for the morning on-the-farm scene in John Steinbeck's *The Red Pony* (1949). But Newman's themes are so emphatic here, they verge on parody. Despite the occasional anachronistic use of synthesizers, the drippy sentimental music creates the same soft-focus version of America Hollywood moguls like Louis B. Mayer falsely championed decades earlier. And indeed Newman's score is steeped in the romantic tradition of old Hollywood, though he recycles the *style* of movie music rather than writing something authentically his own. Newman's heroic fanfares, with all their vacuousness, would ultimately find a home in the Texas Rangers' ballpark in Arlington played after every home-team home run. The score would also earn Newman a second Academy Award nomination for Best Dramatic Score, and win him a 1985 Grammy Award for Best Instrumental.

The ultimate irony of both *Ragtime* and *The Natural* is that the moviemakers misunderstood their source material in the same way Tom Jones, Joe Cocker and Linda Ronstadt misunderstood the Randy Newman songs they covered. In these early scores, Newman was adapting his talents to the screen rather than applying his imagination to the material. And just as he was putting his effort into movie scores, Newman's pop songs were drawing national attention in a different arena. In 1981, Joan Micklin Silver conceived and directed the off-Broadway production *Maybe I'm Doing It Wrong*, a comedy inspired by Newman's music and featuring more than twenty-five of his songs. Meanwhile, on the big screen, Randy Newman was still trying to do it right.

3

While most of Newman's time was spent scoring films, he still made the odd guest appearance on other artists' albums. In 1984, he arranged the synthesizers for Don Henley's *Building the Perfect Beast*, as well as Henley's subsequent single, "Sunset Grill." Joe Walsh had gone out of his way to appear on *Little Criminals*, and Newman returned the favor by playing piano on the title track of Walsh's *The Confessor* (1985). Newman did a few concerts, as well, including Live

Aid in July 1985. Even though he always maligned Billy Joel in interviews, Newman appeared with him at the first Farm Aid concert that fall. Putting their grand pianos back-to-back, they performed "Sail Away," Joel's "Only the Good Die Young" and a scintillating cover of the Lloyd Price version of "Stagger Lee."

A year later, in December, Newman made his fifth appearance on NBC's *Saturday Night Live*. Over the years, Newman had developed a friendship with the show's creator, Lorne Michaels. He appeared on Michaels' short-lived Sunday night NBC comedy program *The New Show* on February 3, 1984, where he not only got to sing, but act with Penny Marshall in a skit about Trivial Pursuit. Now Michaels was cooking up an idea for a film comedy involving *Saturday Night* alumni Steve Martin, Martin Short and Chevy Chase. The film was called *¡Three Amigos!* (1986). Set in 1916, the story involved a trio of has-been B-movie actors who save the Mexican village of Santa Poco from a group of outlaws led by El Guapo ("The Handsome One"). Newman was originally asked to contribute a few songs to the picture, but thanks to cowriter Martin, he ultimately became a contributor. "[H]e knew from Lorne . . . that I might be interested in doing something like this," Newman told *Playboy* in 1987. Maybe Newman should have thought better. *¡Three Amigos!* is a graceless comedy in which director John Landis, whose hits included the clunky *The Blues Brothers* (1980) and the moribund *Trading Places* (1983), attempted to satirize the broad heroism of *The Three Musketeers*. The basic joke of the film is that three actors are mistaken for real-life adventure heroes, but they misunderstand the request for their help as an invitation to do a paid performance rather than actually rid the town of a marauding bandit. In the story, the three horsemen are as dandified as the cowboys in Newman's "Riders in the Rain." When they disappoint the locals of Santa Poco, demonstrating their true cowardice, they become candidates for redemption. Besides the film's trite sentimentality, Landis and the screenwriters also saddled the actors with some desperately unfunny dialogue. "I'll fill you so full of lead that you'll be using your dick as a pencil," Martin threatens El Guapo.

The orchestral score was provided by veteran Elmer Bernstein *(To Kill a Mockingbird, The Magnificent Seven)*, who had worked on a number of Landis films, dating back to *National Lampoon's Animal House* (1978). Besides collaborating on the script, Newman composed some songs for the picture. The main title, "The Ballad of the Three Amigos," sung by the actors, is an uninspired attempt to both parody and pay homage to those rousing numbers that celebrate movie heroes:

> *One for each other*
> *And one for all*
> *The three brave amigos are we*
> *Brother to brother and everyone*
> *A brave amigo*
> *Wherever they need us*
> *Our destinies lead us*
> *Amigos, we're always together.*

The only distinctly comical aspect of the tune is how the three actors hold the "ahh" in "amigos" for what seems like an eternity. "My Little Buttercup," likely inspired by Gilbert and Sullivan's "I'm Called Little Buttercup" from *H.M.S. Pinafore,* is a silly ditty performed in a saloon, where the customers still assume they are three scary hombres. While Chase sits at the piano, Martin and Short perform a dance, choreographed by Shirley Kirkes, to these fey, insipid lyrics:

> *My little buttercup*
> *Has the sweetest smile*
> *Dear little buttercup*
> *Won't you stay awhile*
> *Come with me where moonbeams*
> *Paint the sky*
> *And you and I might linger*
> *In the sweet by-and-by.*

The final Newman track is "Blue Shadows on the Trail," which takes after a children's song you might hear on *Mr. Rogers' Neighborhood.* It also resembles Nilsson's "Little Cowboy," a song Nilsson's mother had sung to him when he was a child. Newman made his acting debut in *¡Three Amigos!* as the voice of "The Singing Bush." The Amigos come across an enchanted sage bush that helps them summon an Invisible Swordsman to find the woman El Guapo kidnapped from Santa Poco. In a cartoon tenor, Newman's hyperanxious shrubbery spits out a catalogue of old standards in the speed-freak manner of Jack Mudurian's 129-song extravaganza, *Downloading the Repertoire*. Newman's selections, while obvious for a western, are perhaps fitting for an artist whose work draws deeply from traditional music — "She'll Be Coming Around the Mountain," "Blow the Man Down" and "Goodnight Ladies." Unfortunately, the best song Newman contributed to *¡Three Amigos!* didn't appear in the movie, showing up instead in demo form on the *Guilty* CD box-set (along with solo versions of "The Ballad of the Three Amigos" and "My Little Buttercup"). "Happy," which Chase was supposed to sing in the Amigo homestead, is a brief taste of typical Newman irony:

> *I woke up this morning*
> *With a smile on my face*
> *And a great big hard-on*
> *For the whole human race*
> *I love everybody*
> *And I want you to know*
> *Got the world by the balls*
> *And I won't let it go*
> *'Cause I'm so fucking happy.*

Newman also recorded a cover of the old thirties standard "Crazy About You" that didn't appear in the film. In the film, the Three Amigos eventually found their courage to rescue the village and the damsel in distress, but unfortunately nobody could rescue the movie. It died a quiet death at the box office.

In 1989, the opportunity arose to work with director Ron Howard, who asked Newman to write the music for *Parenthood*. As a director, Howard has an unusual gift for shifting moods, from the comically endearing *(Night Shift, Splash)*, to the unbearably sentimental *(Cocoon, Willow)*, to the demonstrably dark *(Ransom, The Missing)*. In *Parenthood*, Howard used a little of all three elements. Featuring an ensemble cast, *Parenthood* is a multicharacter study that deals with the ups and downs of family life. Steve Martin and Mary Steenburgen play a couple who love their kids, but are swamped by the responsibilities of raising them, especially when one of their sons turns out to be a slow learner who needs extra care. Dianne Weist, the comic highlight of the picture, plays a single mom trying to deal with her obstreperous teenage daughter (Martha Plimpton) and her amiably goofy boyfriend (Keanu Reeves). Tom Hulce is a prodigal son, constantly in debt from his bad gambling habit, who leans on his elderly father (Jason Robards) to get him out of trouble.

*Parenthood* has some nicely observed details (like the mournful look Robards throws a favorite car he'll never drive again) and some bland homilies (at the end when children are presented as the glue that holds families together). "I liked the picture very much," Newman recalled in the liner notes for the *Guilty* CD box-set. "Considering how important it is to most people, it's unbelievable how few movies examine how difficult it is to be a responsible parent."

For the main title music, as Gil (Steve Martin) and his family walk to the parking lot after a ballgame, Howard decided that he wanted a song. The rest of the movie's score is little more than a mood-altering filler, and Newman's opening tune is terminally bland. In "I Love To See You Smile," Newman returns to the familiar ground of his Metric Music days with another lament for the passing seasons:

> *In the summer*
> *In the springtime*
> *The winter or the fall*
> *The only place I want to be*
> *Is where I can see you smile at me.*

As innocuous as this ragtime shuffle was, "I Love To See You Smile" became one of Newman's most-quoted melodies, appearing in commercials (most notably for Colgate toothpaste), and featured on the short-lived NBC-TV series based on the film. The execrable drama *Milk Money* (1994), where a twelve-year-old kid tries to raise money to buy a hooker (Melanie Griffith) for his father, also used the tune as its opening theme music. Even Homer Simpson gave "I Love To See You Smile" a shot on *The Simpsons Sing the Blues* album.

"The songs I write for movies are less characteristic, because they have to serve the picture," Newman says in defending the composition. "I wouldn't have written 'I was born to make you happy/ I think you're still my style.' [But] I'm glad I did, though." "I Love To See You Smile" does free Newman from the role of untrustworthy narrator. But the problem is the role he inhabits in his movie songs has no character at all. "I put myself in a box," he confesses. "But [with] all this first person stuff, which is the way I've chosen to go exclusively [in my movie songs] . . . I don't have to worry about who I am." "I Love To See You Smile" would be nominated for a Best Original Song Oscar (his second nomination in this category) and Newman would also garner another Best Dramatic Score nomination.

Newman worked with Ron Howard again in the somewhat charming comedy *The Paper* (1994), with Michael Keaton and Glenn Close, an attempt to capture some of the manic humor of classic newspaper films like *His Girl Friday* (1940). Howard's version is a milder, less frantically funny picture about twenty-four hours in the life of a New York City newspaper (based on the *New York Post)*. In the picture, the private lives of the employees come into conflict with the demands of meeting urgent deadlines. The score Newman devised is much more eclectic than the one for *Parenthood*. In the opening credits, against the synthesized ticking of a clock, we hear a percussive pop-jazz arrangement for orchestra and congas that resembles the percolating samba music Henry Mancini originally composed for Orson Welles' *Touch of Evil* (1958). Partway through the arrangement, Newman cleverly uses a synthesizer to approximate the sound of a tapping typewriter. Although it has variety and vibrancy, mixing orchestral passages with R&B and rock, the soundtrack has no more dramatic shape than Newman's score for *Ragtime* did. As with most music for television programs, Newman largely provides filler to patch the story together. The closing credits song, "Make Up Your Mind" (a vast improvement over "I Love To See You Smile"), is a terrific New Orleans R&B shuffle Allen Toussaint would have been proud to produce. Newman's voice (in a duet with Alex Brown) displays a brazen sassiness on lyrics like:

> *Every time things look good*
> *It makes me feel bad*
> *Each time the bird of happiness flies by*
> *Makes me feel so godamned sad*
> *I want to cry,*
> *"Make up your mind!"*

In 1990, TV producer Steven Bochco *(Hill Street Blues)* approached

Newman about contributing some songs for a new ABC police show, *Cop Rock*, which promised something a little different from other police shows. The premise was that all the characters — cops, suspects, lawyers and judges — break spontaneously into song. Newman was intrigued enough to contribute six tunes (still unreleased) to the pilot. The opening theme, "Under the Gun," has some of the raw urgency of "Gone Dead Train" from the *Performance* soundtrack. His first rap song, "In These Streets," preceded "Masterman and Baby J" on *Land of Dreams*. Performed as an ensemble number by a gang, "In These Streets" has some of the nuances Paul Simon attempted on his sublime and largely unheralded *Songs from the Capeman* (1997). "He's Guilty" was performed by a group of jurists and earned an Emmy nomination for Newman. But the strongest song was "Sandman's Coming." Sung to a child by the talented and underappreciated Kathleen Wilhoite, the song is about a mother about to sell her baby to pay for her next fix:

> *It's a great big dirty world*
> *If they say it isn't, they're lyin'*
> *Sandman's coming soon*
> *You know he's coming soon.*

"Sandman's Coming" was later resurrected by Newman for his 1995 musical, *Faust*.

Despite the originality of *Cop Rock,* the show was canceled before the end of its first season. "It just wasn't fated to have an audience," Newman said years later. "You can't take an action thing, and have people singing. The audience wants action." To date, *Cop Rock* remains Newman's last foray into television drama.

### 4

Though Barry Levinson has directed a wide range of material — including *The Natural*, the adventure fantasy *Young Sherlock Holmes* (1985) and the biographical comedy/drama *Good Morning Vietnam* (1987) — he always felt compelled to return to his home turf of Baltimore. Levinson followed *Diner,* which dealt with his own generation of friends, with *Tin Men* (1987), a comedy about his father's generation. In 1990, he decided to retreat even further, to examine his grandfather's generation and how his relatives first came to America. *Avalon* takes place in 1914 just before World War 1, when Levinson's family first immigrated to the United States. In the film, five Jewish brothers from the Krichinsky clan settle in a series of brick row houses, supporting themselves by becoming wallpaper hangers. In time, they raise their kids and become quite successful in their own businesses. Most of the story takes place in the forties, when the children are grown up, the Holocaust is happening in Europe and Jules (Aidan Quinn), the son of family patriarch Sam Krichinsky (Armin Mueller-Stahl), and his cousin Izzy (Kevin Pollak) are house appliance salesmen. *Avalon* dramatizes the contrast between the dreams of the Krichinsky brothers when they first came to America and the radically different modern world their sons inherit.

Levinson's direction here is unfortunately uneven. *Avalon* combines some of the sanctimoniousness of *The Natural* with the finely observed raw humor of *Diner*. Whenever Levinson indulges Sam's lament for the good old days, the film gets tedious and moralizing (television, in Levinson's eyes, is the main culprit in the break-up of the family unit). But he also gets onto the screen some scenes of genuine poignancy. For example, there's a beautifully brittle moment when the brothers argue bitterly about America's random violence after Jules is stabbed by a thief. Jules' wife, Ann (Elizabeth Perkins), is a prickly presence throughout, continuously questioning the views of her husband's parents. Although it's never made clear in the picture, there is a sharp ambivalence at the heart of *Avalon*. Levinson can't resolve the disparity between the fantasy America created by the Jewish immigrants, some of whom became Hollywood moguls, and the real America Levinson grew up in.

For *Avalon*, Newman composed some of the most striking and evocative music he'd written for the screen. Whatever dramatic unity the film has owes much to his ability to create a fluid score. In the opening moments, set on July 4, 1914, as Sam arrives in America, the screen is bathed in the bursting red, white and blue of fireworks. But Newman's score isn't playing ersatz Stephen Foster or Aaron Copland. Instead, he writes a waltz, augmented by a solo piano, that invokes the folk traditions Sam has left behind in the Old World and stands in brilliant contrast to the picture-postcard imagery on screen.

As the family assimilates, Newman subtly weaves more American idioms into the body of his music. Finally, in the end credits, he reprises the waltz, now played by a solo violin. As the story ends, with Sam alone in a nursing home, the tune clearly evokes his first memories of arriving in the new land.

Most of these musical ideas were suggested by Levinson. "Generally, [Newman] would compose after the fact," he recalled. "In this case, with the waltz at the very beginning of the movie, we were somewhere into the middle of the shoot and I called him up. I said, 'Randy, I need some waltz music for the scene when they're getting married, something for them to dance to.' I asked him if he could just knock something out on the piano to use as a temporary track, and that became the main theme." Overall, the score for *Avalon* is subtle, never tugging at our emotions, and yet also lyrical and often moving. In *The Natural,* both the director and composer fell head-first into a sea of sap, but in *Avalon,* with its autobiographical authenticity, perhaps both artists responded to something more substantial. Just two years earlier, Newman had completed *Land of Dreams,* where he had delved into his own family past.

The personal nature of the material may also have moved Levinson to demand more from Newman than he had in their previous effort. Throughout postproduction, Levinson selected musical cues before Newman had even finished the entire score. "He put three other numbers on the tape, so when we began to rough-cut the movie, I ended up putting these against the film in other places," Levinson explains. "In that way the music was fixed early on, which made Randy complain that I'd made things harder for him!" This might help explain why Newman was less than satisfied with the results: he felt the music was mixed so low that you couldn't hear it. "Levinson preferred my music like the sound of grass," he told a Film and TV Music Conference. Despite Levinson's impatience and Newman's irritation, the score gives both the film and the immigrants' aspirations a supple voice.

In 1991, Penny Marshall, whom Newman had met in 1984 as a guest on *The New Show,* asked him to score her new film, *Awakenings,* based on a book by the eccentric and gifted neurologist Oliver Sacks. Once again, however, a powerful dramatic narrative was reduced to a bland, preachy formula. Sacks has a knack for shaping case studies into fascinating essays. In approaching each case, he uses his finely tuned imagination as a springboard to enter the psyche of the person he's writing about. *Awakenings* (1974), a true account, takes place during the spring and summer of 1969, when chronically ill patients who had been in a suspended vegetative state for decades were given what soon looked like a miracle drug. Since some had developed symptoms resembling Parkinson's disease, Sacks decided to give a select number L-dopa, a drug that had the effect of waking them up. Most of the patients were now in middle age, and they were horrified and angry to discover that their whole lives had been "slept away." More upsetting was the fact that, as the effects of the drug began to wear off, they fell back into their stupors. One of Sacks' key subjects was a writer named Leonard who, upon waking, became a charismatic artist with a ribald temperament. Sacks' book is compelling because it's about the sad truth that the imagination can't always bring about miracles. But if Sacks is an eminently inquisitive doctor and writer, Penny Marshall *(Big)* is an imposing director. Her version of *Awakenings*, from a script by Steve Zaillian *(Schindler's List),* is a watered-down and sweetened adaptation that wishes only to believe in miracles. And Newman's score, like his music for *The Natural*, drips with a sanctimony that ultimately helps drown the picture.

Musically, Newman's work on *Awakenings* has a few virtues. The movie begins with a light waltz which echoes the emergence of the disease in Leonard's youth (Robert de Niro plays Leonard as an adult). The delicate melody calls forth childhood songs vaguely remembered, as if they're breaking through the fog of memory. It has the same effect as Elmer Bernstein's lilting theme in the opening of *To Kill a Mockingbird* (1962), where we suddenly enter the childhood memories of Atticus Finch's grown kids. Newman also writes a lovely piano piece for Dexter Gordon called "Dexter's Tune," since his character, Rolando, was once a jazz pianist. But the rest of the score is there to drive Marshall's tugging at the heartstrings. Newman, however, begs to differ with the score's critics. "I think it's about my best score," he remarked proudly, acknowledging the enormous contributions from his orchestrator, Jack Hayes, who had started working with him during *Ragtime*. "I've learned more from him than from anyone else." *Awakenings* garnered a Best Dramatic Score nomination at the Oscars that year.

In 1994, while finishing up Ron Howard's *The Paper*, Newman began work on his first western, Richard Donner's *Maverick*, based on the early sixties TV show about two brothers, Bret and Bart Maverick, nifty gamblers traveling the countryside and getting into trouble. Drawing on a script by William Goldman *(Butch Cassidy and the Sundance Kid),* Donner focuses on Bret Maverick (Mel Gibson), his relationship with Annabelle Bransford (Jodie Foster), another con artist, and aging marshall Zane Cooper (James Garner). The film is filled with cute in-jokes that ultimately render it unbearably precious. Garner, of course, played Bret Maverick on the original TV show, and at one point, a bank is held up by a robber played by Danny Glover, Gibson's detective partner in Donner's *Lethal Weapon* films. To ensure that we get the joke, Donner even has Gibson and Glover seem to recognize each other, with Glover repeating his signature line from *Lethal Weapon:* "I'm too old for this shit."

*Maverick* is shot by the peerless Vilmos Zsigmond *(McCabe and Mrs. Miller, Close Encounters of the Third Kind),* which gives the film a grandeur the story can't begin to match. *Maverick* is the ultimate story of the confidence man, made by people who are too earnest to get a kick out of all the scams. And Gibson, charming as he is, is neither daring nor even very interesting. Foster is funnier and more radiant than she'd ever been previously, and James Garner gives an assured performance, but we end up wanting more of him than we actually get. Despite their age difference, the better — and sexier — love match would have between Foster and Garner. In hindsight, the picture might have been more fun, with more at stake, if Garner had played Bret as an aging gambler, wiser yet still foolhardy.

Newman's score shows some of the same eclecticism he demonstrated in *The Paper,* with a mixture of ragtime, banjo music and orchestrated Appalachian folk idioms. At times it resembles his uncle Alfred's score for *How the West Was Won* (1962) or Bernard Herrmann's sprawling tribute to Americana in *The Kentuckian* (1955). The score is lively and bright even if the film is flat and predictable. But *Maverick* became something of a nightmare for Newman. The moviemakers wanted him to add a banjo to just about every theme, and use the trumpets for "wah-wah" effects in every visual gag. "Directors keep asking for funnier music," Newman sighs. "What is funny music, anyway? I could stick the baton up someone's ass while we were playing, and then at least the orchestra would laugh. . . . The problem is the directors have contempt for the audience. They think they'll never get anything subtle, that it has to be spelled out in simplistic terms. I keep saying that these audiences may not know algebra, but they know movies." Newman did get to add one tune that showed signs of his cleverness called "Tartine de Merde." "I saw [it] as source music in a saloon," he explained. "Some guy singing a medley of his hits. It's afternoon. I tried to get the director and his film editor to add applause, as if each time he went into a new tune they recognized it. The music would be so far down, you really wouldn't notice. It isn't important, but from a showbiz standpoint I love the idea of a guy doing an afternoon saloon tour." Newman also composed a decent country song for the end credits, "Ride Cowboy Ride," with roots in standards like "Lily of the West." Once again, though, it was Newman's dramatic score that received the Oscar nomination.

If *Maverick* was a headache for Newman, his experience scoring Nora Ephron's mystic comic parable, *Michael* (1996), was a complete pain in the ass. Ephron *(Sleepless in Seattle, You've Got Mail)* tells the story of two cynical tabloid reporters (William Hurt, Robert Pastorelli) and an "expert" on angels (Andie McDowell), who follow up a claim by a ditzy old woman (Jean Stapleton) that she has an archangel named Michael (John Travolta) living on her premises. Michael isn't your garden variety angel with a sweet disposition. He smokes, drinks beer, is rather sodden and loves to pick up girls. The story follows these agnostic reporters as they find their faith in the supernatural, while Hurt discovers true love with McDowell. The tune "Feels Like Home," sung by Bonnie Raitt and appearing just before Hurt goes to bed with McDowell, had already been used in Newman's musical, *Faust*. By bringing together these two love-birds, Michael's ill-spent time on Earth is redeemed. Although Ephron seems to get by with her dubious musings on the nature of romance, as in the creepy stalker comedy *Sleepless in Seattle* (1993), she shows no special gift here for the ethereal. *Michael* is a leaden piece of whimsy that falls back on the kind of fake wisdom favored by Hallmark Cards: "You gotta learn to laugh," one character explains. "It's the way to true love." Similarly, when Michael tries to pick up two girls in a bar, he asks Pastorelli, "Remember what John and Paul said?" Pastorelli responds, "The Apostles?" "No," Michael explains. "The Beatles. All you need is love." Throughout the picture, Michael is seen pouring a heaping spoonful of sugar on his food. The analogy to Ephron's script is obvious.

The music Newman wrote for *Michael*, fortunately, isn't syrupy, it's just indistinct. Some of his orchestral arrangements cleverly mix melodies from gospel standards like "Old Time Religion" and "Let Us Gather at the River." But once Newman finished the score, Ephron told him she didn't like classical music. "I wish I'd known that," he later mused. "I was using an orchestra [whereas] I would have used a skiffle band." Like Donner on *Maverick*, Ephron wanted the music to be constantly funny — especially in a scene where Michael brings a dog back from the dead. Newman spent a week trying to get the music for that scene right. "It's not a comedy, I mean, it's not Monty Python," he explained. "So I had to get in this religioso mode, when what I was really thinking was, 'You're an angel and this is what you do? Bring a dog back from the dead?'" Ephron also drove Newman crazy with her infatuation with "temp tracks," temporary music cues (usually borrowed from other sources) that are used only until the composer finishes the original score. On *Michael*, Ephron ended up using so many that Newman's work was barely in evidence. In only one scene did Ephron ask Newman to change the style of the music. "There's a key part in *Michael* where the angel is coming down the stairs," he told James Foley. "I wrote an inspiring piece, but the director didn't like it, wanting it funnier, so I lightened it up. They still didn't like it, and I ended up putting in farting tubas."

One of the few things Newman did enjoy on this project was recording a lovely duet with Valerie Carter. "Heaven Is My Home," complete with angelic choirs, has a gospel flavor — even if the lyrics are something less than inspired: "Spirits all around you everywhere/ You've got to open up your heart." The next year, Newman and Carter teamed up again to record a touching rendition of the late Lowell George's surreal love song "Sailin' Shoes" for the tribute album *Rock & Roll Doctor*.

In 1997, Newman faced an indignity every composer in Hollywood has experienced — he was dumped from a picture. He had written music for the Wolfgang Peterson political thriller *Air Force One*, in which Harrison Ford plays a kidnapped President of the United States, but his score was hijacked a mere eight weeks before the picture was supposed to open. Apparently Peterson felt Newman's score was too slam-bang (an odd accusation given the fever pitch of his melodrama).

Newman was replaced by veteran colleague Jerry Goldsmith, who polished off his contribution in four and a half weeks.

Despite some rough patches with directors, that year Newman would be awarded the inaugural Henry Mancini Award for lifetime achievement in film composing. It was a busy year for Newman: he'd also contributed songs to the live production of *Cats Don't Dance*. With his success as a Hollywood composer growing, Newman now started drawing the attention of Disney.

5

In his *Memoirs of a Useless Man,* the Venetian dramatist Carlo Gozzi said that "dramatic fables" should contain "the great magic of seduction that creates an enchanted illusion of making the impossible appear as truth to the mind and spirit of the spectators." This idea probably best describes the ultimate goal of animation. Even more than dramatic realism, the cartoon demands a suspension of disbelief. And if music is essential to movie drama, it is no less a significant component in animation. As Roy Prendergast accurately pointed out in *Film Music: A Neglected Art,* the element of exaggeration in cartoons already had its antecedent in the eighteenth-century comic operas of Carlo Gozzi and others (like Mozart). The rapid, almost frantic rhythm of *opera buffa* demanded that the music keep pace with the action. This is no less true of animation. Most North American animators looked to the twentieth-century neoclassic style already heard in contemporary artists like Igor Stravinsky, rather than the nineteenth-century romanticism preferred by most Hollywood composers. "In dramatic films of the 1930s and '40s the chromaticism of the nineteenth century was appropriate because of the music's tendency to de-emphasize small-scale musical events, thereby drawing the listener's attention to a larger sense of movement," Prendergast writes. "Cartoons, on the other hand, are usually nothing less than frantic movement consisting of a series of small-scale events, and the music in cartoons plays at least an equal role with the animation and story in establishing the humorous success of events."

In the thirties, the Walt Disney Studios, with their emphasis on the smooth, cultivated style of drawing, had little interest in twentieth century neoclassicism, instead cribbing their soundtracks mostly from the standard repertoire. For example, *The Opry House* featured a Rachmaninoff prelude, while Grieg's "March of the Dwarfs" from *Peer Gynt* turned up in one of their later *Silly Symphonies*. The feature film *Fantasia* (1940) was a desperately commercial attempt by Disney to, as Pauline Kael put it, "combine high art and mass culture." Here, animators merely designed visuals to accompany famous pieces of music. Conducted by Leopold Stokowski, *Fantasia* featured diverse compositions, from Bach's *Toccata and Fugue in D Minor* to Tchaikovsky's *Nutcracker Suite,* accompanying such images as volcanoes erupting and dinosaurs battling. Beethoven's *Pastoral* was even used as the backdrop for female centaurs frolicking like happy peasants. Stravinsky's *The Rite of Spring* was the film's one concession to twentieth-century music. As Kael observed, Disney became the precursor "of the musical processing in [Kubrick's] *2001*." In Disney animated features like *Snow White and the Seven Dwarfs* (1937), *Pinocchio* (1940), *Dumbo* (1941) and *Bambi* (1942), right up to the present day's *Beauty and the Beast* (1991), *Aladdin* (1992) and *The Lion King* (1994), the studio turned away from the practice of pilfering classical scores, and looked more to the tradition of the Broadway musical.

Warner Brothers brought onboard a composer with a completely different approach. Carl Stalling wrote some of the most outrageously impudent material heard this side of Spike Jones. Thanks to Stalling, it wasn't unusual in a Looney Tunes or a Merrie Melodies cartoon to hear a happy collision of bassoons, trombone slides, *mysterioso* strings, violin glissandos and his memorable *"boinnngg!"* sound created on the electric guitar. Together, these instruments created a bold, anarchic sound for some of the wittiest and purest examples of American absurdism. Stalling was born in Lexington, Missouri, in 1898, and his earliest introduction to music was improvising tunes on a toy piano. He fell in love with the movies as a five-year-old, after he saw a screening of *The Great Train Robbery*. By the time he was twelve, he was combining his two passions by playing piano in the local theatre. During the twenties, Stalling conducted his own orchestra in the pit at Kansas City's Isis Theatre. It was there that he met Walt Disney, who offered him a couple of assignments — starring Mickey Mouse. Stalling was so successful at musically enhancing these shorts, Disney brought him to his newly formed studio in Hollywood where Stalling created one of his most famous pieces, the highly imaginative "skeleton dance," used in the first of Disney's many *Silly Symphonies*.

By 1930, Stalling grew restless at Disney and moved to other small animation studios. In 1936, he arrived at Warner Brothers, where a madly inspired team of animators — Bob Clampett, Chuck Jones and Fritz Freleng — were putting together a collection of wiseass animated characters including Bugs Bunny, Daffy Duck, Elmer Fudd and Porky Pig. For twenty-two years, until his retirement in 1958, Stalling was a dissonant jukebox that could play just about every American musical idiom ever invented. Rather than simply raid the classical repertoire, as Disney did to cut costs, Stalling sought out popular songs that Warners could purchase. His idea of popular, though, included ridiculously odd ditties like Raymond Scott's "Dinner Music For a Pack of Hungry Cannibals," or "How Dry I Am?" which he forever linked in our imagination to states of inebriation.

"Set against the historical happenings in American music in the thirties and forties, Stalling's achievements become even more impressive," composer John Zorn wrote in a 1990 appraisal. "Copland's pantonality; [John] Cage beginning to explore the sonic possibilities of the prepared piano with quiet, Satie-inspired music; [Harry] Partch freaking out and building his own instruments based on his own forty-six-tone tuning theories; [Duke] Ellington balancing improvisation and composition with his swinging, harmonically lush big band . . . it was a period of basically conservative American impressionism invaded by the search for new sonic resources."

By the time Randy Newman was approached by Disney to score their animated film *Toy Story* (1995), he had made it pretty clear he wasn't the next Carl Stalling. Newman hewed much closer to the romantic past. Yet Stalling's influence on the cartoon world was unavoidable, and Newman found a way to bridge his wild antics to the more conventional sound Newman had used in his other scores. As he started writing, Newman also began to understand some of the dissimilarities between the worlds of animation and drama. "It's not a huge difference, but the primary difference is that the movement of the characters generally indicates that you've got to do some moving yourself," he explains. In other words, if Michael Keaton falls down in *The Paper*, the score doesn't make "ba-dum-dum" noises. If a character in *Toy Story* does, however, he would likely go "ba-dum-dum." Newman couldn't have picked a better time to score an animated film at Disney, either, thanks to the creative minds at Pixar Animation Studio. Generally speaking, Warner Brothers were perceived as the radical revolutionaries in animation, whereas Disney represented the status quo. But when computer-generated animation — and Newman — came along that line began to blur. Pixar, named after a special graphics computer, combined some of the cutting humor of Warners with the clean, classical animation that defined the Disney aesthetic.

Pixar began as the brainchild of a group of computer graphics experts — Bill Reeves, Alvy Ray Smith and John Lasseter at Lucasfilm. In the mid-eighties, they began to see the computer as a tool for freeing the movement of the animated characters, so they could expand the principles of acting, staging and comic timing in cartoons. Their first animated short, *The Adventures of Andre and Wally B* (1984), featured Andre, a goggle-eyed character with Mickey Mouse hands and a cherub nose, trying to outmaneuver a huge bee. Although their character creations successfully replicated the more traditional hand drawings, they failed to make Andre and Wally B into more than slickly drawn puppets. They were still working out the bugs when George Lucas decided to drop computer graphics, because of the huge expense in time and money. Steve Jobs, cofounder and former (and future) chairman of Apple Computers, bought the controlling interest in Pixar, allowing the trio to continue experimenting. In 1986, they had their first major breakthrough with the short *Luxo Jr.*, directed by Lasseter and Reeves. The piece was just over a minute and a half long and featured two desk lamps — a father and son — tossing a ball back and forth. Through the computer's elegant recreation of motion in the lamps, they were able to establish the emotional bonds between parent and child. *Luxo Jr.* earned Pixar an Academy Award nomination. In 1988, *Tin Toy*, about a tin percussionist who confronts a big, bad slobbering baby, earned Pixar their second Academy Award nomination. Soon Lasseter was considering the possibilities of making a computer-generated animated feature.

In May 1991, Pixar entered into a feature film agreement with Walt Disney Pictures to develop and produce up to three computer-generated animated films, which Disney would then market and distribute. Their first, *Toy Story*, was about a group of toys owned by a suburban boy, Andy, that walked and talked whenever their owner wasn't present. Woody (Tom Hanks) was a cowboy sheriff who began to feel threatened whenever Andy got a new toy for his birthday — this time, a space hero named Buzz Lightyear (Tim Allen). When Woody attempts to eliminate Buzz so he can have Andy to himself, Buzz inadvertently goes missing. The other toys, appalled by Woody's behavior, take umbrage. Woody is then forced to redeem himself by finding Buzz. Unfortunately it's Sid, a young neighborhood sadist who dismantles toys for the sheer merriment of it, who finds Buzz first. By rescuing him, Woody earns the respect of the others and finds a new friend. But Woody and Buzz aren't the whole show. The toys make up a wonderfully motley collection that includes Rex (Wallace Shawn), a neurotic dinosaur; Mr. Potato Head (Don Rickles); Slinky Dog (Jim Varney) and Little Bo Peep (Annie Potts), who is somewhat saucier than her attire would suggest. There's even an Etch A Sketch who plays a part in a nifty joke. As Woody pulls his gun, the Etch A Sketch twirls its knobs: they *draw*.

Director John Lasseter likely believed that if Elton John could be swayed by Disney for *The Lion King*, Newman could be convinced to do *Toy Story*. Newman liked the script but didn't figure the film would be much of a hit. For one thing, by the time John Lasseter hired him, the script had already undergone a complete overhaul. Disney executives were nervous that children weren't going to identify with an insecure cowboy or cheer a boastful action hero in a space suit. Watching the rushes, though, the executives became completely enthralled.

Newman worked out appropriate themes on the piano before assembling a ninety-five-piece orchestra at Culver City, California. In nine weeks, he recorded three songs, a duet and a playful score that fully captured both the comical and the emotionally stirring passages in the film. "For me, probably the funniest part of making these movies is when we're at the scoring stage and Randy's up in front of the [95-piece] orchestra," Lasseter recalled. "We go out and stand among the orchestra while he's performing, and it brings absolute chills every single time. He just gets it. He understood what we were trying to achieve."

To open the film and establish one of the themes, the relationship between kids and their favorite playthings, Newman wrote the affable tune, "You've Got a Friend in Me":

> *You've got a friend in me*
> *When the road looks rough ahead*

*And you're miles and miles*
*From your nice warm bed*
*Just remember what your old pal said*
*Boy, you've got a friend in me.*

Although the song is hardly essential Newman, it isn't emotionally fake, like the music for *The Natural, Awakenings* or a song like "I Love To See You Smile." *Toy Story* has a hipper style and a sometimes darker outlook than other animated features. Sid's surgical experiments, for example, are about as chilling as the stalking zombies in *Night of the Living Dead* (1969). Newman's work in *Toy Story* is both imaginative and pleasant. "I think every time I do a picture like *Toy Story* . . . it takes me places melodically and harmonically that I wouldn't ordinarily go," he explained to Douglas Bell. "I wouldn't normally be as friendly and cuddly as I am [when writing for Disney]. . . . I think it makes my song-writing better."

Newman performed a lovely duet of "You've Got a Friend in Me" with Lyle Lovett over the closing credits. Another *Toy Story* song was a track for Buzz, "I Will Go Sailing No More," in which the space ranger discovers he is only a toy. In the song, Newman captures some of the same pensiveness found in "Texas Girl at the Funeral of Her Father" from *Little Criminals* (the sailing motif is also present in both), and provides a witty touch when he briefly quotes Jerry Goldsmith's trumpet reverie from his main title music for *Patton* (1970). *Toy Story* became the first animated film to receive an Academy Award nomination for Best Screenplay (Joss Whedon, Andrew Stanton, Joel Coen and Alec Sokolow). It earned for Newman yet another Oscar nomination for Best Original Score and Best Song ("You've Got a Friend in Me"). *Toy Story* also received a Golden Globe nomination for Best Picture, and at the animation industry's 1996 Annie Awards won all eight top motion picture honors, including Best Score for Newman.

Disney Studios came knocking at Newman's door again in 1996 to ask him to score an animated feature based on Roald Dahl's children's book *James and the Giant Peach*. Seemingly an odd choice for Disney, Dahl is a British writer famous for his macabre wit and Dickensian sensibility when it came to issues of adult cruelty to kids and the grotesque imaginations of children. Dahl's books became as famous for outraging adult critics as they did for fascinating children. "Parents and schoolteachers are the enemy," he once said. "The adult is the enemy of the child because of the awful process of civilizing this thing that when it is born is an animal with no manners, no moral sense at all." This dynamic is played out in a number of Dahl's books, including *Witches* (1973), where a young boy spending his summer at a holiday resort discovers it is hosting a convention of witches; and *Matilda* (1988), about a girl from a loathsome family who learns self-reliance by tapping into the secret powers she possesses.

*James and the Giant Peach,* which Dahl wrote in 1961, deals with an orphan named James who lives with two repulsive aunts and discovers a magical giant peach filled with various creatures who help him escape to New York. The director of the film, Henry Selick, whose taste is not unlike Dahl's, had already directed the wonderfully bizarre Tim Burton production of *The Nightmare before Christmas* (1993). "I think there's something about Roald Dahl that will always be timeless with kids," Selick theorizes. "It's about kids solving problems. It's about them overcoming odds with a lot of humor, and a lot of invention."

There is a fair bit of both in Selick's adaptation. By combining live action drama and stop-motion animation, he enhances the hyperbole of the original story. Unfortunately, the visual design is not quite as imaginative as one would hope for. *James and the Giant Peach* is strangely earthbound and poorly staged compared to *The Nightmare before Christmas.* The cast, however, compensates somewhat for the visual weaknesses. Paul Terry is agreeable both playing James as a real person and voicing his animated self. His two aunts, Sponge (Miriam Margolyes) and Spiker (Joanna Lumley), are wonderfully inspired comic grotesques, and Pete Postlethwaite is the magic stranger who rescues James by introducing him to the wonders of the peach. Within the fruit, James discovers a spritzing centipede (Richard Dreyfus), a gentleman grasshopper (Simon Callow) with the pompous air of Sir Cedric Hardwicke, a sultry spider (Susan Sarandon), a solicitous ladybug (Jane Leeves) and a desperately troubled earthworm (David Thewlis).

For the score, Newman wrote a number of tunes based on the Roald Dahl lyrics in the book. Perhaps because the story has its roots in Dickens, he composed and arranged in the style of Lionel Bart's score for the Broadway musical *Oliver!* While the songs neatly fit the cadence of Dahl's words, the music is often too conventional for the outlandishness of the story. (Newman's piano demos, some featured on the *Guilty* CD box-set, are a touch more affecting.) In some cases, Newman altered the lyrics to express a more American colloquialism. One example is "Eating the Peach," when all the creatures start devouring the very vessel in which they're riding to New York. In Dahl's original words, the song captures an inkling of Edward Lear's nonsense rhymes:

> *I'm mad for crispy wasp-stings*
> *On a buttered piece of toast*
> *And pickled spines of porcupines*
> *And then a gorgeous roast*
> *Of dragon's flesh, well hung, not fresh.*

Newman's alterations reveal an approach that is distinctly American:

> *I'm crazy 'bout mosquitos*
> *On a piece of buttered toast*
> *And pickled spines of porcupines*
> *And then a great big roast*
> *And dragon's flesh, quite old, not fresh.*

*James and the Giant Peach* isn't a bad movie, but it doesn't reach the epiphanies that one hopes for, either. The score, however, was nominated for an Oscar.

In 1998, Dreamworks released a computer-animated feature called *Antz*, about a neurotic ant named Z (Woody Allen) who has problems conforming to the collective thinking of his colony. *Antz* is essentially a computer-generated animated Woody Allen comedy. It features Sylvester Stallone (who had a bit part as a subway hoodlum in Allen's *Bananas* back in 1971) as Z's macho buddy. Pixar decided to respond with a bug movie of their own. *A Bug's Life* bore some resemblance to the plot for *Antz*, but the computer-generated animation in *A Bug's Life* is more sophisticated and the humor much broader. Flik (Dave Foley) is a misfit ant who's always trying to impress Princess Atta (Julia Louis-Dreyfus), but he continually fails to do anything but draw her wrath. The ant colony is constantly under siege by a grasshopper collective lead by the fascistic Hopper (Kevin Spacey). Besides gathering food for themselves, the ants are forced to satisfy Hopper's clan as well. When Flik accidentally loses the grasshopper stash, he sets out to find help in saving the ants from the wrath of the grasshoppers. He recruits what he believes to be a group of warrior bugs in a bar, only to discover they are an inept and disenchanted circus troupe.

*A Bug's Life* is a screwball comedy with a completely goofy congregation of insects. Denis Leary voices Francis, the ladybug in search of his masculine side. David Hyde Pierce is a stick insect obsessed with having a more substantial frame. Madeline Kahn, in one of her last roles, is an inspiring choice to voice the Gypsy Moth and Dave Foley's Flik is much more appealing than Allen's Z. While both are misfits, Flik is more resourceful; Z is a masochist always retreating to the safety of helplessness. Spacey makes a great villain, too, playing Hopper like he's a Hell's Angel. He's matched by his obsequious brother, Molt, voiced by the desperately funny Richard Kind. And Newman's score is boisterously funny and unabashedly romantic, successfully conjuring up the mood and spirit of Erich Korngold's *Captain Blood* (1935).

If the Pixar films don't provide Newman the opportunity to use fully the sardonic humor of his pop albums, they've still allowed for some clever and witty musical ideas. "In some of the scores I've done, there are sort of old-fashioned kind of romantic scores, like *Awakenings* or *Avalon*, that's what they're supposed to be," Newman told Scott Jordan of *Offbeat Magazine*. "In a picture like *A Bug's Life*, where it isn't there, and it's a big action picture, I can do [left-of-center stuff]." In *A Bug's Life*, Newman balances the two styles quite successfully. Since the writing and overall conception of Pixar's films are predominantly quirky as well as romantic, they provide Newman with a more spacious canvas to work with. *The Natural* and *Awakenings*, by contrast, exist only to manipulate the emotions of the audience by providing moral uplift. *A Bug's Life* was chosen as a Favorite Family Film by the Blockbuster Entertainment Awards in 1999, while Newman's work on the film won him a Grammy Award for Best Instrumental Composition Written for a Motion Picture.

If *Toy Story* (1999) was a comedy about the relationship between children and their toys, *Toy Story 2* is about what happens when kids outgrow them. In the second picture, Woody (Tom Hanks) has been kidnapped by a rare-toy dealer who matches him to a collection marketed on an old TV show (loosely based on *Howdy Doody)*. The set includes Jessie the Cowgirl (Joan Cusack) and Stinky Pete the Prospector (Kelsey Grammer). The dealer intends to sell them to an eager buyer in Japan, but Woody wants to get home to Andy. While Andy is at summer camp, his toy collection (including Buzz Lightyear) sets out to rescue Woody. What gives *Toy Story 2* an added keenness is that Jessie, too, was once treasured by a child named Emily, only to be discarded when Emily grew up. Her plight is rendered movingly in the Newman song "When She Loved Me," sung by Sarah McLachlan:

> *I was left alone*
> *Still I waited for the day*
> *When she'd say*
> *I will always love you.*

*Toy Story 2* includes a number of other intriguing ideas as well. In one scene, Buzz Lightyear plays a video game based on his character. The adult toy dealer is deliberately made to resemble a kid whose attachment to toys is no longer emotional; for him, toys have become strictly commodities. When Woody loses his arm in an accident, you sense how acutely fragile toys really are — especially as they age — which allows the picture to touch on issues of mortality. As entertaining as *Toy Story 2* is, it makes you much more aware of the delicate relationship between children and their inanimate friends. As in *A Bug's Life*, Newman gives *Toy Story 2* as varied a score as any animated film has ever had. In the opening credits, as Buzz works the video game, Newman does playful variations on John Williams' *Star Wars* themes and Strauss' *Also Sprach Zarathustra* (from Kubrick's *2001*). When Andy's toys meet up with a Barbie collection in Al's Toy Barn, Newman cleverly incorporates a few bars from the Safaris' surfing hit, "Wipeout."

For the end credits, Newman invited Robert Goulet to cover "You've Got a Friend in Me" for the soundtrack. When Newman sent the singer the music from the first film, Goulet complained that the CD performance of the song wasn't the same as the version in the film. Newman responded by saying he was being goofy in the film in order to be more in character. Goulet asked if he might do the same, and Newman initially agreed — until he heard the performance. Goulet is a singer with pitch-perfect Broadway precision, but he became wildly exuberant and nutty as the sixty-piece orchestra sawed away behind him. Newman yelled, "Cut!" When Goulet argued, "You told me I could get sloppy," Newman retorted, "I've changed my mind." In 1996, a country tribute to Disney songs featured a charming duet between George Jones and Kathy Mattean on "You've Got a Friend in Me." After the success of the roots soundtrack for the Coen brothers' *Oh Brother Where Art Thou?* (2002), another tribute to Disney songs in the same style, *Oh Mickey Where Art Thou?*, was released in 2003. It featured a fetching bluegrass version of "You've Got a Friend in Me," by Amanda Martin and Lyle Goodman.

"When She Loved Me" not only earned an Oscar nomination, but won a Grammy. As for *Toy Story 2*, it would go on to win the Golden Globe for Best Comedy Picture, making it the first computer-generated animated feature film to step out of its genre and be judged on a par with live-action features. Newman has since gone on to score other animated films. He contributed the song "That'll Do" (sung by Peter Gabriel) for the wonderful sequel *Babe: Pig in the City* (1998), then scored Pixar's *Monster's Inc.* (2001), which won for him his first Academy Award for Best Original Song, "If I Didn't Have You." Although he missed out on *Finding Nemo* (2003), Newman has been called on again to score Pixar's upcoming feature, *Cars* (2005).

When Carl Stalling retired in 1958, he despaired over the state of the art of scoring for animated pictures. "One trouble with cartoons today," he remarked shortly before his death, "is that they have so much dialogue the music doesn't mean much." Newman, a composer famous for writing songs around dramatic ideas, understands the value of dialogue and how music can enhance it. His sense of drama and satire in his music for Pixar not only puts the lie to Stalling's pessimistic outlook, but ultimately does his best hopes proud.

6

In 1999, Randy Newman made Oscar history when he received nominations for his work on three different pictures: *A Bug's Life* (nominated for Best Original Score), *Babe: Pig in the City* for "That'll Do" and *Pleasantville* (also nominated for Best Original Score). The choice of *Pleasantville* was an intriguing one. "What attracted me to the story was that it was about television, which occupies about five hours [a day] of the average American's time," Newman explained. "[Yet] it's the subject of almost no movie that's ever been made." If you discount the moralistic ranting of *Network* (1976), he's probably right. However, there's more at work in *Pleasantville* than a focus on television viewing habits. Although not entirely successful, *Pleasantville*, written and directed by Gary Ross, examines a number of particularly American themes that would unquestionably attract Newman. On a superficial level, it performs a rather bland civics lesson (think of an extended episode of *The Twilight Zone*) contrasting the banality of fifties suburban TV dramas like *Father Knows Best* and *Leave It to Beaver* with the realities of the present day.

Brother and sister David (Tobey Maguire) and Jen (Reese Witherspoon) are the children of divorced parents in the suburbs. While Jen acts out her rebellion by playing the role of the coolest chick around, David longs for the conservative family values expressed on his favorite retrograde television program, *Pleasantville*. One night, with the help of a wizardly TV repairman (Don Knotts), they fall into their television set and into the *Pleasantville* show, becoming "Bud" and "Betty Sue," the son and daughter of George (William H. Macy) and Betty Parker (Joan Allen). Besides being totally in black and white, the world they've entered seems like an idyllic American smalltown. On first glance, it might be the borough of Sam Wood's *King's Row* (1942), except Robert Cummings isn't around to discover Freud and Ronald Reagan isn't getting his legs amputated by a psychopathic doctor played by Charles Coburn. You could even confuse Pleasantville with the Lumberton of David Lynch's *Blue Velvet* (1986), only there's no virginal innocent like Kyle MacLachlan hiding in sultry Isabella Rosselini's closet or Dennis Hopper shouting menacingly that he'll fuck anything that moves. *Pleasantville* isn't a satiric drama about the darker underside of the white picket fence American town. Folks who live in Pleasantville, where sex and violence are as absent as rain, think it's paradise.

Rather than go for a dichotomy between the "fake" and the "real" America, as in *King's Row, Blue Velvet* and other lesser films, *Pleasantville* tries another perspective. David feels right at home in the bosom of his new loving parents — the comfort of a family circle he's never truly known. At first, Jen is aghast at the blandness all around her and desperate to leave. However, when she introduces one of the boys from school to sex, Pleasantville slowly begins to change from black and white to color. The town also transforms into a contentious place where art, music and politics evolve into a living history that changes the lives of everyone — including David and Jen — in unexpected ways. Greil Marcus may well have seized upon the most interesting aspect of *Pleasantville* in a review he wrote for *Esquire*. "The film means to prove that America always contains a secret country, a zombie second self — and that zombie America can be overthrown, in this case with sex and art," Marcus wrote. "It's a fairy tale, but it's not as if it isn't a fairy tale that has already been lived."

Marcus refers to this fairy tale as the "pod" America, the conformist America of the fifties, explored and satirized in black and white with *Invasion of the Body Snatchers* (1956). As Marcus explains it, if *Invasion of the Body Snatchers* is about the horror of how an insipid homogeneity swept America while it was (literally) napping, what happens in *Pleasantville* is the reverse. It's about a "pod" America that's suddenly brought back to colorful life. What's more, in *Pleasantville*, we see an America full of disguises, where masks become metaphors and the quaint America created by Louis B. Mayer and Irving Thalberg is undermined by the vibrant, sometimes frightening one hidden away. This idea is likely what appealed to Randy Newman.

Although this theme is spelled out a little too blatantly in the film, it still manages to reverberate. Brief glimpses of a remembered authentic America burst through the movie's lustrous sheen. The attack by the black and white people on the newly created "coloreds" conjures up every Civil Rights march from Selma to Little Rock. Listening once again to Etta James singing "At Last" just as the teenagers start to discover the joys of sex, you can hear a sigh of satisfaction in her voice that sounds as if it took centuries to be expressed. Dave Brubeck's "Take Five," hardly a startling piece of jazz today, jumps out of the mix with a whole new freshness while eager kids gather at the soda shop. When the opening notes of Miles Davis' "So What" and Buddy Holly's "Rave On" are heard, they don't invoke pangs of nostalgia the way such songs usually do in period films. It's the reverse in *Pleasantville* — you hear them as if it's for the first time, and the music has you looking ahead rather than looking back.

Newman has described his *Pleasantville* score as "wallpaper," but there's more going on in it than he suggests. For starters, it mixes a number of American musical styles smartly and subtly. For most of the black-and-white scenes of families living chaste lives, he uses an eerie tango arrangement, suggesting a ritual dance that's been acted out through the ages. When fire trucks arrive to rescue a cat from a tree, Newman gently lays on the pastoral sound of Copland. On the arrival of Skip Martin, the captain of the basketball team whom Jen introduces to the birds and bees, Newman quietly quotes from the slick, sexy sound of Max Steiner's *A Summer Place* (1959). Most of Newman's artistic life has been concerned with bold attempts to explore the intricacies of the American mask. *Pleasantville* is one of the only movies where he was allowed to address these contradictions, and he does so with vision and enthusiasm.

Newman's next project, *Meet the Parents* (2000), also appeared ideally suited to his temperament. An absurd comedy about an outsider who tries desperately to be accepted, it ultimately betrays its subject by neatly resolving the problem. The outsider, a Jewish nurse in love with a blond WASP, is played by Ben Stiller. Stiller has described his character as "not comfortable in . . . [a] WASPy, Middle American, perfect community. My character is urban, he's intellectual . . . he's circumcised." What's fascinating about Stiller's Jewish angst is that, unlike Woody Allen or Albert Brooks, he isn't motivated by self-hatred or self-deprecation. Stiller doesn't seem anxious about whether he's accepted by Waspy middle America. His humor comes from profound disbelief: he can't understand how anyone, of any culture, could ever consider rejecting him — circumcised or not. The obsessive oddball he plays in *Flirting with Disaster* (1996), for example, only wants to find his real parents, but ends up stunned by the familial chaos he unleashes around him. His forlorn Ted Stroehmann in *There's Something About Mary* (1998) is truly surprised to find himself the reluctant stalker of a loved one. In other words, Stiller doesn't play misfits looking to conform — they believe that the world is going to come around to their way of seeing things. In the case of *Meet the Parents*, at the very least, his character hopes his loved one's parents will.

Stiller's Greg Focker is deeply in love with his girlfriend Pam (Teri Polo) and wants to marry her. But before Greg can propose, Pam finds out her younger sister has announced *her* engagement. He figures that the easiest way to winning Pam's hand lies in spending a weekend with her picture-perfect family and showing them he's the right guy for their daughter. Of course, it all goes completely awry. Pam's formidable father, Jack (Robert De Niro), doesn't think a male nurse with a vulgar-sounding last name is good enough for his first-born. And if that isn't bad enough, Jack is an ex-CIA agent. *Meet the Parents* has a promising premise, but director Jay Roach (who did *Austin Powers: The Spy Who Shagged Me)* never develops the animosity between Jack and Greg beyond the obvious Oedipal rivalry. And since Roach has no real gift for developing the arc of a comedy, he simply strings together gags, as in a television sitcom. The movie audience becomes the laugh track.

Newman's score ends up being a secondary laugh track. The opening credit song, "A Fool in Love," however, has a cute beginning, in which the lyrics are sung in the style of the Ray Conniff singers, commenting on the Dreamworks logo on the screen ("Look at the light coming out of the Earth!/ Look at that boy, sitting on a log!/ Oh, how exciting!"). Unfortunately, the rest of the tune fails to live up to that clever bit of raillery ("When you're a fool in love/ You'll be a fool till the day you die"). If the score proved to be innocuous, there was still the pleasure of hearing Newman perform Fats Domino's "Poor Me" and Muddy Waters' "I've Got My Mojo Working." Newman earned a Best Song nomination for "A Fool in Love" at the 2001 Academy Awards, but lost to Bob Dylan's superior "Things Have Changed," from Curtis Hanson's *Wonder Boys*. Newman also scored the sequel, *Meet the Fockers* (2004), in which Pam's parents meet Greg's (played by Dustin Hoffman and Barbra Streisand).

By 2000, Newman had gained more acclaim through his movie work than he ever had as a pop songwriter. That year alone, he received the Century Award from *Billboard Magazine* in Las Vegas, and the Frederick Lowe Achievement Award at the 12th Annual Nortel Networks Palm Springs International Film Festival in Palm Springs, California. Along with his cousins, Thomas and David, Randy was now assuring for the Newman family a new dynasty in Hollywood. A Newman film score had now been heard in every decade since the thirties.

"The disturbing thing about my whole career is that I know more about this arcane film music than I do about rock music," he once remarked. Despite successfully extending the legacy inherited from his uncle Alfred, Newman had spent much of two decades hidden behind a celluloid mask. His claim, of course, is that it has made his songwriting better. "Probably the reason I now like writing songs, besides the fact that I've lowered my standards, is that I've been doing a lot of film music," he stated with trademark irony in the liner notes to *Guilty: 30 Years of Randy Newman*. Despite the varied nature of his many scores, this particular disguise has afforded Newman limited possibilities.

Becoming a film composer offered Newman more than just financial security, it allowed him the opportunity — and the safety — of reaching a mass audience without having to sacrifice himself in the process. He'd learned from his uncles and his cousins that in Hollywood, film composers perform a disappearing act; they're an anonymous presence vanishing into a picture. His choice of movies is a far more complex story, too, than the old tale of a talented artist selling out. On his pop records, Newman was front and center, taking both the praise and the blame. On a movie, it's the director who takes the hit if it's bad, not the guy who wrote the music. Newman could also find fulfillment in honoring the family tradition. But in removing the untrustworthy narrator from his work, he took away the risk of success, as well as the fear of failure. Given that Newman is an accomplished and skilled composer, his music for *The Natural* and *Awakenings* could blend innocuously into their pictures without debate. Given the terms of the films they're part of, they're unqualified accomplishments. But the failure of a pop song like "Baltimore" or "Pants" draws more critical attention and prompts more interesting questions than the success of a film song like "I Love To See You Smile." You can see Newman struggling with "Baltimore," but not in "I Love To See You Smile." Although Newman's pop work in the eighties was limited to two albums, they were both significant attempts to say something about American culture. And for the first time, he revealed the face behind the mask.

# The Face Behind the Mask

A haunted nostalgia, sometimes sentimental, sometimes irritable, accompanies most quests for America.

— Tom McDonough

I found a way to write about myself that I don't object to — I lied.

— Randy Newman

## 1

Before he began work on *Trouble in Paradise* (1983), his first pop album in four years, Randy Newman was spending more time sitting around watching television and lounging by the pool than he was writing songs. "The gardener had contempt for me," he told Arthur Lubow of *People Magazine*. "He had to water around me." His inactivity was also having a strange effect on his family. "What made me really bad in those days is the kids would go off to school in the morning, and I'd say, 'So long kids, you know, work hard and stuff,' and I just didn't do anything. [My son] Eric didn't know what I did. He

243

thought I got paid for my tan." To solve his own trouble in paradise, Newman rented a room in Los Angeles with a piano and no telephone to disturb him. One of the first songs he wrote and recorded was the appropriately titled "Something To Sing About." Originally known as "A Big Smelly Country Song," it was a hilarious, offbeat tune with a slightly submerged tone of disenchantment. Done in a country-gospel style (imagine a Tammy Wynette arrangement of "He's Got the Whole World in His Hands"), "Something To Sing About" was similar in structure to "Birmingham." Instead of being about a redneck with a sense of pride for his dilapidated city, though, the narrator in "Something To Sing About" boasts with self-satisfied arrogance about the suburban opulence that surrounds him.

Newman taped a demo version of the song in which the vocal is so soft and indistinct that some of the words are virtually unintelligible. It's as if the character in the song is swallowing his pride as much as he is bursting with it. Sure he has six children, money in the bank and a huge house on Elm Street. Of course, he has great neighbors who always get together "when the sun goes down," plus a wife who loves him (and picks him up when he falls). But in the chorus, when Newman sings, "I've got something to sing about/ I've got something that's kinda special," his voice is so tightly constricted he stirs doubt in the listener about all his claims (before the end, however, Newman briefly cracks up, giving away the irony in the song).

"Something To Sing About" is about the delusion of paradise and the false sanctuary offered by utopias. But Newman doesn't pillory his suburbanites for their false morals and bad taste. Unlike the smug attitudes expressed in movies such as *American Beauty* (1999), where the suburban characters are emotionally and sexually crippled by their spiritual emptiness, Newman's song gets at exactly what attracts his characters to their particular lifestyle. He accepts the paradox of their Southern Californian lives in a way Nathanael West couldn't in *The Day of the Locust.* "Something To Sing About" might have been the ideal cut to open *Trouble in Paradise,* but Lenny Waronker didn't agree. "I wanted to record that," Newman told Scott Jordan of *OffBeat Magazine.* "Lenny couldn't stand it. I liked it for evil reasons. I liked how full of himself the guy was." The demo would later be included on the box-set *Guilty: 30 Years of Randy Newman.*

It had been four years since Waronker and Russ Titelman had

joined Newman in the studio to record a pop album, and *Trouble in Paradise* had an appealing theme and vision. Released in early 1983, it took its title from the classic 1932 Ernst Lubitsch comedy. But the subject here wasn't sex, as it was in Lubitsch's superb farce. Instead, *Trouble in Paradise* was a full-blown exploration of what Newman had hinted at on "Something To Sing About." Van Dyke Parks once called Newman "a visitor to a dark place from a very bright place," and that, in part, describes the story here. Newman was contrasting the sunny radiance of Los Angeles with the hidden darkness of places as far and wide as Miami and Capetown. Newman had no illusions about the seedier side of L.A., yet he also wanted to express some of his love for its shiny and hedonistic surface. And, why not? Mikal Gilmore, writing about the album in *Night Beat,* responded immediately to that sentiment. *"[Trouble in Paradise]* tells us that hard truths wouldn't matter much — wouldn't be endurable — without the chance to hit the highway, where the wind can cleanse us of thoughts and the radio can fill the gaps in our feeling the way it fills the shiny, dirty sky around us." In 1985, Manuel Puig, the Argentinean author of *Kiss of the Spider Woman,* told *The New York Times* he saw no reason to be condescending towards Tinseltown's spurious values. "It doesn't matter that the way of life shown by Hollywood was phony," Puig said, reflecting on the dreariness of his early life. "It helped you hope."

On *Trouble in Paradise,* Newman tried to probe the ambiguities that lay at the root of that hope. The germ of the idea was an examination of the sated lives of the rock stars he knew, people who were often obscenely wealthy, but seemed no longer able to indulge fully their riches. "I was talking to Don Henley on a plane," Newman told Christopher Connelly. "He can't charter Lear jets anymore. I said, 'Ah, Jesus, that's tough.' He was laughing, too. Time for belt-tightening. You can't live on a million a year anymore." Here was a theme rich in possibility, but the record itself was uneven, with great songs scattered among mediocre ones. The opening track, "I Love L.A.," was especially disappointing. It was first suggested to Newman by Henley during their airplane conversation. "[He] said, 'Everybody's writing these L.A. breakdown songs, and we're writing about 'Hotel California,' but you're from here, so why don't you write one?' So I did." It starts as a satirical tribute to the city where he was born, borrowing the melody (and some of the lines) of Rodgers and Hart's "The

Lady Is a Tramp." Instead of hating California for being cold and damp, the song hates New York City, where "people are dressed like monkeys." The singer then leaves Chicago to the "Eskimos," and with a "big nasty redhead" by his side, hits the road for Los Angeles, at which point "I Love L.A." becomes an equivocal anthem:

> *Roll down the window, put down the top*
> *Crank up the Beach Boys, baby*
> *Don't let the music stop*
> *We're gonna ride it*
> *Till we can't ride it no more.*

As Lindsey Buckingham and Christine McVie, of Fleetwood Mac, provide background harmonies, members of the rock band Toto supply the groove. Newman offers a scenic tour:

> *Look at that mountain*
> *Look at those trees*
> *Look at that bum over there, man*
> *He's down on his knees.*

In the chorus, Newman shouts "I Love L.A.!" while Buckingham and McVie answer back, "We love it!" The ironies are obvious — the city's excesses hide its squalor — but they're a little too pat. Is this song really a put-down of L.A., or a celebration of it? "It's ambiguous, as all my best songs are," Newman explained to Timothy White. "And you can do it all year 'round, too — unless you can't find the redhead." But instead of grappling with the ambiguity, listeners embraced it as a new song for the city — which isn't all that surprising given the song's lack of bite. By the time he starts endlessly rhyming off street names, the song starts to tailspin:

> *Century Boulevard (We love it)*
> *Victory Boulevard (We love it)*
> *Santa Monica Boulevard (We love it)*
> *Sixth Street (We love it, we love it).*

"There's nothing distinguished on any of those streets," Newman explains. "They're all east-west, and Imperial Highway's got nothing taller on it than I am." In "Rednecks," when Newman overturned the song's joke and listed the Northern neighborhoods and cities where blacks were still living in bondage, the song cut deep and the wounds bled. But when he tries to uncover the urban neglect and indifference on "I Love L.A.," Newman barely breaks the skin. In 1991, on his *Mighty Like a Rose* album, Elvis Costello's similarly impressionistic "The Other Side of Summer" tackled the themes of affluence and indigence with more authority and imagination while proclaiming that "there's malice and there's magic in every season."

"I Love L.A." became the unofficial anthem of the 1984 Los Angeles Summer Olympics, and the Lakers would ultimately include it during their home games. Even Nike incorporated the track into some of their ads. In fact, "I Love L.A." was so endearing to Angelenos, it was placed in a time capsule on December 14, 1984, as a promotion for John Carpenter's gooey sci-fi drama, *Starman*. It could also be heard as Bette Midler motored down the boulevard in Paul Mazursky's sharp satire, *Down and Out in Beverly Hills* (1986) — a movie that conveyed much more successfully the dualities Newman was aiming for in his song. The song was placed in the police parody, *Naked Gun* (1988) and was part of a sick joke in the closing credits of *Volcano* (1997). It also spawned a popular video, shot by Newman's cousin Tim, in which Randy rode in an open convertible through the main boulevards of the city with that same redhead by his side. On the PBS series *Great Streets,* Newman could once again be seen traveling down Sunset in a huge car — but without the nasty redhead. "She's gone back to Cyprus," Newman quipped. The final irony occurred in September 1994, when Newman was presented with keys to the city and an unofficial proclamation recognizing the song's positive impact. By that time, it seems, everybody had forgotten about that bum on his knees throwing up in the street.

"Christmas in Capetown" has Newman returning more confidently to the same area of racial condescension he explored on "Rednecks." Having read some of Nadine Gordimer's books on South Africa, he set out to deal with the scourge of apartheid. The song opens with synthesizers playing what sounds like a benign Christmas carol before we're introduced to the main character. "The guy in 'Capetown' is like a thirty-eight-year-old surfer," Newman told Paul Zollo. "[He's] a little bastard who doesn't like the way things are now." In fact, there's nothing benign about him. Visiting his house is a white girl from England who drinks all this Afrikaner beer and complains about the racism towards blacks. Newman doesn't sing from the point of view of the outraged visitor, but takes on the role of her host:

> *I tell her, Darling, don't talk about something you don't*
> *know anything about.*
> *I tell her, Darling, if you don't like it here go back to your*
> *own miserable country.*

The Capetowner then describes to her the scene he witnesses when he drives his brother to work at the diamond mine. He spots the blacks in long lines carrying their lunch pails "with a picture of *Star Wars* painted on the side." He catches them staring at him "real hard with their big yellow eyes." In a few quick, evocative images, Newman captures the ugly spectre of racism. At the beginning of the song, when he mentions blacks listening to Abba's "Dancing Queen," and here, with the image of *Star Wars* on their lunch boxes, blacks are seen buying into the very dominant culture the narrator feels is slipping away from him. "Christmas in Capetown" ends ominously with a slowed-down reprise of the carol.

"The Blues," which served as the album's first single, is even more innocuous than the title track. Not only did it fail to crack the Top 40, the song didn't cut to the core of its subject. Newman begins by listing a series of tragedies that are the subject matter of a songwriter who's "got the blues." But he quickly shifts to a fan who turns to music for comfort when his father runs off with another woman. Here Newman makes the rare mistake of dismissing the kid's needs rather than satirizing the boy's actions. "I kind of made fun of people who are hurt or sensitive and they go and find solace in music, because I never found any solace, for me it was always like certain work," Newman confesses. "It felt just like a family business, and I felt like I got pushed into it some kind of way. I regret that [song]." Newman's comment helps explain why the character runs to his room where "his piano lay in wait for him" — as it once did for the young Newman. There's little doubt Newman identified with the kid in "The Blues," still he turns the boy's consolation into a burden.

"The Blues" was performed as a duet with Paul Simon, and many listeners felt that *he* was the subject of Newman's put-down. "Nah, it wasn't that way at all," Newman told Liam Lacey of the *Globe & Mail*. "I just played the song for him and he liked it. He's too good a musician to think of it that way and too serious a writer not to be able to laugh at himself." Besides Brian Wilson's touching "In My Room," which takes us to the pure sources of adolescent consolation, the best song about the comfort offered by music was written by Ray Davies of the Kinks in 1978. "Rock & Roll Fantasy" is a superbly evocative tune that movingly acknowledges the needs of the fan while sensitively addressing the band's need to grow beyond the desires of their followers. Though a master satirist himself, Davies doesn't belittle those who treasure their Kinks albums. The song humbly accepts that the band has offered its fans many pleasures over the years.

"Same Girl," which became the B-side of "The Blues" single, is the stronger song. It uses a spare arrangement for piano and strings to tell the tale of a girl with a sunny attitude who hides a dark side — and it hit the mark that "I Love L.A." missed entirely. "'Same Girl' is a sad tune," Newman recalls. "About two junkies in love. Nice music in that tune." In a song as powerfully impressionistic as "Texas Girl at the Funeral of Her Father" and "Ghosts," Newman blends beauty and tragedy so astutely, his own voice cracks ever so slightly when he remembers hers. "Mikey's," on the other hand, is a biting, comical tune which, like "Christmas in Capetown," features a protagonist who's none too pleased that times have changed. The song opens with a Devo-style melody played rapidly on the synthesizers, as the narrator enters Mikey's Bar in North Beach. His first question to Mikey, "Have you seen my Marie?" recalls the dilemma faced by Chuck Berry thirty years earlier in "Memphis, Tennessee." The protagonist is obviously someone who lived in North Beach during the fifties and sixties. Coming to the conclusion that his Marie is nowhere to be found, he starts to see faces he didn't expect to see:

> *Didn't used to be any spades here, now you got 'em*
> *Didn't used to be any Mexicans here, now you got 'em*
> *Didn't used to be any Chinamen here*
> *Didn't used to be this ugly music playing all the time*
> *Where are we, on the moon?*

In this tune, which Newman describes, unassumingly, as being about "a demographic change in North Beach," the singer reminisces about the old days, much like Peter Boyle's bigot in the movie *Joe* (1970), lamenting the loss of a time when you could hear "the fucking 'Duke of Earl'" on the jukebox. Meanwhile, New Wave synthesizers merrily perform an electronic version of "Chopsticks," eventually joined by Jim Horn and Jon Smith's R&B wind section. Clearly the horns, battling it out with the dissonant synths, stand for the nostalgic obsessions of a chap who has not only lost his girl, but still can't figure out what the fuck happened to the Duke of Earl.

"My Life Is Good" is a savage attack on yuppie values in which Newman daringly portrays the privileged one. He masterfully slips once again into the role of untrustworthy narrator, using elements from his own life and background to create an absolutely appalling main character. While bearing some resemblance to the story of "Something To Sing About," the song follows up on the life of the born-again yuppie in "It's Money That I Love." He describes living with his wife and a Mexican maid in Bellair, where their kids go to a Beverly Hills private school. A teacher's complaint about the behavior of their child sends the narrator into a tirade. My life is good, he tells her (calling her an "old bag"), and he doesn't stop there. He brags about some "associates" from New York:

> *I'm gonna take 'em to*
> *Restaurants and everything*
> *Gonna get 'em some*
> *Real good cocaine*
> *They don't get much*
> *Where they come from*
> *And this guy's wife*
> *Is such a pretty brown thing*
> *That I'm liable to give her a poke or two*
> *Whaddaya think of that?*

Before the teacher has time to reply to his outrageous tale, she's offered another story, about his friendship with Bruce Springsteen, who confesses:

*He said, 'Rand, I'm tired*
*How would you like to be the boss for awhile?'*
*Well, yeah!*

Newman takes up the charge as the new Boss, ordering Springsteen's sax player, Clarence Clemmons (played in the song by L.A. session man Ernie Watts), to "blow, Big Man, blow." Clearly Newman has something against Springsteen, whom he'd already taken a shot at on "Pretty Boy."

"I think his reputation artistically is probably inflated a bit," he explained. "But everyone who sees him changes his mind . . . when they see him, it's like they become a pod-person. It's like, 'No, he's *great* man.' I say, 'What do you mean he's great? Yesterday you said it sounded like it came out of a well.' And they say, 'No, man, he's great, he's great.' I don't know what it is. It's like hypnotism." Newman is referring to the many converts Springsteen made to his music through his electrifying live shows, but what likely rankles Newman most is Springsteen's persona as a noble working-class artist. As Newman enjoys playing the roles of characters whose behavior is often repugnant, he probably couldn't resist tweaking an artist who almost always plays the good guy.

"Miami" has an appealing salsa arrangement that's bright and sunny, with mandolins in the chorus that seem to sway in the breeze. But since the song is about the booming drug trade rather than lounging on the beach, Newman's discordant synthesizers produce a crazy party sound that lurks in the background. Newman considers "Miami" (with the help of some buoyant harmony vocal work from Rickie Lee Jones) one of his best songs. Unlike "Louisiana 1927" or "Birmingham," "Miami" is a rare song about an American place that doesn't call up a sense of the past — everything here about Miami, from its glamor to its sordidness, is addressed very much in the present tense. Newman is much sharper on the details, too, than he was in the disappointing "Baltimore" — especially as he describes one of the dealers:

*His name is Medina*
*And he comes from Argentina*
*See that little dog there with him*

> *Well, he treats it just like it was*
> *His little boy.*

More than any other song on *Trouble in Paradise,* this one captures the conflicted nature of Newman's attitude towards these urban paradises.

"Real Emotional Girl" is, like "Marie," another of Newman's romantic numbers many listeners mistake as a straightforward love song. The character in "Real Emotional Girl" gives up intimate details about his new girlfriend to his buddy:

> *She wears her heart on her sleeve*
> *Every little thing you tell her*
> *She'll believe*
> *She really will*
> *She even cries in her sleep.*

Although he's obviously happy to have met someone with such an open heart, there's also something creepy about the way the speaker shares this information. "I saw the guy as sort of a bad guy," Newman told Christopher Connelly. "I don't think you should be relating all those confidences — telling anyone that she cries in her sleep. I think it's like the girl's made another mistake." Her boyfriend shares more details with his best friend. A daddy's girl, she lived at home until she was eighteen, when her father helped her move out. She met a boy who broke her heart so she became very cautious. Despite this, he's discovered that she "turns on easy" and her passions get expressed "like a hurricane." Although listeners were likely seduced by the beautiful ballad arrangement for piano and strings, "Real Emotional Girl" has a protagonist almost as unnerving as the stalker in "Suzanne."

"Take Me Back" is probably the most blatantly personal song Newman wrote before *Land of Dreams.* Here, he talks about growing up in Los Angeles, getting drunk in high school, his infamous car accident and being picked up at the police station by his father. But by the time he reaches adulthood, the story becomes a little less autobiographical. "Take Me Back" is about a fellow who is a huge success until he meets the wrong woman:

*Please take me back*
*I don't wanna live here*
*By this dirty old airport*
*In this greasy little shack*
*Take me back*
*Just give me a chance*
*And we'll start all over again.*

Despite the real details from Newman's past, "Take Me Back" is really a pop confection driven by a pumping Farfisa organ (by David Paich) resembling the carnival sound of Freddie Cannon's "Palisades Park."

"There's a Party at My House" is a new variation on "Mama Told Me Not to Come," but instead of a timid kid caught up in a beguiling seventies orgy, the song depicts the amoral Los Angeles eighties nightlife Bret Easton Ellis would capture two years later in his sordid novel, *Less Than Zero*. While "There's a Party at My House" is done in a swinging fifties rock style, it's a party where nobody's swinging — except the blonde-haired girl with the blue vein right beneath her breast who ends up at the end of a possible sexual assault. Recognizing this ripped-from-the-headlines account differs greatly from the setting in "Mama Told Me Not to Come," Mikal Gilmore noted that the song had the same conflicting emotions that gave "Mama Told Me Not to Come" its comic bite. "The character in 'There's a Party at My House,' who winds up what began as an innocent saturnalia with an implied vision of rape . . . isn't repugnant merely because of his dangerous impulses," Gilmore writes. "[He is] because he speaks to us in a way that can arouse our own desire to join the party." In "Mama Told Me Not to Come," the party offered good drugs and better sex; "There's a Party at My House" involves bad drugs and possibly even rape.

"I'm Different" is a rather lame attempt to capture the defiant independence of much better songs, like the Kinks' "I'm Not Like Everybody Else" and The Crystals' "He's a Rebel." With a female chorus (including Linda Ronstadt, Wendy Waldman and Jennifer Warnes) coyly responding to Newman's gloating, "I'm Different" isn't especially discreet. "Song for the Dead," an anti-war lament for the soldiers of Vietnam, wasn't altogether distinct either. In what would ultimately become the B-side of the "I Love L.A." single, "Song for the Dead" begins as a requiem on the piano almost immediately accompanied by the faint sound of marching drums. By the time the synthesizers bring forth a sea of electronic sludge, a sergeant tells his men — now blown to bits — what they died for:

> *Now our country, boys*
> *Though it's quite far away*
> *Found itself jeopardized*
> *Endangered, boys*
> *By these very gooks*
> *Who lie here beside you*
> *Forever near*
> *Forever.*

While the arrangement is evocative, the song itself has no impact because you don't feel Newman's commitment to the material. "I thought it was safe to come out against Vietnam ten years after the war was over," Newman remarked. In a sense, he was playing it safe in the way he did with "In Germany Before the War." "Song for the Dead" buries the sergeant in so many cheap military platitudes we don't recognize the dead soldiers he's addressing.

Eight years later, in the spring of 1991, Newman would make amends in a song called "Lines in the Sand." The track was never released on an album, but was sent to various radio stations in the wake of the first Gulf War. In many ways, "Lines in the Sand" was Newman's answer to the pieties of the numerous Hollywood stars who became part of "Voices That Care," a tribute to the troops then engaged in Iraq. Newman provided instead a troubling accolade riddled with paradoxes — and it blew "Song for the Dead," with all its self-consciousness, right out of the trenches.

"Newman offered only a certain out-of-fashion stoicism," Greil Marcus wrote in *Mystery Train*. "[It was] an elegy in advance of victory. . . . It was quiet, cold and defeatist. I heard it on the radio, once." Hardly surprising. "Lines in the Sand" is far too disquieting for contemporary commercial radio and its demographically shaped playlists. It doesn't provide any clear lines to follow. But as it wasn't written as a strident and partisan political message, the song strongly embodies the politics of that time. With his voice but a hushed whisper, Newman speaks from within the piety of those sentiments:

*Old sons and daughters*
*Sail across the sea*
*Fight now for justice*
*And liberty*
*Fly across the ocean*
*A friend needs a hand*
*You must try to defend their*
*Lines in the sand.*

In his tribute to the troops, the horrible ironies of war, however, still abound:

*We old men will guide you*
*Though we won't be there beside you*
*We wish you well.*

Accompanied only by his piano and synthesizers, Newman presents a masterful song about war that holds within it the sorrows of victory — the loss, the bloodshed, the injustices — and yet remains a deeply felt testament to the soldiers who fought there. More recently, Newman realized "Lines in the Sand" had a complex relationship to the 2004 war in Iraq. "You *could* write a song about Paul Wolfowitz, who went on a talk show and said something like, 'Once democracy spreads to Iraq. . . .' That's a song right there," he told Barney Hoskyns. "You know, 'the Easter Bunny will come. . . .' It was just so bizarre that an intelligent fellow like that would believe this doctrine to the point of forgetting the weather and the rocks and the sand and the schools teaching people to hate the worst, and what the steps would be for 20-year-old American soldiers on police duty." Which is to say, the prevailing winds always obscure the lines in the sand.

Despite its unevenness, Newman often cites *Trouble in Paradise* as his favorite album. Lenny Waronker agreed, thinking it was brighter and funnier than Newman's earlier records. And *Trouble in Paradise* would be the last Newman pop album that Waronker would helm. "When I became President of Warner Brothers Records, I couldn't produce records anymore — I just couldn't commit the time," Waronker said. "But for a while I managed to produce Randy's scores *[Ragtime,*

*The Natural, Parenthood, Avalon].* They were much more manage-able: we could do them in three weeks." The new album had trouble on the airwaves. Few radio stations initially played "I Love L.A.," and the album itself didn't even make the Top 50, stalling at No. 64 on the *Billboard* chart. Newman quietly returned to recording film scores until, five years later, on *Land of Dreams,* he found he had something new to address — himself.

2

For most of Randy Newman's career, we were used to hearing songs about a variety of American archetypal figures, but we rarely heard songs about him. The initial shock of *Land of Dreams* was that we were no longer hearing outrageous tales about slave traders, stalkers, Southern racists or demagogues. This album caught us up in Newman's own story. "By reflecting on his birth in Los Angeles, the years of infancy and early childhood he spent with his mother in New Orleans while waiting for his dad to return from World War II, the schoolyard ridicule he drew back in L.A. for his eye problems . . . Newman demonstrates how a laboratory of the spirit like America can yield some of the most poignant and unlikely scenarios of self-fulfillment," Timothy White wrote about *Land of Dreams.* On the album, Newman draws on his own early life to address the prevailing themes of contemporary American culture — including racism, disen-franchisement and assimilation. What also changed was his voice, now less masked by his standard drawl. Newman sang in a cadence that was more direct while making the humor in some of the songs more cutting. There was less distance between the singer and his material. But Newman wasn't baring his soul in the way many pop singer-song-writers do, revealing their innermost traumas and longings. *Land of Dreams* instead implies a connection between the personal dreams of Randy Newman, the dreams of the characters in his songs and the dreams of his country.

Since *Trouble in Paradise,* a prescient title, Newman's life had taken a dramatic turn. As he started recording *Land of Dreams,* he was emerging from a period of personal turmoil. In 1985, Newman left his wife Roswitha after eighteen years of marriage. "I don't know why we broke apart," he remarked to Susan Toepfer of *People Magazine.*

"Things like that happen. I will always be her friend and she will always be mine." Their three sons were now grown up. The eldest, Amos, was a record company executive, while Eric was a movie executive and the youngest, John, a senior at Harvard-Westlake in North Hollywood. And now, with longtime friend Lenny Waronker no longer at the controls, Newman had to rely on a flank of producers for *Land of Dreams,* including Mark Knopfler of Dire Straits, Jeff Lynne (formerly of the Electric Light Orchestra), film composer James Newton Howard and Tommy LiPuma. Fortunately, all of this upheaval seemed to galvanize Newman, and he put together his best record since *Born Again.*

The album cover is a photo of Newman as a young child in his full Roy Rogers cowboy regalia, with two toy six-shooters in his hands. The picture seems to be posing a challenge to that other cowboy in the White House, Ronald Reagan, who at the time was taking the country through its *Death Valley Days.* The title of the album, *Land of Dreams,* didn't just refer to the American Dream, but more specifically, to New Orleans, where Newman spent his early childhood. Spencer Williams' 1926 song "Basin Street Blues," popularized by two of New Orleans' finest artists, Louis Armstrong and Louis Prima, introduced the phrase as they celebrated the Big Easy with a shout of unbridled freedom:

> *Won't you come along with me*
> *Down that Mississippi;*
> *We'll take a boat to the land of dreams,*
> *Steam down the river down to New Orleans.*

On the first three songs — "Dixie Flyer," "New Orleans Wins the War" and "Four Eyes" — Newman journeys with us to this land of dreams, giving us an autobiographical account that examines the difficulties of reaching one's aspirations in the Deep South. "Dixie Flyer" tells the story of Newman and his mother making their way to New Orleans to visit her family. "[M]y relatives from Jackson, Miss., came down in a green Hudson to meet us at the station," he told Timothy White. "Yet what I like in that lyric is that they had to have a Gentile drive in those days." Newman is writing from the experience of being Jewish in the segregated South, but he's also satirizing the theme of Jewish assimilation:

*Drinkin' rye whiskey from a flask in the back seat*
*Tryin' to do like the Gentiles do*
*Christ, they wanted to be Gentiles, too*
*Who wouldn't down there, wouldn't you?*
*An American Christian, God damn!*

If Jewish songwriters like Irving Berlin created a dream of America everyone could feel a part of, in "Dixie Flyer" Newman explores the painful reality of segregation in America. "Philip Roth said in one of his books that the second great genius after Moses was Irving Berlin, because he took Christmas ["White Christmas"], the holiest Christian holiday, and made it about the weather, and he took Easter and took all the blood out of it and the bad Jews and made it about fashion ["Easter Parade"]!" Newman commented.

In "New Orleans Wins the War," a lovely ragtime shuffle, he describes living on Willow Street, near the Garden District, and tells how, for the first time, he encountered discrimination against blacks:

*Momma used to take me to Audubon Park*
*Show me the ways of the world*
*She said, "Here comes a white boy, there goes a black one,*
*that one's an octoroon*
*This little cookie here's a macaroon, that big red thing's*
*a red balloon."*

While both songs contain Newman's usual offhand wit, he's also contrasting the pain of Jews and blacks, existing in separate worlds but desperately trying to find ways to fit in and be accepted. Later in the song, Newman informs us that it's 1948, and his father Irving arrives to announce to the city something we'd assume they already knew — that they'd won the war ("Maybe they heard it, maybe not/ Probably they heard it, and just forgot"). Then, using poetic licence and taking up the mantle of the untrustworthy narrator, Newman gives us a tall tale that sees the people of New Orleans building a platform for his father in Jackson Square on which he addresses the gathered throng. But the crowd acts as if it's the Civil War they've just won rather than World War II ("We knew we'd do it/ We done whipped the Yankees").

At this point, two different dreams are being fulfilled. As Irving Newman is lifted high on a pedestal to address the multitudes, Randy (from the viewpoint of a young boy deprived of his father during the war) gets to idealize his dad, while the South, in deliberately confusing the two wars, gets to fulfill its longtime dream of victory.

In the song, Irving decides it's best to get his family out of New Orleans and back to L.A., because the spirit of the South is bound to corrupt his son:

> *People have fun here, and I think they should*
> *But nobody from here ever come to any good*
> *They're gonna pickle him in brandy and tell him he's saved*
> *Then throw fireworks all 'round his grave.*

As he escapes the South for the West Coast at the end of the song, Randy performs a gorgeous R&B shuffle that integrates Jewish and black culture. Here, one can clearly envision Fats Domino rewriting his own version of Irving Berlin's "Blue Skies":

> *Blue, blue morning, blue blue day*
> *All your bad dreams drift away.*

"Four Eyes" deals with the eye problems Newman encountered later in childhood, in a sense turning the malicious humor of "Davy the Fat Boy" and "Short People" on himself. Coming after the pleasant, nostalgic atmosphere of "Dixie Flyer" and "New Orleans Wins the War," "Four Eyes" is profoundly jarring. It opens with the harsh thump of a pounding drum over the melody of a schoolyard rhyme, arranged as a dissonant theme played on the synthesizer. The five-year-old Newman is awakened by his father early one morning to be driven to his first day at school. The hero of "New Orleans Wins the War" is quickly and dramatically brought down to earth as he makes anxious and harsh demands of his son, like a drill sergeant barking orders at a private. Irving has Randy put on the cowboy outfit from the album's cover, and off they go. In the car, he lectures Randy about his expectations of his son, imposing his own dreams in a manner not unlike Randy's own demands on Amos in "Memo to My Son," from *Sail Away*:

*He said, "Son it's time to make us proud of you*
*It's time to do what's right*
*Gonna have to learn to work hard"*
*I said, "Work? What are you talking about?*
*You're not gonna leave me here, are you?"*

As the little bespectacled boy stands all alone on the corner with his Roy Rogers lunch bucket in hand, the other kids gather to mock him:

*They said, "Four eyes! Look like you're still sleeping!"*
*"Four eyes! Look like you're dead!"*
*"Four eyes! Where have you been keeping yourself?"*
*"Look like you been whipped upside the head."*

When the song fades, a chorus of children's voices (like an eerie choral arrangement out of one of Danny Elfman's movie scores) continues to taunt the young Newman as the guitarist plucks out a refrain of "Mary Had a Little Lamb."

Although the texture of these opening three tracks, produced by Knopfler, is largely determined by the fact they deliberately draw on Newman's past, he has altered some of the facts. "I don't remember my first day of school, or whether my dad took me," he recalled later. "He certainly didn't say any of that stuff. . . . But there's a fair amount of truth in it emotionally." In other words, whatever liberties Newman took in the details of these songs, the feeling behind them is authentic, and taken together, they explore the dreams of nations and families, and how they can be fulfilled or dashed. As much as they represent genuine hope for Newman, dreams can also create false expectations. Once Newman establishes this theme in his examination of his childhood, he broadens his scope to address the dreams of the rest of the country.

Done as a Spanish waltz, "Falling in Love," produced by Jeff Lynne, is a pretty straightforward romantic ballad that connects love and religion in the same manner as "Jesus in the Summertime":

*Now you're walkin' in the holy land*
*Yeah, that's you there, walkin' with the king*
*You ask, "What have I done to deserve this?"*
*Why, you haven't done a thing*
*Maybe you're falling in love.*

Newman's backup band for this track was Tom Petty & the Heartbreakers. Petty and Lynne, already part of the Traveling Wilburys, an all-star ensemble that also included George Harrison, Bob Dylan and Roy Orbison, loved creating an informal working environment. Given the variegated harmonies in the Wilburys, Petty figured Newman might as well join up too. "I can't sing in tune like that," Newman told Scott Jordan. "And Petty says to me, 'No, you can do it. With Jeff [Lynne], I didn't think I could do it either, but when I did it with Jeff, we could do it.'" Unfortunately, despite Petty's encouragement, Newman's limited vocal range was beyond Lynne's abilities to compensate. "So I put my hand over my ears like I'd seen people do, and . . . I went, 'Uungh' . . . and I saw Jeff Lynne shaking his head like he smelled something bad," Newman continues. "So he just said, 'Maybe you better sit this one out.'" Perhaps Newman's embarrassment represented poetic justice for Jeff Lynne, the target of Newman's ridicule in "The Story of a Rock & Roll Band," on *Born Again*. "Falling in Love" would later be included in the romantic comedy *Her Alibi* (1989).

"Something Special," an insipid love song produced by film composer James Newton Howard and Tommy LiPuma, had already been featured in the equally feeble Gary Marshall comedy *Overboard* (1987), with Kurt Russell and Goldie Hawn. Although it does have a catchy arrangement, it's a fabricated fantasy of love wherein all obstacles are transcended. "Bad News from Home," by contrast, is a powerful, moody song about romantic treachery that suggests a Jim Thompson pulp novel. A woman abandons her husband, who owns a gas station, in order to join her lover in Mexico. "Bad News from Home" is like "I've Been Wrong Before" reconceived as a film noir:

> *I remember the night she left*
> *I drove to the station in the pouring rain*
> *Sat all night behind my big iron desk*
> *The oil on the water made a rainbow.*

Newman lingers on the word "rainbow" as if he's retracing in his mind the image of her departure. "That song is written from the heart," said Mark Knopfler, who coproduced and played on the track.

"Roll With the Punches" is one of Newman's strongest social critiques. Written a couple of years earlier in 1986 (and first performed that same year on *Saturday Night Live),* it's a fitting addition to *Land of Dreams,* a hard-hitting description of racial inequity in the Reagan era. The song describes a land of deliberately destroyed opportunities:

> *Little black kid come home from school*
> *Put his key in the door*
> *Mr. Rat's on the stairway*
> *Mr. Junkie's lyin' in his own vomit on the floor*
> *You gotta roll with the punches, little black boy*
> *That's what you gotta do.*

"Roll With the Punches" is performed as a catchy ragtime shuffle, but its toughness makes it unlike any other Newman recording. Partway through, the singer suggests that the black boy can just tap his blues away. Newman provides some tap dance rhythms, but they aren't presented as satire (like the music Davy the Fat Boy danced to). Ultimately, in "Roll With the Punches," Newman speaks to the indifference of the Reagan administration towards poverty and drugs in the black community, and to the desperate black youths who were attempting to survive. By the end, Newman's black kid acquiescently taps away, but we can feel the life being beaten out of him as he rolls with the punches.

On "Masterman and Baby J," Newman goes from tapping to rapping — but he doesn't show a great instinct for it. Clearly Newman is trying to dramatize how the despair and disenfranchisement of black urban poverty has led to an incendiary and poetic form of musical expression, but the story of two rappers trying to jump-start their careers is ultimately too glib. "I wanted to write about rap bragging," he explains. "It's amazing how much of it there is." Unfortunately, the tune never goes beyond the bragging to the rage simmering ominously beneath. "Red Bandana" is a much stronger effort, a look at the masks people wear — in particular kids from tough neighborhoods who use bandanas to cover their anger and their pain. This time, Newman reaches for the rawness inside his character. Originally from Buffalo, the young protagonist has traveled the country all the way to Hollywood. When he returns home, he sees his mother and the junkman, who are "both so loaded/ they can hardly stand," and finds his old girlfriend with an ugly-looking dude. He feels completely displaced; whatever dreams he once had are now wasted, replaced by this red bandana — the color of blood.

"Follow the Flag" is a patriotic anthem that satirizes jingoism. "I don't mean a word of it," Newman told Paul Zollo, yet the song isn't performed explicitly as a joke (at least, not in the way a song like "Political Science" was). It's about someone with a desperate need to believe in the values he's been taught his country stands for:

> *They say it's just a dream*
> *That dreamers dreamed*
> *That it's an empty thing that really has no meaning*
> *They say it's all a lie*
> *But it's not a lie*
> *I'm going to follow the flag 'til I die.*

All through *Land of Dreams*, Newman has been both celebrating his country's greatest aspirations and decrying its failings. "Follow the Flag" (whose refrain borrows humorously from "Baby, the Rain Must Fall") pokes fun at the dreamer without necessarily dousing the dream.

It would be easy to mistake "It's Money That Matters" for a rewrite of "It's Money That I Love," but this song isn't a joke. Where "It's Money That I Love" was a deviously funny shot at yuppie privilege, this one is about the spiritual price paid for that privilege. "It's Money That Matters" begins with a nifty joke. A chunky guitar lick from Mark Knopfler, closely resembling one he wrote for Dire Straits' "Money for Nothing," opens the song. That tune, from the *Brothers in Arms* (1985) album, was a satirical attack on MTV and the rock stars whose videos were continually played on the network. In Knopfler's song, a working-class chap who hauls appliances for a living resents doing all this grunt work while all these celebrities get exorbitant salaries for singing and dancing ("Money for nothing/ Chicks for free").

"[Knopfler's] character in ["Money for Nothing"] surprised me," Newman told Paul Zollo. "He's kind of nasty but you [have] sympathy [for] him because he *is* carrying those big appliances. He's bitter but somehow likeable." The character in "It's Money That Matters" is also rather likeable, because unlike the singer in "It's Money That I Love," he isn't celebrating selling out, he's appalled at what he sees:

*All of these people are much brighter than I*
*In any fair system they would flourish and thrive*
*But they barely survive*
*They eke out a living and they barely survive.*

Throughout the song, Newman's character searches for answers to why the world isn't fair — but no one can help him. Finally, he meets someone reminiscent of the self-satisfied yuppie of "My Life Is Good," a fat guy in a red jumpsuit Newman describes as "looking kinda funny." But this plump fellow doesn't mind, because, as he tells the protagonist, he's got a blonde wife, a big house, a big pool in the backyard and another great big pool right beside it. The answer our hero eventually finds is a simple one:

*It's money that matters*
*Now you know that it's true*
*It's money that matters whatever you do.*

It would be safe to assume that the concluding track, "I Want You To Hurt Like I Do," comments on Newman's recent divorce — especially given it's partly about a man who has just abandoned his family. In reality, Newman's sons were now grown men with executive jobs who would hardly feel abandoned by Newman when he left their mother. According to Newman, though, the song was addressing something larger than his own personal life. "'I Want You To Hurt Like I Do' is an authentic rock ballad in the manner of 'We Are the World,'" he remarked sardonically. Back in 1985, close to forty recording artists had gathered to add their voices to a Michael Jackson song called "We Are the World" to raise funds for Ethiopian famine relief. Calling themselves U.S.A. for Africa, they represented a who's who of pop stardom, past and present: Tina Turner, Bob Dylan, Willie Nelson, Lionel Richie, Bruce Springsteen, Diana Ross, Cyndi Lauper, James Ingram, Stevie Wonder, Kenny Rogers, Ray Charles and Michael Jackson. Newman, not surprisingly, was nowhere in sight. Produced by Quincy Jones, who asked that participating artists check their egos at the door, "We Are the World" was, in fact, all *about* ego. Forget that the song's banalities ("There are people dying") reduced a specific tragedy to an obvious generality, "We Are the World" treats the Ethiopians as merely the benefactors of our desire to save ourselves ("There's a choice we're making/ We're saving our own lives"). Moreover, the song suggests, if the stricken Ethiopians will really put their faith in the stars of U.S.A. for Africa, they would achieve their salvation. Newman astutely sniffed out the rancid sentiments in the song. "You see what people do to one another and how things work out and it's like a failure of evolution," he remarked to *Playboy*.

In "I Want You To Hurt Like I Do," Newman rejects the counterfeit dreams and bloated narcissism of "We Are the World." The song opens with a gospel melody played on the organ. A man is telling his current girlfriend he's running out on her just as he once left his wife and children. In fact, he's been running out on people all his life. He tells her that the night he left his family they all cried, including his son. Putting his hand on his boy's shoulder, he said:

> *Sonny, I just want you to hurt like I do*
> *Honest I do, honest I do.*

Here Newman borrows from Sam Cooke's "You Send Me," a song about a man who moves from infatuation to a deep and abiding love ("You send me/ honest you do, honest you do"). But Newman changes the sentiment — this guy can't wait to get away from those he loves. In the second verse, with the help of a choir, the singer extends his reach beyond his loved ones to the rest of the world. He stands on a soapbox and, in a tribute to self-centeredness, declares that it's a "rough rough world" and a "tough tough world." By having the speaker remind us all, in the end, that he wants us to hurt like he does, Newman cuts through the sentimental piety of "We Are the World."

"I know 'we are the world,' but I don't believe it," Newman explained. "I didn't even believe it in the sixties, either." In "I Want You to Hurt Like I Do," Newman provides a link between the selfishness of our private lives, like a father casually walking out on those he loves, and a public world where people choose to ignore, or condescend to, the misery of others. "The song sticks it to the emotional selfishness that travels across generations — how we deal with our imperfect childhoods by making sure we inflict the same grief on everyone around us," wrote Tim Grierson in *Ironminds* magazine.

Grief is an undercurrent running through a record in which, for the first time, Newman's humor cuts to the quick of human vulnerability — including his own. While comparable in scope to both *Sail Away* and *Good Old Boys, Land of Dreams* resonates deeper than both of those records. Newman's irony on the earlier records provided him a certain distance from his subject matter, creating for the listener an air of ambivalence and daring us to figure out what the songs really meant. In *Land of Dreams,* he gets deep inside the material, showing us exactly what it means. We see more of Newman's pained face; it's no longer protected by the mask.

For most of the decade, the true face of the United States had been hidden behind a mask of nostalgia, a false facade commonly described as Ronald Reagan's Morning in America. But for many Americans — especially poor whites and disenfranchised blacks — Reagan's morning was a nightmare. By beginning with the hopes stirred in his youth in the late forties, in *Land of Dreams* Newman found a new and amusing way to examine the jagged realities of the American experience in the eighties. "*Land of Dreams* was about a war that in 1948 was just beginning, a war that was fought in America by blacks and whites in the decades to come," Greil Marcus wrote in *Mystery Train*. "[It's] a war that is worth winning, and that hasn't been won. That was Newman's reply to Ronald Reagan, to his parents, to himself."

The struggle of making *Land of Dreams* was compounded not only by the dissolution of Randy's marriage to Roswitha, but by other events as well. While preparing the album for release, Newman was recovering from the Epstein-Barr virus that had debilitated him during the year of his separation from his wife. "I had this flu there for awhile," Newman told Paul Zollo. "It used to be I would write a song and I'd be invulnerable to anything. . . . But it wasn't lasting me *fifteen minutes* before I'd be feeling bad again." The virus proved a handicap to even moving around. "I couldn't get up a couple of steps without getting out of breath," he told Susan Toepfer of *People*. "But the worst part is in your brain. You just can't think of anything that you look forward to doing. Nothing looks good. [I also tried] the guys with the towels on their heads with [homeopathic medicine]." The true cure, in the end, turned out to be a diet free of fats, oils, sugar, salt, alcohol and caffeine — and daily exercise. Newman wasn't used to feeling so helpless. "My boys could take care of themselves better than I can," Newman told Michelle Green of *People Magazine.* "For me, [it was] Campbell's soup."

Shortly after the release of *Land of Dreams,* Newman lost both of his parents. His mother, Adele, died in the fall, and a year and a half later, Newman lost his father, Irving, to cancer. One unreleased *Land of Dreams* demo — written and performed before their deaths — might well have served as a tribute. But "Days of Heaven," which was dropped from the lineup of *Land of Dreams,* is far from a simple eulogy. This rather mournful song could easily have been composed by the offspring of the couple in Newman's "Love Story":

> *Mom and Dad have passed away*
> *Didn't love you anyway*
> *Just sit up in your room*
> *And cry for hours*
> *Life is short and time is too*
> *And there's nothing you or I can do*
> *But watch the little birds*
> *And smell the pretty flowers*
> *This life is just anticipation*
> *Of days of heaven.*

A number of other unreleased demos came out of the preparation of *Land of Dreams:* "Vicki," performed once at the Third Annual Salute to American Songwriting show in 1978; "Brand New Morning," whose coda was included in "New Orleans Wins the War;" "Little Darling," "Modern Man," "The Longest Night" and "What Have You Done to Me?" appear on the *Guilty* box-set, along with a funnier take of "Masterman and Baby J." As Newman was getting more in touch with his New Orleans musical roots, he also recorded a cover of Fats Domino's optimistic "I'm in Love Again," used in Zelda Barron's amiable coming-of-age film *Shag* (1988). Newman also performed a homage to Arthur Alexander — another legendary New Orleans singer-songwriter — whom The Beatles ("Anna [Go to Him]" and "Soldier of Love") and The Rolling Stones ("You Better Move On") had long admired. Newman would do his own rendition of "You Better Move On" for David Sanborn's NBC musical showcase *Sunday Night.*

*Land of Dreams* had brought Newman's music a fresh vitality; still he returned to writing for films. In the mid-90s, Newman decided to return to a theme very familiar in his work: religion. This time, he would examine it in a genre that was new to him: musical theater.

## 3

For someone who has consistently called himself an atheist, Randy Newman has spent a lot of his career sparring with God. In "I Think He's Hiding," he may poke fun at putting one's faith in an omnipresent Deity, but he still acknowledges there has to be one not to believe. In "Old Man," a dying father is denied the solace in the Lord because he brought up his son as a nonbeliever. But why would he feel the need to write a song that denies a dying old codger the possibility of spiritual comfort, if Newman doesn't at least consider the possibility that an even Older Codger has the whole wide world in His hands? In both "He Gives Us All His Love" and "God's Song (That's Why I Love Mankind)," Newman laughs at the Master's follies, while taking into consideration the possibility that He had to exist in order to make those disasters possible. (Hell, in "God's Song," Newman even inhabits the title role quite comfortably.) Newman's honest ambivalence about devout belief and his own struggle with the concept of spirituality give those particular songs an intangible power because even as declarations of agnosticism, they still resolve nothing. "I have enormous respect for the idea of faith and the power that it has," he told Chris Willman. "I've just never felt it myself. But I would certainly not carry a banner around saying, 'Be an atheist, it's the greatest!' It's not the greatest. But I can think of more good arguments for it than against it." Newman's struggles with those arguments led him to the idea of writing a musical based on Goethe's *Faust*. For those who had followed Newman's work from the beginning, *Faust* was not only perfectly fitting; the story could easily have been the cornerstone of his entire recording career.

The legend of Faust, wherein a man becomes so consumed by his thirst for divine knowledge that he sells his soul to the Devil, has had an enduring appeal. Based loosely on the true story of John Faustus, a necromancer who lived in northern Germany in the mid-sixteenth century, the story also has roots in Dante's *Divine Comedy*, where the journey through hell and purgatory led to the salvation of Divine Love.

Johann Wolfgang Jon Goethe's *Faust* emerged in the Age of Enlightenment in Germany. The play consumed the author for most of his life; he wrote it in two parts, publishing the first half at the age of forty and not completing the second half until 1832, when he was in his early eighties. Goethe conceived *Faust* as a philosophical dramatic poem, a treatise that delved into a number of questions concerning the nature of salvation and damnation. It was a modern myth in which God had become a technological force, a God of progress, the product of an Industrial Revolution which believed industrialization could bring great benefits to humanity.

As a parable, the Faust myth has always fascinated artists. Christopher Marlowe's *The Tragical History of the Life and Death of Doctor Faustus* was written in 1591, three years before the author was killed in a street brawl (it wasn't performed until 1604). It draws predominantly from an original translation of a German chapbook from the end of the Middle Ages entitled "The Damnable Life and Deserved Death of Dr. Faustus" (1587). The allure of Faust struck Mozart in 1775, when he composed his opera *Don Giovanni*, a Don Juan story the composer turned into a Faustian one. Hector Berlioz composed a dramatic cantata, *The Damnation of Faust,* but it was greeted with little enthusiasm when it premiered in Paris in 1846. Charles Gounod, whose previous work had gone largely unnoticed, had his first major success with his opera *Faust* in 1859. Italian composer and painter Arrigo Boito, who found early fame writing librettos for Verdi's *Otello* (1886) and *Falstaff* (1893), turned to Goethe's *Faust* as an inspiration for his opera, *Mefistofele* (1866). When the play was staged in 1868, there was so much controversy surrounding the subject matter a riot broke out in La Scala, prompting police to close down the production. In Igor Stravinsky's chamber work, *L'Histoire du Soldat (A Soldier's Tale)* (1918), the Devil (in disguise) offers a soldier an old book filled with wisdom in exchange for his violin. In 1976, Frank Zappa rewrote Stravinsky's *L'Histoire* as the profane absurdist oratorio "Titties 'n Beer," in which the Devil devours a motorcycle outlaw's girlfriend, plus his case of beer, which he says he'll return in exchange for the biker's soul.

Variations on the Faustian deal have turned up in a number of novels as well. Thomas Mann wrote his version, *Dr. Faustus* (1947), during World War II. Stephen Vincent Benet's short story "The Devil and

Daniel Webster" (1937) has the Devil appearing in New Hampshire as "Mr. Scratch." When the farmer Jabez Stone swears that he would sell his soul to bring in a healthy crop, "Mr. Scratch" is all too pleased to accommodate him. After a prosperous seven years, Stone enlists the help of town hero Daniel Webster to disentangle him from the Devil's bargain. Hans Christian Anderson's *The Little Mermaid* (1836) is *Faust* from a female perspective. His tiny mermaid gives up her only means of expressing herself — her voice — to acquire legs so that she can walk on land and find true love. If she can win the hand of a man in marriage, she will attain an immortal soul. If she fails, she turns into foam on the sea. The musical *Damn Yankees* (1955) tells the story of a baseball fan who sells his soul to see his favorite team, the Washington Senators, win the pennant. Many films, from Brian de Palma's delirious musical *Phantom of the Paradise* (1974) to Taylor Hackford's campy *The Devil's Advocate* (1997), have cleverly adapted the Faust story. Vincente Minnelli's 1953 musical, *The Band Wagon*, is a theatrical parody built around a failed staging of a modern-day *Faust* musical.

The idea of Randy Newman doing a musical about *Faust* was certainly enticing — even though he had expressed little regard for the genre. "It's a stagnant art," he told Margaret Daly of the *Toronto Star* in 1977. "My God, we're talking about a form where *Hair* was supposed to be a breakthrough." But with Newman's roots as deeply entrenched in Tin Pan Alley as they were in rock & roll, it wasn't a huge step from the world of rock to the Broadway musical. And as a child, Newman saw many of the Hollywood musicals his Uncle Alfred had arranged, like *Carousel* and *The King and I*. Newman read Goethe's play in the early eighties, and he immediately understood the appeal. "When I read *Faust* for the first time, I knew at once that I could make it into a musical parody that would tear Goethe's original to the ground," he told Chris Willman. "[I wanted] to have all its wisdom frustrated by the nature of *real* human beings." Rather than make Faust an intelligent German Romantic alchemist seeking profound knowledge, Newman sets his *Faust* in contemporary America and centers on Henry Faust, a grungy kid with an obsession for Nintendo.

"I envisioned [Faust] as a third-year freshman at Notre Dame who didn't know what he wanted," Newman said. "He's like the kids I raised. You know, all those things that sound great to the parents, sound shitty to the kid." In Newman's *Faust,* God was a self-satisfied corporate executive, or, as Newman put it, "a big, relaxed, handsome guy to whom everything comes easy, like Gerald Ford or George Romney." The Devil took the form of an aging, sexually impotent lothario. Newman didn't conceive *Faust* as some grand musical extravaganza about the search for wisdom, and he drew squarely from American musicals that trade in civics lessons — like *West Side Story* or *Bye, Bye Birdie*. "I turned it into sort of a comedy that doesn't focus on good and evil but the good old generation gap," he explained.

Newman's *Faust* was also inspired by a couple of classic Hollywood movies about heaven. *The Green Pastures* (1936) gave us the parables of the Old Testament as detailed by an all-black cast speaking in the idiom of the Old South. Based on Marc Connelly's stage production, drawn from a series of stories by Roark Bradford, *The Green Pastures* was an example of the kind of popular Negro folk art that formed the bedrock of many of Newman's earlier songs. And Raoul Walsh's *The Horn Blows at Midnight* (1945) had a plot that, in some ways, could easily have been the subject of a Newman song. In the film, Jack Benny plays a band trumpeter in heaven who falls asleep and dreams he's a bumbling archangel in possession of Gabriel's horn. With one blast from his mighty trumpet, he could blow up the world — until a very pretty girl distracts him.

When it came to casting his production, Newman selected Don Henley of the Eagles to portray the self-possessed Faust and James Taylor as his mellow and laid-back God. It's perhaps one of life's great ironies that this popular folk singer from the seventies, who personified the most narcissistic impulses in popular music, would end up playing God in a Randy Newman musical. But as Greil Marcus wrote, "The biggest joke [in *Faust*] was Newman, who once made so much of how poorly his records sold in comparison to James Taylor's, was now in a position to give the washed-up Taylor work." Taylor was as surprised as anyone to hear he got the part. "I was daunted by the prospect of playing God, [but] Randy [convinced me that] this particular God was not a very demanding role," Taylor told Chris Willman. "I think his direction said that this was like a Bing Crosby or Arnold Palmer kind of golf-playing white guy, a little bit full of himself — like one of Van Johnson's roles." In Goethe's original play, Faust falls for an ingénue named Gretchen (Newman's ingénue is called Margaret) at the instigation of Mephistopheles. When Faust gets Gretchen pregnant it brings about tragic consequences for all concerned. In the musical, Margaret is played by Linda Ronstadt, a huge Newman fan, who nonetheless has often felt that he's never fully valued singers in the same way he values the orchestra. "I think he holds us in the lowest esteem," Ronstadt has said. "I sometimes think it's because he has so little value for his own vocal abilities." For the role of Martha, a spirited young lady the Devil becomes smitten with, Bonnie Raitt got the nod; Elton John played Angel Rick, a British cherub somewhat pissed with God for ignoring his country's contributions to the betterment of the world. The plum role of the Devil, of course, went to Newman. "The Devil is a [vulgar] gentleman," he remarks. "The Devil is bad, but [Faust] is insensitive."

Despite the initial promise of a contemporary adaptation of *Faust* in the hands of Randy Newman, the production turned out to be an awful disappointment. The musical numbers — filled with Newman's caustic wit — were so carefully laid out, the punch lines were telegraphed ahead of the jokes. The casting was so rigidly set that no one except Henley could fully inhabit the role he or she was given. For instance, James Taylor's God is not only conceived as bland; he *is* bland, so pooped-out he doesn't register as a worthy adversary for Newman's Devil. Playing Satan is also *too* obvious a move for Newman — it's safe territory for a master of disguise. In other words, the role doesn't bring out the daring in Randy Newman — he never amounts to a viable threat. His choice of parts suggests instead he's catering to what he thinks his audience would like to see him do. It's too self-conscious; he's winking at us.

In "God's Song (That's Why I Love Mankind)," Newman took an infinitely more courageous plunge because — despite all the horrors he dredges up on His behalf — he still left God a mystery man. Our devoted faith in Him, in the end, was an unfathomable concept that remained unexplained by God's chuckling indifference to our woes. Newman didn't trade in clever cynicism, as he did while playing the guy with the horns and the pointed tail in *Faust*. In "God's Song," Newman turned God into a confidence man — part snake-oil salesman, part Bible-thumper — someone who tested our resolve. Newman's *Faust* not only sidesteps all the complexities Goethe raised, the story and the other characters are neatly summed up in a few cute phrases or throwaway lyrics. The central problem with *Faust* is that

Newman, who thinks dramatically in his popular songs because he gets to play *all* the characters, doesn't know how to write dramatically for actors. He may have cast performers who best embodied the qualities of the part he'd written, but they did not have the acting skills to develop the characters they were given.

Like Goethe's, Newman's *Faust* consists of two parts. The first begins after God has created the universe and is receiving congratulations from all his angels over his great accomplishment. He leads them in the opening number "Glory Train," a white gospel tune that welcomes everyone into Heaven and forecasts the hard times to come for mankind. Here he can't resist inserting a little joke at James Taylor's expense, briefly quoting from his signature song, "Fire and Rain":

> *I see some hard times coming*
> *Fire and wind and rain*
> *Billions of people, all scared of each other*
> *Hearts full of envy and anger and pain.*

The banality of God's appeal for salvation ("Get on the glory train/ It's rollin' into the station") is compounded by Newman's sly little wisecrack that trains haven't been invented yet. While God commands everyone to stand tall and to "let faith be your guide," he's interrupted by Lucifer, one of God's favorite angels, who accuses Him of being "a master of bullshit." By suggesting fools in the desert with nothing better to do invented both of them, Lucifer gets himself tossed out of Heaven forever. (Since the musical is built on the assumption that God and the Devil *do* indeed exist, Newman's claims that they are figments of our imagination is incongruous, and the Devil's barbed points have no sting.)

After years of reigning successfully in Hell, Lucifer gets nostalgic for life in Heaven — especially since "they now have golf, roller coasters and Hawaiian music." In "You Can't Keep a Good Man Down," he promises to avenge himself for his ouster. Though it's sung by Newman as a New Orleans blues (the Devil's music, after all), the tune lacks the sassiness of a good down-and-dirty blues number. Performed with so much polish, it seems as harmless as "You've Got a Friend in Me."

When the Devil visits with God, he sees that the great deity is about as bored as he is. And in "How Great Our Lord," we see He's running out of answers for all the calamity below:

*Folks up here ask me why*
*Things go so badly down below*
*I tell them when they ask me why*
*I really do not know.*

Finding that God is vulnerable, Lucifer tells Him He made a mistake by creating mankind. By way of proof, he bets the Lord that he can take a human specimen and corrupt him. If the Devil wins, he's allowed back into Heaven; if he loses, God gets the specimen's soul. In "Northern Boy," which opens with stately, pompous coronation music, they consider taking a resident Canadian. First, they focus on Ottawa, the nation's rather staid capitol, but they ultimately have second thoughts:

*Oh Northern boy*
*Clean of limb, clear of eye*
*Unfettered he lives, unfettered he'll die.*

They subsequently agree on Henry Faust (Henley), a schizophrenic student at Notre Dame University in South Bend, Indiana. Faust is introduced with a gliding, shrieking note of heavy metal guitar in "Bless the Children of the World." While the Lord and the Devil are like icons made of straw, Henley takes over the role of Faust and gives it power, authority and soul. Newman conceived Faust as a callow character, so it's ironic that Henley gave the role more personality than any other character in the production. He sings:

*I dream of love, I dream of hate*
*I dream of death and pain*
*But no matter how I try*
*The dream remains the same.*

His dream is filled with "little piggies" slaughtered one by one against the wall, an image that calls up both Charles Manson and the terrorist activities of the Weather Underground.

The Devil meets with Faust and offers him a contract, which he signs without hesitation because he "doesn't like to read on his own time." The Devil takes an instant dislike to him because he not only lacks imagination, he's also "uncultured." However, Lucifer is still convinced he'll win the bet. "The Man" is a rousing duet in which Henry begins to relish the idea of having absolute power. When Henley wraps his voice around the phrase "'scuse me, motherfucker," he slips perfectly into Newman's characteristic drawl — a brilliant touch. It makes sense, too, because Henry has started to adopt some of the Devil's style.

Lucifer discovers that one of God's other angels, Rick, is dissatisfied with the Lord's cavalier treatment of England, his former homeland, in the aptly titled elegy "Little Island":

> *Little Island, Little Island*
> *Glory lost in the mists of time*
> *They will pay for what was done.*

Here Newman tries for the power he achieved on "Louisiana 1927," which gave us a vivid and tragic portrait of a people dispossessed in their own country. Although Elton John gives a sound reading of "Little Island," we never get a specific enough sense of God's indifference to Great Britain to understand fully Rick's bitter resentment.

Soon the Devil starts complaining to God about Faust's character — even calling him a "barbarian." But the Lord is getting worried about their bet, since the last person He wants to see back in Heaven is the Devil. Part One closes with God's response to Lucifer. In "Relax, Enjoy Yourself," as relaxed and content as a Republican rancher in repose, God tries to distract the Devil by putting him at ease:

> *Relax, enjoy yourself*
> *It's all just a wonderful game*
> *There're fruit trees growin' in an open field*
> *And wild roses bloomin' down a country lane*
> *Look around old chum*
> *Slow it down old chum or you never will succeed.*

Meanwhile, the Lord is confronted by an angel child, shot to death on earth in a Tucson Burger King. Lucifer raises the question of why the Lord allowed her to die at all, essentially the same question

Newman asked more effectively in "God's Song." But God's only answer's that His ways are mysterious, which raises Lucifer's ire. "'My ways are mysterious' isn't quite enough for me," Newman told Chris Willman. "I *don't* understand why the 32 Peruvian children go off the hill in the bus." Unfortunately, Taylor's God lacks the depth needed to give this question the full value it demands. Moreover, if Newman had given us a better sense of God and the Devil as two sides of the same coin, this might be an interesting battle raging between them. Instead, Part One closes rather meekly.

Part Two opens with the Lord's attempts to help the self-centered Henry Faust fall in love. He gets Cupid to shoot his arrow at a St. Patrick's Day festivity in South Bend, which also happens to be taking place on Easter Sunday. Faust falls for Margaret, the town's most radiant woman. "Gainesville" opens with one of Newman's distinctively beautiful string arrangements. But when Ronstadt starts to sing, the song immediately falls apart. The poorly constructed opening lines tumble out of Ronstadt's mouth, "I was born in Gainesville, Florida/ And my father was a tailor/ And my mother ran a café near the university."

"[Newman] writes these things that are so outrageously challenging that you have to have 97 octaves to sing them," Ronstadt said in her defense. Newman sympathized. "I can't sing it in a million years," he admits. "I mean, I can, in a stylistic, broken way. The range itself is impossible for me." It was no more possible for Ronstadt (whose vocal range is impressive) because, besides the rhythmless construction, Newman's words also lack their usual lyricism. In "Gainesville," we learn only that Margaret (like the Gretchen in Goethe's *Faust)* is pure of heart, that she has a brother who died and that she is looking to find the perfect man to love her.

Annoyed that God has interfered with Henry's love life, the Devil looks to find a partner for himself. He settles on Martha (Bonnie Raitt), the town siren and a friend of Margaret's. Her song, "Life Has Been Good," is a blues shuffle with Benmont Tench (of Tom Petty's Heartbreakers) providing a little gospel flavor with the Hammond B3 organ. Although Raitt's voice is a little too studied to bring out all of the lyric's lascivious fun, the tune still has an agreeable bounce:

> *Life has been good to me*
> *Well, I admit I've had a ball*

*Life has been good to me*
*I never worry 'bout nothin' at all.*

Given Martha's hedonistic tendencies, the Devil falls for her hard ("as only a middle-aged man can fall for a beautiful but heartless young girl," Newman writes in the liner notes). He seduces her by singing "I Gotta Be Your Man," a New Orleans blues featuring some wild and rapid chord changes that's perhaps too complex for the sentiments it contains ("Let me be your lover boy/ I just wanna hold your hand"). Martha reciprocates with "Feels Like Home," one of Newman's *least* passionate songs, though it also happens to be one of his most popular ones. "Feels Like Home" has the kind of "honest" sentiment that makes you immediately suspicious of the content. "'Feels Like Home' doesn't interest me lyrically at all," Newman confessed to Timothy White. "It's just unfortunate that my taste didn't coincide with the public's tastes." With the untrustworthy narrator absent, Raitt's performance comes across as fake and the lyrics seem wrong for the libidinous Martha:

*If you knew how lonely my life has been*
*And how low I've felt for so long*
*If you knew how I wanted someone*
*To come along*
*And change my world the way you've done*
*Feels like home to me.*

"Feels Like Home," besides appearing in Nora Ephron's disastrous film *Michael,* was recorded by Linda Ronstadt on her 1995 album of the same name. Canadian singer Chantal Kreviazuk also did a solemn reading for her album, *Colour Moving and Still* (1999).

Newman quickly undercuts the earnest sentiment of "Feels Like Home" by having Martha almost immediately dump Lucifer, leaving him to pine away in the next track, "Bleeding All Over the Place." The duet between Newman and Raitt features a call and response that lacks the seductive cooing heard in similar duets performed by Louis Armstrong and Ella Fitzgerald. "Bleeding All Over the Place" begins with Newman quoting Hank Williams' "Why Don't You Love Me" ("Why don't you love me like you used to do?") before the Devil laments his lost love:

*I wander aimlessly, not knowing what to do*
*I've become quite shameless in my love for you*
*I'm trying real hard to understand*
*Have you been sleeping with another man?*

As Lucifer sits in despair, Margaret, against her better instincts, falls for Faust, as we hear in the ballad "My Hero." This rather bland cry of love doesn't do justice to Margaret's newly discovered passion. Newman's lyrics aren't much help, since they sound like something found in a fortune cookie:

*Listen to your heart*
*It will tell you everything*
*Follow it wherever it would go.*

Faust's heart tells him to poison Margaret's protective mother so he can sleep with Margaret. As in Goethe's version, Margaret is impregnated, drawing the ire of her brother, Valentine. With the help of Lucifer, Faust kills Valentine, after which the Devil and Faust leave town for a year.

While they're gone, Margaret has Faust's child, but is so consumed with grief she drowns it in a creek. ("This is the comic high point of Goethe's original play," Newman adds sarcastically in his liner notes, "and one of the most delightfully urbane moments in all of German literature.") Margaret is put on trial for murder, found guilty and sentenced to die at the Indiana State Prison. In jail, she sings "Sandman's Coming" — the same song actress Kathleen Wilhoite, playing a crack addict, performed in the TV show *Cop Rock*. Although Ronstadt's performance is more assured here than on "Gainesville" and "My Hero," it's too poised to summon much of the anguish in the song. Although Margaret is ultimately executed, since she was basically a good person the angels rescue her spirit before she dies. Faust returns to see the consequences of his deeds and asks the Lord for forgiveness. When he takes some of the poison he gave to Margaret's mother, he begins to expire violently. The Lord declares his soul is saved, thus depriving the Devil of victory — and righteously annoying him. After a lengthy depression, Lucifer heads for his alternate Heaven — Las

Vegas. "Happy Ending" closes the musical with a swing number that includes a tasty Hawaiian guitar that twangs intermittently. Here Newman gets to cut loose a little — even if the song merely grinds *Faust* to a halt.

There were several tunes, of varying quality, that Newman cut from the album, including "Each Perfect Day," which described God's rather dull upbringing:

> *The grass is green*
> *The sky is blue*
> *Each perfect day*
> *Is a dream come true.*

"It Was Beautiful" is a pensive ballad God sings to the Devil about His dream of a better life. "Damn Fine Day" was written for a scene in which Faust and the Devil watch the St. Patrick's Day Parade. Newman wanted to fit the Notre Dame Drill Chorus out in bunny suits. "March of the Protestants," a song attacking Catholic values, was to be heard during the actual parade. It has some of the stately pageantry of Miklos Rozsa's "Parade of the Charioteers" from *Ben Hur* (1959). The most ambitious production number was "Love Time." Set during the depression and choreographed to resemble a Busby Berkeley number, "Love Time" features the Devil standing at the top of a staircase looking down on a street scene. He spots a girl in a white nightgown who is being encouraged by a crowd to jump from a bridge and commit suicide. She looks up at the Devil, who also tells her to leap. At her death, she enters a land of love decorated with hearts everywhere ("and four girls looking like Joan Blondell sitting at a table doing their nails," Newman explains). Meanwhile, the Devil, in a Fred Astaire top hat, tap-dances his way over to her — while simultaneously exposing himself to the audience, at which point (in the style of a Fats Waller song) he puts the moves on her:

> *Let's spoon a little*
> *Croon a little*
> *Moon a little*
> *Tune a little*
> *Pretty soon*

*In a little while*
*I'll be all over you*
*It's love time.*

After a brief quote from "Here Comes the Bride," the Devil takes her to bed, but like the character in "Gone Dead Train," he can't get it up. "I'm tired I guess," laments the limp Lucifer as love time quickly turns to down time.

Another rejected song, "Hard Currency," whose melody resembles "The Ballad of the Three Amigos," provides a rather desperate explanation for Martha's exit from the musical. She betrays Margaret by stealing her jewels and plans to take off to Costa Rica to live a more opulent life. Once she "gives her regards to Broadway," she boards a plane and takes off. Originally, Newman also planned to end *Faust* with Spencer Williams' "Basin Street Blues," a tribute to New Orleans that certainly would have been a better destination for the Devil than Las Vegas. Vegas, with its lavish sense of sin, is too easy a target, and it doesn't reverberate for Newman in the way that New Orleans does. New Orleans is *his* land of dreams, and it also conjured up the Devil's music: jazz and blues.

Since most of the musical is taken from Part One of Goethe's parable, Newman sidesteps Goethe's heavily symbolic conclusion. There is no Helen of Troy (whose majestic beauty inspired the play's most celebrated line, about the face that launched a thousand ships), or Care (who tests Faust's resolve in the end and blinds him). Faust's redemption, in which, with the help of Mephistopheles, he reclaims from the sea a submerged piece of land, is a more powerfully poetic ending than Newman's rather lifeless and directionless conception. But the major fault with Newman's *Faust* is that he's wrapped up so tightly with Goethe's version he doesn't truly make the story his own. It lacks the imaginative power, for example, of Brian De Palma's comparable 1974 film, *Phantom of the Paradise*. De Palma sets his musical satire in the contemporary world of rock & roll, while combining the *Phantom of the Opera* and *The Picture of Dorian Gray* with *Faust*. He tells the story of Winslow Leach (William Finley), a composer writing a cantata based on *Faust*. Leach is robbed of his music by Swan (Paul Williams), an entrepreneur looking for the right music to open his rock palace, the Paradise. We soon discover that Swan is under contract to the Devil in a deal to attain eternal youth, which is why he strongly identifies with

Winslow's piece. Swan wants it performed by artists who he thinks have commercial potential. The comically varied bands, all played by the same trio of performers, include The Juicy Fruits, a doo-wop ensemble; The Beach Bums, a surf band; and finally, The Undead, a goth-glam group (complete with Kiss-inspired makeup). When Winslow is maimed (by a record-pressing machine), he stalks the Paradise as a masked phantom, killing anyone who performs *Faust* — except for the singer Phoenix (Jessica Harper), whom he loves.

Where De Palma ingeniously adapts and integrates Goethe's themes into his own Grand Guignol design, Newman rather glibly incorporates the plotline. De Palma daringly sets *Faust* in the corruptible world of rock, which has a long history of recording artists' selling their souls for a hit. The songs (written by the usually smarmy Paul Williams) are also much smarter and wittier than Newman's batch — and they all toy with the themes of *Faust*. "Goodbye, Eddie, Goodbye," sung by the Juicy Fruits, begins by parodying the melodramatic clichés of *West Side Story*. It also echoes the tragic suicide of Johnny Ace, who killed himself in a game of Russian roulette on Christmas Day in 1954, sending his greatest song, "Pledging My Love," to the top of the charts. "Upholstery," sung by the Beach Bums, is a hilarious rewrite of Brian Wilson's "Don't Worry Baby," in which a game of chicken between two guys and their cars turns into a Faustian bargain over pride. "Somebody Super Like You (Beef Construction Song)," sung by The Undead, is an uproarious parody of Nietzsche's Superman reborn as an androgynous Glam God named Beef (cleverly invoking David Bowie in his Ziggy Stardust phase, and played by the peerless Gerrit Graham). In this instance, the rock audience becomes the sacrificial object, but instead of trading their souls, they offer up their limbs to construct Beef and give him life. Faustian themes wind like a river through the numerous musical genres. The composer Winslow is a better dramatic construct than Newman's Faust (although Don Henley is a far more dynamic performer than William Finley). When Winslow becomes the Phantom, his lament has more poignancy, more urgency, than Henry Faust's:

> *To work it out I let them in*
> *All the good guys and the bad guys that I've been*
> *All the devils that disturb me*

> *And the angels that defeated them somehow*
> *Come together in me now.*

Phoenix is a much more worthy (and corruptible) object of desire than Margaret. Ronstadt is never allowed to reach the deeper reserves of desire and sorrow that Jessica Harper's singing does in "Old Souls":

> *Our paths have crossed and parted*
> *This love affair was started long ago*
> *This love survives the ages*
> *In its story lives are pages*
> *Fill them up*
> *May ours turn slow.*

In the end, Paul Williams' Swan is a more ambiguous devil than Newman. Where Newman shakes his tail and becomes cosy with the part, Williams remains mysterious and creepy. His discomforting personality — drawn from his pop songs and past screen roles — blends elusively into the part he's playing. Williams' final song, "The Hell of It," is more self-incriminating than Newman's "Happy Ending." Where Newman's song becomes self-congratulatory, "The Hell of It" includes our own unresolved feelings about Paul Williams, the composer and actor:

> *Good for nothin', bad in bed*
> *Nobody likes you and you're better off dead*
> *Goodbye, we've all come to say goodbye*
> *Born defeated, died in vain*
> *Super destruction, you were hooked on pain*
> *Tho' your music lingers on*
> *All of us are glad you're gone.*

*Phantom of the Paradise* never became the cult classic it deserved to be (it was eclipsed by the inferior *The Rocky Horror Picture Show*), but it remains a great contemporary *Faust* musical. It integrates, with shrewdness and bold imagination, Goethe's themes of damnation and salvation into a contemporary setting. By contrast, Newman's *Faust* is a lethargic piece of craftsmanship with no soul to sell.

In September 1995, Newman released *Faust* on album while announcing a confirmed run at the La Jolla Playhouse in San Diego. During the workshop, James Lapine, Stephen Sondheim's frequent collaborator, originally came in as director. But in the end, he and Newman had differences over the material. "[Lapine] saw it differently, as more serious, sort of earnest and making points," Newman told Chris Willman. "I'm not interested in making any points." Lapine was quickly replaced with Michael Greif *(Rent)*. "Randy's story is satiric and complicated," Greif said in explaining the difference between the Broadway musical and Newman's original cast album. "What producers of musicals on Broadway believe an audience wants is a love story. *Faust* is a very clever, very funny experience that does not demand the same emotional involvement or reward that *Rent* does." Then Newman brought in David Mamet to collaborate on a rewrite of the book. After a moderately successful run at La Jolla, *Faust* opened the Goodman Theatre mainstage season in Chicago in the fall of 1996.

For the stage production, set-designer Thomas Lynch created a number of revolving and sliding panels, while Jan Hartley provided a series of projections, including cartoon thought-bubbles on the panels just above the actors' heads. The stage was divided vertically into Heaven and Hell. Heaven had a deep blue sky and glittering stars, while Hell was bright red, with yellow tongues of flames projected on a stretched fabric. Robert Brustein of *The New Republic* described Lynch's design for Hell as "a cross between an industrial warehouse and a supermarket." Black actor Ken Page, as God, opened the show by singing "Glory Train" in a deep basso voice — a sharp contrast to the wispy vocalizing of James Taylor. A cast of smiling angels, all dressed in white, danced around him. Casting Page as God was an obvious reference to Rex Ingram's "De Lawd" in *The Green Pastures*. A number of scenes written by Mamet were also added to the stage production. For instance, in Hell, Lucifer (David Garrison) is a corporate CEO who goes through the morning mail, stamping memos with edicts like: "Burn," "Bake" or "Fry." The Devil hires a lackey who pops in to tell him that Hitler called, complaining that someone had poisoned his dog again. "Fuck 'im," Lucifer replies. Lucifer also has meetings with God on His golf course where, between swings, God draws on His pipe like Bing Crosby. Kurt Deutsch filled the role of the perpetual stoner Henry

Faust, dancing on his bed belting out energetic rock songs. Bellamy Young gave what reviewer Richard Henzel called "a sweet simplicity" to the part of Margaret, while Sherie Scott, as the siren Martha, performed a striptease to "Damn Fine Day" during the St. Patrick's Day parade. Newman also restored "Hard Currency," the song in which Martha takes off to Costa Rica with Margaret's necklace. In the scene, Newman had half a full-sized plane brought onto the stage while Costa Rican dancers performed a hora around her. Historical figures also turned up in various scenes, including Napoleon, Caligula, Nero and Beethoven (one of Newman's favorite composers).

Newman had hoped to open the production on Broadway that same year but there just weren't sufficient funds to stage it. And the reviews had been pretty mixed. Robert Brustein's pan in *The New Republic*, for example, ended with a backhanded compliment: "I would think Randy Newman's *Faust* has a moderate chance at being a success on Broadway. It is certainly dumb enough." The album was also a commercial failure, barely cracking the *Billboard* chart. "It didn't sell much, and it was hard to find a scapegoat," Newman told Barney Hoskyns. "You know, you had Elton John and Don Henley and Linda Ronstadt on it. There was only one negative involved: me!" Oddly enough, the La Jolla Playhouse production of *Faust* did attract an audience, but it wasn't the crowd that generally attended Newman's concerts. "Sixty-five-year-old women who didn't even know my name really liked *Faust*," Newman told the *Seattle Weekly* with some bemusement. Yet despite the failure of both the album and the show, he still felt he had accomplished something significant. "Everything I know is in it," he told Chris Willman. "I thought it was the best thing I'd ever done, the stage version." His work has always had a theatrical component, so perhaps Newman felt doing a musical was a logical step in fulfilling — and enlarging — that aspect of his work. "I *loved* the theater. All that bullshit about it getting in your blood is true."

In England, there were Newman fans who also had the theater in their blood. A musical revue called *Roll With the Punches: The Songs of Randy Newman* played the Tricycle Theatre in London in the summer of 1996. Directed by Chris Bond, with musical direction from Terry Mortimer, the eighty-five-minute show starred George Costigan, Belinda Lang and Paul J. Medford, and featured a collection of songs framed by a boy-meets-girl story. With no more than three lines spoken between numbers, the revue featured a vast selection of material — from the familiar "I Love L.A." to the less recognizable "Take Me Back," and including "Sail Away," "Falling in Love," "Guilty" and "Pants." Costigan portrayed Newman while Lang played Marie (inspired, obviously, by the song), Medford turned up as the bartender from "Mikey" and Ray Shell played God (in "God's Song (That's Why I Love Mankind)").

Where Chris Bond and Terry Mortimer reached for the dramatic and theatrical aspect of Newman's best songs, Newman's *Faust* attempted to compress the major themes of his songs into a popular theatrical concept. Its failure was less about overreaching ambition, however, than it was a failure of imagination and a retreat into the safe and familiar. Rather than drawing on Newman's strengths, the stage musical underlined his weaknesses. The ambiguity of Newman's brilliant disguise became merely shtick, a cute and clever mask to hide behind. But for an artist as restless and bold as Newman, failure never turns into an admission of defeat. As he continued writing film soundtracks, a concept album was taking form that would soon put the devil back into his daring.

# 4

One night in the late seventies, on their network TV show, Donny and Marie Osmond decided to perform a nostalgic tribute to the glorious days of our youth. Decked out in spangles and bell-bottoms, the duo picked a contemporary pop standard they believed caught the mood of nostalgia. As they began, they traded lines of the song as if exchanging precious memories:

> *You're everlasting summer*
> *You can see it fadin' fast*
> *So you grab a piece of somethin'*
> *That you think is gonna last*
> *Well, you wouldn't know a diamond*
> *If you held it in your hand*
> *The things you think are precious*
> *I can't understand.*

Despite the bitter and acrimonious tone of the lyrics, the siblings' performance was upbeat and grossly energetic. They exchanged smiles, tossed individual lines to each other and reached out their hands as if eagerly anticipating their high school reunion. By the time they reached the chorus and were singing in harmony, their mood turned exuberant:

> *Are you reelin' in the years*
> *Stowin' away the time*
> *Are you gatherin' up the tears*
> *Have you had enough of mine?*

You probably recognize the song they selected as their tribute to the past: Steely Dan's 1972 hit "Reelin' in the Years." Hardly conceived as a bouquet of roses to the good ol' days, "Reelin' in the Years" was in fact a viciously satiric attack on those who do get misty over a walk down memory lane. But Donny and Marie responded only to the effervescent bounce in the melody. Just as Randy Newman songs have left many performers woefully misinterpreting "Sail Away" or "You Can Leave Your Hat On," Steely Dan have also pulled the wool over the eyes of other artists and their fans. Though it's rarely talked about, Steely Dan and Randy Newman are, in fact, kindred spirits.

While Newman was putting the finishing touches on *Sail Away* in 1972, two frustrated songwriters from New York City, Donald Fagen and Walter Becker, decided to form a band. The pair met in 1967 at Bard College, discovering a mutual love for both black jazz and black humor while the rest of the college was grooving to Vanilla Fudge. Once Fagen graduated (and Becker got booted out), they decided to enter a partnership as songwriters. They first sought out the Brill Building, where they sold a few songs, including "I Mean to Shine" (covered by Barbra Streisand). But they soon found their sardonic sense of humor made it impossible to continue writing pop ballads designed to be hit records. In 1970, the duo abandoned songwriting and acquired employment as roadies for Jay & the Americans. But life on the road soon bored them, and they began writing songs at ABC Records, a label that took an interest in them and encouraged Fagen and Becker to record their own stuff.

They quickly assembled a band from studio musicians they liked and called it Steely Dan, after a dildo coined by William Burroughs in his novel *Naked Lunch* (1959). Nobody seemed to get that little joke, so they took the prank further by composing obtuse, sardonic songs adorned by crisp and commercially friendly melodies. Underneath Steely Dan's smooth jazz arrangements lay some pretty deranged comic stories. "We think of our records as comedy records to some degree," Fagen told *The New York Times* in 2003. "There wasn't really any model for that sort of thing, with the possible exception of Frank Zappa. But when we first started, people thought our style belied the actual content of the lyrics. So they thought we were just some sort of sincere California band. I guess that's the secret of subversion." It's this subversion that links Steely Dan's music to Randy Newman. While stylistically different, they have a shared sensibility: Steely Dan was the brainchild of two wiseass Jewish writers who drank at the same watering hole as Newman. In *Avant Rock: Experimental Music from the Beatles to Björk*, Bill Martin writes: "What really makes the Steely Dan vision . . . is a synthesis of jazz-rock with a sound from the first decades of the 20th century, a sound that I associate with Cole Porter, the Gershwin Brothers and Duke Ellington — I would call this sound 'music deco.' As with the art deco movement in design and architecture, music deco is innovation developed from popular materials. And, as with art deco, there is a definite Jewish side to music deco, or a synthesis of Jewish and African-American influences."

While incorporating such influences, Steely Dan also became masters of disguise and believers in the untrustworthy narrator. Besides the neatly veiled but anti-nostalgic "Reelin' in the Years," from *Can't Buy a Thrill* (1972), the band produced a number of deceptively perverse songs that miraculously found their way onto the radio. "Show Biz Kids," with its catchy, funky melody, took a well-aimed shot at the Hollywood rich and poor — not to mention their fans. Look closely, and "Rikki Don't Lose That Number," which borrowed its seductive jazz melody from Horace Silver's "Song for My Father," is really about a transvestite. Likewise "The Fez," with its exotic dance rhythms, is actually a lighthearted advisory about wearing condoms. "Pretzel Logic," which accurately describes the swastika, partly takes on the subject of Adolph Hitler. "Any World (That I'm Welcome To)" is a powerful critique of conventional life with a melody so beguiling you can sometimes hear the song playing in the most conventional of places — like a supermarket.

When Newman recorded his *Bad Love* album in 1999, he may not have had Steely Dan on his mind, but it's hard to imagine this particular record without them. The scabrous intelligence at work on *Bad Love* shares Steely Dan's curmudgeonly view of human nature and is as comically detached as some of their albums. *Bad Love,* Newman's first release on Dreamworks Records, was a sharply focused album. Where he had seemed utterly lost and indistinct on *Faust,* his powers of observation were at their sharpest and most bittersweet here. "There's a thread running through it," Newman explains. "[There's] some kind of pathological love in most of these songs." As it turns out, true love was happening in his life. In 1990, Newman wed 35-year-old Gretchen Preece, a receptionist in the building where his office once was, with whom he had been having the affair that ultimately ended his marriage to Roswitha. Preece initially had her doubts about getting involved with Newman. "I thought it was possible that it was aberrant behaviour — that I chased her *because* she ran away," Newman recalls. "She treated me worse than anybody. And I felt, well I hope there's something else there, till the day I married her. And it's worked out fine." According to Newman, he fell in love with Gretchen because she laughed at his jokes. Within a few years, he and his new bride had two kids, Patrick and Alice, and purchased a house in Brentwood.

On *Bad Love,* Newman put together a new production team that included Mitchell Froom and Tchad Blake, who had also worked with Elvis Costello, Suzanne Vega and Los Lobos. He had been introduced to Froom by Lenny Waronker, who had recently made the switch from Warner Brothers to Dreamworks. "We're a small company," Waronker told Bernard Weintraub in *The New York Times.* "Every record counts with us." Newman was very happy with the recommendation. "Mitchell is a very, very good musician — he's got perfect pitch," Newman remarked. "And he added a great deal with what he did on keyboards. He's proficient in an area I don't care that much about — basic tracks." The presence of Froom meant Newman was left to do the arrangements and conduct the orchestra. He also helped Newman improve in certain areas where he was already proficient. "Mitchell made me feel comfortable about my singing and playing," Newman said. "He realizes that I do what I do and it's okay if it's not technically perfect. It's my style." *Bad Love* was one of Newman's happiest experiences making a record — and you can certainly hear the exhilaration on the album. "It was quick and yet we didn't lower our standards," he said of the record.

After thirty years with Warner Brothers, *Bad Love* marked the first label change in Newman's career. But while it was a big deal for Newman, Warners didn't seem to care. "I've sent Warners an amusing letter of resignation and I haven't heard anything. It's like trying to find a general to surrender to," Newman said after signing the Dreamworks contract. Dreamworks, however, didn't prove any more cordial to Newman than Warners had been. "I haven't heard from them [either]! The people I'm leaving don't give a shit that I'm leaving and the people I'm coming to don't give a shit that I'm coming!" By the time *Bad Love* was released, Dreamworks' cavalier attitude towards Newman had led to bad blood.

The album opens with the autobiographical song "My Country," which explores the pervasive effect television had on Randy's family as he was growing up. "[This song] is probably the closest to autobiographical that I've ever written," he told Michael Enright of the CBC. "What our family did growing up was watch *The Jackie Gleason Show* and *Phil Silvers* and we would bounce what we had to say off the screen." Whereas in earlier songs like "Love Story" and "So Long Dad," Newman created fictional American families to explore the intricate relationships within them, on "My Country" he was drawing more directly on his own. "The family time was consumed every night with watching television: my mother in a chair, dad on the sofa, me lying on the floor and my brother sitting behind me," Newman recalls. The song opens with what initially sounds like a nostalgic yearning for family togetherness. But before long, we come to realize it's really about how a family is fractured and distracted:

> *We were watching and we couldn't look away*
> *We all know what we look like*
> *You know what I mean*
> *We wouldn't have it any other way.*

Whatever emotions aren't expressed face to face, or hurled at the television screen, are buried instead:

*Feelings might go unexpressed*
*I think that's probably for the best*
*Dig too deep who knows what you will find.*

But Newman doesn't moralize about how television breaks up the sanctity of the family in the way Barry Levinson did in *Avalon*. Instead he is showing us, in a satirical manner, how TV has altered the intimate way families once related to each other. When he describes his home scene as "my country," Newman's also poking fun at the dynamics of his tiny nuclear family. Television offers us a window on the world at large — the actual country out there — but all they can do is project onto the TV screen the things they can't say to each other. When the kids in the song grow up and move out, they all get televisions of their own. But still they come over to the family house to join Mom and Pop watching the tube. "The guy in the song doesn't understand why his kids would come over to his house," Newman told Michael Enright. "He thinks, 'They have their own TVs; why do they want to come over and watch mine? If you have a television, why would you go any-where?' That's where this person lives — it's his country, televisionland." "My Country" anticipates some of the themes later explored in Newman's score for *Pleasantville*.

Newman has described "Shame" as a song about "a love with no accounting for dignity," about the intangible power younger women have over older men. Set in New Orleans, "Shame" is a blues shuffle that resembles *Faust*'s "I Gotta Be Your Man," which has the Devil desperately trying to score with Martha. But "Shame" is an infinitely better song, and the character here is so bamboozled by love he con-fuses it with infatuation — he's even reduced to begging. "'Shame' is a character you're familiar with in literature," Newman told Barney Hoskyns. "There must be somebody like that in Eudora Welty or Faulkner. A Southern guy who's old and sort of smooth but not smart enough to be *really* smooth, and with a bad temper. He's got the Lexus and he's got money and he lives in the Quarter, but this kid's killing him. If you fall for a 22-year-old, as powerful as you are, it can destroy you. And I love that that exists, in a way." The song has its antecedent in Steely Dan's "Hey Nineteen," from the 1981 album *Gaucho*. In that song, the protagonist is a middle-aged man trying to pick up a nubile creature at a rock club, but can't find any way to communicate with her. The funniest aspect of the song may be his misconception that he can score with her if he plays her an Aretha Franklin song, a singer she is likely too young to recognize.

"Shame" expresses with shrewd wit the terror of a once powerful man succumbing to the ravages of old age:

> *You know what it feels like*
> *To have to get up in the middle of the night*
> *And sit down to take a piss?*
> *You do know?*
> *So you say.*

Newman successfully accomplishes in "Shame" what he set out to do in the unreleased "Good Morning," from *Johnny Cutler's Birthday*. There he created conflicting emotions within the same song by staging an argument between Marie and Johnny. In "Shame," Newman uses a female chorus (borrowed from Shirley & Company's disco classic, "Shame, Shame, Shame," but used comically) as his adversary, continually interrupting and admonishing him. Like Johnny chiding Marie in "Good Morning," Newman's voice vainly attempts to shut them up.

Back in the sixties, Mick Jagger told *Disc Magazine* something of his fears of getting old while still performing. "I've worked out that I'd be fifty in 1984," he said. "I'd be dead! Horrible isn't it. . . . I can see myself coming onstage in my black, windowed, invalid carriage with a stick. Then I turn around, wiggle my bottom at the audience and say something like 'Now here's an old song you might remember called 'Satisfaction.'" In 2004, Jagger's still out there wiggling his bottom, his nightmare come horribly true. In "I'm Dead (But I Don't Know It)," Newman parodies Jagger's worst fears — and the worst excesses of the dozens of ancient rock stars who won't abandon the stage:

> *I have nothing to say*
> *But I'm going to say it anyway*
> *Thirty years upon a stage*
> *And I hear the people say*
> *Why won't he go away?*

"I'll quit when I think I'm slipping," Newman told Arthur Lubow of *People*. "Everyone was saying 15 years ago, when they were twenty-five,

'Oh, I'll never be doing this when I'm forty. There's no chance.' Well, no one's leaving the stage."

Newman ingeniously employs every rock cliché here — as he did in "The Story of a Rock & Roll Band" on *Born Again* — using percussion sounds played backwards and duelling guitars straight out of Van Halen's "Ain't Talking About Love" and the Kinks' "All Day and All of the Night." Newman says the song is about "a kind of blinding self-love" and sees it as a cautionary tale about himself. "The career path in rock & roll is usually: people do their best work then fade out," he told Alan Taylor of *The Sunday Herald*. "I watch myself very closely for signs of decay, and they're all around me, but I don't think the work has suffered, maybe because of the movies, because you have to show up and do something every day."

"Every Time It Rains" is one of the few conventional love songs on the record, and it could just as easily have fit into Newman's early period at Metric Music. Written for Michael Jackson, who never recorded it, it's a sombre ballad for piano and acoustic guitar (augmented with a sumptuous string section) that contains some of Newman's most plaintive lyrics:

> *Every time it rains*
> *And summer showers soak the ground*
> *I watch the rain come pouring down*
> *And I call out your name.*

Like "Marie" and "Feels Like Home," Newman finds "Every Time It Rains" uncharacteristic of his work. "It's really the type of song I don't write — a straightforward love song," he explains. "But I'm glad I get a chance to get out of myself a little bit and do something like this. It wouldn't surprise me if 'Every Time It Rains' were the easiest to take for people who've never heard me before." The song would be covered faithfully — as an easier-to-take number — by Joe Cocker on his 2002 release *Respect Yourself*.

"The Great Nations of Europe," based on Alfred Crosby's 1993 book, *European Ecological Imperialism: The Biological Expansion of Europe, 900–1900*, is the other side of the coin represented by "Political Science" — only this time countries across the Atlantic get skewered. Crosby argues that when Europeans colonized New Zealand, Australia and North America, the plants and animals they brought with them carried diseases that wiped out the natives. Newman sets his hilariously pompous march in the 16th century, just as Europe begins gleefully pillaging each new land she encounters:

> *The Grand Canary Islands*
> *First land to which they came*
> *They slaughtered all the canaries*
> *Which gave the land its name.*

While describing the sudden disappearance of Guanches natives ("You've never seen anyone so gone," he sings emphatically), Newman sends out his clarion cry:

> *Hide your wives and daughters*
> *Hide your groceries too*
> *Great nations of Europe coming through.*

Newman deftly dances his way through history, casually calling up Columbus and Balboa, who is introduced to natives that he's told are gay (at which point, Newman warns us to hide our sons as well). From there the song takes a daring leap into Africa where HIV begins to loom large. "The Great Nations of Europe," despite its subject matter, is surprisingly free of rancor. Newman didn't feel, however, that he'd humanized the song enough. "I thought it was going to be one of the best I've written," he told Jim Macnie of the *Providence Phoenix*. "[But it's] . . . like I'm standing there with a pointer in my hand pointing at history." Despite Newman's reservations, "The Great Nations of Europe" is less a formal history lesson than a wicked romp through human folly.

"The One You Love" is a song about the fragile bonds of commitment that shares some of the romantic ambivalence of his 1970 track "Let Me Go." Like "Shame," it's also about a love that can't sustain itself. The character in "The One You Love" keeps trying to define the perfect woman, but he constantly gets tripped up by actions he can't control and feelings he doesn't anticipate:

*She can hurt you*
*With the sound of her voice*
*You can leave her*
*But you got no choice*
*You can't leave her, man*
*You're just a prisoner*
*Of the one you love.*

"The One You Love," a blues shuffle with a delectable R&B chorus of female vocalists, isn't about the yearning and heartbreak of young love. Rather, it's a song written by an older, experienced man with a keen sense of his own mortality. "My wife [Gretchen] and I had a turbulent courtship, and she scared me half the time," Newman recalls. "I'd talk to her on the phone, and maybe when she hung up she'd say, 'Okay, bye.' And I'd think, 'Uh-oh' — it was a bad goodbye. I was like forty-eight years old or something, and a bad goodbye would just kill me." "The One You Love" is a cutting song about the loved ones you could die for.

In *The Social Contract* (1762) Jean-Jacques Rousseau lamented that man is born free but everywhere was still in chains, a dilemma that would haunt philosophers and political idealists long after him, including Karl Marx. In "The World Isn't Fair," Newman gets to the heart of that contradiction in his own inimitable way, conjuring up the ghost of Marx and casually introducing him to the dystopian world that emerged in his wake. "It's a truism to say it: the world isn't fair," he explained to James Keast of *Exclaim!* "You know, why don't school-teachers get a million dollars, [instead of] Madonna? Oh, I don't know. Why? Gee, God's ways are mysterious." Newman opens the song with music that suggests a coronation. Then he begins to tell the story of the rise of a public-spirited man, concentrating on the early details of his life (including the dreams of *The Communist Manifesto*). He even provides a simple summary of Marx's dense critique of capitalism:

*There'll be no exploitation*
*Of the worker or his kin*
*No discrimination 'cause the color of your skin*
*No more private property*
*It would not be allowed.*

Newman also slips in a little joke about the inevitability of Marx's theories:

> *No one could rise too high*
> *No one could sink too low*
> *Or go under completely*
> *Like some we all know.*

"The World Isn't Fair" is a terrific companion piece to "My Life Is Good." While the song is about Karl Marx, it's told by a beneficiary of the spoils of capitalism. As a demonstration of the ways in which the world isn't fair, the narrator takes Marx to a private school orientation, where a number of beautiful women are arrayed for the night. But instead of equally dazzling companions on their arms, their partners are "froggish men":

> *Were you to kiss one Karl*
> *Nary a prince would there be.*

The idea for the song came to Newman when he went to his own kid's school orientation and saw beautiful women ("looking like Gwyneth Paltrow") partnered with "all these old guys who look like me." Joining the ranks of "It's Money That I Love," the song also skewers liberal values. "You start out as a nice liberal and you think bad people will be punished for their misdeeds, or at least the undeserving people should not and will not profit," Newman said. "But it just doesn't turn out that way. So I imagined explaining this to Karl Marx." In the song, Newman perceptively takes Marx's egalitarian political philosophy and applies it to the politics of sex, demonstrating how unfair the world really is, even in matters of love. While Newman goes on to describe to Marx the tyranny and bloodshed of the communist systems built in his name, Newman also draws a somewhat sarcastic portrait of his preferred life in America:

> *I'm glad I'm living in the land of the free*
> *Where the rich just get richer*

*And the poor you never have to see*
*It would depress us, Karl*
*Because we care*
*That the world isn't fair.*

Newman touches brilliantly on the paradox of American capitalism, which creates its own misery as it holds out promise to those less fortunate in the world. After all, both communism and American democracy were the products of idealistic dreamers. In "The World Isn't Fair," Newman accepts this reality — especially in American life — without necessarily condoning it. "This republic was founded on an unworldly assumption, a denial of 'the facts of life,'" Mary McCarthy wrote in an essay about American democracy included in *On the Contrary* (1962). "It is manifestly untrue that all men are created equal; interpreted in worldly terms, this doctrine has resulted in a pseudo-equality, that is, in standardization, in an equality of things rather than persons. The inalienable rights to life, liberty and the pursuit of happiness appear, in practice, to have become the inalienable right to a bathtub, a flush toilet and a can of Spam." Newman's yuppie interprets those "inalienable rights" in much the same way. He lives out his freedom happily insulated by the material goods he feels the American Dream owes him. Because of the peculiar chemistry of human nature, Newman confidently tells us the world can never be fair.

"Big Hat, No Cattle" is a country and western song about a confidence man with plenty of bluster and nothing up his sleeve. In this oddly funny, incisive examination of self-deception, Newman was inspired by Geoffrey Wolff's memoir, *The Duke of Deception* (1990). Wolff traces the life of his father, someone who appeared to be living an exemplary life, but turned out to be a fraud in every way. "I'm talking about people who base a whole life on lying, people who have cards that say 'producer,' or 'CEO, Cloverdale Music,'" Newman said in explaining the song. "What does it cost to have cards printed up with anything you want? Nothing." Like a great novelist, Newman reads between the lines of the character's delusions and rationalizations:

*Oft times I wondered what I might have become*
*Had I buckled down and really tried*

*But when it came down to the wire*
*I called my family to my side*
*Stood up straight, threw my head back, and I lied, lied, lied.*

"Big Hat, No Cattle" later turned up in the soundtrack of *Jurassic Park III* (2001).

"Better Off Dead" deals with a bad romantic partnership: the singer gets hung up on a woman who could not care less about him:

*Someone who doesn't want you*
*But won't let go*
*Someone who thinks you're crazy*
*And tells you so*
*Over and over and over*
*If that happens to you*
*You'd be better off dead.*

Arranged as a Latin samba, "Better Off Dead" gets a little too cute at times, as when Newman claims that when someone doesn't want you "it ramifies your head." "I know some critic is going to think I don't know what the word ramify means, or how to use it," he says. "I made up an alternate verb form of it here, like a made-up R&B word, like the 'puppetudes' of love. I wanted to say how there would be ramifications from something that happens to your head in this kind of relationship. I should have said 'blamifies' or something to make it really obvious I was playing with the word, but I just didn't give a fuck."

"I Miss You" is a song written for his ex-wife, Roswitha. Inspired by Neil Young's "Look Out For My Love," in which the adoring singer stalks his former lover like a ghost, "I Miss You," which borrows some of its melody from *Born Again's* "Ghosts," is a nakedly passionate plea for both acknowledgement and forgiveness:

*I wanted to thank you for the good years*
*And apologize for the rough ones*
*You must be laughing yourself sick*
*Up there in Idaho*
*But I wanted to write you one*

*Before I quit*
*And this one's it.*

In the process, Newman doesn't spare himself. He makes it clear that in his career he always made his own Faustian bargain, sacrificing those he cared for most ("I'd sell my soul and your souls for a song"). "'I Miss You' is genuine," Newman explained. "I love my ex-wife . . . she knows me . . . we were married eighteen years and I never wrote a song about her in all that time." Roswitha remarried in 1992, which begs the question as to what her reaction to the song would be. "I never really talked with her in depth," Newman told John Sakamoto of *The Toronto Sun*. "People could tell you it's just being forty. . . . I just never thought that it would ever happen to me. I mean, my first wife did nothing to provoke it. We never had any trouble. I got married at 23 and we were different. . . . The second [wife] is more like me." When Newman and Gretchen were on their honeymoon in Italy, he asked her if she would like to get to know Roswitha and she agreed. They finally met after the honeymoon at Michael's Restaurant in Santa Monica.

"Going Home" is a quiet lament for World War 1 which still manages to reverberate. No more complex musically than "Caroline," it's the story of a man who's lying in the trenches and who loves his country and his girl. "World War 1 fascinates me because it was such a shock to the world," Newman says. "Nothing before or since has come close. It was a horrible, horrible event. It was modern weaponry and cavalry and then tanks. They fought for four years over a hundred yards, some ridiculously small amount of ground. It's the stupidest event in history." The song was first recorded in 1977 in demo form as "Going Home (1918)," and was originally intended for inclusion on *Little Criminals*. On *Bad Love*, Newman and Froom keep it stripped down to a piano demo, but they process it through equalization to sound like an old 78. "I know Mitchell [Froom's] going to get blamed in some review for using all these effects, but we did it because I simply can't sing the thing," Newman explains.

*Bad Love* concludes with "I Want Everyone To Like Me," first recorded as a demo around the time of *Land of Dreams*. It's a bald parody of our obsession with being accepted by others ("I want everyone to approve of me/ To disapprove of me/ Makes me feel so sad/ So I could run to embrace them"). Arranged as a bouncy little jazz number with some Django Reinhardt-style swing guitar, the song expresses an obvious motivation of anyone interested in getting into show business. "Anyone in show business can say [I want everyone to like me] with a straight face," Newman told John Sakamoto. "Though you don't [usually] *say* it." Since Newman's body of work is steeped in ambiguity, he can either play against the song's true sentiments, or play it straight. Of course, like any popular artist, he wants to be liked. But given some of the songs in his catalogue, the attitudes he expresses and the people he sometimes sings about: how is a listener supposed to *like* someone like Randy Newman?

"There have been times in my life where I wondered whether I was saying things I really thought or felt or meant, or whether I was saying things to make people like me," he explains. "I first started worrying about it when I was in the sixth grade, and I still don't know the answer."

*Bad Love* is the culmination of the self-revelatory work Newman began on *Land of Dreams*. By now Newman's mask had taken on characteristics of the face beneath it, but he had been spending much of the decade writing film scores and nobody seemed to know what to do with *Bad Love* — even his record label. By 1999, Newman was mostly familiar to people because of *Toy Story*. "You know, people like 'You've Got a Friend in Me,' which I wrote for a movie so it's not saying 'fart' or 'piss' in it," Newman explains. "They're not inferior songs . . . but 'Davy the Fat Boy' or 'Shame' or 'Better Off Dead' [are] the things that interest me." But they didn't interest the record company enough to promote Newman's new album. *Bad Love* may have been a boldly funny collection of songs about how love is an absurdist farce, but that didn't keep it from going largely unnoticed. And given the strict, conventional radio playlists in the late nineties, what station would find room for offbeat songs like "The Great Nations of Europe" or "The World Isn't Fair"?

Of course, *Bad Love* was not about selling radio-friendly love songs. Newman doesn't titillate the listener with innuendo like a Britney Spears hit, his songs get into the messy, more unsettling dynamics among lovers, families and friends. "It was the best record I ever made," Newman told Aaron Wherry of *The National Post*. "[But it] sold like 80,000 [copies]." In Canada, the sales figures were even more dismal: "The record company did nothing apparently, it sold 800 records." As a result, after only one record, Dreamworks dropped

Newman from their roster. Yet even after the misstep of *Faust*, Newman was reaching new depths as a recording artist, finding ways to reveal more of himself without jeopardizing the dramatic irony that gave his songs their vitality and humor.

"My next step would be to try to enter the twenty-first century musically," Newman told Timothy White. "Pop music still hasn't reached what classical music has done in the twentieth century — I mean, [Igor] Stravinsky was a long time ago. You could do it. . . . I believe I could do it, just out of interest, just to see, but I would sell even less records." Moving into the new century, Newman would find personal and professional acclaim waiting in film music rather than in the pop world. But that was okay. He already knew the world wasn't fair. He was now about to find out just how lonely it would be at the top.

# Lonely at the Top

The mask is more real than the face. It isn't hiding anything.

— Bob Dylan

The best prophet of the future is the past.

— Chinese proverb

### 1

When the twenty-first century began, Randy Newman had already
been in the music business for more than forty years. It had been thirty
years since he'd sat in that studio playing "Lonely at the Top" for
Frank Sinatra. At that time, Newman was a young songwriter, barely
a singer and a virtual unknown as an American artist, and Sinatra was
in the twilight of his career as a master interpreter of American songs.
By 2000, Sinatra was gone, and Newman had a body of work that put
him at least closer to the top than he was when he'd met Ol' Blue Eyes.
He'd had a series of critically acclaimed albums, including *Sail Away*

and *Good Old Boys,* commercial successes like *Little Criminals,* underrated gems like *Born Again* and a deeply satisfying autobiographical record, *Land of Dreams.* He'd written a musical and, to this point, had received thirteen Academy Award nominations for his film scores. He'd been honored a year earlier by Rhino Records with a four-disc box-set called *Guilty: 30 Years of Randy Newman,* a vast selection of studio recordings, demos, singles and movie scores that showed the fascinating arc of an already eclectic career. Newman had also rebounded from the commercial debacle of *Bad Love,* his first recording of original songs in over a decade. At the end of the twentieth century, Newman realized "Lonely at the Top" may have been something of a prophesy for himself. He might have been closer to the top of his game, but it was indeed a lonely place to be.

Despite his absence on the charts and lack of radio airplay, Newman was becoming more of an iconic figure in American culture. As if to illustrate to what degree that was true, a stage production called *The Education of Randy Newman* was mounted. The musical, conceived by music arranger Michael Roth (who'd worked with Newman on *Faust)* and dramaturge Jerry Patch, recreated the life of the composer through forty of his songs. "It wasn't my idea, really," Newman told Bob Mehr of the *Seattle Weekly.* "There have been three or four different shows done based on my songs — revues mostly. But I believe this is the best one."

Set in New Orleans and Los Angeles, the musical is modeled on the famous memoir *The Education of Henry Adams* (1907). Adams, born in Boston in 1838, was the son of the American diplomat Charles Francis Adams and the grandson of President John Quincy Adams. He was an historian who described his polemical autobiography as an "accidental education," a chronicle of a storied career and a spiritual quest for knowledge. *The Education of Henry Adams* is a third-person account with fascinating and riveting vignettes of an American at home and abroad. Altogether, it is a thorough examination of the restlessness of the American mind.

Besides recounting his time at Harvard and his graduate school days in Berlin, Adams describes how he followed his father to Washington in 1860. Adams takes us nimbly through the divisive Civil War, two traumatic assassinations (Presidents Lincoln and McKinley) and the effect of the Industrial Revolution on American culture. His digressions are often gems of acquired wisdom. Contemplating the relations between America and Europe in the mid-nineteenth century, Adams wrote: "The American mind exasperated the European as a buzz saw might exasperate a pine forest." He described Lincoln as "a long, awkward figure" with "a plain, ploughed face; a mind absent in part, and in part evidently worried by white kid gloves; features that expressed neither self-satisfaction nor any other familiar Americanism. . . ."

While writing *The Education of Randy Newman*, Roth and Patch likely saw great similarities between Adams' irreverent, deeply philosophical observations and Newman's songs. For one thing, Adams' use of the third person patterns Newman's style of songwriting. Whereas Adams' skepticism appears cordial next to Newman's, they do share a humanistic view of life. Both hated school and believed education was not a formal exercise, but something gained through experience, observation and intelligent interpretation. *The Education of Randy Newman* had its world premiere at South Coast Repertory in Los Angeles on May 26, 2000. A two-act musical directed by Myron Johnson, it featured a modest ensemble (Jennifer Leigh Warren, Gregg Henry, John Lathan, Alison Smith, Jordan Bennet, Sherry Hursey and Scott Waara) playing a number of characters featured in Newman's songs.

Unfortunately, according to Steven Leigh Morris in the *LA Weekly,* the production was comparable to a stodgy lecture. The story revolves around a composer (Waara) who resembles Newman, taking a colorful excursion through a selection of Newman songs to learn about the American Dream. While Morris acknowledges *The Education of Randy Newman*'s attempts to draw an intricate portrait of America using Newman's songs, in his opinion, the work gets buried in theatrical props and clichés. For example in Act One, an ode to the South, the emphatic and poetic power of "Louisiana, 1927" is "treated as a school lesson, with the narrator-teacher (Warren) twanging her suspenders and chirping to her brightly costumed wards as though pouring jelly beans all over the song's plaintive lament." Alison Smith played one of the children mesmerized by the police parade in "Jolly Coppers on Parade," but according to Morris, the song's intent was lost: "The child gets patted on the head by Mom, and you'd think the song had been sponsored by some police union." All through the piece, various visual props were employed that douse any potential irony. "Follow the Flag" used endless visual sequences of the Stars and

Stripes. For "I Love L.A.," Johnson flashed photos of all the referenced landmarks as if they were cue cards. In a sense, the untrustworthy narrator of Newman's songs had been replaced in this musical by a trustworthy one. "Newman's work has been frequently misunderstood for the same reason that many plays are misunderstood: because audiences are unable to distinguish between a character and its author, between an argument and the unspoken, underlying reasons that a character would raise that argument," Morris writes. In 2002, with some alterations, the play would run again at the Act Theatre in Seattle. Newman's pop work was still being misunderstood, but his movie music was finally on the verge of being celebrated.

## 2

Perhaps it was a sign of things to come, but shortly after the opening of *The Education of Randy Newman,* Newman started to win awards. On December 4, 2000, Newman received the Billboard Century Award at the MGM Grand Hotel in Las Vegas, presented to him by his friend Don Henley. Two years later, Newman would win the award he dearly coveted. At the Seventy-Fourth Academy Awards at the Staples Center in Los Angeles on Sunday, March 24, 2002, a memorable evening was in store. It was a night Hollywood — long devoted to churning out versions of the American Dream — would address (as well as neatly avoid) many aspects of those factory illusions. There was controversy, an elegant tribute to black American culture, an honorary award to Robert Redford, founder of the Sundance Film Festival, the first Oscar-nomination category for Best Animated Film and a surprised winner in Randy Newman.

The controversy surrounded one of the films nominated for Best Picture, Ron Howard's *A Beautiful Mind*. It was the story of the Nobel Prize-winning mathematician John Forbes Nash Jr. (Russell Crowe), a scientific genius who happened also to be a paranoid schizophrenic. At the onset of his mental disturbance — which created pure havoc in his personal life — Nash developed theories on equilibrium that won him the Nobel Prize in 1994. On film, these complex dramatic elements, explored with great insight in Sylvia Nasar's 1998 biography, became gross simplifications. There was so much contention surrounding *A Beautiful Mind,* which ultimately won Best Picture, it prompted host

Whoopi Goldberg to comment, "So much mud has been thrown this year, all the nominees look black."

The mud-slinging proved a minor distraction. Instead, Goldberg's point about black nominees mirrored a landmark night for black performers in Hollywood. There was much to celebrate. For starters, there was the gracious and humbling tribute to one of America's greatest black actors: the groundbreaking Sidney Poitier. Denzel Washington, who would win for Best Actor in *Training Day*, remarked, "Forty years I've been chasing Sidney and what do they do — they go and give it to him on the same night." Halle Berry would also win Best Actress for her role in *Monster's Ball,* but where both Washington and Poitier were elegant in their acceptance speeches, Berry turned it into a soapbox for a long, rambling, often incoherent rant about how she was "a vessel" for all black actresses. "This moment is so much bigger than me," she exclaimed. "This is for every nameless, faceless woman of color for whom the door has been opened."

But if this edition of the Academy Awards was a night of pride for black actors celebrating how far they had come in Hollywood, for one of the Jewish artists, a cultural descendant of the people who created the industry, it was a rather sheepish and guilty affair. Woody Allen was called upon to introduce a tribute to films about New York. With the possible exception of Spike Lee or Martin Scorsese, choosing Allen made perfect sense, considering the many varied, loving movies he'd made set in the Big Apple. But instead of adopting a celebratory mood, the man who had won an Oscar for *Annie Hall* in 1977 (but never showed up to claim it) walked onstage as if he'd been pegged by security as a terrorist. "When the Academy called, I panicked," he explained nervously. "I thought they might want their Oscar back and the pawn shop has been out of business for awhile."

Unlike Allen, Randy Newman had no Oscar to give back. On the contrary, he had come to believe he'd never get one. When he finally did win, for Best Original Song ("If I Didn't Have You," from *Monsters Inc.),* he had already endured sixteen nominations without a prize. By 2002, Newman had won three Grammys, an Emmy and was scheduled to be inducted into the Songwriters Hall of Fame in June. But the Oscar (which had also eluded his Uncle Alfred many times) seemed beyond his grasp, and he was well aware his mark of futility had already tied him with art director Roland Anderson *(Breakfast at*

*Tiffany's)* and film composer Alex North *(A Streetcar Named Desire, Spartacus),* for the longest of all-time. The inevitability of Newman losing every year had some folks referring to him as the Susan Lucci of the Oscars — though like Newman, Lucci eventually did get her Emmy. Reporters like David Bianculli, in the *New York Daily News,* expressed exhaustion with seeing Newman carted out each year just to get hammered. "This isn't the Grammys," he wrote. "Much as I love Randy Newman, having him return each year to sing a song that doesn't win isn't the best use of our time, or his, or Oscar's."

Curiously, *Monsters Inc.* was the least interesting of the Pixar animated films Randy Newman scored. Where the two *Toy Story* films and *A Bug's Life* had an impish tone to match their sweetly inspired scripts, *Monsters Inc.* was a tad maudlin. Set in the city of Monstropolis, the story concerned a corporation who hired various monsters to enter the bedrooms of sleeping children through their closet doors, and scare them each night. One strict rule was that the kids could never learn about the existence of the corporation. Each shift then becomes a contest for the biggest quota of "scares." The current leader is Sully (John Goodman), a Bigfoot monster who is nothing but a cutie pie at heart. His trainer is Mikey (Billy Crystal), a huge eye fashioned with little legs, and a big mouth. Challenging Sully for the most frights is Randall (Steve Buscemi), a lizard monster with the personality of a snake. One night, as Sully tries to deliver some of Mikey's paperwork, he accidentally brings a young child, Boo (Mary Gibbs), back with him into the workplace. While Randall tries to find a way to cheat his way to the top, he discovers Sully's little accident and tries to tip off management so he can become champ. As Sully and Mikey try to hide Boo from Randall, Sully comes to love the little girl and lose his desire to scare other kids.

Some of the little details in *Monsters Inc.* are inventive. For example, the street corner intersections have signs that read "Stalk" and "Don't Stalk." There's a scene in which the monsters arrive to work that wittily parodies the scene of the astronauts walking in unison to Bill Conti's triumphant march in Philip Kaufman's *The Right Stuff* (1983). A popular restaurant is called Harryhausen's, in tribute to the great animator Ray Harryhausen, who worked on such films as *The 7th Voyage of Sinbad* (1958) and *Mysterious Island* (1961). But the love story that develops between Sully and Boo verges on Disney kitsch.

"If I Didn't Have You," which celebrates the friendship between Sully and Mikey, is a weaker version of the duet "You've Got a Friend in Me" from *Toy Story*. Sung by Crystal and Goodman, the song is arranged for a small jazz combo and resembles, in style, a meeting between Al Jolson and Louis Armstrong:

> (Sully) *If I were a rich man with a million or two*
> (Mikey) *I'd live in a penthouse in a room with a view*
> (Sully) *And if I were handsome . . .*
> (Mikey) *No way*
> (Sully) *It could happen*
> *These dreams could come true*
> *I wouldn't have nothing*
> *If I didn't have you.*

"If I Didn't Have You" is good-natured, but only in the most innocuous way. It lacks the crafty wordplay and the friskiness one associates with Newman's work.

Newman was nominated that evening for two awards, but given the strong work done by Howard Shore in *The Lord of the Rings,* he didn't expect to win Best Original Score. He also knew he was up against some stiff competition in the Original Song category — Sting's rather tepid Golden Globe-winning tune, "Until," from the equally bland *Kate and Leopold;* Paul McCartney's insipid ballad "Vanilla Sky" from the equally meaningless film of the same title; Diane Warren's strident "There You'll Be" from the overwrought *Pearl Harbor;* and Enya's ethereal "May It Be" from *The Lord of the Rings: The Fellowship of the Ring.* As expected, early on Newman lost his bid for Best Original Score, which, as expected, went to Howard Shore. Later in the program, after all the nominees had performed their original songs, Newman did "If I Didn't Have You" as a duet with John Goodman.

When Jennifer Lopez took to the stage to announce the winner, she began with a remark once attributed to lyricist Ira Gershwin about a love affair: "A romance won't end on a sorrowful note though in the morning you will be gone," she quoted. "The song may be ended, but as a songwriter wrote, the melody lingers on and on." After listing the nominees, she quickly got to the winner. When Lopez read Newman's name, her words were drowned out by a wave of enthusiasm that seemed to sweep the air right out of the room. People cheered and applauded, rising to their feet, as much in relief as in tribute of an artist they felt was long overdue. Goodman, in particular, had a huge cherubic grin on his face. For his part, Newman appeared shaken by the response. Where earlier in the program Woody Allen had hidden behind his patented self-deprecation, Newman immediately overturned any attempt to sympathize with his Oscar draught. "Thank you," he deadpanned. "I don't want your pity." As the audience began to settle down, Newman started having fun, using his trademark irony to deal with the years of frustration. "I want to thank, first of all, the music branch for giving me so many chances to be humiliated over the years," he began.

When Newman thanked the orchestra, it was obvious that many of the musicians who had performed his scores appreciated the gesture. "When he won the Oscar, the orchestra stood up in the pit for him," recalls Sandy DeCrescent, the contractor for musicians of Local 47 (Los Angeles). "And we were told not to do any of that if he won, because we're not supposed to show any prejudice. But that's a measure of the respect that the musicians have for him." The musicians jumping to their feet only added to Newman's astonishment. "It moved me more than I'd thought it would," he told Barney Hoskyns. "The people I'd always *wanted* to respect me, it was clear that they did." Newman didn't appear sure as to whether he should continue joking or cave in to the joy of winning. "I'm absolutely astounded that I've won for this — though the picture deserves recognition." Rather than discuss what made the Pixar films so unique, Newman simply noted that they'd made four pictures in a row that were good. "Peter Weir did that once," he remarked as if in a daze, "but I can't remember another instance exactly." Newman's best moment, though, came when it appeared that the orchestra would start playing their usual music cue warning long-winded winners to vacate the podium. He couldn't resist taking a little dig at them. "Are you really going to play in four seconds?" he asked in astonishment. "Don't play," he ordered. "It's been so long."

It had been so long. Coming shortly after the commercial disappointment of *Bad Love,* winning the Oscar quickly reminded Newman he was indeed respected among his peers. He immediately focused on what he wanted to say. Newman first expressed thanks to Milos

Forman and Barry Levinson, the men most responsible for bringing him into the world of film scoring. As *Monsters Inc.* was a Pixar picture, he also acknowledged John Lasseter, who hired him for *Toy Story*. After thanking the musicians, Newman naturally had to find a way to acknowledge having been given this award by someone as stunning as Jennifer Lopez. The man who had penned "Shame" and "Bleeding All Over the Place" went on to say that he'll probably never get to heaven, but having Lopez give him the prize might be as close as he'd ever get. When he left the stage, Newman held the statue in a virtual death grip. By the end of the evening, it was sound man Kevin O'Connell, who was nominated, and lost, for *Pearl Harbor,* who now had the dubious pleasure of owning the record for futility, with his 15 unsuccessful nominations.

In comparing Allen and Newman's response to the Oscars that evening, both men had always been cultural outsiders. Newman found his way into the Hollywood mainstream by the sheer fate of family lineage. Allen had rejected the vulgarity of Hollywood, much as a snob takes refuge in refinement. But Newman, with his sardonic detachment, could protect himself from Hollywood's corrupting influence. He could even enjoy some of its spoils. "Vulgarity is not as destructive to an artist as snobbery," Pauline Kael once wrote in defence of Norman Jewison's adaptation of *Fiddler on the Roof* (1971). The biggest irony might have been that Woody Allen had won his Oscar for *Annie Hall* — his poison-pen letter to Tinseltown.

In the spring of 2002, Newman quickly recovered from Oscar fever to find himself inducted into the Songwriters Hall of Fame along with Sting, Michael Jackson, Ashford & Simpson and Barry Manilow. When asked by *People Magazine* which artist's plaques he would like to flank his, he told them "Carole King and Stevie Wonder on either side. And Irving Berlin above." Later in the year, Newman began work on director Gary Ross' new picture, *Seabiscuit* — the story of a cinderella racehorse. Although Newman had developed a happy, creative working relationship with Ross five years earlier on *Pleasantville,* his experience on *Seabiscuit* turned out not to be so pleasant. The source of the film was Laura Hillenbrand's lively, informative 2001 biography of the same name. An illuminating examination of both the career of this unlikely champion and the renewal of America itself in the wake of the Great Depression, her book was about overcoming enormous handicaps. Ross designed his picture as thoughtful, populist entertainment, a horse-racing thriller filled with American archetypal characters. In the movie, Charles Howard (Jeff Bridges) is an entrepreneur who loses everything in the Depression, including his family. Johnny "Red" Pollard (Tobey Maguire), an intelligent, literate and bitter young man, has also lost his family. What he does best is fight and ride horses. Tom Smith (Chris Cooper) is a past-it horse trainer put out to pasture, until he discovers Seabiscuit, a horse that, while possessing considerable talent, has lost his edge.

Ross doesn't fall into the trap of doling out movie corn, but he can't harvest a story with much depth or complexity. In fact, he's tied it into a structure that forbids it. *Seabiscuit* is shaped as a piece of old-fashioned craftsmanship about a horse who heals the wounds of a bleeding nation and the people who trained and rode him. At first, its overriding metaphor is summed up in Smith's first evaluation of the horse. "He's forgotten what he was born to do," Smith says calmly. "He just needs to learn how to be a horse again." By the end, Pollard expresses the film's sentiment more literally. "You know, everybody thinks we found this broken-down horse and fixed him. But we didn't. He fixed us — every one of us. I guess in a way we kinda fixed each other, too." *Seabiscuit* is spelled out in such broad strokes that, at times, the story seems removed from the particulars of drama. The actors do manage to compensate somewhat for the leanness of the story — despite their sketchy characters. Bridges brings an all-American brashness tinged with an unquenchable sadness, while Maguire builds Pollard's resilience on a fragile foundation of bitter disillusionment. Cooper peerlessly personifies the silent, sturdy cowboy who has become an intricate part of American mythology.

As a director, Ross is one of those rare artists who has more interesting ideas than he knows how to dramatize (a weakness partly disguised by the originality of *Pleasantville*). In *Seabiscuit*, Ross never fully illuminates the transition America takes from the Jazz Age into the age of the migrant camps. Instead, he relies on still photos and the painfully prosaic narration of David McCullough. As for Newman's score, it has the same eclecticism he demonstrated in *Maverick*. When Howard buys his ranch, Newman provides a light American pastoral arrangement. For Seabiscuit's first race, he introduces swinging bluegrass sounds. When the horse heads to Mexico, a mariachi band fills the soundtrack. All through the picture, Newman nimbly mixes musical genres — shifting effortlessly from country to jazz — to provide as much color as possible. For Seabiscuit's last race in Santa Anita in 1940, however, Ross apparently wanted more heroic strains from the orchestra — and Newman balked at the suggestion.

"It was the worst experience of my life," he told Greil Marcus. "I was going to take my name off of it." When no accommodation could be reached, Newman walked from the picture instead, with the last fifteen minutes ultimately scored by someone else. "[The director] just wanted everything slowed down. They had five sessions after I left. I could not stand dealing with him anymore." What began as a promising working relationship quickly soured to the point where Newman could barely look at *Seabiscuit*. "I went to the theater and saw it," he recalls. "I had never seen the last reel. And it was just absolutely grating — the music that was written for it. It was like taking body blows. The person sitting next to me must have thought I was crazy. I was like, 'Uhhh. Ohhh.'"

In August 2003, still recovering from those body blows, Newman wrote the theme song for the hit TV series *Monk,* with Tony Shaloub as an obsessive-compulsive Columbo-style San Francisco detective. "It's a Jungle Out There," which gives perfect voice to Monk's myriad phobias, replaced Jeff Beal's original Emmy Award-nominated jazz guitar theme music. "If you could think of any popular artist who speaks in Monk's voice, and whose music could reflect the tone and sensibility of *Monk,* it would be Randy Newman," executive producer David Hoberman remarked in defense of his new replacement. Not all *Monk* fans were happy, even expressing their displeasure with an Internet petition. Beal essentially agreed with the petition. "Monk wouldn't like this," he told Jon Burlingame of *Daily Variety.* "If there's one thing an obsessive-compulsive person doesn't like, it's change." Change was in the wind, though, for Randy Newman. Given the tributes and stage musicals mounted in his honor, it was time to look back. In the fall of 2003, signed to a new label, Randy Newman found he had something new to say about something old.

3

On November 3, 1992, the day Bill Clinton was elected President of the United States, fifty-one-year-old Bob Dylan released an album of cover songs with a different story to tell. Unlike the opaque *Self Portrait*, which deliberately cannibalized the canon of American pop, *Good As I Been To You* was a collection of traditional folk and blues tracks much like those that had served as inspiration to the Dylan of thirty years earlier. After a couple of decades of haphazard recordings and vain attempts to still appear relevant, Dylan's trademark disguise had become nothing more than a redundant series of masks revealing very little of the man behind them. But on this new record, the cover was both naked and revealing.

"Bob Dylan's face stared from the record racks like a bitter warning," wrote Nick Hasted in *Uncut*. "In the era of youth-worship he had helped create, he looked shockingly decayed, the 1960s picture of Dorian Gray. But the album's title added a complicating slant of knowing approach. Good as I been to you, look how you've treated me. Good as I been to you, what more do you want?"

The record gave listeners an unlikely excursion through the past, where we could hear Dylan catch up to the meaning in songs that much earlier had launched his meteoric career. Stripped down to their bare essentials (with Dylan alone on his acoustic guitar and harmonica), these seasoned ballads found a clearly defined home in the present. They also told a story about an America where promises can be made as easily as they can be broken. However, as Pauline Kael once commented on Warren Beatty's idealistic film *Reds* (1982), "Promises that couldn't be kept are not the same as promises broken." You could hear that distinction on every track on *Good As I Been To You,* especially "Black Jack Davey," a rewrite of Clarence Ashley's haunting ballad "House Carpenter," in which a married woman is tempted from her husband's side only to die tragically with her new lover. Whether you were listening to Dylan's take on Stephen Foster's "Hard Times" or the Mississippi Sheiks' "Sittin' On Top of the World," it was soon clear that this record raised questions about the hope for spiritual and cultural rejuvenation that carried Bill Clinton into the White House.

When Dylan followed up *Good As I Been to You* a year later with a similar collection, *World Gone Wrong,* Greil Marcus concluded that these two records had "removed him from the prison of his own career and returned him . . . to the world at large."

It's doubtful Randy Newman was consciously removing himself from the prison of his own career when he sat down to record *The Randy Newman Songbook, Volume One* in 2003. But it's also hard not to think that in returning to his past, Newman (like Dylan) had found something new to say about himself and his work. "It wasn't something I would have thought to do necessarily — memorialize my own songs," he told David Wild. "It's kind of interesting to me to do this project because it does play to history in a way." Playing to history afforded Newman an opportunity to organize some key songs, along with some rarities, and design a map that would summarize the basic themes he had been exploring his entire career. Ultimately, the album would tell an explicitly American story of ambition ("Lonely at the Top"), retribution ("God's Song (That's Why I Love Mankind)," "Louisiana 1927"), racism ("Sail Away," "Rednecks"), injustice ("The World Isn't Fair") and isolation ("Living Without You," "I Think It's Going to Rain Today"). On *The Randy Newman Songbook, Volume One*, the portrait of America Newman drew became, in the words of Melville scholar Tony Tanner, "a place of vertiginous activity and radical uncertainty of direction." But, at the same time, *The Randy Newman Songbook, Volume One* displayed a certainty of direction for Newman, the artist, reassessing his life and music as he approached the delicate age of sixty. In revisiting his old songs, he could claim them in the present and delve deeper into their meaning.

Newman stripped away the adornments from the original arrangements and presented himself alone on the piano, sounding more candid than he did on *Land of Dreams*. He begins with a short fragment of "Dexter's Tune," the mournful tribute to Dexter Gordon from the score to *Awakenings*, before launching into "Lonely at the Top." The song is no longer the simple ironic joke it was when the songwriter composed it for Frank Sinatra. Since Newman is as established now as Sinatra was then, there's a pathos in the performance that wasn't evident when Newman included it on *Randy Newman Live* and *Sail Away*. He can't even laugh sarcastically at the line, "and all the money that I've made." Newman sings as if he knows this song now from the inside.

It's also lonely at the top for the deity of "God's Song (That's Why I Love Mankind)," which Newman performs with more gravity than he did on the version on *Sail Away*. Here he measures each word as if considering the weight of the consequences of God's actions. The original version contained the anger and defiance of an artist railing at the futility of faith. Here the song becomes a painful admission of God's indifference. "God's Song" has some of the spiritual force of Mahalia Jackson's recording of the traditional gospel number "Trouble of the World." Her deeply resonating performance, which has the power to convert the most hardened skeptic, reveals to us a true believer whose total faith in God leaves her satisfied and finished with the trouble of this world. Newman brings the same determined passion to his story of someone appalled by God's indifference to the troubles of this world. It's hard to imagine Newman could have gotten any further into one of his greatest songs, but on this recording, he improves on the original.

Newman also revisits "Louisiana 1927," this time without the sadly evocative string arrangement that once opened it. Following "God's Song," Newman examines the consequences of an act of God. When he gets to the line, "they're trying to wash us away," the indignation in his voice has been replaced by regret. "Let Me Go," an unreleased song from the 1970 film *The Pursuit of Happiness,* is a story of the fear of being loved. "I hadn't thought about the song in twenty years," Newman told Colin Devenish in *Rolling Stone.* "It's not one of my best songs, but it feels good where it is on the record." Sung by an older Newman, who has experienced a painful divorce, "Let Me Go" expresses many of the anxieties associated with romantic commitment. In particular, it examines the common fear a man has that he'll be consumed by the woman who loves him — a quality shared with Paul Simon's equally conflicted "Slip Slidin' Away":

> *I know a man*
> *He came from my hometown*
> *He wore his passion for his woman like a thorny crown.*
> *He said, "Delores, I live in fear.*
> *My love for you is so overpowering*
> *I'm afraid I will disappear."*
> *Slip Slidin' Away.*

Newman follows "Let Me Go" with a solid, urgent performance of "Rednecks." "'Rednecks,' of course, is aggressive," he remarks. "You can't sit and eat potato chips and have it on in the background at a party." As the song ends, Newman supplies a small coda from *Avalon* before leading directly into a forlorn reading of "Living Without You." When he first recorded it on *Randy Newman Creates Something New Under the Sun,* the orchestration was so sublime it almost overwhelmed the simplicity of the song's story. On *The Randy Newman Songbook, Volume One,* with the tune stripped down to its stark longings, Newman sounds as if he's feeling the full force of desolation.

Considering the many recorded versions there are of "I Think It's Going to Rain Today," it's astonishing that it can still sound so fresh. While Newman's never been fond of it, his most recent performance may be the definitive version, slowing down the tempo so that each word is supported on the notes played on the piano. While originally written as a parody of the solipsism expressed in many popular songs, Newman saturates his with the remorse of someone who understands the pain of human neglect, transcending the song's clever ambiguity and making it deeply moving. By stripping "You Can Leave Your Hat On" of its blues band arrangement, Newman brings the pathetic perversities even closer to the surface. The discordant notes on the piano beautifully underscore the turbulent anxieties of the little man with the huge hard-on. On "It's Money That I Love," Newman gives himself over completely to the outrageousness of the song. It's an exuberant performance that embraces decadent behavior so gleefully, it makes the tune all that more appalling. (Unfortunately, Newman felt the need to upgrade the age of the song's hooker from sixteen to nineteen.) Even if this version of "It's Money That I Love" lacks the richness offered by the synth horns and female chorus in the original, the tune is still an expression of low cunning at its most ingenious.

As great as the original performance of "Marie" is on *Good Old Boys,* Johnny Cutler's drunkenness, as he expresses love for his wife, was nothing more than a convincing affectation. The version here finds Newman getting so far into the song that he sounds convincingly drunk while he's singing it.

A short instrumental excerpt from the gorgeous "When She Loved Me," from *Toy Story 2,* sets up a quartet of political songs. If the early part of the album introduced us to the squabbling citizens of Newman's land of dreams, these four songs tell us what that dream is all about. "Sail Away" begins as his powerful lament to the horrors of the slave trade — the point where America begins to exist for Randy Newman. Starting with the iniquity that brought blacks to the new frontier, Newman follows with "The World Isn't Fair," his tale about Karl Marx and his dreams for a more equitable world. Of course the narrator in the song, who speaks to Marx, is a well-off American living off the inequities of the capitalist dream. "Political Science" follows, a ticklish performance of his jingoistic parody which found new resonance in the present — given the ongoing war in Iraq. Now, when the singer talks about how no one likes America — including "Old Europe" — it could be viewed as an indictment of the right-wing idealism of the Bush administration. (Only it's doubtful that, after dropping their bombs on their enemies, Bush or Vice President Dick Cheney would care for the singer's Japanese kimonos or Italian shoes.) Just to show that "Old Europe" isn't any more virtuous than America, Newman completes the sequence with "The Great Nations of Europe." By positioning this track after "Political Science," Newman shows that America began in the shadow of European conquest, an escape from persecution that, in turn, led to persecution in the new land. Hearing the four songs together draws a fragile picture of the nation's tainted hopes, outrageous aspirations and absurd yearnings.

After his political quartet, Newman continues with "In Germany Before the War," a song about a pedophile who murders his victim. On *Little Criminals,* the ironies in the song were painfully obvious — even the melody was self-consciously embroidered in Kurt Weill-like orchestration. The performance here is much more spare and eerie — even if the subject matter still draws conspicuous links between sexual perversity and fascism. The central flaw in the song was always that Newman never got inside his child-killer. Yet even if he still doesn't get there, he at least sounds like he can't get the killer's image out of his head. He sings with the tentativeness of a man wrestling with ghosts he can't exorcise — so we can't shake the creepy emotions his story dredges up in us. The album ends with a small selection of the main theme from *Ragtime.* In bookending the album with themes from his movie music, Newman makes us aware that the selection of songs form the scenes from a movie — the Randy Newman film.

*The Randy Newman Songbook, Volume One* was issued on Nonesuch Records in the early fall of 2003. Nonesuch was founded in the mid-sixties by Jac Holtzan (founder of Elektra Records). Initially,

Nonesuch sought out the unacknowledged corners of the classical world before making the leap into world music in 1967. During the seventies and eighties, Nonesuch built a pop repertoire of non-mainstream acts including the Kronos Quartet, Emmylou Harris, David Byrne, Bill Frissell, Wilco, Youssou N'Dour, Joni Mitchell and, now, Randy Newman. "It's a little like doing your own memorial record," Newman told Elysa Gardner of *USA Today* in describing the album. "It's like being Hendrix, but not waiting till you're dead." Titling the album *The Randy Newman Songbook, Volume One* was also a cheeky attempt to borrow from the famous songbooks of iconic American composers such as Gershwin, Porter and Berlin. Quite removed from his brief nightmare at Dreamworks, Newman felt right at home at Nonesuch. And Mitchell Froom, who had helmed *Bad Love*, signed on for production duties. "Thankfully, Mitchell suggested a number of key changes so I wasn't croaking at people on songs like 'Marie' and 'Living Without You,'" Newman told David Wild. "I think I sing better now, which is one of the reasons I didn't mind doing this album." As the timbre of his voice was always the key to understanding the paradoxical components of his songs, Newman recognized how essential its expressiveness was to this record. "Singing's the kind of thing you get better at until you start your irrevocable decline," he remarks. "Now I have scheduled my irrevocable decline, but it's not for another couple of years." With time firmly on his side, Randy Newman was itching to take to the road — as if starting all over again.

4

Shortly before he died, journalist Timothy White wrote these words about Randy Newman: "By identifying the misfit, the unsung outsider and sincere antagonist in the American social landscape and acknowledging their intrinsic dignity and courage, by proving that one can possess an even quirkier vocal presence than Jimmy Durante or Bob Dylan and still croon as effectively as Bing Crosby, Hoagy Carmichael or Fats Domino, and by marshalling his considerable powers of melody and poetry to step outside the circle of pop-rock decorum and tell the plain truth on himself and his milieu, Randy Newman has become one of the most brilliant and indispensable artists in American popular music."

Yet as indispensable as he has become, he still poses a dilemma for many people — when he registers at all. After all, Newman's still hardly a household name. Some recall "Short People," and think of him as this odd little novelty act. Others may cite "You've Got a Friend in Me" from *Toy Story*, and perceive him as some comfy children's songwriter (until, that is, you told them that he also wrote a song called "I Want You To Hurt Like I Do"). In the summer of 2004, when Kiefer Sutherland was sighted doing a striptease in a New Zealand nightspot, the news report read that he'd performed it to the Tom Jones song, "You Can Leave Your Hat On." Many remain unaware of the man who wrote and originally sang it. Among other misfits, however, Newman is a legend, a termite artist biting into the American mainstream. He has a fan following that even dubs itself "Little Criminals."

The discomforting presence of Randy Newman also inspired the creators of the animated TV show *Family Guy* to parody him. In one episode, the world was coming to an end and the Griffin family went desperately looking for a place to collect themselves. All they could find, in the end, was an isolated house in which Randy Newman sat — all alone — at his piano observing every little mundane detail around him and turning them into songs. Such parodies make it clear that no matter how marginal Newman is for mainstream pop audiences, he has also established a particular brand — a specific image — on the fringes.

Years earlier, when Newman would shuffle over to his piano onstage, he was something of an anomaly in the world of rock. While most pop stars made desperate attempts to look hip, often dressing as outlandishly as possible, Newman's wardrobe was as un-hip as one could possibly go. Huge, square eyeglass frames. A pair of old jeans and a black short-sleeve button-down shirt. Tennis shoes. Back in the late sixties, of course, this was seen as refreshing, as heartening as watching Woody Allen mock the oppressive WASP beefcake image which is so sadly back in vogue today. Like Allen, Newman played to the harmless image of the nebbish as a way of working intelligence into his art. Watching Newman shuffle over to his piano, in those same clothes today, feels more like a concession to a familiar and easy pose. The disguise was once transparent, today it's so visible, it sometimes hides the artist.

Newman's disguise works best when it keeps the ambiguity alive in his music. When Newman toured that fall in support of *The Randy Newman Songbook, Volume One,* he wrestled with an image he'd spent years creating. He made his way over to his piano in the same shambling manner he always did. But although the set of tunes was familiar, Newman made sure they were never predictable. His catalogue of material could now speak to any point in time. When Hurricane Isabel had hit an area of Washington, D.C., before a scheduled concert, he played "Louisiana, 1927" to remind Washington audiences of the continuity of history. Newman seemed to be saying that we gain our best perspective on tragedy when it is infused with the elements of complex circumstance. When he performed "Rednecks," Newman had to acknowledge that sometimes a song can have little impact on those very complex circumstances. "All the songs I've written about racism have solved the problem," he told the crowd sarcastically. "It's all gone." Before singing "Political Science," where he sings of American officials deciding to finally drop the Big One, he remarked, "They finally listened to me." Sometimes he reverted to popular shtick. "Take it," he said to the imaginary band during the instrumental break in "Birmingham." "I'm too cheap to have one," he told the audience, "so I have to resort to stuff like that." Newman has resorted to that gag on many a night to get a quick laugh. His many fans would find a welcoming warmth in it.

But as he concluded the show with "I'm Dead (But I Don't Know It)," his "tribute" to antiquated rock stars who won't go away, there was a built-in awareness that those geriatric cases were now his peers. "Nobody has retired," he said to the laughing crowd. "There are more people around from the sixties than from the nineties, and I don't know why." Of course, he knew the tune could just as easily be indicting himself, but unlike the Moody Blues, or the revamped Jethro Tull, Newman's presence has been too elusive to be weighed down by hubris. After all, his career wasn't shaped by pop stardom.

"Lack of really big commercial success maybe has contributed to longevity," Newman told Bravo! in 2003. "When you're under the radar, maybe it's easier to go on a long time. Considering the type of stuff I do, that's so outside the mainstream in some ways, I've been very fortunate in how well I've done." Operating under the radar has been the strategy of Newman's brilliant disguise all along. As an artist in popular music, however, he'll periodically court great acclaim as well. "When the history books are written about this time period, Randy will be up there," Lenny Waronker told Robert Wilonsky of the *Dallas Observer*. "To me, what he has done is successful. I always believe he will have some kind of real commercial success. It's hard for him to understand this, but as long as he's working and as long as he cares, he can't go wrong. Those songs are timeless."

Could Newman ever find the commercial success of a Celine Dion or Sting? It's doubtful. His grating, cranky voice, for one thing, practically guarantees he will always operate best under that radar. As for the subject matter in his songs, it will always play havoc with those who ignore his untrustworthy narrator. During the winter of 2003, Newman was in the United Kingdom for a profile film by Channel Four's Jon Ronson. While getting his makeup applied before the shoot, he had a rather welcoming encounter. "I was doing this TV show yesterday and there was this makeup girl who made me up for a few days," he told Barney Hoskyns. "We'd talk and we'd go at the same speed 'cause she was smart, but then I started playing 'My Life Is Good.' And I could see she was going, 'What the hell? *This* is what he does?!'" Yes. But this is what he always does. "It's like, you gotta be there at the beginning and you gotta be listening to get what I'm doing," he explains.

For those who have always listened, and to those who will listen, they'll hear in his music an American dreamer who never tries to find comfort in the dream. Newman doesn't sing of the quaint America found in director Phil Alden Robinson's *Field of Dreams* (1989), in which a farmer builds a baseball diamond on his land in an effort to heal the ruptured values of his country and family. That's a vapid and nostalgic America which urges conformity to the moral values it sets before us. Newman's America is far too ambiguous and contradictory to be described in such a simplistic way. Newman's America encompasses all things we don't find warm and comforting — and that includes the misfits and outsiders he sings about. "The real American day hasn't begun yet," D.H. Lawrence wrote in 1924. "American consciousness has so far been a false dawn. . . . You have got to pull the democratic and idealistic clothes off American utterance and see what you can of the dusky body of IT underneath."

The life and music of Randy Newman represent an avid quest to dig deeply into that dusky body of American utterance. To be an American dreamer, his songs continue to remind us, means learning how to live with the unresolvable truths of what those dreams mean. This is both his hardship to endure and our challenge to embrace.

---

# Bibliography and Sources

The individual source notes for each chapter are listed at: www.ecwpress.com.

## Books

Adams, Henry. *The Education of Henry Adams* (Oxford University Press, 1999).

Barry, John M. *Rising Tide: The Great Mississippi Flood of 1927 and How it Changed America* (Simon & Shuster, 1998).

Bier, Jesse. *The Rise and Fall of American Humour* (Holt Rinehart and Winston, 1968).

Bierce, Ambrose, ed. by David E. Schultz and S.T. Joshi. *The Devil's Dictionary (New Unabridged Edition)* (University of Georgia Press, 2001).

Bruce, Lenny, ed. by John Cohen. *The Essential Lenny Bruce* (Ballentine Books, 1967).

Christgau, Robert. *Grown Up Wrong* (Harvard University Press, 1998).

Chusid, Irwin. *Songs in the Key of Z* (a cappella, 2000).

Commager, Henry Steele. *The American Mind* (Yale, 1949).

Cornyn, Stan, with Paul Scanlon. *Exploding: The Highs, Hits, Hype, Heroes, and Hustlers of the Warner Music Group* (Harper Collins, 2002).

Doctorow, E.L. *Ragtime* (Random House, 1975).

Dostoevsky, Fyodor. *The Brothers Karamazov* (Penguin Edition, 1982).

Eisler, Hanns. *Composing For the Films* (Oxford University Press, 1947).

Epstein, Lawrence J. *The Haunted Smile: The Story of Jewish Comedians in America* (Perseus Books Group, 2001).

Fiedler, Leslie. *Cross the Border, Close the Gap* (Stein & Day, 1972).

Furia, Philip. *The Poets of Tin Pan Alley: A History of America's Great Lyricists* (Oxford University Press, 1990).

Gabler, Neal. *An Empire of Their Own: How the Jews Invented Hollywood* (Crown Publishers, 1988).

Gilmore, Mikal. *Shot in the Heart* (Doubleday, 1993).

—. *Night Beat* (Doubleday, 1998).

Gozzi, Carlo. *Memoirs of a Useless Man* (Oxford University Press, 1962).

Grout, Donald J. *A History of Western Music* (W.W. Norton, 1973).

Heylin, Clinton, ed. *The Penguin Book of Rock & Roll Writing* (Viking, 1992).

Hoberman J., and Jeffrey Shandler. *Entertaining America: Jews, Movies and Broadcasting* (Princeton University Press, 2003).

Hoskyns, Barney. *Waiting For the Sun: Strange Days, Weird Scenes, and the Sound of Los Angeles* (St Martin's Griffin, 1996).

Howe, Irving. *World of Our Fathers* (Touchstone, 1976).

Jansen, David A. *Encyclopedia of Tin Pan Alley* (Routledge, 2003).

Kael, Pauline. *I Lost it at the Movies* (Little Brown, 1965).

—. *Deeper Into Movies* (Little, Brown, 1973).

—. *Taking It All In* (Holt, Rinehart & Winston, 1984).

—. *State of the Art* (Dutton, 1985).

—. *5001 Nights at the Movies* (Henry Holt, 1991).

Laing, Dave. *One-Chord Wonders: Power and Meaning in Punk Rock* (Milton Keynes Publishers, 1985).

Lawrence, D.H. *Studies in Classic American Literature* (Penguin Paperback Edition, 1971).

Levinson, Barry, ed. by David Thompson. *Levinson on Levinson* (Faber and Faber, 1992).

Leyda, Jay. *The Melville Log* (Harcourt Brace & C, 1951).

Lindberg, Gary. *The Confidence Man in American Literature* (Oxford University Press, 1982).

Marcus, Greil. *Mystery Train: Images of America in Rock 'N' Roll Music* (Fourth Revised Edition). (Penguin Books, 1997).

—. *Invisible Republic: Bob Dylan's Basement Tapes* (Henry Holt, 1997).

—. *Double Trouble* (Henry Holt, 2000).

Martin, Bill. *Avant Rock: Experimental Music from the Beatles to Björk* (Open Court Press, 2002).

MacDonald, Lawrence E. *The Invisible Art of Film Music* (Ardsley House, 1998).

Malamud, Bernard. *The Natural* (Farrar, Straus & Giroux, 1952).

Matterson, Stephen. *Introduction to Herman Melville's The Confidence Man* (Penguin Classics Paperback Edition, 1990).

May, Rollo. *The Cry For Myth* (Delta, 1991).

McCarthy, Mary. *On the Contrary* (A.M. Heath & Co., 1962).

McDonald, Ian. *The People's Music* (Random House, 2003).

Melnick, Jeffrey. *A Right to Sing the Blues* (Harvard University Press, 1999).

Melville, Herman. *The Confidence Man* (Oxford University Press, 1982).

—. (Penguin Classics Paperback Edition, 1990).

Miller, Jim, ed. *Rolling Stone Illustrated History of Rock & Roll* (Random House/Rolling Stone Press, 1980).

Mosley, Walter. *Devil in a Blue Dress* (Serpent's Tail Press, 1990).

Newton. Huey P. *Revolutionary Suicide* (Ballantine Books, 1973).

Phillips, Julia. *You'll Never Eat Lunch in This Town Again* (New American Library, 1991).

Prendergast, Roy. *Film Music: A Neglected Art* (Norton, 1977).

Ricks, Christopher, ed. with William Vance. *The Faber Book of America* (Faber & Faber, 1992).

Rourke, Constance. *American Humor: A Study of the National Character* (Harcourt Press, 1931).

Singer, Isaac Bashevis. *Enemies, A Love Story* (Farrar, Straus & Giroux, 1972).

Tanner, Tony. *Introduction to Herman Melville's The Confidence Man* (Oxford University Press, 1989).

Thomas, Tony. *Music For the Movies* (Barnes, Tantivy, 1973).

Thoreau, Henry David. *Main Woods* (Pavilion Press, 2003).

Tocqueville, Alexis de. *Democracy in America* (Colonial Press, 1900).

Warren, Robert Penn. *All the King's Men* (Harcourt Press, 2005).

West. Nathanael. *The Day of the Locust* (Signet re-issue, 1983).

Wyman, Bill. *Rolling With the Stones* (DK Publishing, 2002).

Willis, Ellen. *Beginning to See the Light: Pieces of a Decade* (Knopf, 1981).

Zappa, Frank. *The Real Frank Zappa Book* (Poseidon Press, 1989).

Zollo, Paul. *Songwriters on Songwriting: Expanded Edition* (De Capo Press, 1997).

## Articles

Bell, Douglas, "Randy and the Giant Career Path," Toronto *Globe and Mail*, December 7, 1996.

Bianculli, David, "Here's Hoping Oscar is Serious About a Shorter Running Time," *The New York Daily News*, March 23, 2002.

Brustein, Robert, Review of *Faust*, *The New Republic*, November 18, 1996.

Burlingame, Jon, "Favorite Little Ditty Tuned Out From Monk," *Daily Variety*, August 21, 2003.

Case, Brian, "Talk with Randy Newman," *New Music Express*, 1978.

Connelly, Christopher, "Randy Newman Isn't Kidding," *Rolling Stone*, March 31, 1983.

Cott, Jonathan, "Randy Newman: His Only Hero Was Roy Capanella," *Rolling Stone*, November 12, 1970.

Courrier, Kevin, unpublished interview with Greil Marcus, February 22, 1991.

Cromelin, Richard, "Press Packet for *Little Criminals*," 1977.

—. "Interview with Randy Newman and John Lasseter," *The Los Angeles Times*, November 3, 2001.

Crouse, Timothy, Review of *Randy Newman Live*, *Rolling Stone*, August 19, 1972.

Dahl, Roald, "Roald Dahl: Books and Writers," Amazon.com.

Daley, Dan, "Randy Newman's *Sail Away*," *Mix Magazine*, June 1, 2003.

Daly, Margaret, "Reclusive Randy Newman's Still A Knot of Contradictions," *Toronto Star*, Saturday, October 8, 1977.

DeCrescent, Sandy, "Always a Bridesmaid...and Finally a Bride," *International Musician*, May, 2002.

Devenish, Colin, "Newman Sings His Songbook," *Rolling Stone*, October 1, 2003.

Elder, Sean, "Brilliant Careers: Randy Newman," Salon, August 24, 1999.

Foley, James, "Randy Newman at the Film & TV Music Composers Conference," February 22, 1997.

Frontain, Raymond-Jean, "Profile on Lorenz Hart," *Girlfriends Magazine*.

Galupo, Scott, Review of Randy Newman concert, *The Washington Times*, September 25, 2003.

Gardner, Elysa, "Randy Newman Back in Business," *USA Today*, September 9, 2003.

Goddard, Peter, "Randy Newman Fights Back at the Man," *Toronto Star*, Saturday, March 12, 1983.

Green, Michelle, "The Devil's Advocate," *People*, October 30, 1995.

Greenwald, Matthew, "Interview with Van Dyke Parks," *The Tracking Angle*, Summer, 1996.

Grierson, Ralph, "Always a Bridesmaid...and Finally a Bride," *International Musician*, May, 2002.

Grierson, Tim, "Old People We Love: Randy Newman," *Ironminds Magazine*, July 20, 2000.

Hampson, Sarah, "Go On and Love Me, I Don't Care," Toronto *Globe and Mail*, November 29, 2003.

Hasted, Nick, "Random Shots at the Face of Time," *Uncut: Legends #1: Bob Dylan*, October, 2003.

Holden, Stephen, Review of *Sail Away*, *Rolling Stone*, July 6, 1972.

—. Review of *Born Again*, "Two Minsanthropes: Randy Newman and Stephen Sondheim attack the world," *Rolling Stone*, October 4, 1979.

—. "Can a Pop Composer Help Out Broadway?," *The New York Times*, September 24, 1995.

Hoskyns, Barney, "I Love You...You C**t!" *Mojo*, August, 1998.

—. "Interview with Randy Newman: Is Randy Newman the Old Eminem?," *Rock's Backpages*, September, 2003.

Hurtt, Michael, "The Godfather," *Mojo*, May 2004.

James, Clive, "Randy Newman — The Hoarse Foreman of the Apocalypse," *Cream Magazine*, June 1973.

Jordan, Scott, "Backtalk with Randy Newman," *OffBeat Magazine*, November, 1998.

Kaplan, Erin Aubry. "White Man With Attitude," *LA Weekly*, November 23-29, 2001.

Keast, James, "Randy Newman: The Underdog," *Exclaim!* , July 1, 1999.

Kligman, David, "'Short People' Songwriter Celebrates 30 Years of Music," Associated Press, November 17, 1998.

Lacey, Liam, "Mingling the Comic and the Serious," Toronto *Globe and Mail*, March 5, 1983.

Levitin, Daniel, in conversation with Lenny Waronker, unacknowledged Internet source, 1998.

Love, Damien, "A Simple Twist of Fate," *Uncut*, June 2004.

Lubow, Arthur, "Randy Newman: Tired of Being a Cult Figure," *People*, May 2, 1983.

Lydon, Susan, "Randy Newman — Out of Cole Porter, Hoagy Carmichael, Bob Dylan, Groucho Marx, Mark Twain, and Randy Newman," *The New York Times Magazine*, November 5, 1972.

Macnie, Jim, "His Life is Good," *Providence Phoenix*, June 22-29, 2000.

Mehr, Bob, "At School With Randy Newman," *Seattle Weekly*, October 16-22, 2002.

Male, Andrew, "Last Night a Record Changed My Life," *Mojo*, November 2003.

Marcus, Greil, Review of Bob Dylan's *Self Portrait*, *Rolling Stone*, July 23, 1970.

—. Review of *Little Criminals*, *Rolling Stone*, December 1, 1977.

—. Interview with Elvis Costello, *Rolling Stone*, September 2, 1982.

—. Review of *Pleasantville*, *Esquire*, March, 1999.

—. "Real Life Top Ten," Salon, September 17, 2001.

—. "Real Life Top Ten," Salon, June 24, 2002.

—. "Days Between Stations: Thirty Years Ago, Randy Newman Satirically Sang, 'It's Lonely at the Top'," Interview, November, 2003.

Maslin, Janet, "Randy Newman — The Moral is Implicit," *The New York Times*, Sunday, September 25, 1977.

McGrath, Paul, "Newman Loves the Giant He Loves To Ridicule," Toronto *Globe and Mail*, Monday, October 10, 1977.

Mehr, Bob, "At School with Randy Newman," *The Seattle Weekly*, October 16-22, 2002.

Montgomery, Scott, Kevin Walsh and Gary Norris, "The Invisible Randy Newman: The Metric Music to Reprise Years," *Goldmine*, September, 1995.

Morris, Steven Leigh, "Maybe They're Doing It Wrong: Why Randy Newman's New Musical Goes Limp," *LA Weekly*, June 23-29, 2000.

Mulcahy, Alex, "Review of *The Randy Newman Songbook, Volume One*," Dimple, December 5, 2003.

Newman, Randy, "The Playboy Interview," *Playboy*, January 1987.

—. Interview with *The Economist*, January 27, 1996.

—. "Guilt By Association: Cross-examining Randy Newman, the culpable composer," Amazon.com, 1998.

—. "Press packet for *Bad Love*," Dreamworks Records, 1999.

—. Web interview prior to Ally McBeal episode, May 22, 2000.

—. "Q & A with Randy Newman," online chat, February 8, 2001.

—. "Pop Quiz with Randy Newman," *People*, April 15, 2002.

Niester, Alan, "From Freud to Short People," Toronto *Globe and Mail*, Thursday, June 15, 1978.

Norris, Gary. *Pants*, the Randy Newman newsletter.

Pareles, Jon, "Song For All Occasions, But Sparing Ground Zero," *The New York Times*, 2001.

Patch, Jerry, Continuing Education: SCR and One of America's Top Songwriters Take a Look at 20th Century America, South Coast Repertory program notes.

Pond, Steve, "The Old Sensitive Randy Newman is Gone For Good," *Rolling Stone*, January 21, 1982.

Puig, Manuel, interview for *Kiss of the Spider Woman*, *The New York Times*, August 1985.

*Rolling Stone*, Random Notes, October 30, 1980.

Sakamoto, John. "The Randy Newman Q & A," *The Toronto Sun*, June 29, 1999.

Scheurer, Timothy, "Brother, Can You Spare a Dime?," FortuneCity.com.

Simmons, Sylvie, "Smile? Don't Mind If I Do...," *Mojo*, March 2004.

Strauss, Neil, "The Pop Life: Interview with Steely Dan," *The New York Times*, June 12, 2003.

Taylor, Alan, "Animated and Short," *Sunday Herald*, September 28, 2003.

Tosches, Nick, "Who Killed the Hit Machine?," *Vanity Fair*, November 2002.

Toepfer, Susan, "Randy Newman Seeks Comfort in His Land of Dreams," *People*, December 5, 1988.

Turner, Steve, "Randy and Reid: Mutual Admiration," *Beat Instrumental*, February, 1972.

Weintraub, Bernard, interview with Lenny Waronker, *The New York Times*, March 21, 2002.

Wener, Ben, "Newman By Nilsson Quite Simply Sings," *The Orange County Register*, June 27, 2000.

Wherry, Aaron, "Well, since they asked....," *National Post*, November 24, 2003.

White, Timothy, "Randy Newman's America: A Portrait of the Artist," *Billboard Magazine*, December 9, 2000.

Wild, David, "The Importance of Being Randy," randynewman.com.

Williams, Ralph Vaughn. "Film Music," *Film Music Notes*, Vol. 6, No. 3, 1946.

Williams, Richard, "Review of Randy Newman concert," *Melody Maker*, October 1970.

Wilonsky, Robert, "Maybe He's Doing it Wrong," *Dallas Observer*, November 5, 1998.

Winchell, Mark Royden, "The Dream of the South," University of South Carolina Press, 2004.

Winkler, Peter, "Randy Newman's Americana," *Popular Music*, Volume 7/1, January 1988.

Young, Charles M, "Randy Newman Snubs God," *Rolling Stone*, November 17, 1977.

## Radio and Television

Bossin, Rob, "Interview with Randy Newman," The Entertainers, CBC Radio, May 4, 1978.

Burn, Ken, Ken Burn's America: Huey Long, PBS, 1985.

Edwards, Bob, "Interview with Randy Newman," Morning Edition, National Public Radio, October 8, 2003.

Enright, Michael, "Interview with Randy Newman," Morningside, CBC Radio, 1999.

Newman, Randy. "Artist of the Month." Bravo!, December, 2003.

*Wait, Wait, Don't Tell Me*, National Public Radio show, taped at Cal Tech Campus in Los Angeles on February 28, 2002, aired on March 2, 2002.

## CD, DVD and LP Liner Notes

Armstrong, Curtis, liner notes for CD re-issue, *Nilsson Sings Newman: 30th Anniversary Edition*, Buddha Records, 2000.

Cook, Page, liner notes to CD re-issue, *Captain From Castille: The Classic Film Scores of Alfred Newman*, Charles Gerhardt conducting the National Philharmonic Orchestra, RCA Records, 1973.

Eden, Dawn, liner notes for CD box-set, *The Harry Nilsson Anthology*, RCA Records, 1994.

Feldman, Jim, liner notes for CD, *Dusty in Memphis*, Rhino Records, 1992.

Hoerburger, Rob, liner notes for CD box-set anthology, *The Dusty Springfield Anthology*, Mercury Records, 1997.

Kooper, Al and Danny Kapilian, liner notes for Harry Nilsson tribute CD, *For the Love of Harry: Everybody Sings Nilsson*, BMG Music, 1995.

Morthland, John, liner notes for CD, *Sweet Soul Queen of New Orleans: The Irma Thomas Collection*, Razor & Tie, 1996.

Negron, Chuck and Cory Wells, liner notes for CD box-set anthology, *Celebrate: The Three Dog Night Story, 1963–1975*, MCA Records, 1993.

Newman, Randy, liner notes for CD box-set anthology, *Guilty: 30 Years of Randy Newman*, Rhino Records, 1998.

—. Commentary track on DVD release of *Pleasantville*, New Line Video, 1999.

—. Liner note tribute for CD re-issue, *Nilsson Sings Newman: 30th Anniversary Edition*, Buddha Records, 2000.

—. Liner notes for CD re-issue, *Sail Away*, Rhino Records, 2002.

Selick, Henry, featurette for the DVD *James and the Giant Peach*, Disney Video, 1996.

Smith, Roger, liner notes for CD re-issue, *Harry/Nilsson Sings Newman*, BMG Music, 1999.

Tharpe, Sister Rosetta, "Strange Things Happening Everyday," quoted in liner notes for CD box-set anthology, *Martin Scorsese Presents The Blues: A Musical Journey*, Hip-O Records, 2003.

Thomas, Tony, interview with Alfred Newman for LP liner notes, *Alfred Newman — Hollywood Maestro*, Citadel Records, 1976.

Waronker, Lenny, liner notes for CD box-set anthology, *Guilty: 30 Years of Randy Newman*, Rhino Records, 1998.

White, Timothy, "Bet No One Ever Hurt This Bad: The Importance of Being Randy Newman," liner notes for CD box-set anthology, *Guilty: 30 Years of Randy Newman*, Rhino Records, 1998.

Wild, David, liner notes for CD re-issue, *Sail Away*, Rhino Records, 2002.

—. Liner notes for CD re-issue, *Good Old Boys*, Rhino Records, 2002.

Willman, Chris, liner notes for CD re-issue of *Faust*, Rhino Records, 2003.

Zorn, John, liner notes for CD, *The Carl Stalling Project: Music From the Warner Brothers Cartoon 1936–1958*, Warner Brothers, 1990.

# Index